Ur **|||‖|‖|‖‖|‖‖‖|‖‖|‖‖|‖** g
D1277304 n

DISCARD

Third Edition

Under-standing the film

An introduction
to film appreciation

Ron Johnson & Jan Bone

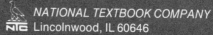
NATIONAL TEXTBOOK COMPANY
Lincolnwood, IL 60646

791.43
JOHNSON
1986

Copyright © 1986, 1981, 1976 by National Textbook Company.
4255 West Touhy Avenue, Lincolnwood, IL 60646
Library of Congress Catalog Number: **80-80893**
All rights reserved. No part of this book
may be reproduced, stored in a retrieval
system, or transmitted in any form or by
any means, electronic, mechanical,
photocopying, recording or otherwise,
without prior permission of National Textbook Company. Manufactured in the
United States of America.

5 6 7 8 9 RD 9 8 7 6 5 4 3 2 1

Quality   10/14/87   14.95 per paper

Acknowledgements

Chris Angelos, Bernard Balmuth, Jacob Bloom, Boss Film Corporation, Joanne Brokaw, Bill Burton, Kenneth C. Clark, Scott Conrad, John DeCuir, John Dern, Richard Edlund, Nancy Eichler, Dan Gire, Jerry Greenberg, Michael Gross, Gerry Hanson, Alan Heim, Paul Hirsch, James Howe, Sheldon Kahn, Steve Mills, Marina Mittrione, Rick Nicita, Ivy Orta, Ronald L. Perkins, Shawna Reninger, Lloyd Rutski, Cynthia and Roy Scheider, Walt Schillinger, Syd Silverman, Patrick Stockstill, Terri Tafreshi, and Jack Valenti. Special thanks to Ivan Reitman, producer/director of *Ghostbusters;* to Saul Zaentz, producer of *Amadeus;* and to Sam Spiegel, producer of *The African Queen,* for their help and cooperation.

Academy of Motion Picture Arts and Sciences, CBS, Columbia Pictures, Contemporary Films/McGraw-Hill, Horizon Management Inc., Janus Films Inc., Lucasfilm Ltd., Motion Picture Association of America, Museum of Modern Art/Film Stills Archive, National Film Board of Canada, Paramount Pictures Corporation, Phillips Petroleum Company, Pyramid Films, RKO General Incorporated, Screen Actors Guild, Tri-Star Pictures, 20th Century-Fox Film Corporation, Universal Pictures, Variety, Walt Disney Productions, and Warner Bros., Inc.

I especially wish to acknowledge the publishing team that encouraged me in the processing of this edition. My appreciation to book designer, Tamra Campbell, and to editors Judith Clayton and Judith M. Kiolbassa.

And special thanks to our families for their help, encouragement, and patience: Francys Johnson, Amy, Julie, Marc, and Teri; and Dave Bone, Jon and Sandra, Jeannie and Chris, Bob and Jan, Dan and Betsy.

Contents

Professional Profiles

A film represents the creative efforts of many people, working as a highly skilled team to bring a concept to the screen. Throughout *Understanding the Film* veteran professionals have shared their work experiences with you in order to help you understand the complex business of moviemaking. Each individual has tried to describe his or her particular craft in a way that shows you the job's responsibilities and requirements. This element of the text is called a "Professional Profile."

As you read these "Profiles" you will come to see that the most remarkable thing about these talented men and women is the joy and pride they feel about their work. They *like* film. They want *you* to like and appreciate film. Their profiles offer you a behind-the-scenes look at the fascinating world of the motion picture.

A complete list of the "Professional Profiles" and where they may be found throughout the text follows.

Foreword

Any book which intelligently and lovingly, explores and advances the appreciation of movies as an art form and as entertainment is a book that ought to be read.

I am persistently optimistic for the future of stories told on film or tape. I am even more certain that the theater with its wide screen, amply nourished with luminance, its state-of-the-art stereophonic sensual sound, with its comfortable seats, with an audience ready to laugh, cry, to be held in suspense, or to be exalted by the sounds and sights of the human condition, offers the viewer an epic entertainment experience that cannot be duplicated in the living room of any home.

Understanding the Film: An Introduction to Film Appreciation introduces you to many of the men and women whose large talents and professional craftsmanship inhabit the screens of theaters all over the world. I think you will "see" film in ways that never crossed your consciousness before.

Jack Valenti

President
Motion Picture Association of America

Introduction

This edition of *Understanding the Film* deals with a fascinating subject, but one with which we are so familiar that we tend to take it for granted. Unfortunately, the more we do take things for granted, the less we appreciate them.

This is true for most of us as moviegoers. We are entertained, but rarely do we allow ourselves to really understand or perceive what is happening. We are involved, but how often do we really consider a motion picture as a kind of message or communication that is being transmitted to us through a most unique medium? Finally, when we do comment on a movie, are we really evaluating it in terms of whether its message was valid or meaningful? Do we consider whether it was transmitted effectively in terms of film technique? When we do begin to think and act along these lines, the hour or two we spend in front of the screen becomes even more enjoyable. In truth, our satisfaction can be so heightened and the medium, itself, so much more appreciated, that we become more selective. No longer are we simply *moviegoers*. Rather, we will have become *film viewers*. This is the aim of this book.

A few more words about *Understanding the Film*. First, as you will see, we feel that in order for you to develop the kind of interest in movies we would like, this book cannot deal only with the "oldies" even though they are classics. And so, we have given contemporary movies equal or greater "billing." Second, we feel that in order to really understand the film, you have got to know more about how movies are made. We have presented one scene from *Ghostbusters* from the actual script right through to editing. In addition, we have included a chapter on film editing, an integral part of the film process. Finally, we think you would benefit by getting to know the people involved in the film business, from the producer all the way through the person whose job it is to promote a film. To get a "sense" of how they feel about their work, throughout this book we feature closeups of people who have spent their lives in the motion picture industry. Put this all together, and we trust you will find *Understanding the Film* a book as refreshing and illuminating as a really good movie.

1

The Most Popular
Art Form

What Is Film?

There you are, sitting with a friend, in a movie theater. Around you are many other people, most of them young people about 16 to 24 years old. As you eat your buttered popcorn, your eyes are glued to the 30-foot-wide screen in front of you. Occasionally you and your friend say something to each other about the action taking place on the giant screen. However, most of the time your mind—and maybe even your body—is intricately involved with the events taking place on the screen.

When the action on the screen and the reaction in your mind are united as one, "film" is taking place. What we mean by this is that *communication* is taking place. The communication began with the person who created the idea for the film. This person, the filmmaker, has used film as the medium* for communicating the idea. When you understand the message of the filmmaker, communication has taken place.

We usually think of *film* as the moving image on the screen or the celluloid running through the projector. However, just as a book is nothing but words until someone reads it, a film is nothing but tiny pictures until someone sees it.

So a film is really two entities. It is a long strip of celluloid with small pictures on it, which is projected, with the aid of light and a lens, onto a screen. Film is also a kind of communication between the filmmaker and the audience.

Why Are Films So Popular?

Film today is an art form, along with such other art forms as painting, sculpture, music, writing, architecture, dance, and theater. The art of the film is a continuing endeavor by creative people to find ways to express themselves and to communicate their ideas.

The very nature of the film medium itself perpetuates its popularity. The size of the image, the use of color, the stars in the film, and the interest in popular story lines all contribute to film's universal acceptance and popularity.

---

*medium: the element that the artist uses to express his or her ideas.

There are at least five reasons for the popularity of film as the 20th-century art form:

1. It is easy to become involved in a film because there seems to be little to do except let it pour into your head. Your chair is soft. You lean back. You're munching buttered popcorn. The theater is dark, except for the moving image, 30 x 15 feet in size. You're watching Harrison Ford in *Indiana Jones and the Temple of Doom*. In the midst of a confrontation between Ford and a suave Chinese gangster who wants the diamond our hero has obtained for him, Ford has been tricked into swallowing poison. The Shanghai nightclub suddenly erupts with gunfire, and Ford and singer Kate Capshaw are scrambling on the floor. He's searching for the antidote; she's looking for the giant diamond amid a cascade of ice cubes. They crash through a window, check their fall by sliding down an awning, and drop into a car piloted by Ford's young sidekick, Short Round, so tiny that he needs blocks strapped to his feet to reach the gas pedal. At the airport, the trio board a waiting tri-motor for their escape. As the pilot taxis down the runway, the camera cuts to the plane's insignia. Suddenly . . . you drop your popcorn as you realize the plane is owned by the gangster trying to kill Ford.

2. Films seem to be real, as if the action were taking place as you watch. That is why when you are telling someone about a film you have seen, you often say, "I saw the most amazing movie last night—*Starman*. Have you seen it yet? An Alien comes to observe life on earth and gets stranded near the home of a young widow. His people tell him their mother ship will pick him up in three days at Meteor Crater, more than 2000 miles away. Starman, the Alien, clones the human form of Jenny's recently deceased husband. He has only three days to reach Arizona, and the U.S. Army is chasing him."

Take another look at the quote in the last paragraph. The first two verbs are in the past tense. They imply that you saw *Starman* at an earlier time. Nevertheless the verbs you use to describe the film are in the present tense, implying that Starman, the widow, and the mother ship all exist right now. You are describing the film's action as if it is still happening.

Harrison Ford has starred in five of the ten top-grossing films of all time. Ford's whip and hat became trademarks of his roles as adventuresome archaeologist Indiana Jones. (Indiana Jones and the Temple of Doom © *Lucasfilm Ltd.* *(LFL) 1984. All Rights Reserved. Courtesy of Lucasfilm Ltd.)*

3. Films are a part of our culture, and they influence how we think and what we do. It is "chic" to be able to talk to others about the Terror Dogs in *Ghostbusters,* the tornado in *Places in the Heart,* the jungles of Colombia in *Romancing the Stone,* or the young girl's audition in *Flashdance.* A kind of "belonging" and a closer relationship develops among people when they talk about mutual experiences. When people talk about films, they like to believe they are experts. They speak with authority as they tell each other their opinions and reactions.

Films influence people in many of the fads, clothing styles, mannerisms, and lifestyles that they copy from actors and actresses—the twitching of the matchstick by Warren Beatty in *Bonnie and Clyde,* the kung fu tricks of Bruce Lee, and even the hair and dress styles from *The Great Gatsby.*

During the fifties, Marlon Brando's cool, nonchalant, controlled method of acting was imitated by thousands of young people. Typical teenage boys could be seen standing on a street corner, thumbs hanging on tight jean pockets, a cigarette hanging from narrow lips, and head lowered with slightly closed eyes looking up. This body posture and mannerism was straight out of *The Wild One* or *On the Waterfront,* from the characters identified with Marlo Brando. It was the "cool look," still with us today, but personified by more different actors and a greater variety of films: Robert Redford and Paul Newman in *The Sting;* Clint Eastwood in *Pale Rider;* John Travolta in *Saturday Night Fever, Grease,* or *Urban Cowboy;* Burt Reynolds in *Smokey and the Bandit* or *Rough Cut;* or Roger Moore in *A View to Kill.*

4. Throughout the history of motion pictures, people have gone to movies because they are a way of escaping the realities of life, if only for a short time. A movie allows you to experience undreamed-of excitement, adventure, drama, comedy, and romance in your own not-very-exciting life. Movies, after all, are not real. But they *seem* very real. Sometimes, especially if a movie is well done, you forget to distinguish between reality and fantasy while you're watching. You can experience many of the same emotional feelings as the characters in the movies.

During the Depression of the 1930s, thousands

Films become shared experiences as we discuss scenes like Gozer's Temple and the Terror Dogs with others who've seen *Ghostbusters*, one of the most popular comedies of all time. (Ghostbusters © *1984 Columbia Pictures Inc. All Rights Reserved. Courtesy of Columbia Pictures.)*

of people flocked to movie theaters to see beautiful women and handsome men tap-dance across gigantic, lavish stages in the pure-escape films of Busby Berkeley. During this era, people needed to be entertained. They wanted to forget the realities of their gloomy and cheerless lives at the height of the Depression. During these years, the "star system" became important, because people preferred to think and dream about the supposedly glamorous and exciting lives their heroes and heroines were leading.

Sometimes everyday life is just boring or confusing or frustrating, rather than grim, but movies still give us an escape to another world.

Perhaps it isn't a coincidence that during the recession and widespread unemployment of the middle 1970s, people flocked to see spectacular "disaster" films like *The Poseidon Adventure* and *The Towering Inferno.* These exciting, if improbable, films provided a sure way to forget less dramatic problems. So did the always popular spy, adventure, and crime films, from *Godfather I* and *II* to *Murder on the Orient Express.*

Films of the eighties are bringing people back

into the theaters. Box-office hits like *Tootsie, Ghostbusters,* and *Beverly Hills Cop;* critically acclaimed films like *Amadeus* and *A Passage To India;* heartwarming movies like *The Karate Kid* and *The Natural;* and of course the science-fiction trilogy of *Star Wars, The Empire Strikes Back,* and *The Return of the Jedi* are making moviegoing popular once again.

5. Hollywood filmmakers create a tremendously entertaining and captivating product, and they know how to get people into the theater. Motion pictures (including movies shown on television and cable, and available for video rental) may well be one of the most common subjects of conversation among certain groups of people. Movies are fun to see. They seem so exciting! Because of this immediacy, we are caught up in adventure (*Raiders of the Lost Ark*), jealousy (*Amadeus*), and compelling drama (*The Killing Fields*).

Because film has the ability, through the marvelous interplay of technique and mood, to transport us in time, it can also reflect the society of an earlier day. David Lean gave us a vivid picture of Czarist Russia in the opening scenes of *Doctor Zhivago.* Twenty years later, in *A Passage to India*, he showed us two worlds and two cultures of 1928 India, using the emotional and deeply personal story of a sensitive young woman and a young man to illustrate class conflict.

Because *Amadeus*, the brilliant film about the rivalry of Mozart and Salieri, court composer, was shot on location in Czechoslovakia, director Milos Forman and producer Saul Zaentz were able to use many 200-year-old buildings and treasures to portray the complexities of the Austro-Hungarian Empire.

"Time has stood still in Prague," says Forman. "There are wonderful palaces whose interiors are preserved as museums that are just breathtaking."

Amadeus uses the interiors of six different palaces as locations, often stocked with antique furniture from dozens of other buildings, including inlaid cabinets and tables.

For the scenes in the Emperor Joseph's palace, the sixteenth-century Archiepiscopalace in Prague was used. Gobelin tapestries, rich with designs showing the discovery of the New World, hung on the walls. The actor portraying the Emperor sat on gold furniture from the summer palace of the Schwarzenbergs. Mozart and Salieri are shown playing on one-of-a-kind pianos that are virtually beyond price.

This insistence on absolute authenticity that marked every phase of the *Amadeus* production extended to period costumes, wigs, dress and manners at court, the uniforms of the servants, and the garb of people in the street.

Depression audiences flocked to see *Gold Diggers of 1933*, typical of the lavish musicals that provided escape from hard times. *(The Museum of Modern Art/Film Stills Archive.)*

Movies Are Big Business

Theatrical movie-going continues to be big business, despite the competition of broadcast and cable television, VCRs, and other forms of entertainment. The Motion Picture Association of America (MPAA), industry trade association, says that a box office gross of $4,030.6 million in 1984 represents a 7.0 percent change since 1983, which had set a record-breaking gross of $3,766.0 million.

With over a $4 billion gross in 1984 box-office

Year	Box Office Gross (million)	Yearly Percent Change
1984	$4,030.6	+ 7.0%
1983	3,766.0	+ 9.1%
1982	3,452.7	+ 16.4%
1981	2,965.6	+ 7.9%
1980	2,748.5	− 2.6%

Through the magic of films like *Amadeus,* we "see" the universal emotions of ambition and youthful exuberance set in the rigid patterns of court society. Here, F. Murray Abraham as Antonio Salieri, conducts one of his compositions, while brooding over the young Mozart's rapidly growing popularity. (Amadeus © *1984 The Saul Zaentz Company. All Rights Reserved.*)

gross receipts, according to MPAA, movie going in theaters is obviously here to stay. Though television has influenced the movie habit, and though sales of movies on video cassette are climbing, the movie theater as generations of Americans have known it is scarcely going out of business. In fact, the MPAA says there were 20,200 hardtop/conventional theater screens in 1984, a 6.9 percent increase over 1983. Drive-in screens were down to 2,832, with 20 fewer screens than in 1983.

Throughout the first eight months of 1984, the motion picture industry employed an average of 216,050 people, compared to 210,088 during the same period in 1983. Production and Services

personnel increased to 96,275, compared to 83,400. Distribution employees averaged 10,288, compared to 1983 figures of 10,375. Theater employment, however, dropped to 109,488, down from 116,313 in 1983.

In 1983, the latest year for which figures are available, a total of $828.8 million was spent to advertise motion pictures in newspapers, on television, on radio, and in magazines. Newspapers had a 71.4 percent share of the advertising dollar; network television came next, with 15.9 percent; followed by local television (9.4 percent), radio (2.7 percent), and magazines (0.6 percent.)

In 1984, the MPAA computerized tracking system identified 87 distributors, including MPAA member companies, who released 398 new features and 122 reissues, for a total of 520 films. The average negative cost of new features financed in whole or in part by the nine MPAA companies and released in 1984 was $14.4 million, compared with 1983's cost level of $11.9 million. The median cost (half the films cost more; half the films cost less) was $11.5 million per film, up slightly from $10.807 million in 1983.

Foreign revenues, of course, are in addition to these figures, which represent United States theater box-office grosses. Feature films often are huge box-office successes abroad. *Grease, Close Encounters of the Third Kind,* and—more recently—*Ghostbusters* have been extremely popular in foreign countries. Producer/director Ivan Reitman made a special tour of Japan and Europe to help promote *Ghostbusters,* a strategy which certainly contributed to the film's total revenues.

Made-for-television movies, too, have markets outside the United States. Television executive Steve Mills, whose CBS Motion Pictures for Television and Mini-series Division is responsible for over 50 completed films per year, says the contracts CBS makes with producers often call for films to be shown twice on the CBS network in a three- or four-year period. "We'll pay the producer $2 milion, even though it costs $2½ or $3 million to make the picture," Mills says. "Then the rights revert to the producer, who can easily make up any deficits through foreign sales."

Foreign-produced films distributed in the United States have their United States grosses included in the U.S. Theatrical Economic Review.

Such pictures as Australia's *Mad Max,* its highly popular sequel, *Road Warrior,* and *Mad Max II; My Brilliant Career;* West Germany's *Paris, Texas,* which won The Golden Palm Award in 1984's international film festival in Cannes, and *Das Boot;* Russia's *Wartime Romance;* Argentina's *Camila;* and Israel's *Beyond the Walls* all have enjoyed critical and box-office acclaim.

Who Goes To See Films?

Film-going used to be a family affair, but television and video cassette recorders are changing viewers' habits. By 1985, more than 40 million American homes had cable television, and *Time* estimated that 17 million VCRs were in use. In January 1983, the U.S. Supreme Court ruled that the home taping of broadcast programming does not violate copyright laws, a decision which sanctioned what millions already were doing. However, MPAA President Jack Valenti attacked the practice. "A dismal concern of American creative people is the ability of the video cassette recorder to make multiple and incessant copies of movies and television material without the permission of the copyright owner, or any compensation to the producers of that entertainment," he told a German film-industry luncheon in Munich.

By early 1985, an estimated 5,000 films had been released on video cassette, and more were on the way. MGM dusted off *Gone with the Wind*—though the film's first video cassettes were produced with the "wrong" version of Dixie accompanying the opening screen credits and had to be redone. *Raiders of the Lost Ark* (at a pre-Christmas price of $24.95) became the bestselling video cassette of all time. Movies of the forties and fifties (*Painted Desert, Flying Deuces,* and nearly a hundred other titles) at $19.95 were offered by Waldenbooks, a large nationwide chain of retail bookstores. Movies could be rented, sometimes for as little as $1 per night, from a wide variety of outlets: photography stores, video or electronics dealers, and even grocery supermarket chains.

Yet people are still seeing movies in traditional theaters. Despite a 5 percent drop in attendance from the previous year, 115 million moviegoers age 12 and older paid admission in 1984. An MPAA survey in August, 1984 showed that 51 percent of teenagers (12–17 years old) went to the movies at least once a month, and an additional 34 percent went occasionally. Most moviegoers are under 40, and they account for 85 percent of total yearly admissions. Single persons go to movies more frequently (at least once a month) than do married adults, and a higher percentage of adults with children under 18 go to the movies more frequently or occasionally than adults without children. More males than females tend to be frequent moviegoers, and moviegoing continues to increase with higher levels of education.

Which Films are the Most Popular?

One of the more effective ways to find out which films are currently being seen by the largest number of viewers is to check *Variety. Variety,* a weekly tabloid newspaper covering many areas of the entertainment business, is available on many newsstands and in most public libraries. Each week, this newspaper tells its readers, in its own special colorful terms, how top films are doing.

'Fields' Potent 150G, Bost.-Prov.;
'Falcon' 125½G, 'Cop' Brisk 157G

is a *Variety* headline that tells readers *The Killing Fields,* Academy-Award nominated drama of southeast Asia, is doing brisk business in the Boston–Providence (R.I) market during the week preceding February 6, 1985. *The Falcon and the Snowman,* Orion's non-fiction spy story, is running a close second, bringing a box-office gross of $125,000, and *Beverly Hills Cop,* the Eddie Murphy comedy, is pulling in $157,000.

Variety's Philadelphia correspondent says, "*Beverly Hills Cop* continues to ankle along displaying great lags with a $162,000 ninth week via 17 lookeries."

From Los Angeles, *Variety* correspondent Richard Klein reports that "*Beverly Hills Cop* (which looks to $312,000 at 20 in ninth) kept its

****

ALL-TIME FILM RENTAL CHAMPS
(OF U.S.-CANADA MARKET)

****

Following is listed *Variety's* annually updated roster of All-Time Rental Champion Films, pictures which have paid $4,000,000 or more in domestic film rentals to the distributor. (Film rentals are that portion of boxoffice ticket sale grosses remitted by exhibitors to the film's distributor.)

This list contains many changes of figures, both upward and downward, reflecting corrected and updated information provided since last year's report. Dollar changes do not necessarily reflect boxoffice activity solely during 1984, but include changes in prior years' data. New films released in 1983 and 1984 that qualify have been added to the list, and several films have been dropped from the chart, latter due to corrections which reduced their rentals totals below the $4,000,000 minimum. (Data are through December 1984.)

The rentals figures listed here are absolute dollar figures for each film, reflecting actual amounts received by the distributors (estimated in the case of pictures in current release), not adulterated or adjusted to reflect inflation. They are listed in descending order by level of performance, though pictures released in different eras cannot be compared directly due to a variety of factors. (The same data are presented in alphabetical order by film title in the Intl. Film Annual Issue printed each May.)

Ticket price inflation favors recent films in terms of their rentals performance, as does the new phenomenon of saturation releases in which 800 or more prints are used to debut a picture. On the other hand, the movie-going population (and frequency of attendance) was much greater in earlier periods (especially before 1950), and the older films have the advantage of numerous reissues adding to their totals. (The newest pictures have, with very few exceptions, no reissue potential and, of course, less time elapsed to benefit from a reissue.)

Readers are cautioned that using a simple multiplying factor based on the Consumer Price Index or Average Ticket Price per year to adjust the following actual figures for inflation may lead to misleading results. A better method is to make head-to-head comparisons only between films released during the same time period.

Worldwide film rentals, as well as domestic or worldwide figures for total boxoffice ticket sale grosses, are not used in tabulating the list of boxoffice champions because these figures are not available on a comprehensive basis covering all films.

Readers who query *Variety* in search of the worldwide rentals, b.o. gross, or even admissions head-count figures should be aware of the difficulty in obtaining such information. This is reflected by the frequent use of *Variety*-reported *domestic rentals* figures in periodicals and reference books printed overseas, where worldwide data, independently gathered, would be more appropriate to the discussion.

Collection of worldwide data is particularly difficult since major distributors only report it for hit films and not the relative flops and, increasingly, a top film is being distributed territorially by dozens of individual distributors, due to the growth of the independent producer and presale financing.

A sizable contingent of older releases is round-figure estimated at the minimum $4,000,000 level, though more exact data would be distinctly preferable. There is an emphatic reluctance on the part of film companies to revise figures (with the possible exception of Buena Vista) following a film's initial release and major re-release.

Some of the older films have had considerable subsequent income, but it is rarely reported. The total for Fox' "The Rocky Horror Picture Show" has been updated recently, reflecting several years of continuous midnight showings.

Note: Film title is followed by name of director, producer or production company, original distributing company plus present distributor, if different (e.g., MGM/UA), plus differing U.S. and Canadian distribs in the case of some foreign-made films; year of release; and total rentals received to date.

Title Director-Producer-Distributor	Total Rentals
E.T. The Extra-Terrestrial (S. Spielberg; S. Spielberg/K. Kennedy; U; 1982)	$209,976,989
Star Wars (G. Lucas; G. Kurtz; Fox; 1977)	193,500,000
Return Of The Jedi (R. Marquand; H. Kazanjian/G. Lucas/Lucasfilm Ltd.; Fox; 1983)	165,500,000
The Empire Strikes Back (I. Kershner; G. Lucas/G. Kurtz; Fox; 1980)	141,600,000
Jaws (S. Spielberg; R. Zanuck/D. Brown; U; 1975)	129,961,081
Ghostbusters (I. Reitman; Col; 1984)	127,000,000
Raiders Of The Lost Ark (S. Spielberg; F. Marshall/H. Kazanjian/G. Lucas; Par; 1981)	115,598,000
Indiana Jones And The Temple of Doom (S. Spielberg; R. Watts/G. Lucas/F. Marshall; Par; 1984)	109,000,000
Grease (R. Kleiser; R. Stigwood/A. Carr; Par; 1978)	96,300,000
Tootsie (S. Pollack; S. Pollack/D. Richards; Col; 1982)	95,197,000
The Exorcist (W. Friedkin; W.P. Blatty; WB; 1973)	89,000,000
The Godfather (F.F. Coppola; A. Ruddy; Par; 1972)	86,275,000
Superman (R. Donner; P. Spengler; WB; 1978)	82,800,000
Close Encounters Of The Third Kind (S. Spielberg; J. & M. Phillips; Col; 1977/1980)	82,750,000
The Sound Of Music (R. Wise; Fox; 1965)	79,748,000
Gremlins (J. Dante; M. Finnell/S. Spielberg/F. Marshall/K. Kennedy; 1984)	78,500,000
The Sting (G.R. Hill; T. Bill/M. & J. Phillips; U; 1973)	78,198,608
Gone With ████████ (V. Fleming; D. Selznick; MGM/█████	76,700,000
Satur██████████ Stigwood; Par; 197█	74,100,000

Title Director-Producer-Distributor	Total Rentals
The Best Little Whorehouse In Texas (C. Higgins; T. Miller/E. Milkis/R. Boyett; RKO/U; 1982)	47,549,136
Doctor Zhivago (D. Lean; C. Ponti; MGM/UA; 1965)	46,550,000
Butch Cassidy And The Sundance Kid (G.R. Hill; J. Foreman; Fox; 1969)	46,039,000
Airport (G. Seaton; R. Hunter; U; 1970)	45,281,020
Mary Poppins (R. Stevenson; W. Disney; BV; 1964)	45,000,000
The Jerk (C. Reiner; D. Picker/W.E. McEuen; U; 1979)	43,350,787
The Ten Commandments (C.B. DeMille; Par; 1956)	43,000,000
The Poseidon Adventure (R. Neame; I. Allen; Fox; 1972)	42,000,000
Arthur (S. Gordon; R. Greenhut; Orion/WB; 1981)	42,000,000
Rocky II (S. Stallone; R. Chartoff/I. Winkler; UA; 1979)	41,879,000
The Goodbye Girl (H. Ross; R. Stark; MGM/WB; 1977)	41,800,000
The Karate Kid (J. Avildsen; J. Weintraub; Col; 1984)	41,700,000
Snow White (Anim; W. Disney; RKO/BV; 1937)	41,400,000
Stripes (I. Reitman; D. Goldberg/I. Reitman; Col; 1981)	40,877,000
Airplane (J. Abrahams/D. Zucker/J. Zucker; H.W. Koch/J. Davison; Par; 1980)	40,610,000
Trading Places (J. Landis; A. Russo; Par; 1983)	40,600,000
Any Which Way You Can (B. Van Horn; F. Manes; WB; 1980)	40,500,000
Fiddler On The Roof (N. Jewison; UA; 1971)	40,498,669
Alien (R. Scott; G. Carroll/D. Giler/W. Hill; Fox; 1979)	40,300,000
Star Trek II: The Wrath Of Khan (N. Meyer; R. Sallin/H. Bennett; Par; 1982)	40,000,000
Coal Miner's Dau████ (M. Apted; R. Larson; U; 1980)	39,959,367
Smoke████████████████████ Moonjean;	

© 1985, Variety. Reprinted with permission.

9

perfect record intact this weekend of decisive vistories here, while *The Falcon and the Snowman* ($185,000 at 10 in second) held on to runnerup slot.''

After you've read a few *Variety* stories, you catch on quickly to the language the paper uses to describe how well pictures are doing. In New York City, *Variety* reports on *The Cotton Club,* ''No reservations necessary as tooter, tap-dancers, thrushes and hitmen move into low-Gere with $90,000 at 32 after $209,798 at 62.''

A Passage to India's New York City grosses are described as ''East meets West for a wide-breaking $369,000 in sixth trip to 77 after a Rajah-like $166,334 at eight.''

Translated, this means that Francis Ford Coppola's *The Cotton Club,* which stars Richard Gere in a gangster-nightclub film, has been playing at 62 theaters, but this week has dropped to 32, with a corresponding financial decrease in box-office receipts. *A Passage to India,* David Lean's Oscar-nominated film, is currently playing at many more theaters than the preceding week, with box-office receipts more than doubled.

Each week, *Variety* publishes a full-page chart that lists the 50 top-grossing films of the week; their titles, distributors, revenues for the preceding week; and their rank based on financial income.

Each January, *Variety* publishes a list of ''Alltime Film Rental Champs of U.S.-Canada Market,'' which lists pictures that have paid $4 million or more in domestic film rentals to the distributor. Because of inflation, and of saturated release in which 800 or more prints are used to introduce a picture, recent films are favored in the list. It is not possible to use the Consumer Price Index or similar formula to adjust *Variety's* actual figures for inflation, as the results would be misleading. Worldwide film rentals aren't used to tabulate the box-office champions list, because such rental figures are not available for all films on a comprehensive basis.

As *Variety* listed the top films in January 1985, the *Star Wars* trilogy (*Star Wars, Return of the Jedi,* and *The Empire Strikes Back*) were firmly in second, third, and fourth place, trailing *E.T.: The Extra-Terrestrial,* with *Jaws,* the 1975 Spielberg hit, in fifth place.

Ivan Reitman's *Ghostbusters,* which *Variety*

terms the comedy hit of all time, was sixth, followed by Lucasfilm's *Raiders of the Lost Ark* and *Indiana Jones and the Temple of Doom. Grease,* the 1978 John Travolta/Oliva Newton-John musical parodying the fifties, and *Tootsie,* which featured Dustin Hoffman in drag, completed the top ten.

The movie industry attempts to keep constant tabs on the changing tastes, habits, fads, moods, feelings, and social climates of the generation that sees movies most. Producers must be constantly aware of what movies people will want to see. Since the industry is investing millions of dollars into each movie, producers must be alert to pick up new trends in a fickle audience. In addition, they must be able to guess—in a risky market—what the competition is planning. Sometimes several movies are made around a similar theme. If they are released too close together, the success of each picture may be diluted by the others, even if the films are well reviewed and well received. During the Christmas 1984 season, the simultaneous play of *Dune, 2010,* and *Starman* tended to dilute the potential box office for sci-fi films and possibly reduce the gross of each picture. In most cases, getting a film from concept to theater showing takes 18 months to two years, and often, substantially longer. For instance, *A Chorus Line,* the behind-scenes soul-baring struggles of 17 dancers vying for roles in a Broadway musical, was released in late 1985. Yet Universal originally bought screen rights ten years earlier, selling them to Polygram in 1980. *Variety* reported that producers Cy Feuer and Ernest Martin paid $100,000 of their own money to screenwriter Arnold Schulman for a first draft. Eventually a production deal was worked out with Embassy, which financed the picture. Director Richard Attenborough (*Gandhi*) estimated the film's cost at $24 million: $9 million for development and $15 million for production.

Is the Most Popular Best?

If we believe *Variety,* popularity is synonymous with ''best'' and ''financial success.'' Sometimes this is true. *The Killing Fields,* second on the *Variety* chart of 50 top-grossing films in mid-February 1985, with a sample gross of $1,373,542 for the

The motif of masked people runs throughout *Amadeus,* paralleling Mozart's own preoccupation with disguise. Here, Tom Hulce as Mozart captures the exuberance of the game-playing, rebellious man-child whose 626 known compositions before his death at 35 included 23 operas, 66 arias, and 20 masses. (*Amadeus* ©*1984 The Saul Zaentz Company. All Rights Reserved.*)

Sally Field's struggle, as a widow and mother, to save her family and farm by harvesting the cotton crop won her the second Academy Award of her career. Also nominated as Best Actress for similar roles were Jessica Lange (*Country*) and Sissy Spacek (*The River*). (Places In the Heart © 1984 Tri-Star Pictures. All Rights Reserved.)

week ending February 6, received 13 Academy Award nominations, including "best picture."

Amadeus, Saul Zaentz's adaptation of Peter Schaeffer's play about jealousy and bitterness in the world of Mozart, was another Academy Award nominee for "best picture" and had 10 additional nominations. Yet during the same time period, *Amadeus* grossed only $482,850.

Does this mean *The Killing Fields* was a "better" picture than *Amadeus*?

Not necessarily.

Because Orion Pictures, which distributed *Amadeus*, felt the film would appeal to more discriminating audiences, the film initially had limited platform release. As word-of-mouth recommendations spread and as the film received outstanding reviews, broader distribution began.

Amadeus illustrated the popularity of American films abroad. In Norway, one top theater with 1158 seats reported over 90 percent capacity during the film's first 55 days. Said Knut Bohwim of Kommunes Film Central, "This means one-sixth of the population of Oslo has seen the picture." In Switzerland, Martin Hellstern of Rialto Film reported that 11th-week grosses were 50 percent better than the first. And within weeks of the Oscar nominations, *Amadeus* opened in Australia, Great Britian, Israel, Italy, Japan and the Far East, Portugal, South America, and Spain.

Film popularity, then, depends on more than "film quality" and is affected by many variables, including distribution and timing. Jane Fonda's *The China Syndrome*, which dealt with a hypothetical near-meltdown at a nuclear plant, opened within days of the real Three Mile Island accident. No one knows exactly how much effect audience concerns had on the film's popularity, but it seems safe to say the coincidence helped.

On the other hand, timing of release may have hurt the three "save the farm" dramas that opened in late 1984. *Places in the Heart* (Sally Field), *Country* (Jessica Lange), and *The River* (Sissy Spacek) had somewhat similar themes of a strong woman struggling to keep the family farm from going under. Each film received good reviews. But box-office success for any one of the films might have been greater without the competition for essentially the same audience.

We have been accustomed to accepting movies as best if they are the most popular. We seem to think *Raiders of the Lost Ark* must be a great movie because so many people went to see it. Perhaps *Raiders* and its sequel, *Indiana Jones and the Temple of Doom,* are great motion pictures, especially in their creative use of fantasy and special effects. Maybe one standard we can use to judge a movie's quality is the enormous numbers of people who go to see it. But the number of people who go to see *Raiders*—or any other film—does not, by itself, prove anything about the movie's quality. Instead, it proves only its popularity. In later chapters, we shall investigate what criteria we can use to judge a film's excellence.

Promotional advertising and skillful marketing techniques are used to persuade us that because "everyone" is seeing the movie, the film itself must be worthwhile. Marketing tie-ins of posters, T-shirts, lunchboxes, toys, calendars, and other merchandise—while bringing revenue to the film's distributors through strict licensing agreements—help remind us that we "should" see the film if we want to keep up with current trends.

Often these tie-ins are aimed at children. Ralston Purina introduced *Gremlins*™ Sweetened Cereal to coincide with the popularity of Steven Spielberg's film. "Please send me my 'Gizmo™' toy," said a boxtop coupon. "I have enclosed my check/money order for $9.95 plus two Gremlins™ brand cereal proofs of purchase." The box also suggested that youngsters should order 'Gizmo™' today. "He comes in his very own shoe box, just as you see him in the movie. Be sure to keep him out of bright light, don't get him wet, and never, NEVER feed him after midnight!"

One of the most successful promotional tie-ins between product and film came with *E.T.: The Extra-Terrestrial*. As Brian Herman, media relations manager for Hershey Foods Corporation, tells the story, "The studio had approached another candy company before they called us, but found no interest. In August, 1981, 10 months before the picture opened, we were told Reese's Pieces might be used in the film. Of course, Universal did not need our permission to photograph the product. However, we were asked to decide if we wanted to be involved in promoting both the film and Reese's Pieces through a licensing arrangement. The candy was due for national distribution, so we agreed.

"By June, 1982, when the film *E.T.: The Extra-Terrestrial* was released, we arranged to have Reese's Pieces in 800 movie theaters around the country. If you bought a bag, you'd get a free *E.T.* sticker. We put proof-of-purchase certificates on our packages so people could write in for an *E.T.* poster or T-shirt."

Herman says that although subsequent sales have leveled off, there was an initial sales increase of approximately 65 percent, due primarily to the film.

General Mills offered *E.T.* peanut butter and chocolate-flavored crispy, sweetened wheat and barley cereal, describing it as "E.T.'s favorite flavors." People who sent five *E.T.* Cereal Universal Product Code symbols could get a 1984 Grammy Award-winning 33⅓ record album with narration by Michael Jackson. Musical selections from the original motion picture were also available on cassette tape, as was a large 20-page storybook with over 40 full-color pictures from the movie. Also available: a 22 x 22-inch full color glossy poster of E.T. and Michael Jackson.

On the box was a maze, suggesting youngsters help E.T. find his favorite cereal. The maze included such hazards as chocolate peaks, peanut patch, milky marsh, and crunchy caverns.

Licensing and merchandising have become big business, not only for Warner Bros. (*Gremlins*) and Universal Studios (*E.T.: The Extra-Terrestrial*), but for Twentieth Century-Fox. *AdWeek's* Midwest Edition reports that Fox has 385 domestic agreements covering more than 3000 products. The rate of return for the studio ranges between 5 and 10 percent on each product sale, in addition to a substantial fee for the initial agreement.

"You want a certain amount of exposure," says Chuck Ashman, president of Twentieth Century-Fox Licensing, whose company has 25 agents in the United States and 53 agents in other countries to handle licensing. "You're constantly looking for new ways to reach your consumer without having to pay the prohibitive network costs."

AdWeek writer Betsy Sharkey says Fox licenses spin-off merchandise and promotions from the popular television series, *Dynasty,* aimed at the upscale consumer market. There's a *Dynasty* line of collectible dolls at $10,000 each; a *Dynasty* line of crystal and silver designed by Gorham; and a *Dynasty* boutique in Beverly Hills. Krystle Carrington's new "baby" was introduced at the February 1985 Toy Fair, complete with designer wardrobe and $200 crystal-and-silver baby bottle.

Charles of the Ritz reportedly spent $10 million developing a line of Krystle fragrances, priced at $150/ounce. Marshall Field's, the Chicago-based department store chain, expects to sell $250,000 of Forever Krystle perfume and colognes.

Motion picture/television retailing tie-ins are proving beneficial for Field's, says public affairs director Paul Costello. The Chicago store held a 1500-person black tie buffet dinner (and hospital benefit) to introduce the *Dynasty* designer collection and perfume. More than 5000 people viewed the Nolan Miller designs in the three weeks they were displayed. Marshall Field's Christmas 1984 windows were decorated as "Christmas with the Carringtons."

To publicize *Dune,* the $40-million science fiction film, Marshall Field's created a multi-visual effect with the picture's sound track and original design sketches. Ten original costumes from the film were displayed, along with pieces of the original furniture. *Dune* author Frank Herbert was imported for book autographing.

Twentieth Century-Fox licensed sportswear, sleepwear, and children's clothing as a promotion for *Johnny Dangerously,* a gangster film starring Michael Keaton. For three weeks after the film opened in December 1984, 500 shopping center windows in 500 cities were promoting the *Johnny Dangerously* line.

Clearly, licensing and merchandising is big business—an $8 billion annual bonanza, according to *AdWeek.* Here's what they reported had been arranged for *2010,* even before the film opened.

Author Frank Herbert made a promotional tour helping to publicize *Dune,* the high-budget film based on his bestselling novel. Department stores like Chicago's Marshall Field's borrowed some of the film's costumes to create a popular exhibit. *(Courtesy of Marshall Field's.)*

2010 Licensing Agreements*

- Simon & Schuster: *The Official Art of 2010* paperback

- Allando fashions: Line of futuristic jackets, jumpsuits, key chains, and jewelry

- Allison Manufacturing: *2010* T-shirts and pajamas being distributed through J. C. Penney, Target, K-mart and other mass merchandisers

- IJE Kidstuff: Children's record and book sets

* © 1984 *ADWEEK.* All rights reserved. Used with permission.

- TSR Inc.: Adventure games and toy figures based on *2010*

- Marvel: Series of *2010* comic books, including a special $2 edition

- Ballentine Books: Re-release of author Arthur Clarke's *2010: Odyssey Two* and the release of *The Odyssey File,* excerpts from conversations between Clarke and director Peter Hyams, in paperback

- Roach Inc.: Caps, embroidered and puff-ink models, distributed through mass merchandisers including K-mart and J. C. Penney

- Sandylion Stickers: 2-D and 3-D holograph stickers

- One Stop Posters: *2010: The Year We Make Contact* buttons

- Starlog Magazine: *2010*, magazine with newsstand distribution

- Starmakers: *2010* posters, puzzles, and stickers

- George Fenmore Associates: *2010* souvenir program for in-theater sales

Many of us, also, are influenced by what critics say about films. Previews of *Witness,* along with generally good reviews, shown on television stations in advance of the film's opening, were undoubtedly partly responsible for long lines at the box office. If critics we like because of their past recommendations tell us we should go see a film, or that we'll enjoy it, their endorsements may tip the scale when we decide which movie to see.

If your local critics don't like the movie, the publicity agent often manages to find an out-of-towner who does. Sometimes, even though local reviews are good, the ads feature nationally recognized names. For instance, the *Chicago Sun-Times'* Roger Ebert, the only movie critic to win a Pulitzer Prize, describes Peter Weir's *Witness* as, "Thrilling and touching, and exciting, and scary and romantic, and it never puts one foot wrong. This movie is really good. Harrison Ford has never given a better performance in a movie." But ads for *Witness* also quote *Newsweek's* Jack Kroll, "A feast of ravishing images and suspenseful rhythms. Harrison Ford is tough, sweet, romantic, brooding, masculine—more like the easy-flowing old movie stars than almost anybody in his generation," and *Glamour's* Joy Boyum, "A love story, thriller, and journey into quaint Americana all rolled into one enormously powerful film."

Ads for *The Breakfast Club*, the Dede Allen-edited chronicle of five high school students who meet for detention, remind viewers that *The Breakfast Club* is "entertaining, effective and strong . . . with excellent acting." The quote comes from William Wolf of Gannet Newspapers. Also part of the ad is Joel Siegel's statement that *"The Breakfast Club* is definitely the best in its class."* Siegel is critic for ABC-TV, *Good Morning, America.*

Striking pictures in newspaper ads and exciting sequences or clips shown in television ads catch our attention. Using popular stars for the film is another technique of promoting attendance, even though the "star" system of the thirties and forties, when major studios put players under long-term contracts and developed their careers through series of pictures, no longer operates. Clark Gable, John Wayne, Humphrey Bogart, Judy Garland, Shirley Temple, and Marilyn Monroe were all stars who could pull in large audiences on the strength of their box-office appeal.

Today, there are fewer "bankable" stars, and actors and actresses who qualify—that is, who can attract financing on the strength of their proven box-office appeal—can often command enormous salaries. Clint Eastwood, Harrison Ford, Robert Redford, Jack Nicholson, Paul Newman, Roy Scheider, and Dustin Hoffman—especially after the success of his performance in *Tootsie*—have no difficulty in being offered their choices of top scripts. Jane Fonda and Barbra Streisand also have this ability to attract investors, who recognize not only the ability of the stars, but also the near-certainty that any film they appear in will make money.

The Academy Awards

The most effective promotion a movie can receive is to be nominated for an Academy Award (an Oscar) from the Academy of Motion Picture Arts and Sciences, a by-invitation-only organization of approximately 4800 veteran film professionals, representing 14 branches of the film industry.

In order to be nominated, a film has to open in Los Angeles before December 31 of the year for which it's being considered. It must play in L.A. for seven consecutive days to paying audiences and have at least two shows a day during that time. Next, producers of those films must submit to the Academy an official bulletin listing screen credits, especially in technical categories. Films are then listed in a bulletin the Academy sends its members.

An Academy member in a particular branch—directing, for example—lists and ranks the top five pictures from the list for "best direction" and returns the ballot to the accounting firm of Price Waterhouse, which tallies results. In addition, all voting Academy members rank their top five choices for "best picture."

By mid-February, the nominees are announced. Often pictures are nominated for several awards. The Killing Fields was nominated for best picture, best director (Roland Joffe), best actor (Sam Waterston), best supporting actor (Dr. Haing S. Ngor), best screenplay based on material from another medium (Bruce Robinson), best film editing (Jim Clark), and best cinematography (Chris Menges).

A Passage to India was nominated for 11 awards: best performance by an actress in a lead role (Judy Davis) and in a supporting role (Dame Peggy Ashcroft), art direction, cinematography, costume design, directing, film editing, original score, best picture, sound, and screenplay based on material from another medium.

A special screening schedule at the Academy theater in Beverly Hills is set up, so members can attend. If they want to vote for "best foreign language film" or "best documentary features," members must see each of the five films nominated in those categories, and register their attendance at those Academy screenings. Before "Oscar" balloting takes place, producers often run "for your consideration..." ads in Hollywood trade papers, reminding Academy members of all the nominations their films have gathered.

Finally, a ballot listing all categories is mailed to the Academy's voting members. They have a week to make their decisions and send results directly to Price Waterhouse. This time, unlike the nominating procedure, they can vote in almost all categories—that is, a director can vote for "best performance by an actor in a supporting role." Only those who have seen all the foreign language films or documentary features can vote in those categories.

The Academy produces the Oscar telecast with a specially appointed production team. Millions of viewers, each remembering the films they've particularly enjoyed, watch the various presenters ask the Price Waterhouse representative for "the envelope, please."

If a film and its makers win several Oscars, there is usually no doubt that it will then become successful, at least in a money-making sense. The Academy Awards are more than a popularity contest, however. Academy library head Patrick Stockstill says research studies show some correlation between box-office grosses and Oscar winners. However, he feels that because voting is limited to Academy members—all veteran professionals—technical and artistic achievements are indeed recognized.

Though the movie choices shown on television may be numerous, especially if we don't mind staying up till 3 A.M., the number of commerical movies we can go to a theater and see at any given time is limited. Obviously, in small cities and towns where there are only one or two theaters, the choice is very limited. However, even in larger cities, our choice of commercial movies is much smaller than you might imagine. The same movie may be playing simultaneously at seven or eight nearby theaters.

If moviegoers basically are being fed a limited diet of movies with little diversity, we may continue to think that the movies being produced are the best. We simply don't have enough experience seeing different kinds of movies to make critical judgments.

We must realize that the major filmmaking companies are similar in many ways to the major automobile-producing companies. Both groups are in business to make a profit. That's their most important motive. Everything else comes

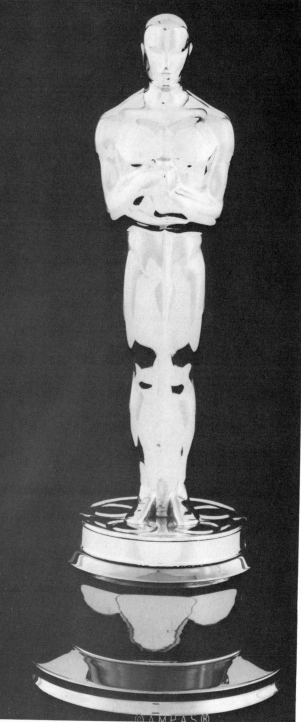

Presented annually since 1927-28 for outstanding achievements in filmmaking, the Oscar, awarded by the American Academy of Motion Picture Arts and Sciences, has come to symbolize success. (©*Academy of Motion Picture Arts and Sciences.*)

second. The auto makers placed safety and pollution controls far down their list of priorities until they were forced to build better and safer cars. Similarly, Hollywood will continue to produce the kinds of movies we see unless—or until—we demand something else. Even though producers would have us believe otherwise, Hollywood places profits first, above creativity, on its list of priorities. It will gladly sacrifice creativity if doing so means more revenue.

The most popular movies, then, are not always "best." We should try to be discriminating in our choice of movies, and not rely solely on popularity to indicate which films are "best." One of the objectives of studying the film is to become aware of some techniques in viewing movies that will help *you* decide whether a movie is worthwhile or not.

Film Is the World

Nearly 400 years ago, William Shakespeare said, "All the world's a stage." However, it wasn't until the invention of the motion picture that his words really came true.

Motion picture photographers sometimes describe their craft with the slogan, "Give us a place to put the camera, and we'll film the world." This description came true in 1969 when the first astronauts on the moon filmed the earth.

The moving picture camera can make a flower bloom before our eyes. It can capture the grace and beauty of a flying bird and the skill of a pole-vaulter making a jump. The moving image can transport us to any place on earth, or beyond, or underneath, or even out of the galaxy.

The camera can see the world through other people's eyes.

A thousand words can be written about a girl's beauty. Yet a picture of her face, showing her responding emotionally, tells us so much more about what she is like. Although there are some things that film cannot do easily, such as show us what a person is thinking, it often can show us much more, with much more conviction, than words can.

Film is the art of the world that we can share easily with all other people. A film scene of a child's smelling a flower means nearly the same thing to the Russian, Japanese, French, African, and American audience.

Film is *now*. It is in tune with the present. It helps us look at our world in a new way. Director D. W. Griffith, known best for *Birth of a Nation,* once said, "The task I am trying to achieve is, above all, to make you see."

Film shows us what it is like to be human.

Reflections and Activities

To the students, from the authors of *Understanding the Film:* Film is a current and ongoing art form that sometimes requires careful thought and reflection if it is to be understood. At the end of each chapter of *Understanding the Film* is a group of REFLECTIONS and ACTIVITIES.

REFLECTIONS are suggestions to guide your thinking about films. Reach each reflection carefully and consider the question it asks; also consider your own experiences and opinions. You might even consider your feelings as you reflect. Answering a REFLECTION, if only to yourself, will help you gain a greater and more peronal understanding of the film.

The ACTIVITIES are designed to get you actively involved in film appreciation. Some may be simple, other activities may be difficult. All the activities are planned to help you satisfy your curiosity about films and to improve your understanding of them.

Reflections

1. The last time you saw a movie in a theater, did you notice how the other people in the theater behaved? Did the audience as a whole react to certain scenes in the film? Was there scenery that only a few people reacted to? How do you think the behavior of the other people in the theater affects how you feel about a film?

2. Where does a *film* take place? How are the emulsion moving through the projector, what you see and hear on the screen, and what you feel about the film related?

3. Suppose you do not like a film, or perhaps do not understand it. Is this the fault of the filmmaker? Or is it your failure as an audience? Are there other possible reasons you might not like a film?

4. Why are some films more popular than others? What factors influence a film's popularity? Is audience reaction the only factor? What kinds of external influences can affect popularity?

5. What is an *action* movie? What is it about a film that makes it an *action* film?

6. When you discuss a film, do you always discuss it as if it were happening now? Why do you suppose this happens?

7. In what ways might films influence our society and our culture? Can you give any examples of influential films? Explain why you feel these films have influence.

8. Do you feel you have to see the latest film?

9. Many films are an escape from reality. What kinds of films allow people to escape? Do you always want to see the same kind of movie when you want to escape?

10. How do you decide which films to see? What influences you the most—friends? advertisements? reviews? something to do? or subject matter?

11. What kinds of films do you consider to be the most popular right now?

12. Are the most popular films the best films? Or have you found that there are some films that are very good but are not box-office successes?

13. What is a good film? What criteria do you use to decide?

14. What is the difference between film and literature? What can film do that literature cannot? What can literature do that film cannot?

15. Explain the meaning of the following statement: "Film shows us what it is like to be human."

Activities

1. Obtain about 25 plain index cards. Draw a simple action scene on each card. Make each

scene a little different. When the cards are flipped quickly the scene will appear to move. Examples: a person diving into a pool, a person dancing, and abstract designs of circles or triangles.

2. You can buy clear 16 mm film from a photographic supply center. Draw directly on the film with markers or paint. You will be drawing a movie. (Be sure not to draw between the sprocket holes.) Thread a projector with your film and watch the result of your creativity.

3. Research the history of motion pictures. The library will have materials on the early movies and early movie idols. Present the history in an oral or written report.

4. Conduct a one-week survey in your school to determine the most popular current films. Compare your list with the one in *Variety* for that week.

5. Look at a 16mm projector and observe how it works. Did you know that the film actually stops in the projector in order to project one frame on the screen?

6. Obtain a copy of *Variety* at your school or public library. The language in *Variety* is particularly colorful and geared for the entertainment industry. Pick a short article, or part of an article, and rewrite it in standard English. Why do you think *Variety*, a trade paper, uses colorful language and jargon?

7. Find some specific examples of how film influenced the behavior of people thirty or sixty years ago. This information can be found in older books describing film. Ask your librarian for help. Write a short report describing what you've discovered.

8. Collect advertisements of movies from newspapers or magazines. Notice the techniques used to get you into the theater: catchy drawings and titles, names of stars, phrases, catchy movie titles, quotes from reviews, etc. Bring in your advertisements and compare them with those your classmates collected.

9. Conduct a survey to find out how often students see films. Also ask what factors would encourage them to see films more frequently. Write your findings in a short report.

10. Look for a quote from a movie review in a movie advertisement in your newspaper. Then, find the original review. (The name of the newspaper or magazine where the review was printed will be mentioned in the advertisement. Magazine reviews are indexed under the heading "Motion Picture Reviews" in the *Reader's Guide* and listed in *The Magazine Index*.) Check to see if the critic really liked the movie, as the ad implies, or if he or she was quoted out of context.

Further Reading: *Check your library.*

Kaplan, Mike, ed. *Variety International Showbusiness Reference 1983,* New York: Garland Publishing, 1984.

—*Variety Major U.S. Showbusiness Awards,* New York: Garland Publishing, 1982.

—*Variety International Motion Picture Marketplace 1982–83,* New York: Garland Publishing, 1982.

Knight, Arthur. *The Liveliest Art,* New York: New American Library, 1979.

Monoco, James. *American Film Now: The People, The Power, The Money, The Movies,* revised edition, New York: New American Library, 1984.

Shipman, David. *The Story of Cinema: A Complete Narrative History from the Beginnings to the Present,* New York: St. Martin, 1984.

The Annual Index to Motion Picture Credits (published yearly) and *The Academy Players Directory* (published three times a year) are made available from the Academy of Motion Picture Arts and Sciences, 8949 Wilshire Blvd., Beverly Hills, CA 90211.

The Producer

Howard Kazanjian's filmmaking career began when, at 12, his parents gave him a movie camera, and he began creating neighborhood epics. A graduate of the University of Southern California Film School (where fellow students included George Lucas, Randal Kleiser, John Milius, and Gary Kurtz), Kazanjian then completed the Directors Guild Training Program.

As assistant director on Camelot *(Joshua Logan);* Finian's Rainbow *(Francis Ford Coppola);* The Wild Bunch *(Sam Peckinpah);* The Arrangement *(Elia Kazan);* The Front Page *(Billy Wilder);* The Hindenburg *(Robert Wise); and* Family Plot *(Alfred Hitchcock), Kazanjian worked with Hollywood's legendary directors.*

Asked by George Lucas to produce More American Graffiti, *Kazanjian then shared the responsibilities of executive producer with Lucas on* Raiders of the Lost Ark, *moving on to produce* Return of the Jedi, *the third film in the* Star Wars *trilogy.*

The producer's job can be as challenging and as complex as you want to make it. The producer creates the film.

Many producers today find a project or idea they like. They hire a writer to create a treatment or screenplay, and later, hire the director. Because the average feature film today costs around $14 million, they look for financing. If a major studio is putting up the money, it has a say in how the screenplay reads and may demand final approval before deciding to make the picture. A producer can also take the screenplay to a foreign distributor and trade those rights for a guarantee; can sell off cable rights to a company like HBO; can sell off worldwide or domestic video rights to a cassette-producing company. Then the producer can tell a studio, "I've raised half the money. Give me the rest of what I need, along with money for prints and advertising."

It's not easy. You need a good screenplay and a track record. People who put up the money don't bet on a horse race without knowing the horse and rider.

Most producers hire the writer and the director. Sometimes the studio gives its blessing; sometimes it insists on someone you don't want. Besides these people, I personally hire the production designer, the director of photography, and key personnel . . . right down to the special effects people and the makeup artist.

You pick a distributor that can get you the best theaters. You work with distributors in promotion and advertising, and even marketing.

Howard Kazanjian. *(Lucasfilm Ltd. (LFL) © 1983. All Rights Reserved. Courtesy of Lucasfilm Ltd.)*

Some producers follow a picture through every aspect of filmmaking. I monitor the quality of the prints, and their security, so we're not ripped off. When a film like *Raiders* or *Jedi* plays abroad, I like to see that the translation is done correctly . . . making sure the voice that's used in Sweden or Japan or Italy *sounds* like Harrison Ford and that American slang expressions are translated properly, so the audience understands the subtle meaning of dialogue.

A producer always is close to the budget . . . always involved in decisions with financial implications. Sometimes you have to spend more money. Maybe you use $40,000 for helicopters that weren't planned seven months ago. But you trade off. You eliminate 40 people in tuxedos in a downtown restaurant and find that an intimate table at a window overlooking the lake tells the story better than a lavish scene.

Should a picture with sand dunes be shot in Palmdale, near Los Angeles, in Yuma, or in Tunisia? Should interiors be done in England or Mexico for financial and creative reasons, or be shot on a Hollywood sound stage? By controlling the budget—crossing art with arithmetic—the producer makes those decisions.

With *Raiders of the Lost Ark*, our challenge was to do a great picture for $20 million. We had a wonderful screenplay, full of action; a creative executive producer; a very creative director. We worked with fire, water, miniatures, and snakes. We shot in Africa, England, and the United States, including Hawaii. We worked in Tunisia, where climate and working conditions were difficult.

It's the producer's responsibility to watch the daily costs of the picture, to make decisions and advise the director on what should be eliminated, altered, or adjusted. Hopefully, creative minds can make the savings, yet get the end results you want.

On *Raiders*, Steven Spielberg originally asked for 2,000 extras and sets built over 50 acres in Tunisia at the secret digs. We were budgeted for a maximum of 300 extras for three days, 200 extras for two days, and 100 extras for several weeks.

We were both in England, in pre-production. I had the art department place one-inch plastic soldiers all over a large model of the set and called Steven in. "My God," he said. "This is ridiculous. We can't have 2,000 extras. Let's cut it down." Then we wiped all the soldiers off the board. Steven studied the set and cut the area in half.

We were able to save $750,000. Although it was Steven's decision, psychologically I set it up. Once we got to Tunisia, we found the decision to use fewer extras was a wise one, because of problems with health, sanitation, transportation, feeding, wardrobe, and props. And we had a better look on screen.

Return of the Jedi, probably the most difficult picture ever made, required offices in San Rafael, labs in Los Angeles, a huge office complex and stages in London, offices and construction in Yuma, and another office complex in Crescent City, California, where preparation on the redwoods began a full year before photography. We scouted foreign countries for various locations. We were in constant communications between designers, art department, and the special effects house. Since producing is creative as well as monetary, I was responsible for the money. I had to coordinate everything.

On big-scale pictures, it's three years of round-the-clock, seven-days-a-week struggle. You're never on your own. You can't go home at night without the phone ringing, with decisions to be made.

It's hard work. On location, I'm often picked up at 6 A.M. to get to the set by 8 for shooting. I'm always at the studios till 8 at night. I read scripts at home on weekends.

On *Jedi*, George Lucas and I spent a full year in post production. We started each morning at 7 A.M., saw dailies at 8 A.M., and usually lived in film or sound cutting rooms all day.

Even when I'm not in production, the pace continues. One day last week, I met with a major studio in the morning, a toy licensing company at noon, a film insurance conference after lunch—all before going to my office.

You have to love it. Film people are crazy and wonderful, and the work is always challenging. The competition is fierce. It's not all Hollywood in dark glasses and a Mercedes. It's motivating others to do their best work . . . maintaining law and order on the set . . . meeting the schedule without hidden overruns. And in the end, when the audience likes the film, it's creative and self-satisfying.

2

The World of Film

Who Makes Movies?

Peter Bogdanovich, director of *Paper Moon* and *The Last Picture Show,* said, "The screen is nothing but a sheet with light and shadows on it—complete illusion. The magic lantern projects two-dimensional images on a blank screen, and it's spellbinding."

People all over the world *are* spellbound by the lights and shadows of motion projected upon a screen. The fascination may range from our sophisticated acceptance to the wonderment of primitive people seeing projected moving images for the first time.

The Chinese government has crews of film projectionists who carry a portable projector, screen, and propaganda films to thousands of rural villages.

The Japanese film industry cranks out more films each year than any country in the world.

The Soviet Union has more movie theaters than any other country. They also produced the most expensive film ever made—*War and Peace,* which reportedly cost more than $96,000,000 and which runs for 7 hours and 13 minutes. More than 165,000 uniforms had to be made. The re-creation of a battle lasted approximately the same length as the real battle.

Many factors influence a film's earnings. Rentals in the United States and Canada (called domestic earnings), rentals abroad, television licensing arrangements with domestic and foreign networks all must be taken into account. The release pattern selected for a film (the number of theaters showing the picture) affects earnings. So do percentage deals between theater owners and motion picture companies on revenue and publicity expenditures affect final figures.

Whole industries have developed within this world of film. The major Hollywood film production companies, such as 20th-Century Fox, Paramount, MGM, Universal, and Columbia, generally produce entertainment films. Most foreign countries have their own "Hollywoods." The names of actors and actresses are used to raise millions of dollars to finance movie productions. Michael Deeley, past president of EMI, commented, "We use big-name stars because they indicate a certain size and class of picture, and we tend to deal in more visual themes—which is a fancy way of saying we like action. Among the stars considered bankable on an international basis are Barbra Streisand, Jane Fonda, Jacqueline Bisset, Harrison Ford, Paul Newman, Robert Redford, Clint Eastwood, and Roy Scheider."

Irwin Allen, producer of such films as *The Poseidon Adventure* and *Towering Inferno,* observed "If you're spending $10–15 million on a picture, or more, you cannot make the movie for just the American audience. My pictures always made more money in the foreign markets than at home. You have to give foreign audiences spectacle and action that need no translation. My pictures could almost be shown without the dialogue. Make a picture with lots of action, stick in plenty of stars, and you'll get people into the theater in foreign countries."

Most films are produced with television in mind. The film is sold to television and the 16 mm market (schools, churches, hospitals, etc.) and made available in video cassettes.

Networks and local television stations produce their own news films and documentaries, though most are now created directly on videotape.

There are thousands of small film and video production companies across the United States and around the world that produce professional television commercials and sales-oriented films and tapes for business and industry. Many of these small companies also produce entertainment and educational films and tapes. Thousands of students in colleges, universities, high schools, and grade schools create their own films.

Companies that manufacture raw film, such as Eastman Kodak and Ansco, have grown into gigantic corporations. Almost anywhere in the world, you can find processing laboratories.

Why Make Films?

A film is made for many different reasons—to entertain, to educate, to make money, to do something creative, or simply to preserve the images (and now the sounds) of family occasions.

But the most basic reason why people have created this gigantic industry is that films communicate. Filmmakers use their skills and tech-

Dinosaur, the prize-winning short film by Will Vinton uses chalk line drawings and three-dimensional animation. The technique of cutting back and forth captures the audience interest while illustrating scientific facts. *(Courtesy of Pyramid Films.)*

niques to create a film because they have a message to communicate. Films communicate an intangible, immediate presence that can entertain, inform, and instruct all at the same time.

Films entertain

The most popular kind of film, as discussed earlier, seems to be the entertainment-type film. People sometimes say, "I only go to see entertaining films," meaning that they are the only films fun to watch. But let's broaden our definition of the word "entertaining" to include many more films—in fact, let us include *all* films.

The reason for this is that many films do not fall within the narrow, "fun" definition. For some people, an entertaining film is frivolity, neither educational nor very enlightening. Seen only in the theater or on television, it may have less quality and less artistic achievement.

But *all* films should be considered entertaining because they are an *agreeable occupation of the mind.*

Films teach

Films shown in schools are often referred to as "educational" films. This term makes students shudder and think of films called *Improving Your Punctuation, How to Conduct a Discussion, The American Revolution,* or *Alcohol and the Human Body.* In recent years, however, schools have begun to demand films that educate and inform students better.

As a result, the quality of educational films has improved tremendously. One hopeful sign is that most of the newer short "educational" films are visually exciting. The filmmakers and, more important, the producers, are discovering that today's sophisticated, television-oriented students want to see good films.

The primary objective of an educational film is to teach the audience in a planned and organized manner. This is not to say that an educational film is not entertaining, or that entertaining film is not educational. The significance is that the principal intent of many educational films is to persuade, to educate, to teach.

25

Documentaries such as *Dare the Wildest River,* shot on the Colorado River, often use establishing shots to give viewers a sense of participation and adventure. (*Courtesy of Pyramid Films.*)

Although many people think of film as only those pictures in theatrical release, short films designed for classroom and student use are seen by millions of viewers. (*Search for Solutions. Photo Courtesy of Phillips Petroleum Company.*)

Films inform

Films also can tell us about something new and make us aware of recent ideas. They are intellectually stimulating. Films furnish people with knowledge about how to perceive something new that was otherwise unknown. We learn from our total environment, and film is a part of it.

All films are entertaining, informative and educational in some way. However, most films have more of one quality than of the others, because filmmakers have various reasons for making a particular film. For instance, the filmmaker's primary objective in creating an entertaining film is to provide entertainment. If the film is informational or instructional in any way, it wasn't the main purpose. However, the film may make profound visual statements about life or the human condition. For example, *Rocky* was probably planned by Sylvester Stallone, writer and star, and John Avildsen, the director, as pure entertainment. Nevertheless, we can certainly gain profound emotional and intellectual knowledge from the fictional story. *Rocky* expands our hori-

zons; it helps us to know more about the world we live in. Stallone may not have set out to make *Rocky* to be instructive, but we can learn from it.

On the other hand, some types of films are intended to inform and instruct, though they may also entertain.

Since 1975, Phillips Petroleum Company has underwritten production and circulation of the *American Enterprise* film series. Using history rather than abstract economic concepts, the 29-minute films look at the free enterprise system from five viewpoints: Land, People, Innovation, Organization, and Government. Playback Associates, Inc., of New York City, produced the series with the guidance of nine leading economics professors. Says Dr. William Parker, professor of economics at Yale University, "What we see here is an attempt to forge a new educational tool that combines the vividness of an entertainment film with the accuracy and balance of a primary economics text. With wide circulation, this series can make a not inconsiderable difference in public understanding of economic ideas."

Eight thousand film prints of the *American En-*

Search for Solutions. *Photo Courtesy of Phillips Petroleum Company.*

terprise series have been circulated on a free loan basis to schools, along with a comprehensive teaching kit. They have been shown over 1.7 million times to 54.6 million viewers in the classroom. Phillips allows schools to duplicate videotapes of each film without charge. The company has donated a number of prints to junior and senior high school media centers. *American Enterprise* was the first educational series to reach one million students a month in the classroom.

Since 1979, Phillips Petroleum Company has provided a series of nine 18-minute films, *The Search for Solutions,* which explore the problem-solving process and illustrate that science is fun. Films are also targeted to secondary students, particularly women and minorities, to encourage them to consider a career in science, engineering, and technology.

The 14,000 prints of *The Search for Solutions* that Phillips underwrites are seen by an average monthly classroom audience of 1.7 million students. By spring 1985, these films had been shown 3.5 million times to a classroom audience of 98 million. Additionally, they have been shown twice on the Public Broadcasting System network. Phillips says this film series has been booked by over 72 percent of all high schools in the United States.

In each series, the only credit to Phillips is a three-second silent credit at the end of each film and a small credit line in teaching materials.

Genre of Films

There are probably as many genre of films as there are people who make them. Some genre, or types of films, are science fiction, western, gangster, adventure, police, fantasy, war, horror, musical, cartoon, comedy, disaster, and romantic films. We could also include in our genre of films: documentary, experimental, educational, and industrial films, women's films, Black films, Latino films, foreign films, propaganda, nature films, and newsreels.

As you can see, it is difficult to categorize film so that everyone will know what is being talked about. Confusion abounds. For example, what is the difference between cartoons and animated films? Can a western also be a comedy? A foreign film can be any of our genre of films, and it is only foreign depending on where you live. What is a women's film? Is it a film with only women it it, or is it made by a woman? Does it matter? To some people, it must matter, because the women's film is sometimes described in print.

Imagine a police officer chasing a gangster who became trapped in a time warp. Both characters are sent back to 1870; then they are discovered by Indians who are in the middle of a war with the local ranchers. In this short outline, we have used the police, gangster, science fiction, fanasy, war, and western genre. If we show the film outside of the country of origin, it is foreign. It is certainly educational. You might even discover more genres. The plot of our imaginary film isn't so unusual when it is compared to recent films such as *Time After Time* and *The Island.*

The problem is that it is difficult to put film into boxes. However, in order to make sense out of chaos, we have put films into some sort of categories. There are some terms that may help you think about film genre. Several kinds or genre of film are listed in the following list. You may think of more. Using the films you know, try to make relationships between the various genres, and define what the terms mean to you.

Some of these terms for genre of film need to be explored further so that you can understand their place in the world of film.

Science Fiction Films
Fantasy Films
Adventure Films
Horror Films
Musicals
Independent Films
Nature Films
Hispanic Films
Comedies
Experimental Films
Disaster Films
Police Films
Westerns
Industrial Films
Documentaries
Black Films
Romances
Propaganda Films
Foreign Films
War Films
Newsreels
Gangster Films
Women's Films
Cartoons

Documentary Films

Documentary films certainly inform and instruct the viewer. They also entertain, although perhaps not in an amusing way. What is entertaining in a documentary film usually relates to the realism and beauty it conveys to the viewer. The viewer can sometimes identify deeply with the people in a documentary film.

According to the Academy of Motion Picture Arts and Sciences: "Documentary films are defined as those that deal with historical, social, scientific, or economic subjects, either photographed in actual occurrence or re-enacted, and where the emphasis is more on factual content than on entertainment."

The word "documentary" was first used by John Grierson, an early documentary filmmaker in England, in a review he wrote of the film *Moana* created by Robert Flaherty, another early documentarian. Grierson called documentary filmmaking, "a creative treatment of reality."

Within the history of documentary films, there are six major types:

Newsreel

The newsreel was introduced years ago as a short subject between double features in the theater. Today television has made use of the newsreel film in daily news broadcasts.

Social action

These documentary films are similar to propaganda films, since they usually express a point of view. Grierson insisted that documentary films should be about real social problems, not about actors in a "problem" story. Documentaries should be about life, and life itself the source of the ideas, research, and filmmaking.

Propaganda

Propaganda films are structured and emotionally appealing, persuading us to form conclusions that are not necessarily part of the intellectual process. Many of the early films made in the Soviet Union, even the masterpieces of Eisenstein, were propaganda supporting the Russian Revolution. Nazi Germany also produced many propaganda films, notably Riefenstahl's famous *Triumph of the Will*. Many other countries, especially in wartime, have encouraged the making of patriotic propaganda films.

Television commercials are also good examples of propaganda. Within just a few seconds, the commercial must persuade the audience to buy or do something. Most commercials use all three approaches—they persuade, but some inform and also entertain.

Naturalist

This type of documentary film is concerned with the natural and primitive parts of our world—primitive peoples and nature.

The emotions a short film like *Flavio* call forth in viewers can become a starting point for classroom discussion. Gordon Parks, a gifted and sensitive photographer, captures the plaintiveness of poverty in this documentary. *(Courtesy of Contemporary Films/McGraw-Hill.)*

Realistic

The realistic documentary attempts to portray life as it is. Sometimes, through manipulation of the film in the editing process, it is possible to create an aspect of life that is not really real. Because the filmmaker has this control over the documentary, he may sacrifice objectivity and lose a part of what is real.

Lyrical

A lyrical documentary is simply a further extension in the manipulation of pieces of film to create a film-poem.

New Documentary Techniques

In the early 1960s new kinds of cameras and tape recorders were invented that allowed filmmakers much more freedom. Earlier filmmakers had to rely on bulky, heavy equipment, but now cameras can be powered by batteries. Today there also is a tape recorder capable of excellent sound recording that will even fit in a coat pocket. This enabled the documentary filmmaker to create *cinema verité,* or direct cinema. The filmmaker can go almost anywhere and do almost anything. The new style allows filmmakers to record events actually as they happen, with sound. This type of documentary is part of realistic filmmaking. In addition, new, light, portable video recorders are allowing film or videomakers to create on-the-spot visual recordings of nearly every event conceivable.

Famous documentary films include *Nanook of the North* (1922), Flaherty's film about an Eskimo family's fight for survival; *Night Mail* (1936), a poetic British film about a mail train; *The River* (1937), a Depression-era film about the Mississippi River area and its people; *Harvest of Shame,* a television documentary about the conditions among migrant laborers who harvest farm crops. The recent documentary film list can also include *Gimme Shelter* and *Woodstock.*

Some people feel that documentary films include even many commercially successful feature films. They would include such films as *The Godfather,* describing it as a documentary film about organized crime; and *Sounder,* a documentary film about a black family during the Depression.

Other people object, saying that a documenary film must deal with reality. Films like *The Godfather* and *Sounder* are only fictional accounts of reality. Robert Flaherty did discover Nanook and semidirected the Eskimo to do various pieces of action in the film. Flaherty also edited the film the way he wanted, as do fictional filmmakers. On the other hand, the film deals only with real people in their native setting.

A very influential present-day *cinema verité* filmmaker, Frederick Wiseman, does essentially the same thing that Flaherty did in the editing room. He chooses pieces of film and arranges them in the order he wants. The results—*High School, Law and Order, Basic Training,* and *Hospital*—are very much like reality. Yet Wiseman has manipulated the film to convey a message.

No filmmaker can be completely objective about a film. Various decisions must be made as where to put the camera, what exposure to use, how long to keep the camera operating, which scene to use when editing, where to put the scene, and so on. As soon as a decision is made, the filmmaker begins to lose objectivity. The decision, then, is how much objectivity should there be?

Animated Films

Animated films are created in a number of ways. The basic technique is to shoot one frame of a single drawn image or desired movement at a time, continuing the process as long as desired. The end result is a film showing a continual flow of movement.

One of the first animated films appeared in 1908—Winsor McCay's *Gertie, the Trained Dino-*

One of the earliest makers of documentaries, Robert Flaherty, shot *Nanook of the North* on location, developing his own film while in the Arctic. Though present-day Eskimo life has changed greatly, Flaherty's film gives us glimpses of a stark existence in which the fight for survival becomes a daily struggle. *(The Museum of Modern Art/Film Stills Archive.)*

The most famous mouse of all time, beloved Mickey, became a sorcerer's apprentice in *Fantasia*. Though its initial release was disappointing, the film's re-release has earned millions, and many experts now consider it one of the greatest animated films ever made. (Fantasia © *Walt Disney Productions.*)

saur. By 1917, newspaper cartoon strips such as the *Katzenjammer Kids, Krazy Kat,* and *Bringing Up Father* were popular with audiences.

Although he was not the first animated-film producer, Walt Disney is probably the best-known animated filmmaker. Disney created Mickey Mouse, Donald Duck, Goofy, and a host of other cartoon characters that have delighted audiences for decades. Further, Disney did much to develop the art of animation. In *The Art of Walt Disney,* Christopher Finch describes Disney: "His great abilities lay in the area of ideas—conceiving them, developing them, and seeing them through to a successful conclusion . . . he was, at his best, one of the most vigorous and innovative filmmakers in the entire history of the cinema."

Some of the most successful animated films have come from the Disney studios: *The Old Mill, Snow White and the Seven Dwarfs* (the first feature-length animated film), *Pinnochio, Fanta-*sia, *Dumbo, Bambi, Cinderella, One Hundred and One Dalmations, The Jungle Book,* other features, featurettes, and hundreds of short animations.

Other well-known animators include Walter Lantz—Bugs Bunny, Porky Pig, and Elmer Fudd—and Max Fleisher—Betty Boop, Popeye the Sailor, and the second feature-length animation, *Gulliver's Travels.*

Recently, animated films appreciated by the general public include the Beatles' *Yellow Submarine* and Bakshi's *Lord of the Rings.*

Animated films are very expensive to make, especially when they are done well. They are time-consuming, often taking large staffs of artists several years to complete. Recent experiments with animation completed by computers may result in a greater number of animated films.

Television uses animated series for morning programming and specials for holiday programming. Many of these films use only the most basic elements of movement in order to save on expenses. Nevertheless, many excellent animated programs on television may be a promise of even better animations in the future.

The National Film Board of Canada and Zagreb Studios in Yugoslavia have opened up the opportunity for animators to communicate via the moving animated image. Some of these films include *Walking, The Egg,* and *The Wall.*

Some artists have experimented with a form of animation called *pixilation.* The artist takes one frame and moves the subject a little, then shoots another frame, and so forth through the entire film. Some artists have used real people, such as Norman McLaren in *Neighbors* and *A Chairy Tale.* In these cases, the filmmaker has the person move a little bit for each frame. The results can be very funny, with people appearing to be skating on one leg, moving down the street while sitting, or moving while standing at attention.

Other artists have used the same technique with different media including sand, water colors, G.I. Joe dolls, and clay. Filmmaker and artist Will Vinton has used clay to create the very real films *Closed Mondays, Mountain Music,* and *Rip Van Winkle,* as well as The Nome King in *Return to Oz.*

Kinestasis is another form of animation. This technique uses many 3- or 4-frame shots of a still photograph, drawing, or a picture. The result is a very rapid series of pictures that appear to "flash by." Charles Braverman created *The Sixties,* using this technique in part. He also made *An American Time Capsule,* which is a history of the United States in four minutes. Braverman's *Condensed Cream of the Beatles* is one of the best films using kinestasis. *Frank Film,* which won an Academy Award, is really thousands of images cut from pictures in magazines and then animated by using kinestasis.

"Independent" Films

In filmmaking, the term "independent" has more than one meaning. Under the old studio system in the thirties and forties, producers were affiliated with a major studio. Promising young actors and actresses were placed under contract by studios and groomed for stardom, with lessons in

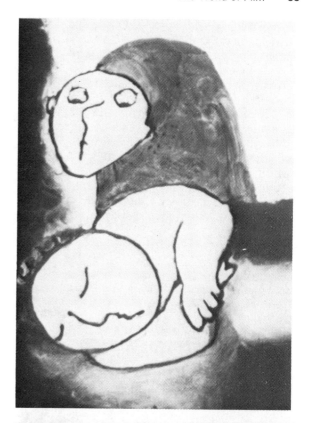

Animators use differing techniques to carry a film's message. *The Street,* (top), and *Animated Motion, Part 4* (bottom), demonstrate the versatility of animation. *(Courtesy of National Film Board of Canada.)*

acting, singing, and dancing. Often, like Debbie Reynolds and Elizabeth Taylor, they were placed under long-term contract, with options renewable at the studio's discretion.

Today, many pictures are made by filmmakers who work initially outside the studio system to plan a movie. Once financing and distribution have been arranged, the projects get under way.

After the double-barreled success of *Frances* and *Tootsie* (for which she won an Academy Award), Jessica Lange decided to develop her property. The result? *Country*, a critically acclaimed drama of an Iowa farm family struggling to overcome seemingly insurmountable obstacles.

Canada's Norman McLaren, famous film artist, uses the universal craft of mime to illustrate that man is never totally master of his situation. *A Chairy Tale* is as popular today as when it was first created. *(These are scenes from the National Film Board of Canada production* A Chairy Tale.*)*

Along with screenwriter/co-producer William D. Wittliff, Lange fleshed out the basic plot for *Country*, the story of a courageous farmer's wife who attempts to keep her family united through the forced foreclosure of her land. Lange and Wittliff met with Walt Disney Picture officials and secured financing for the film. It was decided that *Country* would be the second movie to be released by Touchstone Films, Disney's new subsidiary. Lange and Wittliff became co-producers, with William Beaudine, Jr. as line producer.

Independent film producer Saul Zaentz (*Amadeus*) came to films through the music business, going on the road in 1954 with Duke Ellington, Dave Brubeck, Gerry Mulligan, and Stan Getz. He joined the legendary Weiss Brothers and their offbeat label, Fantasy Records, eventually bought them out, and moved the company to Berkeley. Today, Fantasy, combined with The Saul Zaentz Company, occupies a square block of a seven-story complex fully equipped with state-of-the-art recording studios, mixing and film editing facilities, where many contemporary movies, including *The Right Stuff,* were edited.

Jim Henson's Muppets, created for television, proved even more popular on film. *The Muppets Take Manhattan* was a sequel to the financially-successful *The Muppet Movie.* (© *1984 Tri-Star Pictures. All Rights Reserved.*)

Zaentz's involvement in film production came when he co-produced the Oscar-winning *One Flew Over the Cuckoo's Nest* with Michael Douglas, a project with unusual business and contractual complications. Though Zaentz believes there are many intelligent and creative producers in Hollywood, he prefers to be independent.

"When you're an independent producer, whether you're in Hollywood or in Berkeley," says Zaentz, whose credits include *The Lord of the Rings* and the cult film *Payday,* "it means you have your own script, your own director. No one can tell you, 'Let's have an up ending with Mozart not dying—we don't want to depress the audience.' You have something to say about the theaters where *Amadeus* will play, about the advertising, the publicity. This eliminates a lot of dissatisfactions if the picture doesn't do business, because you can't pass the buck and

blame it on 'those people who didn't put any money or thought into promoting it.'

"The idea is to do everything you can to make the picture a success and get it released. Then the public will tell you if it's a success. If you're an independent, you can make sure the film gets proper advertising, is shown in the right houses, and gets good distribution."

Independent producers often arrange distribution through companies such as Orion Pictures (*Amadeus, The Cotton Club*) or Tri-Star Pictures (*Places in the Heart, The Natural, The Muppets Take Manhattan*). 20th Century-Fox financed and distributed *Star Wars,* produced by George Lucas's own company.

The term "independent" can also refer to a personal film made by an independent filmmaker. Often these films have small audiences and are not shown in major theaters. Some have become

35

cult films. Others are hardly known outside a small circle of viewers.

Sometimes these films are called *experimental,* but that implies some sort of scientific trial-and-error investigation. The filmmakers who create these films are not scientists. They are artists trying to express themselves.

The World of Film

During the Middle Ages books were used and controlled by a few individuals and institutions of power. Only members of royalty and the Church had books. Books were expensive to reproduce; each book had to be copied by hand. Common people could not afford books, and, so, were kept illiterate. With the invention of the printing press and moveable type, however, books became available to everyone.

Similarly, film and television were once too expensive for the ordinary person. The industry was controlled by a few individuals and institutions. Today, with the development of relatively inexpensive super-8 cameras, video cameras, pay-TV, cable television, and video cassettes, dominance of the industry by large institutions is disappearing. It is possible now for a person to create his or her own film or videotape. Even the terms *film* and *videotape* are beginning to lose their meaning, when what we really mean is the moving image.

The world of film allows several generations of people around the globe to experience and remember movies. Some of the movies entertain, some inform, some educate, but all of the movies become a shared memory.

As people look back in their lives, they remember a line, a scene, or perhaps a sequence from a well-liked movie. These recollections, like the recollections associated with a melody or song, bring memories of happiness, sadness, joy, fear, and even hate. These memories may suggest long-ago relationships: a favorite date, the time when the crowd saw a horror movie, or when the soda spilled all over your friend's lap.

Many of your grandparents or perhaps great-grandparents still remember Charlie Chaplin struggling frantically to get out of the little shack before it plunges over the cliff (*The Gold Rush,*

1925), the charge of the South against the North (*The Birth of a Nation,* 1915), and Al Jolson singing "You Ain't Seen Nothin' Yet!" (*The Jazz Singer,* 1927).

Younger people remember King Kong breaking his chains and the crowd going wild in the theater (*King Kong,* 1932), James Stewart's patriotic speech on the floor of the Senate (*Mr. Smith Goes to Washington,* 1939), Groucho Marx's eyebrows, cigar, and put-downs (*A Night at the Opera,* 1938).

Maybe your parents or grandparents remember Eva Marie Saint hanging over a cliff grasping Cary Grant's arm as he struggles to pull her to safety (*North by Northwest,* 1950); Marlon Brando walking angrily down to the corrupt union official's office building, followed by a large crowd of men, yelling challenges to Lee J. Cobb (*On the Waterfront,* 1951); and Gene Kelly, splashing, dancing, and singing in the rain (*Singin' In the Rain,* 1952).

Because movies are shown frequently on broadcast and cable television, and released on video cassette, you may be more familiar than you realize with movie favorites. How often have you seen the war room or the battle sequences in *Sink the Bismarck,* the Munchkins in *The Wizard of Oz,* the attack on Fort Knox in *Goldfinger,* the man-eating plants in *Days of the Triffids,* the Ascot races in *My Fair Lady,* or the bar in *Casablanca*?

How many times have you watched Julie Andrews making a game out of singing the scale (*Sound of Music*) or Dustin Hoffman signing autographs as soap-opera star Dorothy Michaels (*Tootsie*) or Harrison Ford escaping from the forces of evil (*Star Wars* trilogy)?

Chances are you've seen these films time and time again on television, just as your parents and grandparents may have seen them first in the movie theater. Did you share the same experience? Some people say no.

Pulitzer Prize-winning movie critic Roger Ebert believes strongly there's something special about seeing a film in a theater. As he writes in *A Kiss Is Still a Kiss,* "Like most other people whose tastes began to form before television became the dominant entertainment medium, I have a simple idea of what it means to go to the movies. You buy your ticket and take a seat in a large, dark room with hundreds of strangers. You slide down in your seat and make yourself comfortable. On the screen in front of you, the movie image appears—enormous and overwhelming. If the movie is a good one, you allow yourself to be absorbed in its fantasy, and its dreams become part of your memories.''

To Ebert, a film seen on television or VCR is never quite so magical or appealing. You may or may not agree with him. But one thing is certain. Even as you and a generation of people after you watch films, you will see the same plots, the same characters, the same chase scenes, the same sex and nude scenes, the same violent and fast-paced action sequences as your parents and grandparents did. The new generation will see, in essence, the same product but with a new title.

Film Festivals

Another part of the world of film are the film festivals, which started in the 1940s and 1950s. The Venice Biennale had shown a regular exhibition beginning as early as 1932, but it was only after 1946 that festivals began to appear all over the world.

C-3PO and Han Solo have become ''friends'' to millions of viewers who have seen the *Star Wars* trilogy in theaters, on television, or on videocassettes. Harrison Ford's attempts to muffle C-3POs comments at a critical moment bring chuckles from audiences. (The Empire Strikes Back © *Lucasfilm Ltd. (LFL) 1980. All Rights Reserved. Courtesy of Lucasfilm Ltd.*)

Film festivals give international exposure to talented filmmakers. They offer a chance to see the best commercial and artistic films from all over the world. The most prestigious of the festivals are those in Cannes (France), Venice, New York, San Francisco, and Chicago.

Awards

Beyond receiving recognition at festivals, films can receive various awards. In the United States, the best known are these:

Academy Awards

Oscars are awarded for 27 different achievements, including best actor and actress, best picture, best director, best supporting actor and actress, best cinematography, etc. They are given by the Academy of Motion Picture Arts and Sciences.

New York Critic's Award

The best picture, director, actors, and actresses are chosen unanimously by 15 critics from the New York daily newspapers.

Among those receiving the golden Oscar statuettes at the 57th Annual Academy Awards for the 1984 film *Amadeus* were best director, Milos Forman (left), and best producer, Saul Zaentz (right). Millions of viewers around the world watched the annual telecast honoring the year's best films, performances, and technical achievements. (©*Academy of Motion Picture Arts and Sciences.*)

National Board of Review

The "10 best" honor is awarded annually by the Board's Committee on Exceptional Films.

As you see more films and discuss them, you should begin to see the value of films that entertain, inform, and instruct. If you find it difficult to differentiate between the three types, remember that they often overlap. In addition, the real value of seeing and understanding the film is to value it for its own worth.

Rating the Movies

While the movie industry has developed ways of rating a film's overall excellence and technical achievement, the audience also needs to know something about the suitability of the movie's content. Parents want to know if a movie can be viewed by younger children or teenagers. Adults may want to know if a film contains excessive violence, profanity, or explicit sexual scenes. For these and other reasons, a voluntary movie rating system has evolved to rate film content for the theater-going public.

Development of the Ratings Code

The rating system developed gradually as America's social and economic upheaval brought about a revision of mores and customs. For many years, the Production Code Administration (also known as the Hays office) policed movies at the source in Hollywood. It was the movies' answer to the Catholic Legion of Decency, formed in 1933, whose members pledged to abstain from attending immoral movies.

In 1938, the Department of Justice filed an antitrust suit against the major concerns in the production-distribution and exhibition fields, accusing them of dominating exhibition through a virtual monopoly ownership of key "first-run" theaters, and of acting in collusion to exploit this advantage. Ten years later, the United States Supreme Court decided against the defendants, and the final consent decree was signed by Loew, Inc., in 1952.

"When the big studios relinquished their theaters, the power that existed in the Hays office and the Hollywood establishment was forever broken," says Jack Valenti, president (since 1966) of the Motion Picture Association of America (MPAA). "From that collapse of authority came, slowly, the onward thrust of the filmmaker to have a larger share in the creative command decisions. The result of society's change—marked by insurrection on the campus, rise in women's liberation, protest of the young, questioning of church, doubts about the institution of marriage, and the crumbling of social traditions—was the emergence of a new kind of American movie. Frank and open, it was made by filmmakers subject to very few self-imposed restraints."

Valenti's first controversy as MPAA president came a few weeks after his installation when he, MPAA top attorney Louis Nizer, and Warner Bros. head Jack Warner met to view the next-to-final cut of *Who's Afraid of Virginia Woolf?*, in which, for the first time on screen, sexually explicit language was used. Valenti succeeded in getting the language deleted before release but realized an unsettling new era in film was beginning.

"I was afraid we would lurch from crisis to crisis without any suitable solutions in sight," he remembers.

Several months later, Metro-Goldwyn-Mayer marketed the Antonioni film *Blow-Up,* a film with nudity. The Production Code Administration in California had denied the seal of approval. Valenti backed the decision. MGM, however, distributed the film through a subsidiary company, flouting the voluntary agreement of MPAA member companies that none of them would distribute a film without a Code seal.

In April 1968, the United States Supreme Court upheld the constitutional power of states and cities to prevent the exposure of children to books and films which could not be denied to adults.

Within weeks, Valenti began discussing plans for a movie rating system, bringing together the National Association of Theater Owners; the governing committee of the International Film Importers & Distributors of America; guilds of actors, writers, directors, and producers; craft unions, critics, religious organizations, and heads of MPAA member companies. By November 1968, the voluntary film-rating system of the motion picture industry had started.

The Production Code Administration and its rigid restrictions, in effect for nearly 40 years, was dismantled. Instead, the MPAA would rate movies for parents who could then make an informed decision on whether their children should attend.

Valenti saw the new plan as a compromise—a way to give filmmakers the right to say what they chose in their own manner and form without anyone forcing them to cut one millimeter of film or threatening to refuse them exhibition. At the same time, he felt a public obligation to let parents know in advance what kind of movie was being shown at the local theater.

"Under the rating program, filmmakers became free to tell stories in their way without anyone thwarting them," Valenti explains. "The price they would pay for that freedom was the possible restriction on viewing by children. I believe that freedom of the screen is not defined by whether or not children must see everything filmmakers conceive."

How Ratings Are Determined

Ratings are decided by a full-time Rating Board of seven persons, located in California. For more than 10 years, Richard Heffner, a Rutgers University professor of communications and public policy, has served as chairman. Says Heffner, "Our function is not to impose ideologies, morality, psychology, or aesthetics, but to make an educated estimation of what most parents would think a movie should be rated."

Board members need no special qualifications, except a love of movies and the capacity to put themselves in the role of most parents and view a film as parents trying to decide whether their younger children ought to see a specific movie.

No one is forced to submit a film to the Board for rating, but nearly all responsible producers do. Most makers of pornographic movies do not submit their films. Instead, within the rules of the rating system, they self-apply an X rating and market their films.

Not all movies are rated. An erotic adventure film, *Bolero*, by Bo and John Derek, was reportedly given an X rating in 1984 by the Board; but the Dereks chose to distribute it without a rating.

If a film does not have a rating, however, many television stations and newspapers will not accept advertising for the movie. Some theater chains will not show such films.

The symbols G, PG, PG-13, and R are certification marks of MPAA. They cannot be used by any company which has not officially submitted its film for rating. They may not be self-applied. About 85 percent of the exhibitors in America subscribe to the rating program.

After viewing and group discussion, the Board votes on the rating. Each member spells out reasons for the rating in each of the several categories: theme, violence, language, nudity, and sex, and rates the film overall, based on the category assessments. The final rating is decided by majority vote.

Under the rules, the film's producer has a right to ask why a particular rating was given. If a producer chooses, he or she can edit the film to try for a less severe rating. The re-edited film is screened again by the Board, and a new vote is taken. If producers wish, they can appeal the decision to the Rating Appeals Board—a panel of 22 men and women from MPAA and two other trade organizations, representing exhibitors and distributors.

After the film is screened for the Appeals Board, both the producer and the Rating Board chairman present their case and have a chance for rebuttal. After lengthy discussion and questioning, the Appeals Board takes a secret ballot. If two-thirds of those present agree, the Rating Board decision is overturned.

In fall, 1983, Brian DePalma's gangster film, *Scarface*, originally received an X rating, primarily for violence; but the Appeals Board changed it to R. In June, 1984, *Time* reported that *Terror in the Aisles*, a film Universal planned to release, composed of scenes from past horror movies, had its original X rating upheld by the Appeals board.

What the Ratings Mean

G: "General Audiences—all ages admitted."

This is a film which contains nothing in theme, language, nudity and sex, or violence which would, in the view of the Rating Board, be offensive to parents whose younger children view the film. The G rating is not a certificate of approval and does not signify a children's film. Some profoundly significant films are rated G (for example, *A Man for All Seasons.*)

Some language may go beyond polite conversation, but words are common everyday expressions. No stronger words are present in G-rated films. Violence is at a minimum. Nudity and sex scenes are not present.

Many producers today are not making G-rated movies. In the year ending October 1983, only 12 such films were released. In 1985, however, G-rated *That's Dancing,* with Gene Kelly's narration and clips of great dance sequences received generally favorable reviews and attracted good audiences.

PG: "Parental Guidance Suggested. Some material may not be suitable for children."

The label PG states that parents may consider some material unsuitable for their children, but the parent must make this decision. There may be some profanity in these films. There may be violence, but there is not cumulative horror or violence.

A PG-rated film contains no explicit sex, although there may be some indication of sensuality. Brief nudity may appear in PG-rated films, but anything beyond that puts the film into R.

PG-13: "Parents are strongly cautioned to give special guidance for attendance of children under 13. Some material may be inappropriate for young children."

A PG-13 film is one which, in the view of the Rating Board, goes beyond the boundaries of the PG-rating, but does not quite fit within the restricted R category. If nudity is sexually oriented, the film will not be rated PG-13. If violence is rough or persistent, the film is rated R. A film's single use of one of the harsher sexually derived words, though only as an expletive, requires the Rating Board to give the film at least a PG-13 rat-

ing. More than one such expletive requires the Rating Board to issue an R rating. So does even one of these words used in a sexual context.

The PG-13 rating, begun in summer 1984, may have been triggered by critics' response to *Indiana Jones and the Temple of Doom*, in which a man's heart is ripped out of his chest and he's lowered into a fiery pit, and to *Gremlins*, in which a mother churns up one creature in a food processor and explodes another gremlin in a microwave oven.

Both pictures were extremely popular, but parents and critics complained loudly that the original PG rating for both films didn't warn them sufficiently not to let young children see the movies. *Milwaukee Journal* critic Douglas Armstrong's call-in radio show received large numbers of calls from unhappy parents.

The hue and cry on *Indiana Jones* and *Gremlins* may have brought about a long-overdue look at the rating system. MPAA Rating Board Chairman Richard Heffner defends the "PG-13" category this way: "Parents generally don't treat pre-teenagers as they do older brothers and sisters. The rating system shouldn't either."

R: "Restricted, under 17s require accompanying parent or guardian."

This film contains some adult-type material: language, violence, nudity, sexuality, or other content. The language may be rough, and the violence may be hard. While explicit sex is not to be found in R-rated films, nudity and lovemaking may be involved.

X: "No one under 17 admitted."

This X-rating (Marlon Brando's *Last Tango in Paris* is an example) does not necessarily mean obscene or pornographic in terms of sex or violence. Courts, and not the Rating Board, decide legally whether a film is obscene or pornographic. The reason for not admitting children to X-rated films can be the accumulation of brutal or sexually connected language, or of explicit sex or excessive and sadistic violence.

Reflections

1. Do you see a variety of films, or do you usually see the same kind of film each time you go to the theater or see a movie on television?

2. Are all films entertaining? Do different films entertain in the same way?

3. In what ways does a film communicate? Is there a difference between entertainment and communication?

4. What are some of the ways in which a film entertains, teaches, and informs?

5. What do you think John Grieson meant when he said, "Documentary films are a creative treatment of reality?" Think about the documentaries you have seen to help you answer this question.

6. How do documentary filmmakers manipulate reality?

7. How many of the different genre of documentary films have you seen?

8. What is propaganda? Are the films that we see in any way propaganda? Perhaps you would rather call this idea simply the story or plot of the movie. If so, why do we become so attached to certain kinds of movies, movie stars, or messages they communicate?

9. Are television commercials a kind of propaganda? Do they serve any purpose other than getting us to buy a particular product?

10. What is a *cinema verité* film? What do you think it means when we say that a film was shot in the style of *cinema verité?*

11. Filmmakers have a control over the films they make. We call this objectiveness. Generally, how objective is the documentary filmmaker vs. a feature filmmaker of story films?

12. What is the filmmaker trying to do in the creative process of making an independent film?

Activities

1. Find out how animated films are made. There are a number of books in the library that will explain the techniques involved. Present an illustrated report.

2. What films are popular in foreign countries? Use *Variety* to research your answer.

3. Plan a documentary film of a school play, a sports event, a birthday party, or a community activity. Write an outline of the action, sequence, and characters. If possible, actually film your documentary and show it to your classmates.

4. Create a two-minute animated film. Be sure you can name and explain the technique you use.

5. To create a short-story film, gather ideas from all around you. Write down a brief description or outline. The everyday lives of the people you know make excellent stories. (All you have to do is figure out how to put it on film. There is no such thing as an uninteresting idea, just uninteresting films.)

6. If you've made some films, you might want to enter your film in a film festival. There are many super-8 film festivals. Many are described in *Filmmaker's Newsletter* and *Super-8 Filmmaker.*

7. If you live near a large city, chances are that the city has a film festival. Community colleges or universities also may have them. Attend a film festival. The films shown will be very different from the usual films you see in the local theater.

8. Ask your teacher if you can look through some film catalogs. Sometimes, the audiovisual department in your school has many copies of film catalogs. Your public library may also have film catalogs. Choose several films you would like to see.

Further Reading: *Check your library.*

Alexander, W. *Film on the Left: American Documentary Film From 1931–1942,* Princeton, NJ: Princeton University Press, 1981.

Flaherty, Frances H. *Odyssey of a Film-Maker: The Robert Flaherty Story,* Threshold, VT, 1984.

Fordin, Hugh. *The Movies' Greatest Musicals: Produced in Hollywood, USA by the Freed Unit,* New York: Ungar Publishing Co., Inc., 1984.

Frayling, Christopher. *Spaghetti Westerns: Cowboys & Europeans from Karl May to Sergio Leone,* Boston: Routledge, 1981.

Kaminsky, Stuart M. *American Film Genres,* 2nd edition, Chicago: Nelson-Hall, 1984.

Lenburg, Jeff. *The Great Cartoon Directors,* Jefferson, NC: McFarland & Co., 1983.

Schatz, Thomas. *Hollywood Genres: Formulas, Filmmaking & The Studio System.* Philadelphia, PA: Temple University Press, 1981.

Umphlett, Wiley L. *The Movies Go to College: Hollywood & The World of The College-Life Film,* Cranbury, NJ: Fairleigh Dickinson University Press, 1984.

Notes

1. Paul McKuskey, *Movies: Conversations with Peter Bogdanovich* (Harcourt Brace Jovanovich, Inc., 1974).

2. *The Art of Walt Disney* by Christopher Finch (Abrams, New York, 1973).

3. *An Introduction to the American Underground Film* by Sheldon Renan (E. P. Dutton and Company, New York, 1967).

The Screenwriter

While still attending high school in Los Angeles, Larry Gelbart was writing radio material for Danny Thomas, then a fledgling comedian on Fanny Brice's Maxwell House Coffee Time show. Gelbart's prolific and varied background includes writing for Bob Hope's early films (The Lemon Drop Kid, Paleface); television with Hope, Sid Caesar, and many others; Broadway shows (A Funny Thing Happened On the Way to the Forum), a few uncredited Italian films, and the television pilot for M*A*S*H.

Gelbart was co-producer of M*A*S*H and wrote many of the scripts for its first four seasons. As his role with the show wound down, he sought creative challenges: Sly Fox, a Broadway adaptation of Ben Johnson's Volpone; the screenplay for Oh God!, which he adapted from Avery Corman's novel; Movie Movie; Tootsie; Neighbors; Blame It on Rio, and the 1985 Academy Awards show.

The way a writer sells a studio or independent producer a film idea varies with the stature, reputation, and trust the writer enjoys. It's possible to get an okay to do a script on a one-sentence description, if it catches the fancy and imagination of an executive. It's much more likely, however, that you'll submit an idea in two to three pages, introducing the characters and detailing what the film is about. Sometimes you meet the executive face to face across his desk. Other production executives may be there: representatives from story development, or story analysis.

It's rare for a writer to get instant approval. The usual response is, "Let us get back to you." That's understandable; they're putting themselves on the line for millions of dollars.

Studios only see scripts submitted by agents. But of all the positions in the motion picture industry, the writer may have the easiest job getting in. It's cheaper to read a script than to give an actor a screen test or to give a director a picture to film.

A script goes through many stages, some minor, some radical. There are always compromises. There are few places in the creative world, apart from film, where there is as much participation by nonauthors. No painter has collaborators who say you need a little more red or who suggest that your design should be square, rather than circular.

Screenwriters have a great many cooks eager to help them with their broth. The lucky writer can make changes—not just to be accommodating and hold

Larry Gelbart

onto the job and the credit, but because he or she genuinely agrees the changes improve the script. Then it's not a painful process. But that doesn't usually happen.

For over 40 years I've been writing with dark, soft pencils and legal tablets. Now, I'm collaborating with my son on a project, using his computer. I try to bring a screenplay in at about 120 pages.

Until the writer's work starts to go before the cameras, all the writer uses to express ideas are words. When you begin collaborating with the director and cast, you begin to pare. You see that the story can be told in more cinematic terms without losing anything.

Some pictures can be written quickly. But *Tootsie* started almost 10 years before it came to the screen. By the time I became involved, there had already been four drafts. Crossdressing as a theme goes back 3000 years, to Plautus, a

Roman playwright. But it has to be more than just a sight joke. Klinger didn't get into a dress in *M*A*S*H* for laughs but, rather, to escape the war. If Dustin Hoffman's character wore women's clothes, we needed to say something pertinent as well. My biggest contribution to *Tootsie* was the idea that being a woman made a much better man out of him. That became the keystone for the screenplay, rather than having him simply look silly and find himself in awkward situations.

Hoffman and I worked closely together for a year before filming began. We talked over how he would feel as a woman...his feelings as a frustrated and unsuccessful actor...the personal point of view he wanted to bring to the film.

I'm a great believer in research. I spent time at *General Hospital,* watching them tape, seeing how they really did it, rather than taking cheap shots at soap opera.

If a screenwriter is highly enough regarded, he or she will be consulted on casting. Once the director is chosen and the cast selected, the writer may need to alter the script. Sometimes the script clearly benefits by using the actor's established personality.

Sometimes, though, the screenwriter runs up against the actor's ego. Clark Gable, once set to play in a film called *Submarine,* disagreed with the writer's ending. "Clark Gable," he said loftily, "does not go down with the sub." He didn't.

Unless you have another capacity on a film, such as directing or producing, it's unusual for the screenwriter to be present on the set. You may be nearby in your office and asked to come over if a bit of new dialogue is needed, but the script is pretty much fixed when you sign off on the project. Usually changes occur when scenes are changed. Something written to be filmed inside may be shot outside, for instance, necessitating dialogue changes.

Then the writer is at the mercy of the company, and can only hope that new material or changes are consistent with the writer's original vision. I've never been totally pleased by the final version of my pictures, because so many hands are laid on during production.

The writer and the producer see the movie differently. The producer thinks about cost and raising money and schedules and budget.

But as the writer, long before you start to write, you "see" the movie running through a Moviola in your head, organizing itself, breaking down into scenes that will tell the story. Not unlike a private sneak preview.

3

Viewing the Film: The First Level of Understanding

Film Images

Black-garbed figures are walking through the waving fields of grain. Superimposed on the screen are the words, "Pennsylvania, 1984." The scene cuts to a church service, with the pastor speaking in German. A shot of the coffin, a medium shot of a row of solemn mourners, a long shot showing a woman—the new widow—surrounded protectively by a group of white-capped Amish. It is the opening sequence of *Witness,* Peter Weir's compelling drama of two different worlds only a few miles apart.

The bikes are racing around the college track in Bloomington. The audience in the bleachers is rooting for their favorite team. The audience in the theater is rooting for the "cutters." One of the cutters is literally tied to the bike as he rides back into the race. He passes one bike after another. The crowd in the bleachers roars. Some of the people in the movie theater yell, too! The cutters win. We wanted them to win. The filmmaker did not fail us. (*Breaking Away,* 1979)

Even when described in words, film scenes seem exciting. Some people who try to describe the dramatic excitement and realism of films call this the "magic of movies." But it is really not magic. The dynamic excitement and realism of every story-line movie you have ever seen were created by people. The films seem real to you because you are caught up in visual techniques. They seem to be "magic" simply because the action happens so fast and seems so lifelike.

Some people would rather *not* understand the "magic of movies" because they are afraid they will not enjoy films as much. However, if you seriously attempt to understand how a filmmaker uses techniques to influence the ways you understand and perceive film, you will discover even greater enjoyment and reward in the films that you see. The first step in understanding film is understanding how we *see* visual images.

When you see the word *fish,* you understand it means an animal that swims in the water. Your mind puts together the four written letters that are symbols for sounds and comes up with the word *fish.* Perhaps you think of a fish hooked on a line from a fishing pole or swimming in your aquarium. No matter what your mental image is, you have taken it from the letters *F-I-S-H,* sym-

bols printed on paper. These symbols mean something to people who understand how to "translate" them into an agreed-on interpretation. Even if you had learned a different set of symbols because your native language was not English, you would still imagine similar mental pictures.

On the other hand, when you see a picture of a fish, you understand immediately that it *is* a fish. Even though the picture of a fish is also a symbol, it is much less abstract. Nearly anyone who sees a picture of a fish will understand what it represents.

People have used pictures for thousands of years to communicate messages and ideas. The filmmaker's use of a picture to communicate is not new, but something else is.

If you analyze much of the art of early people, you will notice a striving for movement. Early people drew many pictures of their exploits on the walls of caves where they lived. Many of the paintings illustrated a desire to show motion. Many pictures and sculptures by ancient artists were attempts to show movement.

But the work the artist created could not move and appear real until a special machine for this purpose was invented. Pictures that move—motion pictures—were the first time that art was combined with a machine to create an altogether new and different art form that communicates using *moving* visual images.

The Language of Film

It soon became apparent to those who studied the new art form that film, like speech and writing, has a language. But the language of film is much easier to learn and to understand. Perhaps the difference is best illustrated like this.

You probably noticed that there were some aspects of the written action that were not told very well. This is because the images show us what is happening much better than the written description. You may conclude that visual pictures or images always communicate much better than words, written or spoken. However, this is not true either. Writing, speech, and visual images all communicate within their own particular spheres very well, with some overlapping.

The juxtaposition of traditional and modern ways creates conflict and heightens the drama of *Witness*. Kelly McGillis, as an Amish widow who shelters Harrison Ford, is attracted to the ''worldly'' Philadelphia cop-on-the-run. (*Witness* Copyright © 1985 PARA-MOUNT PICTURES CORPORATION. ALL RIGHTS RESERVED. COURTESY OF PARAMOUNT PICTURES.)

The major difference is that visual images stimulate our perceptions *directly,* while written and spoken words stimulate our perceptions *indirectly.* When we read a word or a sentence, we must first "translate" the symbols to discover the meaning. The letters F-I-S-H don't mean "fish" until we put them together. Preschoolers who haven't learned to read are handicapped in their understanding if they have to spell out F-I-S-H every time they encounter the word and then try to translate it. We can do it more quickly because of our past experience, but we are still translating symbols before we understand the meaning. When we see a *picture* of a fish, however, so complex a translation is not needed. We understand the image directly.

Another difference between the spoken word, the written word, and the visual image relates to how easily we assimilate and learn to perceive the communication. When you were about a year old, you began to learn that different things in your world had names. You learned these names and gradually began to learn to speak. At about the age of three or four, some children begin to learn to read simple words. By the age of six, nearly all children are being taught to read in school. In this process, we learn that words represent ideas, and as we grow older, we put them together to represent more and more complex ideas.

At about the same age that we learn to speak, most of us are exposed to moving images on television. We assimilate and learn to understand these images differently. Certainly infants see various kinds of movements and images that are at first meaningless. Soon, however, children discover that the little moving people on the TV screen are similar to pictures in books—except that they move. The images are even like real people, except that they are smaller. Gradually, children accept what they see on the screen as real. They do not question the techniques the television camera operator has used to influence the way they perceive the images on the screen. They are infatuated—caught up in a continuous moving array of images that directly stimulate their perceptions with little conscious effort on their part.

Some people—perhaps most people—never go beyond this level of receiving the visual image. They learn to watch the screen, but they never reach new levels of perceiving the visual image. Most people do not realize that there is anything more to watching television or a film than simply letting it pour into their heads.

One important objective in the study of film is learning to perceive and understand various aspects of the language of the moving image. Just as people who never learn to read are said to be illiterate, people who have poor visual perceptions are visually illiterate.

Seeing Film

As you investigate your experience in seeing film, you need to consider three aspects.

1. *Learning to be more perceptive.* It is possible to learn to be more perceptive. As an Indian boy grew to manhood, he learned to observe various details in his environment and to understand their meaning: a slight indentation in soft dirt, a pebble turned over, a tuft of hair. These things were important in his everyday life. Similarly, a child today learns to be perceptive about everything that affects his or her senses. Many of these things may not seem important, though, and we stop noticing them. As we grow older, our environment may seem to become commonplace and mediocre because it is so familiar. Present-day young people have been characterized as experiencing too much of life too soon. Therefore, some people believe, young people need more stimulation to affect the senses than did teens in an earlier, less-conditioned generation. This is why, they say, that many recent films have been more violent, more visually and emotionally shocking—to provide audiences with that extra excitement.

You can learn to be more perceptive by specifically setting out to sharpen your skills, as you might try to improve other skills, like playing the guitar or skiing.

fish

- Learn the elements of your environment that influence your perceptions (these are discussed in chapter 4). As you see films, keep those influences in mind.

- Try to be more perceptive about the films you see. Look hard. Let your mind be filled with the visual images you see and the dialogue and music that you hear. Try to recall the various elements you have just seen. Attempt to find relationships between each of the diverse parts.

- Learn to understand the meanings of the techniques the filmmaker uses (Chapter 5) to influence the way you see a film. Look for these various techniques in the films you see, but remember that the total film is the technique the filmmaker is using to communicate the message. Don't get so bogged down looking for a high-angle shot, a cut and matching shot, or a montage that you lose track of what the film is communicating. As you see more films and seriously try to improve your perceptive skills, more and more aspects of films will fit into place. Try to relate similar things you have seen in different films.

- Perhaps the most valuable technique in learning to be more perceptive is to discuss the film you have seen with others. By expressing your-

Adolph Caesar (right) disciplines Larry Riley (center) as Art Evans (left) looks on in Columbia Pictures' *A Soldier's Story*, a sensitive story of racism in the military. Perceptive viewers find films such as this can make them more aware of their personal responses to social issues. (A Soldier's Story © *1984. Thorn EMI Films Finance PLC. All Rights Reserved.*)

self in words, you will be increasing your ability to perceive film. It is sometimes helpful to have a discussion leader, such as a teacher trained in the study of film.

In discussing film, it is very helpful if the group agrees to allow anything to be said. If members of the group can exchange ideas in a completely free atmosphere, the perceptive skills of each group member can grow.

The exercise of talking with people about films you've seen together will be very valuable in increasing your perceptive skills. Discussing films is not an exercise in "flower-making," that is, it is not a time when everyone sits around and says nice things about the film. Discussion should be part of a process of continual growth in perceiving films better.

2. *Learning to appreciate the aesthetic qualities of film.* Sometimes it is difficult to distinguish between films we like personally and films that have been acclaimed for their more *aesthetic* quality—for being works of art. Even a person trained in the artistic and aesthetic qualities of film as an art form may have trouble seeing a film's supposed artistic merit. Later, we shall discuss in more detail the criteria used to evaluate the merit of films. At this point, however, try to recognize that it is possible for you to learn to appreciate many films you otherwise might not have liked by learning to notice and understand their aesthetic qualities.

Perhaps the most important element in learning to see the artistry in film is to learn first to observe the beauty of the world and the things in it that usually go unnoticed: a spider spinning a web, a drop of water on a leaf, the clouds, the interactions of people, the smell of a newly baked apple pie, the sound of blowing leaves in a tree. If you can, or already do, appreciate everyday beauty with all your senses, then you can learn to see the aesthetic beauty in film.

Second, you can learn to accept the aesthetic beauty of films. It doesn't mean you cannot question. Questioning is the beginning of learning and understanding. But do not refuse to accept because you do not understand.

3. *Learning to identify and measure your responses to film.* After you see a film, attempt to verbalize it in your mind, finding words that describe what you have seen. This is sometimes very difficult, especially when you have seen a particularly moving film. The difference between thinking verbally and using images to understand may be an important problem for a generation raised on television. Younger, television-oriented people may sometimes find it difficult to find words to describe their thoughts. Therefore, you should make every effort to think out words that describe your experience as you see film.

After you begin to discuss the films you have seen, you will begin to notice your own responses. You should notice that you usually respond to a film both intellectually and emotionally. However, on closer analysis, you may find that most of your responses are intellectualized, perhaps because we generally do not like showing our emotional feelings in public. But you still should be able to describe your original emotional feelings when you saw the film.

As you discuss the film or think about it later, try to determine how the filmmaker used various techniques to influence your emotions. As you continue to discuss the films you see and to learn more about film technique, try to observe and identify growth in your perceptive and aesthetic skills. The most valuable part of learning anything is your ability to recognize your own growth and understanding of the subject.

Reflections

1. What is *observation*?

2. After reading Chapter 3, do you believe it is possible to learn to improve your observation of films?

3. In what ways does the visual image communicate? Do you prefer the written word or the visual image? Is one method of communication always better than the other? Why?

4. Try to recall various film sequences. Why did you remember these sequences rather than others? Check with friends. Do they remember

the same sequences? Why might different people remember different film sequences?

5. How would you evaluate your class discussions about film? Do you participate in the discussions? Are there ways the discussions could be improved?

6. Why is it important in a film-study class to discuss the films you see?

7. What is meant by the word *aesthetic?* Is it possible to learn to be more aesthetic?

8. How can you measure your own responses to film? Have you noticed any changes in your responses as you mature?

Activities

1. Read a poem or short story and then note the differences between the two mediums.

2. Find a piece of music that you like and create a film around it. The music can be instrumental.

3. Director Milos Forman (*Amadeus, One Flew Over the Cuckoo's Nest*) says a film based on a play is actually a new work—an entirely different fulfillment of the same impulse that has created the original. Read a play, see the film version, and note the differences between the two mediums. (*Amadeus,*

A Soldier's Story, and *The Miracle Worker* are just a few of the many examples.)

Further Reading: *Check your library.*

Bluestone, George. *Novels into Films,* University of California Press, 1966.

Brosman, John. *Movie Magic: The Story of Special Effects in the Cinema,* St. Martins Press, 1974.

Felsen, Henry Gregor. *Three Plus Three,* Scott, Foresman and Company, 1970. Comments by the author of three short stories that he converted into film scripts.

Gibson, William. *The Miracle Worker, New York, Knopf, 1957.*

Kuhns, William. *The Moving Picture Book,* Pflaum/Standard, 1975, "Toward a Psychology of the Movies: A Commentary by Buster Keaton," pp. 264–265.

Miller, Gabriel. *Screening the Novel: Rediscovered American Fiction in Film,* New York. Ungar, Frederick, 1980.

Monasco, James. *How to Read a Film: the Art, Technology, Language, History, and Theory of Film and Media.* rev. ed., New York, Oxford University Press, Inc., 1981.

Shaffer, Peter. *Peter Shaffer's Amadeus*, New York, Harper and Row, 1981.

Ivan Reitman (foreground). (©1984, Columbia Pictures Industries, Inc. All Rights Reserved.)

The Director

Producer/director Ivan Reitman, acclaimed for contemporary comedy, (National Lampoon's Animal House, Meatballs, and Stripes), is a native Czech whose family fled to Canada when he was four. As a college student, he won a music prize in a national student competition for the Canadian Centennial, produced and directed several shorts that were aired on Canadian television, and started the

New Cinema of Canada, *a nontheatrical film distribution company. After success- ful stage productions in Toronto and New York, followed by producing* Animal House *(1978), Reitman returned to directing.* Meatballs *and* Stripes *teamed him with Bill Murray and co-writer Harold Ramis. In 1983, Reitman returned to Broad- way to produce and direct* Merlin, *the hit musical magic show that brought him a Tony nomination.*

Actor Dan Aykroyd first brought his Ghostbusters *script to Reitman in May 1983. "I thought it was a wonderful idea," the director says, "but I wanted it to be a little more realistic." Three drafts later, with Ramis and Aykroyd co-writing the screenplay,* Ghostbusters *became the first major comedy with large-scale spe- cial effects—nearly 200 of them.* Variety *reported in January 1985 that as of that date,* Ghostbusters *had become the top-grossing comedy of all time. By Decem- ber 31, 1984,* Variety *said, the film had earned a whopping $127,000,000 in domestic rentals (the portion of the box-office gross that's paid to the distributor) for the United States and Canada, making it one of the ten largest grossing pic- tures in cinema history.*

The director is creative captain of the ship. That means making large decisions and tiny, minute decisions.

The script is like a Bible that the director has to translate and make alive. Directors have to take written dialogue and screen directions from the pages and get them to look as if it's really happening, so somehow a viewer can suspend disbelief when watching the film. Audiences must believe everything they see is true and going on before their eyes.

Big decisions include fixing the script to the point where the director is satisfied and directing the actors so they perform the screen play satisfactorily. Little decisions include every decision—from wardrobe, hair style, and makeup, to set location and the color of the paint on the walls.

Every decision calls for keeping an eye on costs. For example, when you're shooting on location, on which side of the street should electrical and supply trucks be parked so they won't be in the shot? If you've picked the wrong side of the street, you spend two costly hours moving trucks.

As director, you've got to make these decisions quickly, because you've got 150 people on your crew, and 20 people in charge of them. The set dresser, who adds anything from paint to shrubbery to signs to cars so the set looks like is should, comes up to learn which side of the street you're shooting on, so he can plan the work. If you're only filming in one direction, you don't have to dress both sides.

All these small decisions translate into money. A director has to move fast, to meet the schedule, to make *yes* or *no* decisions on hundreds of things not originally called for in the budget. Film is a financially based art form. A creative director has to combine imagination with practicality.

Most successful directors work very hard. My day starts with my arrival on the set at 6 or 7 A.M. I've probably laid out the first shot the night before, dis- cussing alternatives with the director of photography and key personnel: the pro- duction designer, the art director, and the production manager. I talk to the actors before they go to make-up and wardrobe and block the scene. We plan where to stand up, where to move, how to play the lines. I show the entire crew what the general shape of the scene will be. I define the master shot and set the first camera position. We'll discuss the mood: whether it's dark or light, dramatic or scary.

While the cameras are being set up and the actors are getting ready, I'll meet with the writers. "Can you give us an idea how to strengthen this line? It needs more weight, so the audience will understand."

Before you know it, two hours will have gone by, and the cameraman is ready to shoot. By then, I'll have answered at least a dozen questions from wardrobe—should the clothes be creased or dirty? Should the actor be sweating? Should the hair be out of place? The continuity person checks each actor for the match from scene to scene. If the camera is moving during the shot, I'll ride the camera or walk the scene. The actors rehearse again, and everything quiets down. You don't overrehearse comedy, so it doesn't go stale.

During the take—after they yell, "Quiet!"—I watch intensely, with almost tunnel vision. As soon as I finish a take, I'll announce whether we'll print it. Usually a director has a sense of what is right, or of how performances can be improved.

Sometimes I'll change blocking or adjust the script. Although I might shoot as many as 20 takes, I usually average eight or nine and print three or four. We get the master shot and make sure we have choices on closeups. We do reaction shots and highlights, so the scene will have a life and rhythm. I average 10 to 12 of these setups in one day on a Hollywood feature.

After six hours of filming, there's a half-hour noon break with the catering truck. We go back to it after lunch. The shooting day is 12 hours long.

Then—at 6 or 7 P.M.—I plan the next day's work. If I'm going to be filming in a jail or at a different location, I'm driven there to see it. We may take a fast look with the cameraman. After we break for dinner, the editor and I go to the screening room to check the rushes from the previous day. I'll indicate the takes we'll probably use, or run rough, assembled footage. Often, there's a last-minute phone conversation with other actors or writers about what is going on. When I finally get to bed, I'll read and study what I have to do the next day.

When I'm on location, I work six days a week; in California, I'll work five days a week and use the extra day for major creative conferences or script changes. From the time I know I'm going to make a film, it usually takes three months to prepare, three months to shoot, and four months to finish. I'm meticulous about editing and post-production. I'm involved in all the editing decisions and the mixing room and in checking the color of all the prints. I've toured Japan and all Europe, giving press conferences on *Ghostbusters* because it's important to help sell a film. If you make movies that people don't go to, you stop making movies.

A sense of humor is very important for a director. Everything that can go wrong, usually does. Patience is significant, because a lot of filmmaking requires waiting around. You have to push, but if you push too much, you destroy more than you create.

A director has to work hard at the mechanics. Then the vision comes through. Successful filmmaking is a craft. Directors need a good sense of overall architecture so they can fit disparate pieces together like a jigsaw puzzle or a chess game.

It's the director's job to tell the story and to move people—to work creatively with talented and sensitive actors, and to make the film speak with a cohesive voice.

4

Perceiving the Film: The Next Level of Understanding

Perception

Look around you right now. What do you see? Do you see anything you didn't see before?

Probably you are somewhere you know very well. In fact, this place may have become so familiar to you that everything associated with it is boring and uninteresting. You may find it difficult to see anything new. "I asked a friend who had just returned from a long walk in the woods what she had observed. 'Nothing in particular,' she replied.

"How was that possible?" I asked myself. "I, who cannot hear or see, find hundreds of things to interest me through mere touch. I feel the delicate symmetry of a leaf. I pass my hands lovingly about the rough, shaggy bark of a pine. Occasionally, if I am very fortunate, I place my hand gently on a small tree and feel the happy quiver of a bird in full song."

Helen Keller, who was both deaf and blind, and who was the subject of the play, film, and television movie entitled *The Miracle Worker,* speaks eloquently for beauty in the world around us and for the precious gift of sight and hearing.

In a movie for television called *The City,* Anthony

Although John Malkovich portrayed a blind boarder in *Places of the Heart,* his sensitive perception allowed him to "see" Sally Field's struggles as a young Depression-era widow. (©*1984 Tri-Star Pictures. All Rights Reserved.*)

Films such as *The High Sierra,* which explores the beauty of the world of John Muir, enrich our lives by letting us "see" beauty in unfamiliar surroundings. Though most of us may never visit this rugged mountain country, we can appreciate its loveliness. (*Courtesy of Pyramid Films.*)

Quinn played the mayor. During one scene in this long, dramatic, political-action movie, the mayor is photographing a tree when a group of university students recognize him. They ask him what he is doing. He replies that he is taking a picture of a tree.

"Why photograph that tree?" they ask. "It's like any other tree!"

The mayor looks at them and then looks around at all the other trees in the park, pointing out how each tree is unique.

"The trouble today," he tells the students, "is that people have stopped looking at trees."

Many of us have stopped looking at trees. Perhaps, as we get older, the beauty and uniqueness of many aspects of our environment escape our attention. Watch a small child's first taste of ice cream, first touch of snow, first look at the ocean, or first sight of a newborn puppy. There is a curious excitement and genuine animated fascination in a child's discoveries that most older people lack.

Film Helps Us to See

Film is an analysis of the obvious. It helps us to *see* something that has always been there and to see it in a new way.

The word *see* means more than *look at.* It means also the way in which we perceive or understand. Therefore, film allows us to see something from a new perspective—from a new point of view. This is part of the dramatic excitement of films. Film allows us to see things in our world with new insight.

Perhaps every film made allows us to see better, but some films do this more skillfully than others. For example, the lyrical documentary film *Glass* shows us how glassblowers blow molten glass into beautiful and elegant finished pieces. It also compares the old way of blowing glass into jugs, bottles, and other handcrafted glassware with machines that mass-produce bottles.

In the film *Mint Tea,* the filmmaker shows us what it is like to be lonely in a crowd.

Some techniques of film have been used for many years. Montage, a progression of scenes, vividly portrays the horror of the massacre on the Odessa steps in Eisenstein's *Potemkin,* a film classic. (*The Museum of Modern Art/Film Stills Archive.*)

The director of *Jeremiah Johnson* visually describes to us the rugged textures of a mountain man's life.

The great Russian director Eisenstein was trying to show us the tyranny of Czarist Russia in *Potemkin.*

In *Rodeo,* the slow motion sequences allow us to see the agony and the violent action of the cowboy versus the animal in an almost poetic manner. Yet we are subconsciously aware that time has been slowed down and that the torture is really happening faster.

Perception: A Puzzle

The room is darkened. The projector is turned on and light floods the screen. A film begins. You are watching a film with twenty-four other people. No one says a word throughout the entire film showing. The film ends and the lights are turned

on. Now, here's the puzzle: Since everyone saw the same film, at the same time, in the same room, then everyone saw the same film.

right? . . . .wrong!

Certainly everyone saw the same bits of movement, the same reflected images. However, one part of the puzzle was left out on purpose. Not to trick you, but to get you to think about a most important element in seeing and studying films.

The part left out? Well, you see, two of the people watching the film were Russian; three were young people, 8, 14, and 17 years old; five were Australian aborigines; fourteen were female; seven were told the film wasn't very good; and six were told it was an award winner. There were nineteen people who had eaten lunch shortly before the film began. Four had missed lunch be-

cause the cafeteria was too crowded. One person had a cold, and two people believed guns should be registered by the government. One person fell asleep ten minutes after the film started.

The act of seeing a film takes place in the mind. The twenty-four people mentioned saw the film, but they all perceived and understood the film in their individual minds.

The two Russians, though they spoke no English, perceived the film fairly well because it was very visual. That is, it had many parts that meant something to them visually, without the dialogue. The 8-year-old perceived the film well in many parts. However, her 14- and 17-year-old friends understood it on a different level of perception because they had more life experience and were able to recognize parts that escaped the younger child. They didn't necessarily perceive the film *better,* but they saw it in broader terms and through different eyes. Even these two people

perceived it differently, because the 14-year-old liked automobiles and the 17-year-old didn't.

The native aborigines perceived only a dog that was shown barking in front of a house at one point in the film. They knew what dogs were because they had wild dogs in Australia. Without the technological experience we have, the tall buildings and busy freeways failed to mean anything to them.

Fourteen of the people were female; ten were male. Women and girls, men and boys often see things differently because of different backgrounds and experiences.

The seven who were told the film wasn't very good did differ in their perceptions from the six who were told the film was an award winner. These people were preconditioned, so that their understanding of the film was changed even before it started.

The nineteen people with full stomachs hardly noticed the dinner scene, but the four individuals who skipped lunch missed the whole next sequence in the film because they were still thinking about the chocolate cake.

Since the person with the cold was feeling dragged out and depressed, he failed to understand many of the very funny jokes.

The film had nothing to do with guns, but the two people who believed in strict gun control were rigid in many other ways. They felt the film was saying unkind things about the government.

The person who fell asleep missed nearly all the film. But he did perceive a sort of low hum and was startled in his sleep when, in the film, a car backfired while pulling out of the driveway.

But what about you?

You were the twenty-fifth person. What did you perceive?

Whatever it was . . . it wasn't like what anyone else perceived. *Everyone sees films (and all of life) differently.*

What exactly is perception? What influences it?

Perception is understanding what takes place in the brain. All the things observed by one or more of your senses and comprehended by your brain have a different, special meaning to each individual person. Because films are about life and are a microcosm of the world you live in, it is important in the study of film to understand how you are influenced by what you see and hear in a film.

Twelve Factors That Influence What We See

Involuntary Attention

After school one day, you are walking your dog along a fairly busy road. Suddenly, as a car races by, the driver blasts the horn! You nearly leap out of your skin, and your dog yelps.

Both you and your dog's perceptions were suddenly influenced by a loud sound. Your mind was far away from the passing cars. Your attention was involuntarily disrupted.

You spend most of your daily life *not* paying attention to all the little details. We'd probably all become basket cases if we did try to take in every tiny detail of life. We have learned, for the most part, to pay attention only to the things that have some meaning for us. Occasionally, however, we are jarred by an involuntary sight or sound and are startled and surprised.

Filmmakers like Alfred Hitchcock understand this psychological fact and deliberately take advantage of it. Hitchcock planned his films to lull our attention in one part of the film, so we will be suddenly surprised or shocked in the following scene.

Voluntary Attention

Whenever you pay attention to one specific activity rather than another, you are voluntarily choosing between alternatives. You follow the plot in a film because it interests you. As more and more alternative choices in the plot structure become apparent, your attention refocuses. Or perhaps one of your favorite actresses has a small role in a film. In certain scenes, you might *voluntarily* watch her performance more carefully than the main characters.

Intensity and Size

On a clear night, look into the sky. Some stars seem to be brighter than others. They seem to stand out from the clusters of stars surrounding them. They are more intense. You notice them first.

Some sounds—for instance, the deep vibrations of a ship's horn or the roar of a car without a muffler—are also more intense. These sounds stand out distinctly from the background noise.

You are more likely to notice a house trailer on a road than a bicycle. You'll take a second look at a 16-year-old, 200-pound football player among a group of 7-year-olds. The house trailer and the football player are larger than their surrounding environment. You noticed them first because of their size.

In films, if the filmmaker wants us particularly to notice one kind of sound, it will be louder than the other sounds when various sounds are mixed together. In the short film *An Occurrence at Owl Creek Bridge,* the condemned man lies on his back on the bank of a stream after swimming away from the Union soldiers. When he begins to hear the sounds of birds and insects, the volume becomes slightly louder. Suddenly a shell explodes near him, and the sounds of nature disappear. The filmmaker changes the direction of our attention by changing, first, the volume and later the sounds themselves. Similarly, the filmmaker may set the camera so that the knife the murderer is going to use lies in the foreground, near the camera. In both examples, the filmmaker is aware of intensity and size and uses these factors to influence what our senses perceive.

Novelty or Contrast

If you were walking down the street one day and suddenly you saw in the crowd a man walking toward you wearing a pink suit with yellow lace on the sleeves and vest, he would be a novelty.

You see a group of people all going in the same direction into a gateway at a football game. But as you observe the flow of people, you notice that one individual is trying to make his way through the crowd in the opposite direction. That one individual stands out from the people moving toward him.

Likewise, filmmakers try to make their films stand out by finding a unique angle—something to set their particular film apart from the crowd. *Rocky* was a hit because audiences could easily identify with the hero's need to be a winner and his struggle to overcome almost unsurmountable

In this deliberately underplayed scene from *Witness,* young Amish widow Kelly McGillis is introduced to the pleasures of dancing by Philadelphia policeman Harrison Ford. The setting: a Pennsylvania barn late at night, the music from Ford's car radio, highlights the attraction between them. (Witness *Copyright* © *1985 Paramount Pictures Corporation. All Rights Reserved. Courtesy Of Paramount Pictures.*)

odds. *On Golden Pond* was a heart-warming story of a family's love and concern for each other and the difficulties each member found in admitting and expressing their emotions. *Tootsie* used the gimmick of a man pretending to be a woman as a device to allow Dustin Hoffman—and the audience—to realize how stereotyped our attitudes about "male" and "female" roles often

Genre films often are released in cycles, as filmmakers try to capture audience interest by repeating themes. Science fiction, Westerns, and—in the Thirties—gangster films like *Little Caesar* have all had their day as "most popular." (Little Caesar © 1930 First National Pictures Inc., renewed 1958.)

are. *Witness* used a clash of cultures and life styles set in modern day Pennsylvania to appeal to the audience's yearning for life away from the violence of the city.

Throughout the history of movies, filmmakers have tried to outdo the films made before in a similar genre. In 1930, Edward G. Robinson created the film character of the ruthless gangster in *Little Caesar*. Only a few months later, James Cagney appeared as the sadistic killer in *The Public Enemy*. Gangster pictures followed one after another as this new genre of film became popular—in fact, fifty gangster films were released in the year 1931!

The superior filmmaker will use novelty and contrast to help make a film more interesting and exciting. One kind of novelty will come from using a great variety of techniques, such as different kinds of shots, angles, length of scenes, zooms, follow shots, and so forth. However, the filmmaker tries to keep in mind the fine line between novelty and triteness. After a while, most people get bored by seeing the same story with different faces. Many people get tired of hearing foul language or seeing too much violence and sex on the screen. "Gimmicky" techniques like slow motion and zoom shots become trite if used too often.

Movement

Moving things are noticed before things that are still. The moving object seems to attract our attention quickly. Moving things have fascinated people through the ages. Even in the cave drawings of ancient people and in the drawings of the Egyptians, movement was an integral part of art. But it wasn't until the motion picture camera and projector were invented that art could really move.

Perhaps we're fascinated by movement because the whole world moves. Leaves on trees move in the wind. Cars whiz by at speeds that would have terrified our ancestors. Even when things don't move, they can appear to move if we are moving.

Filmmakers are aware that film is a moving artform. They constantly attempt to find ways to keep the film moving.

Understanding the Film

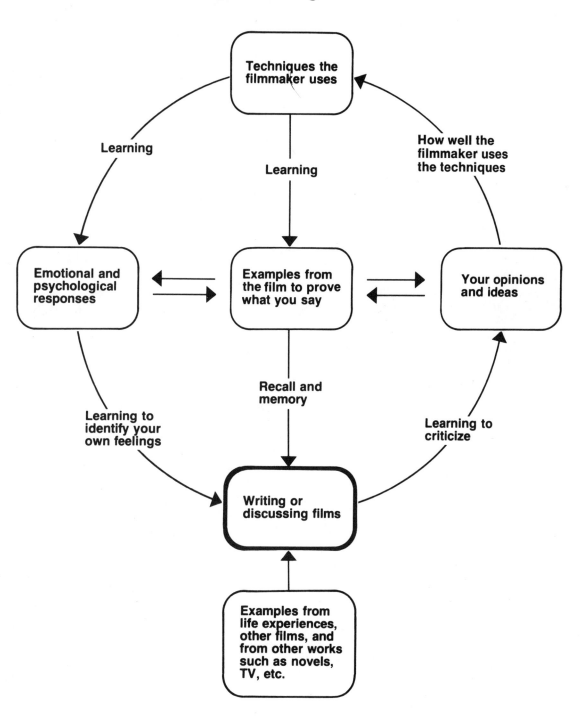

Plot and theme are two major elements in film. In *Amadeus,* the plot shows the dying Mozart (Tom Hulce) dictating the *Requiem* to Salieri (F. Murray Abraham), but the theme of jealousy and confrontation runs throughout the film. (Amadeus © *1984 The Saul Zaentz Company. All Rights Reserved.*)

Motivation

When we feel like doing something, we are *motivated.* Our motivation depends a great deal on our voluntary and involuntary attention and on our past experience.

One kind of attraction is to use popular box-office stars like Bill Murray, Dan Aykroyd, Harrison Ford, and Jessica Lange. Another is to show a lot of action and violence. The *plot* (what happens in the story) may be very exciting and interesting. The *theme* (what the film is about) may have significant, expressive, and eloquent interpretation. For instance, in *Amadeus,* the universal theme of mediocrity in confrontation with genius pits jealousy-maddened court composer Salieri against Mozart, whom Salieri calls "this clownish, giggling, repulsive buffoon . . . this blasphemous oaf."

We become concerned and engrossed. The filmmaker uses other techniques to hold our at-tention and to motivate us to continue watching the film: color, beautiful dissolves, fast cutting from one scene to many successive scenes, low- and high-angle shots, close-ups, beautiful long shots, and so on.

Filmmakers realize that if they want to keep the audience interested in continuing to watch the film, they must be able to motivate us to become involved in it.

Set

As individuals become older, they become more set in their patterns of thinking. They tend to continue thinking along older and more familiar patterns. These thought patterns form complex views about the world familiar to the individual, influencing even seemingly unrelated issues. In *The Greening of America,* Charles Reich says:

Ask a stranger on a bus or airplane about psychiatry

or redwoods or police or taxes or morals or war, and you can guess with fair accuracy his views on all the rest of these topics and many others besides, even though they are seemingly unrelated. If he thinks wilderness areas should be "developed" he is quite likely to favor punitive treatment for campus disruptions. If he is enthusiastic about hunting wild animals, he probably believes that the American economic system rests on individual business activity, and has an aversion to people with long hair.

When we see films, we should keep in mind that "set" is a part of all human beings. It is a kind of influence that gets in the way and doesn't allow us to see clearly the ideas presented in films.

Past Experience

When we see a film, we are bringing with us our total past life experience. Many of our present recognitions and decisions about our environment are made instantly, based on the influence of our past experiences. We can only make the decision to perceive a specific part when we have recognized parts or more of the whole.

You don't recognize a leg as part of a chair until you see the whole chair, or at least most of it. You would not perceive a chicken in the same way as most everyone else if you had never seen a chicken before. You might recognize it as a bird if you had seen other birds before.

If you have had little experience with more sophisticated films, you may find concepts, ideas, and visual images and techniques that are unfamiliar. However, as you see more films, you begin to build a background of past experiences that will enable you to make connections and see relationships.

Your Mind and Body

Just before your film class, you have an argument with your biology teacher. When you enter the film class, you are still pretty angry. You sit down, the film starts, and you are still fuming.

Because of your mental attitude, you certainly will not perceive the film the same as you would have before the confrontation with the teacher.

You may be supersensitive to certain things in the film, or your mind may still be on the argument, or you may just be too angry to concentrate on anything.

The physical condition of your body also influences how you perceive films. You perceive the films you see differently if your film study class comes before rather than after lunch. If you have a cold, if you didn't have enough sleep the night before, if you gave or got a kiss just before your film class—all these are factors influencing your perception of the film you see.

Your Surroundings

The physical condition of the room helps influence how you perceive a film. The room may be cold or warm or hot, the air fresh or stuffy. If you are uncomfortable, your perceptions will be affected. The placement of your seat in relation to the screen and other seats in the room can influence your perceptions. The light may be partially on or the room may be totally black. The placement of the projector in the room determines the size of the image, which is another factor in how you perceive the film.

Conformity

Perhaps the factor that influences your perceptions most is conformity. People are very much influenced by other people. Although most people like to think of themselves as individuals, and many like to think they are nonconformists, most psychologists agree that people are influenced by others because of their inner need for acceptance. This psychological need may vary during growth for various individuals, changing the extent to which they can be influenced by others' opinions.

As you view films, try to discover how you yourself sometimes conform. For instance, you may say you see what others in your class say they saw in a film, because you are not sure enough of what *you* saw. However, many times you will not recognize this factor influencing your perception. It is a part of you that is very difficult to recognize (and to accept) when it is pointed out to you. Nevertheless, it exists.

Through the magic of film, viewers can become more perceptive to ideas and can begin to examine their own values. *Leisure,* an animated film that traces the history of spare time suggests that the way we choose to spend leisure may influence the direction of society. (Leisure. *Courtesy of Pyramid Films.*)

Prejudices

In a short film called *The Sixties,* there is a scene of some teenagers of 1965 doing the Twist. It never fails to bring a laugh.

If you see a documentary film about primitive people, watch their ways of eating and food-gathering and hunting, and think to yourself, "You wouldn't catch me eating those things," you are guilty of a form of prejudice called *ethnocentrism.* It is the tendency by one group of people to think of the customs of others in terms of their own customs—and to find them odd, or even wrong, if they are different.

When your film teacher shows you a film you don't understand, and you say "That was a dumb, boring film," you are guilty of being biased because your experience has been largely with films you understood. Usually our first reaction to something we don't understand is to blame the unfamiliar or puzzling experience

rather than ourselves. But prejudice is really prejudging things with partial and, in most cases, inaccurate information.

Each individual watching a film sees it in his or her own unique way. No two people will see and hear *exactly* the same thing. Even the mistakes we make in interpreting how various techniques influence our perceptions are explained by the factors that influence what we see. By learning the language filmmakers use to communicate to us, we can grow in our understanding of ourselves and of film.

Perhaps it is helpful to understand that as a person views a film, the mind puts together the film and the sum total of everything we are. To better understand the process of film communication and the perception that takes place in the mind, note the chart found on page 65. Look closely at the chart and compare the illustrations with the description that follows.

The filmmaker is the sender of a film message

to his or her audience. If the audience, or receiver, understands the message, communication is said to have taken place.

However, as we described during this chapter, there are many factors that may influence how the audience perceives the message or film that the filmmaker has created. Sometimes the problem of understanding the film is within the viewer, at other times, the problem is within the film. No matter where the problem of understanding lies, the way the film is perceived by the audience ultimately allows the audience to complete the art of communication.

When we write, discuss, or think about a film, we are influenced by the problems inherent in our own selves, the problems inherent in the film, other films, novels, TV programs, our total life experience, and the 12 factors suggested in this chapter that influence our perceptions.

Our opinions and ideas concerning the film can grow and mature as we learn how to criticize the film. We express our criticism and opinions of the techniques the filmmaker uses to prove what we are thinking or saying, based upon examples from the film. We learn how the filmmaker uses the techniques in the film by recalling various examples from the film. Our emotional and psychological responses to the film are learned by understanding how the filmmaker uses the techniques to influence our perceptions of the film. We can learn to identify our feelings as we write, discuss, or think about film.

Reflections

1. What do you think Anthony Quinn meant when he said, "The trouble today is that most people have stopped looking at trees." Do we rush around so much today that we fail to notice the beauty around us? What is beauty? How do we see and express beauty?

2. Do the films we see today communicate beauty? Can you think of examples of films that showed you beauty? Are there beautiful ideas, too?

3. Do many of the films that we see in the theater demonstrate a need in our lives for more and more thrills? Can you think of examples?

4. What does *seeing* really mean in our discussions of the text?

5. Can you think of examples in your own experience of each of the 12 factors that influence the way we see films?

Activities

1. Check out the diagram found on page 65 and see if you really understand what it is that happens to you when you see film. It is certainly complex, isn't it?

2. Look at the world around you when you leave school today. Is there something new and different, or perhaps something beautiful, that you never noticed before?

3. Cut out pictures you consider beautiful and make a collage.

4. Look for interesting subjects, including people, to photograph. You can use a movie camera to do the same thing.

Further Reading: *Check your library.*

Almendros, Nestor. *A Man with a Camera* (translated by Belash, Rachel P.), Farrar, Strauss & Giroux, Inc., New York, 1984.

Note

1. Charles Reich, *The Greening of America* (New York: Bantam Books, 1971), p. 14.

The Production Designer

Much of the "magic of the movies" depends on the effectiveness and believability of the scenery, sets, and backgrounds where a film takes place. These are the responsibility of the production designer.

Production designer Charles Rosen majored in drama at the University of Oklahoma and earned his Master of Fine Arts degree in Theatrical Design at Yale University. After a career in legitimate theater and television work in New York, he came to Hollywood. Among his many films are Invasion of the Body Snatchers, The Producers *(Mel Brooks' spoof with its famous "Springtime for Hitler" number),* Taxi Driver, Charly, My Favorite Year, Flashdance, *and* The River.

The production designer is the architect of the film. It's structuring color, structuring a look. It's coordination. Production design is a marriage of all the elements needed, while satisfying the requirements of the particular film.

The production designer is in total control of the visual aspects of the picture, working closely with the art director and set decorator, overseeing all the visual details, even down to the costumes, making sure the style and period of the film are "right" for the look the director wants.

This control is diversified through many departments, under the direction of the production designer, and each person has certain responsibilities.

For instance, the set decorator will get a china cabinet for a dining room. The property master gets the action props—everything that moves, is held, or is handled. If the family eats from the dishes during the dinner sequence, they are action props and his or her responsibility. If, however, the dishes remain in the china cabinet or background and are not moved, the set decorator is responsible for choosing them. Either way, the production designer bears the ultimate responsibility of seeing that the dishes are "right" for the look of the picture.

The production designer is one of the first people hired to work on a film, often months ahead of shooting. Nearly all pictures require searching for locations, even if many scenes are shot at the studio. The production designer looks for places that give the "feel" and "atmosphere" the director has chosen for the film. The audience must never doubt for a moment that they're in the location, even if the production designer has to duplicate that location on a Hollywood sound stage.

Charles Rosen (The River ©1985 Universal City Studios, Inc.)

Reviews for *Flashdance* said Pittsburgh had never looked so good. We chose Pittsburgh for the steel industry and the hills. Yet we shot there for only 10 days, using most of the footage for the titles. The bridges over the rivers became the opening scene. For the construction sequence over the titles, we found an abandoned subway tunnel. We brought in scaffolding and equipment. We put water on the walls. We shot the outside of the Carnegie Museum where they went to the concert, and used a long lens for the romantic sequence when they walk through the abandoned steel mill. Everything else was created in Los Angeles.

Sometimes the requirements for a particular film are very specific. When I did *The River,* the story involved the flooding of a farm. I needed farmland with levees, a valley that came right down to the river, a road right against the hillside that also went across the valley, and a place where the farmer's house could be built between the river and the road.

Weather was a problem. I couldn't take the film to Pennsylvania or upstate New York, because it was already May and the growing season was too short to plant the corn crop we needed for the story.

Finally, I found a wild tract of land four miles below a dam controlled by the Tennessee Valley Authority. To get the flat 65 acres we needed, we had to buy a hilltop and 400 acres. We used giant bulldozers to take down every tree on the flat portion.

Then the TVA engineered a levee for us, computing water flows scientifically. We built a levee down the entire length of the property, and a dam at the end of the levee.

The shooting schedule required us to film at night for two weeks. The TVA sold us extra water each night—water enough to make the river five feet higher than the farm, with the water held by the levee.

I arranged for experts from the University of Tennessee Agricultural Dept., the USDA, and the best local farmers to advise us on the 60 acres of corn we planted. We had specialists in bugs and weeds helping us. That corn was so polished and "manicured" that in scenes where we needed weeds, we had to transplant them by hand!

As production designer for *The River,* I had to involve myself not only with finding the right location and with farming techniques, but also with the look of a small family farm, with country auctions and the deprivations of a farmwife. We created an 1860 farmhouse and old log farm structures. What better way to sell the family heritage than to show a house obviously put up by great grandfather? We not only built the "old" house but showed it as it would have been renovated in the 1950s.

A production designer is a sociologist. He or she has to know costumes, mores, manners—to know what you're dealing with in terms of materials and fabrics and colors for a particular period in a particular location at a particular time of year. You can't have just a vague idea. You need specific training.

Under your planning and supervision, illustrators do paintings and storyboard artists do continuity and draftsmen design sets. The production designer is responsible for bringing it all together and styling everything in the image that works best for that specific film.

If the production designer has done a good job, you won't notice all these things. It's like background music. The visual impact of the film must never strike a jarring note.

5

The Language
of Film

The Filmmaker's Magic

Do you like to see films because they are exciting, with lots of adventure and fast action? Do you like films because they seem so real? Do you like comedies, spy stories, and westerns, or do you like modern dramas best? Or does it depend on the particular film?

When a filmmaker begins to create the film itself, he or she has a choice of a great variety of techniques to tell the story or communicate the message. This chapter is designed to help you learn and understand better the films you see. It should help you enjoy films more and to appreciate the effort that is put into the making of all films.

For an outsider, watching a film being made can be confusing and even dull. Most of the time it may seem that nothing is happening. When something does happen, it is over practically before you know it.

Films are created in bits and pieces. Then the bits and pieces are put together in an order that the filmmaker hopes will make sense to the viewer. If the order in the finished film does make sense to us, we call it realistic and accept it as being real, even though it is not. It seems real to us because we have come to accept the techniques the filmmaker uses to create the impression of reality.

For example, we see a scene of a man inside a room. He walks to a door, opens it, and leaves the room. In the next scene, we see him in a car through the driver's window. The car is moving down a busy highway. The next scene is only one-fourth of a second long, showing a three-frame flashback to the same man talking angrily with a woman. Then we see the man driving again. There is a long dissolve of this scene into the next scene. The camera is high, looking down on the car as it comes toward the camera. The car pulls to the curb and stops. The man gets out and quickly hurries into the entrance of a nearby building.

Most of us would accept this 30-second sequence as being real. We have seen scenes like it in many films. But there are several elements in the sequence that are not real at all. If we had seen this sequence in *real time* (that is, the time we live in), it might have taken 45 minutes or

longer. The man might even have gotten in a traffic jam, which could have stretched the real time even further.

The filmmaker has conveniently let us see only bits of the action—the parts when the man leaves the room, drives the car, and enters the building. There is also a flashback when he is talking angrily to a woman. This is not real. Certainly we think of things which have happened to us in the past, but we can't see the "memories" of other people.

There are other unreal aspects to the sequence. Can you name some?

Film Techniques

The filmmaker uses visual or "filmic" techniques to communicate a message. Filmmakers are in the business of creating most films so they will convince you that what you are seeing and hearing is real.

The filmmaker's techniques involve camerawork—the kind of film and lenses used as well as camera placement, focusing, and timing—lighting, sets, and actors. The film may have music, natural sound, no sound, or other various combinations. When the filmmaker has completed shooting the film, it will be cut into many hundreds, sometimes thousands, of pieces and then put back in an order that will seem real and convincing.

Camera Work

The basic element in almost all films is the *shot*. This is a single piece of film that may be as short as one frame or as long as an entire film. The *shot*, when incorporated in the film, continues until the filmmaker decides to change to another shot.

A *scene* is similar to a shot in almost every

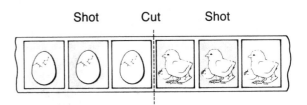

Shot   Cut   Shot

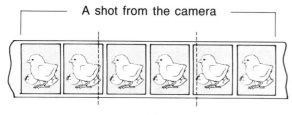

A shot from the camera

A scene in the film

way except that the film editor (the person who creates the order out of the pieces of film) has cut the shot to the length wanted. Therefore, in a finished film, the shot becomes a scene.

A group of related scenes that are edited together make up a *sequence*. The *cut* is used to change our attention from one scene to another. As we watch the film, the change from one scene to the next is called a *transition*.

The joining of one scene with another scene, how scenes follow one other, may seem a simple enough notion, but the cut in a film is one of the most powerful of the filmmaker's techniques. It allows us, as we view a scene, to move in time and in space. For example, if we watch a scene of a man climbing into bed and falling asleep and in the next scene we see him at a table eating breakfast, we may assume that an entire night has passed. The simple transition from one scene to the next has made us believe seven or eight hours have passed.

Similarly, in another scene, a woman is busy peeling potatoes. She discovers that she doesn't have enough potatoes. She removes her apron, puts on her coat, and goes to the door. In the next scene we see the woman walking into a supermarket. This time, the simple transition makes us believe that the woman has traveled several blocks or miles.

There is no problem in accepting these two concepts—we are so accustomed to seeing this technique in every movie we see.

The simple transition may be powerful in another way: the juxtaposition of one scene to another unrelated scene. The Russian filmmakers Lev Kuleshov and Vsevolod Pudovkin discovered soon after the turn of the century that when two unrelated scenes are cut together, or spliced, an entirely new idea may result.

Arthur Knight in *The Liveliest Art* explains:

"Perhaps the most famous of Kuleshov's experiments—also recorded by Pudovkin—was one involving an old film with the actor Mozhukhin. From it, Kuleshov obtained a closeup in which Mozhukhin appeared perfectly expressionless. He inserted this same shot at various points in another film: first he juxtaposed the expressionless actor's closeup to a plate of soup; once he placed the closeup next to a child playing contentedly with a teddy bear; a third time, the expressionless scene was placed next to a shot of an old woman lying dead in her coffin. Audiences shown the experimental reel praised Mozhukhin's performances: his look of hunger, his delight on seeing the child, and his grief over the dead woman. For Kuleshov, however, this was a conclusive demonstration that it is not only a single image, but the juxtaposition of images that creates the emotional tone of a sequence."

One scene alone usually doesn't mean too much. However, when spliced to another scene, the combined results can create an idea that neither scene could have accomplished alone.

You are watching a film and suddenly the character appears to jump partway across the screen. The character continues to move until the shot changes to another shot. Where does the shot end? Technically the shot ends at the *jump-cut*. A jump-cut may be a break in a film which has been repaired. Since several frames have been cut out, the character seems to jump suddenly across the screen.

A jump-cut may also be caused by stopping the camera for a split second and then continuing to film the action. Like the removal of a few frames in a shot, stopping the camera even for one or two frames causes a jump-cut. Sometimes it is fun to make jump-cuts on purpose because characters can be made to disappear like magic.

The filmmaker uses different kinds of shots to create variations. An *establishing shot* often comes at the beginning of a sequence to orient the audience with the general surroundings. The establishing shot is also known as a *long shot*. Then, as contrast, a filmmaker will often use a *medium shot* followed by a *close shot*, or *closeup*. There is no rule that governs how much is shown in these basic shots, because the contrast between them relates to the subject. For example, if a long shot of the Sears Tower in

Veteran filmmaker David Lean is noted for his use of establishing shots as a device to bring viewers into another culture and time. In *Dr. Zhivago* and (here) in *A Passage to India,* the long shots set the scene for the personal relationships that develop during the film. (Passage to India © *1984 Columbia Pictures Industries, Inc. All Rights Reserved.*)

Chicago included the entire building, then a closeup shot of the building may include as much as half the entire lower level. However, if we consider a shot of the human face as a long shot, then, in contrast, the eye would be a closeup.

For example, imagine that during your last summer vacation, you and your family made a visit to Yellowstone National Park. While there, you were lucky enough to get a medium-close shot of a bear walking on all four legs toward the camera. Then the bear stands on his hind legs. At this point a figure comes into the scene on the right side of the screen for one second. The shot ends with the bear opening his mouth for a peanut the figure has thrown.

Some months later you and some of your friends have decided to make a film for an assignment. At one point in the film, the main char-

acter is frightened by something while walking in a woody area. You and your friends discuss various possible creatures that could fill the requirements. Suddenly you remember the shot of the bear you took last summer.

The next day you bring the shot and show it to your friends. They like it, but don't know what to do with the part where the figure comes into the shot for a second.

"Let's go ahead and make the film, and I'll do the editing. I have an idea," you say.

So you begin your film. When you come to the part where your character is frightened, you make sure the following shots are made: A close shot of your character's face looking frightened. A close shot of his hand gripped tightly around a heavy stick he is carrying. A medium shot of the character turning and running away.

When you edit the film, this is how the shots

are made into scenes and put together. (There is more than one way to edit this, too.) The first scene in this sequence shows the main character walking along a forest path. The next scene uses part of the bear scene, in which the bear rises up on his hind legs, followed by the scene of the character's frightened face. You decided not to use the scene of his hand gripping the stick because the film was better without it. So the scene that follows is the one of the bear walking toward the camera. The final scene shows the character turning and running away.

The scenes of the person and the bear are not really related except by the way they are edited together in the completed film. Placed in juxtaposition, the scenes interact with each other to create the desired effect—fright. Note that the figure that came into the original shot of the bear is left out. Also, the part of the shot where the bear stands up on his hind legs is used first, while the part where he opens his mouth, is not used. A part of the shot of the bear walking toward the camera is used last to suggest fear—fear in the main character, and fear in the audience, be-

The medium shot is a device filmmakers use to focus attention on a scene and bring the audiences closer to the action. Here, director Robert Benton uses a medium shot to suggest the emotional relationship between Ed Harris and Amy Madigan, partners in an extramarital affair in *Places In The Heart*. (Places In the Heart ©1984 Tri-Star Pictures. All Rights Reserved.)

The closeup shot is often used for contrast, and helps audiences to identify intimately with the character being portrayed. In *Places In The Heart,* the closeup of young Gennie James is deliberately used to create feelings of warmth and caring in audiences. (Places In the Heart ©1984 Tri-Star Pictures. All Rights Reserved.).

cause they are watching the scenes of the bear through the eyes of the main character.

This is one way motion pictures give the viewer the illusion of reality, of being a part of the film. The filmmaker builds one scene on another in a continuing creative effort to put together the entire film.

Scenes in a film are the building blocks of sequences, which make up the entire film. They can be compared to sentences which make up paragraphs that create an entire story. Each scene is related to the others so they will communicate the desired effect to the audience.

There is also no rule governing the order of the three shots. Filmmakers use all three in varying orders to create interest.

Long shots, medium shots, and closeup shots may be used to create various feelings and moods in the audience. Sometimes a closeup shot may create a feeling of intimacy with the actor or better identification. Sometimes, as in many of Hitchcock's films, closeup shots create suspense. In contrast, many filmmakers use a long shot to convey the idea of alienation or the feeling of loneliness.

All the techniques used by filmmakers, however, depend on many other factors in the film. The ideas described here to illustrate how various techniques may be used are only suggestions. Each technique must eventually relate to the entire film.

As you watch film, especially if you are seeing a picture for the second time, you may be conscious of a particular device—the *point of view shot*. Steven Spielberg used this technique brilliantly in *Jaws*. At the opening of the film, we see a girl swimming in the ocean. Suddenly there's a cut to a shot from a camera at the bottom of the water, looking up at the girl.

We don't see the shark. Instead, we see the girl from the *shark's* point of view. We see her feet dangling in the water. The camera moves closer and closer. Finally, we cut to a surface camera, and we see the girl react to the shark's attack.

Through the camera placement, Spielberg implies that there is another element in the scene—the shark. Because of the point of view shot that shows us the girl *through the shark's eyes*, he makes us imagine that something else, something menacing, is there.

You can often find the point of view shot used in a horror picture. Someone, usually a young girl, is photographed alone in a house, usually at night. Then there's a cut to a shot of the girl as seen through a doorway at a distance. The implication to the audience is that someone is watching her.

In *The Empire Strikes Back*, point of view shots are used to get inside Luke Skywalker's mind, in much the same way that the technique of interior monologue is used in a novel. Physically, you can understand what Luke is seeing, and what he is reacting to.

"For instance, when Luke goes into the carbon freezing chamber in Cloud City, he hears Darth Vader's voice," recalls *Empire* editor Paul Hirsch.

"He looks around. We cut from the closeup of Luke to a long shot of Vader at the top of the stairs. Then we cut back to Luke, as he starts resolutely forward.

"Because the shot of Vader is bracketed with closeups of Luke, it becomes a point of view shot. It helps the audience to identify with Luke, and to see Vader through his eyes.

"Point of view shots also enabled us to achieve the two crashes in *Empire*," says Hirsch, "when Luke's speeder crashes in front of a walker in the snow, and when the X-wing crashes in the bog on Dagobah. We couldn't convincingly show an objective shot of these ships crashing. Instead, George Lucas and Irvin Kershner chose to use a point of view shot from inside the cockpit. In each case, by using this device, we were able to make the crashes look real, as well as to let the audience share Luke's experience of them."

Another series of shots used by filmmakers involves camera angles. There are three basic angles. *High-angle shots* look down on the subject, as when Gary Cooper in *High Noon* walks down an empty street to face a killer. *Low-angle shots*, in which the camera is looking up, sometimes tell us the character is domineering and powerful. In *Citizen Kane*, the many low-angle shots of Orson Welles give a feeling of strength and power. *Flat-angle shots* (or *eye-level shots*) are in the same height and angle as the subject.

The camera can move, too, as many beginning filmmakers find out. Sometimes they move it too much. However, when used properly, camera movement can add a lot to the audience's understanding and appreciation of a film. A *pan* from left to right or right to left may help the audience orient itself. The camera simply pivots, usually on a tripod, sideways in either direction. A *tilt* is similar to a pan except that the camera pivots up or down. Either a pan or a tilt may be used to follow someone while the camera stays in one place. In a *travel* or *follow shot*, the camera moves with the subject.

Filmmakers also can use different camera lenses to influence what you see and feel while watching a film. In *The Graduate*, director Mike Nichols used a telephoto lens to film Dustin Hoffman running toward the camera. Nichols was trying to convey the near-nightmare feelings of Hoffman, who is trying to reach a church before his girl marries someone else. He runs and runs, but doesn't seem to get anywhere. Nichols could have used slow motion here, but it probably would not have worked as well, perhaps because slow motion is used often, and, perhaps overused.

A telephoto lens makes the image appear flat, with everything in the frame compressed. In that shot, Hoffman doesn't seem to be getting closer because the lens has compressed the distance.

Another lens, used more often than the telephoto, is the wide angle. With this lens, the filmmaker does not have to be so careful about focus, since everything is in focus from a few feet to infinity.

A zoom lens combines many lenses in one. It can be set in any position from telephoto to wide angle. With the zoom lens, the camera is stationary, while the image appears to be quickly getting larger and closer or moving farther away.

Sometimes the filmmaker moves the camera itself toward or away from the subject in a *dolly shot*. When you see the results on the screen, everything appears to be moving to the side and away from all four edges of the screen. The dolly shot is used in preference to a zoom shot when more control over the movement is desired. Since the zoom lens wasn't invented until 1948, filmmakers before then relied entirely on the dolly shot. Also, the zoom lens effect is considered to be more artificial and mechanical. A dolly shot is noticed less by the audience.

The last basic camera movement is a *boom shot*. Usually the camera and cameraman are placed on a large boom which can move in any direction.

In the famous chase scene in *Bullitt*, there were actually *three* cars speeding, crashing, and bouncing over the hills of San Francisco: the car Steve McQueen was in, the car the "bad guys" were in, and the cameraman's car. In effect, the audience was riding in that third car.

The point to remember is that we, the audience, are seeing all the action through the eye of a camera. Behind the camera are not only the camera operator but a group of people helping to make it look real. Perhaps when you begin to notice mistakes (and they are made in films from all over the world), you will understand.

In *Executive Action*, a microphone on a boom lowers too far and can be seen at the top of the frame. In an old western film with Jimmy Stewart called *Bend in the River*, you don't need to look hard to see a jet plane streak in a long shot scene of a number of covered wagons winding across a landscape.

Optical Effects

Besides camera techniques, filmmakers use various optical effects. Most of these effects are done in a film laboratory with an optical printer. This sophisticated and very expensive machine is simply a projector aimed directly at a camera. The technician has complete control of the optical printer and can do amazing feats. For example, many of the startling effects in such films as *The Exorcist, The Other,* and *2001: A Space Odyssey* were done by optical printers.

Filmmakers use optical effects to influence how we see films, just as they use other techniques discussed so far. A *fade-out* at the end of several sequences tells us a segment has ended. A *fade-in* tells that a new segment is beginning. During a fade-out, the image grows darker until it is black. A fade-in is just the opposite. The scene starts out black. It grows lighter until it reaches the proper exposure.

A *dissolve* is really a fade-out and a fade-in overlapped to create an image that appears to mix one into the other. Filmmakers use dissolves as transitions to show the passage of time from one scene to the next.

An optical effect that seems to be much used today is *slow motion.* Slow motion can be created by speeding up the film in the camera. That is, more frames per second are taken than is normal. Therefore, more action is being recorded faster. When the film is played back at a normal rate, the result is slow motion. Normally, 24 frames are exposed per second. This speed can be increased so that several million frames per second are being exposed, and a bullet can be seen leaving the barrel of a gun. Or the speed can be decreased so that only one frame is exposed every 25 seconds. In this effect, the sun will appear to rise very rapidly, or a flower will bloom before our eyes like magic.

The filmmaker uses slow motion for a number of reasons, often to describe the details better or to show the beauty of the subject. Two short films are excellent examples of the use of slow motion. *Dream of Wild Horses* is a beautiful, poetic film emphasizing the beauty and grace of wild horses. In *Rodeo,* the filmmaker uses slow motion to show us the beauty and the agony of rodeo Brahma bull-riding. In the science fiction feature film *Westworld,* parts of fight sequences were filmed in slow motion to show the dramatic, violent action between man and robot.

During the battle on the ice planet Hoth in *The Empire Strikes Back,* slow motion was used in some of the sequences involving the walkers. These gigantic war machines, the Empire's All Terrain Armored Transports, were stalking the Rebel forces on four jointed legs, firing cannons and laser blots. Rebel pilots harpoon a walker, flying their snow-speeder around and around the legs of the 50-foot-high machine, tangling them in cable as if the pilots were roping a calf.

"Though the walker appeared to be 50 feet tall," recalls Richard Edlund, co-director of special visual effects (with Brian Johnson) on *Empire,* "it actually was only four feet high. When it tumbled over, we had to make it fall convincingly. We couldn't just make it fall at normal speed. Our solution was to use a slow motion camera and photograph it at 100 frames a second—a very high rate of speed. That technique made the walker take a much longer time to crash, and helped to reinforce the effect of its tremendous size."

Another of the many techniques that filmmakers use to create a special audience reaction or to call attention to a particular part of the film is multiple framing.

"In *The Empire Strikes Back,*" says its editor, Paul Hirsch, "we triple-framed the sequence inside the tree cave on Dagobah, where Luke Skywalker has a vision of Darth Vader and cuts off his head.

"Originally the scene was shot at normal speed. Then in order to slow it down and to make it more 'other-worldly,' we triple-framed it, rephotographing each frame of film three times at an optical house. Triple-framing is not as smooth as slow motion, but it produces the same pace as slow motion.

"There is a risk in a sequence such as this. Cutting off someone's head is obviously a trick, and slowing down the action gives the audience more time to analyze how the trick is done. Yet, having that extra time does give the audience a longer look at the fight between Luke and Darth Vader, which symbolizes Luke's own struggle between The Force and the Dark Side."

Other optical effects include *wipes,* when one scene moves another scene off the screen; *freeze frames,* which stop and thereby emphasize a particular frame; and *swish pans,* in which the camera pans rapidly between scenes, creating rapid pacing.

Point of View

The filmmaker, similar to the author of a short story or novel, can use various points of view. However the filmmaker can move from first person, to second person, and to a third person within the same film and even the same sequence. This allows us to identify with first, one character and then, another. It allows the filmmaker to return us to an earlier time in a flashback; it allows us to see what a character sees. This is called a subjective point of view.

For example, in *Witness,* an 8-year-old Amish boy whose father has just died is exploring the Philadelphia Amtrack station. It is, perhaps, his first trip to the "outside" world. We see him glance towards his mother, waiting on a bench, an unfamiliar sight in her black cloak and bonnet. Then the camera moves at child's-eye level, letting us see what the boy sees. We "walk" as he walks, looking at a gigantic, gold-covered statue. Next the camera cuts to an overhead shot, looking down from high up in the rafters, at the statue and the small boy.

The camera has made us *first,* a disinterested spectator, observing the boy as a stranger in the station might see him; *second,* the boy himself, noticing unfamiliar sights and focusing on them with the wide-eyed wonder of unsophisticated childhood; and *third,* an omniscient, overseeing, objective witness ourselves, much like an abstract figure of justice.

The carefully planned and photographed sequence foreshadows events to come, estab-

The camera tracks young Lukas Haas in wide-eyed wonder as he explores the Philadelphia train station. By placing the camera at Lukas' eye level, director Peter Weir has made all of us witnesses to the brutal murder helping us to share the boy's terror. (Witness *Copyright © 1985* PARAMOUNT PICTURES CORPORATION. ALL RIGHTS RESERVED. COURTESY OF PARAMOUNT PICTURES.)

lishing the boy's mood of careful observance. Through sensitive camera work, we, the audience, become *involved* and identify with the boy. Like him, we become witnesses. We cannot remain detached.

Editing

Perhaps the most important technique a filmmaker uses to influence our reaction to a film is *editing.* Many beginning filmmakers believe editing is just the removal of unwanted scenes such as out-of-focus or badly lighted shots. However, editing is much more crucial and valuable

Cynthia Scheider, editor of *Breaking Away* and *Eyewitness*, and winner of a television editor's award for PBS' *Life on the Mississippi*, was awarded an honorary Doctor of Humane Letters from Franklin & Marshall college for her contributions to film. Scheider edited *Fair Is Fair*, a Tri-Star Pictures release about a group of teens in Texas who accidentally shoot a man. (*Courtesy of Franklin & Marshall College.*)

in the making of the finished film. Next to the actual photography, editing shots into the order a filmmaker wants is perhaps the most important part of creating a film.

Editing is so important that whole books have been written on this subject.

Creative editing involves cutting scenes so the action flows smoothly. We see a character walk to a door, open it, and start to go through to the other side. The viewpoint changes to inside the room, and we see the character continue on into the room. The action is smooth. There is one continuous flow of movement from outside to inside. This is called *matching action*. When the shots were originally filmed, the filmmaker *overshot*. At first the camera was on the outside of the room, filming the character walking to the door, opening it, and going through. Filming continued until the character was past the place where the director planned a scene cut. Then ac-

tion was repeated, this time with the camera inside the room. When the camera *rolls* (starts), the character comes on through the doorway into the room.

When the film editor gets the film, he or she cuts the two shots into two scenes. The first scene ends exactly at the point where the character goes through the doorway. The second scene begins exactly at the point where the character left off at the end of the first scene. The action is smooth and we hardly notice a change of camera position, let alone a cut between two scenes.

Another term used to describe the process of scenes appearing one after another is *montage.* Each of the scenes passes by quickly, but each scene is connected by similar ideas.

One classic use of *montage* occurs in *Citizen Kane.* Orson Welles and Ruth Warrick, playing husband and wife, start the sequence by having breakfast at opposite ends of a conventionally sized dining table. As the sequence progresses, the table becomes longer and more stretched out. By the end of the scenes, we see the couple reading separate newspapers and obviously paying no attention to each other. The montage has served its purpose: to give viewers a quick understanding of the couple's growing indifference, to tell without dialogue the reason behind the marriage break-up, and to move the plot along without digressing.

Montage can be a way of helping the viewer to perceive a situation—*showing* rather than *telling*—and of forcing the viewer's intellectual and emotional involvement with the story.

Near the beginning of Peter Weir's *Witness,* we see a horse-drawn buggy driven by two bearded, broad-hatted Amish farmers. We see a closeup of their faces. The camera pulls back, and we realize the buggy is holding up a line of modern cars. We cut to a long shot of the horse and buggy being crowded by a huge diesel-smoking semitrailer. The final shot in the sequence shows the horse-drawn buggy waiting patiently at a red light, in the middle of city traffic and facing a garish Dairy Queen. Weir has used the juxtaposition of images and the montage to dramatize the film's theme: the conflict of the quiet, determined Amish culture with the hustle-and-bustle of modern life. It is a theme he will return to again and again, as Harrison Ford, playing a tough Philadelphia detective on the run from drug-dealing, corrupt cops, hides out on an Amish farm.

All editing, if it is to appear real, must be smooth and flow with the action. For most films, much more footage is shot than is used in the film you see. The film not used in the final print is called the *out-takes.*

The editor must be aware of the *rhythm, tempo,* and *pacing* of the film. Rhythm, tempo, and pacing have to do with the movement in the film, the way the film is edited, and the nature of the subject being filmed. These three terms relate to the music, the poetry, the movement of artistically edited images.

Rhythm is the "beat" that we feel as we see the edited images pass by. Tempo is the rate of the rhythm, or how fast the rhythm moves. Pacing is the various changes in tempo and rhythm that take place in the film.

Orson Welles shot a series of scenes depicting a couple breakfasting together to illustrate the growing distance between them, and the eventual breakup of their marriage. His skillful editing juxtaposed those scenes into a dramatic montage. (Citizen Kane ©*RKO General Incorporated.*)

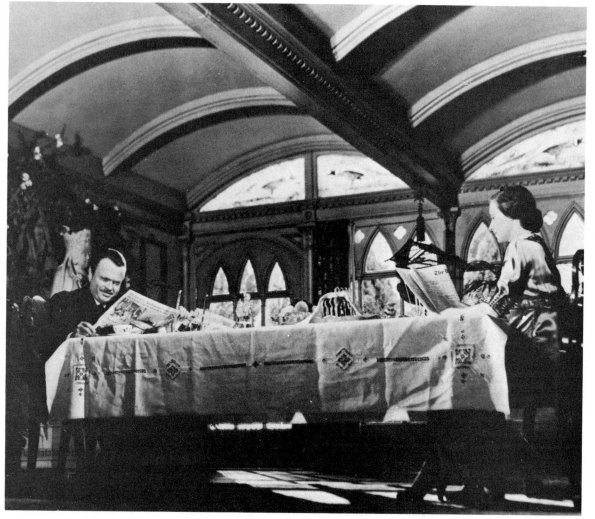

Old ways and modern ways meet as Philadelphia policemen Brent Jennings and Harrison Ford question Lukas Haas and his grieving, newly-widowed mother about a murder the boy has witnessed. In later scenes from *Witness,* director Peter Weir uses the unhurried tempo of Amish farm life as a contrast to the fast-paced modern world. (Witness *Copyright* © *1985 Paramount Pictures Corporation. All Rights Reserved. Courtesy Of Paramount Pictures.*)

Two basic techniques a film editor uses are *cut-ins* and *cut-aways.*

In a cut-in, some detail of the main action is cut into the middle of another scene. For instance, a medium shot shows several characters talking. Suddenly one of them steps back in terror. At this point there is a cut-in of the actor's face. The cut-in is also a closeup.

A cut-away cuts to another bit of action which involves the first scene. In the same shot as in the example above, one of the characters turns and looks off screen in terror. What she sees is

what we see next—a cut-away to a man entering a room, holding a gun.

By juxtaposing bits and pieces of film that have been carefully planned and shot, a film editor can do all sorts of tricks. When Paul Hirsch edited *Carrie,* there was a scene in which Piper Laurie, as the deranged religious fanatic who tried to kill her daughter, cornered Sissy Spacek in their kitchen. Carrie, who could move things without touching them, made all the kitchen knives and tools fly up and stop her mother. The motion of the knives, of course, had been previously shot on a number of separate pieces of film, but skillful editing made them look as if they were each responding to Carrie's commands and flying through the air to attack the mother. The scene is totally believable, except, of course, that it's impossible.

Lighting

Another important technique used by filmmakers is the creative use of light. Lighting placed low, for instance, gives actors a sinister look, as in horror movies such as *Frankenstein, Ben,* and *The Other.* Lighting that is dimmed may make the same actors look depressed or sad.

All film needs light in order for us to see the projected image on the screen. Lighting can be one of the most powerful techniques used by filmmakers. In addition, objects and people create shadows when in front of the lights. A shadow of a knife across a face and the shadow of a woman slowly enveloping a man are examples of shadow techniques.

To make the classic film *King Kong,* the gorilla model was photographed, moved slightly, and photographed again, with the process repeated many times. In 1985, a spoof of the picture showing a model taming a ferocious gorilla was filmed for an insurance company's television commercial. (King Kong ©*RKO General Incorporated.*)

In addition, lighting calls our attention to one part of the image; it may divide it in half, or it may leave something in the foreground or background lit with dark images in contrast.

Color

Color is probably liked best by most young people. However, color used together with black-and-white is also a technique the filmmaker can decide to employ.

Black-and-white is sometimes used for films that attempt to convey feelings of sadness, gloom, and melancholy, as in *Requiem for a Heavyweight.* This technique is also used to depict a time long ago, as in *Paper Moon.* In old films, black-and-white was used because color hadn't been invented, or later, because it was cheaper.

Color is used to give a feeling of reality and brightness. It adds depth and more dimension to the film, even though well-photographed black-and-white films may do similar things.

Composition

The filmmaker will compose the scene very carefully, paying attention to, for example, where a lamp is placed in relation to the two actors. The filmmaker will make sure that the image balances. There is no rule to composition. Usually, the frame or image is composed so that it pleases the eye, emphasizes something, or so that it will describe a tension between lights and darks, between colors, shapes, and vertical and horizontal figures. Often, the frame is composed to add depth or a feeling of dimension.

Sound

Sometimes we become so much a part of the film that we do not notice the sound, which adds another dimension. Most of the normal sounds you hear in real life are employed to make the film seem real. But unless you go around with an earplug in your ear hooked to a transistor radio, one important kind of film sound, music, is not the usual background for events in real life.

However, music does play an important part in most films you see. Music influences our emotions perhaps only second to the film itself.

Adding music not only enhances the excitement, but can also involve our emotions and intensify how we feel about what is happening. The rhythm is right with the movement. Remember the beautiful waltz of ''The Blue Danube'' in *2001: A Space Odyssey,* as man-made space stations and vehicles slowly move in orbit toward each other? ''Lara's Theme'' in *Dr. Zhivago* adds to the romance of this story of revolutionary Russia.

When the moving images exactly coincide with the sound, filmmakers say that they are *synchronized.* Synchronized sound adds much to the realism of a film. So do the right *sound effects.* Most of the extraneous sounds—a creaking door, cars passing, a police siren, wind, bells chiming —are not recorded at the time of filming. These sound effects are dubbed in later to add realism.

Special Effects

Another technique that filmmakers use to communicate images is special effects. This technique is hard to film.

When we think of special effects, we usually think of *Star Wars, The Empire Strikes Back, Return of the Jedi, Indiana Jones and the Temple of Doom,* and *Ghostbusters.*

Leo Janus, in ''Special Science Creates Illusions in Sci-Fi Spectacles'' explains: ''Through special effects, improbable events are made sufficiently dramatic to force an audience to suspend disbelief. Indeed, for many caught up in such shocking films as *Jaws, Towering Inferno,* or *Earthquake,* the boundaries between screen and reality have by no means been self-evident.''

All kinds of models and various miniatures are used in creating special effects. In addition, complex photographic techniques such as matte painting, front and rear projection, slow and fast frames per second, animation, beam-splitting mirrors, special optics, special processing, infra-red film, traveling mattes, and many more are used to create special effects. Special effects can often convince us that a spaceship is traveling through the galaxy. It is a useful tool of filmmakers in their quest to create fantasy for us.

Special effects have developed into a highly-technical, sophisticated branch of film, and Richard Edlund, Academy Award nominee for *Ghostbusters* and *2010* is considered one of the top innovators. Here Edlund checks a camera angle while he and Brian Johnson supervise the complex special effects needed for *The Empire Strikes Back.* (The Empire Strikes Back, *Courtesy of Lucasfilm, Ltd.,* ©*Lucasfilm, Ltd. (LFL) 1980. All Rights Reserved.*)

One of the decade's outstanding films, just as *Star Wars,* its predecessor, had been, is *The Empire Strikes Back.* Author and executive producer George Lucas conceives the epic adventure as a 9-part saga spanning 40 years, with *Star Wars* and *The Empire Strikes Back* as the first two parts of the middle trilogy and *Return of the Jedi* as the third.

Both technically brilliant films have been hailed by critics and audiences for their special photographic effects. But though 20th Century-Fox backed *Star Wars, Empire* was a self-financed Lucasfilm production. Its effects, miniatures, and opticals were an in-house operation—the responsibility of another Lucas company, Industrial Light and Magic (ILM).

Special photographic effects, like those in the two films, are not new to motion pictures. In fact, George Méliès showed astronauts planning a lunar trip, building a projectile, being shot off to the moon, landing in the eye of the man in the moon (who wept a large tear), and descending into a lunar crater—all in Méliès's *A Trip to the Moon,* filmed in 1902.

Richard Edlund, Oscar-winner for *Star Wars* and co-supervisor (with Brian Johnson) of special visual effects on *Empire,* helped set up ILM in Marin County near San Francisco, picking department heads and technicians for the tremendous task.

"Here at ILM, George Lucas worked closely with us on special effects. Right from the beginning, we had storyboards of every shot. We knew what we could do, what we *thought* we could do, and what we would be trying for the first time. Because planning was so detailed, we knew in advance just how many space shots and how many starfield shots we needed. We kept asking, 'What's the tempo of the sequence? How does each shot work with the next shot?' We knew what we were going to do. We were not just pointing the cameras. . . .

"Much of what we were doing was prototype work which had never been done before. We had to work on a rigid timetable. It was crucial for us to understand the magnitude of the project and the momentum we had to maintain. Every day we had to get five shots—pieces of film which lasted four seconds each on screen—out and on camera in order to keep *Empire* on schedule."

Key to much of *Empire's* filming was a highly sophisticated optical printer, that enables film to be rephotographed a number of times. The printer, designed and built especially for this picture, cost over $500,000.

"There were nearly 2,000 separately photographed elements involved in *Empire,*" Edlund says. "An element is an image that is photographed as a separate piece of film. Even though a shot might only last four seconds on screen, it still had an average of five separate elements, and had to be run through the optical printer several times."

One of *Empire's* most complicated sequences showed the *Millennium Falcon,* piloted by Han

One shot in this complex sequence had 25 separately photographed elements. To produce the special effects in the *Star Wars* trilogy of films, new techniques and equipment were worked out. (The Empire Strikes Back, *Courtesy of Lucasfilm, Ltd.,* © *Lucasfilm, Ltd., (LFL) 1980. All Rights Reserved.*)

Solo, flying through an asteroid belt and pursued by Imperial TIE fighters. "One shot in this sequence," Edlund explains, "had 25 separately photographed elements. There were space ships, background asteroids, and foreground asteroids that all had to be photographed separately. There were also separate shots of stars, lasers, shadows, and explosions. All 25 of these elements had to be put together in one composite shot. Every element had to have perfect color balance, so it could blend into one shot without being noticed. Every element had to have no matte lines. Even with over 100 pieces of film in-

volved, it took only four tries through the optical printer to get that shot right."

Some optical effects for *Empire* were done on the outside, according to editor Paul Hirsch. When Princess Leia and Chewbacca were being chased by stormtroopers in Cloud City, the laser pistol sequences were opticals, produced by an outside house. So were the lightsaber, or laser sword, shots in the duel between Vader and Luke. The paintings and composites, however, were done at ILM.

Animation techniques at ILM were extremely important to *Empire,* says Edlund. "When a spaceship or asteroid flies by, and you see the shadow traveling underneath, that's done by animation.''

Audiences, however, may not consciously realize just how skillfully these sequences had to be crafted and inserted into the film. ''Even 10-year-olds have seen a good deal of film,'' Edlund explains. ''They're very aware of when something is wrong with a shot; they may not know just why, or where special effects didn't quite work, but they do know when it doesn't look right. Since people are so sophisticated these days

about visual images, our work has to be technically perfect if we are to make part of the film believable and not jar the viewer or call attention to our material. If the special-effect shot looks phony, we've let the director down and stopped the momentum of the drama.''

Rotoscoping, another animation technique, also was used in *Empire.* ''Suppose there is a spaceship flying over the surface of a planet, shooting lasers or dropping bombs. We project each frame of film and plot it on a separate piece of paper that is carefully held in place. The spaceship is

Lightsaber shots for *Empire* were produced outside, then integrated with paintings, composites, and live action footage. Special effects in the *Star Wars* trilogy were among the most elaborate ever conceived and produced. (The Empire Strikes Back, *Courtesy of Lucasfilm, Ltd., ©Lucasfilm, Ltd., (LFL) 1980. All Rights Reserved.*)

outlined. Then we draw a series of lasers coming out of the ship. Next, we rephotograph with the same camera originally used for projecting the ship. Thus it aligns perfectly with the scene when composited in the printer."

Stop-motion animation was used for the Tauntaun, the beast that Luke rode while on patrol on the ice planet Hoth. "There was a full-size version you saw in close shots," Edlund re-

Though the Tauntaun ridden by Luke Skywalker (Mark Hamill) was a full-sized model, other Tauntaun shots used a 12-inch puppet, photographed in stop-motion animation. (Photo: George Whitear.) (The Empire Strikes Back ©1980 Lucasfilm, Ltd. (LFL). All Rights Reserved. Courtesy of Lucasfilm, Ltd.)

calls. "But when the whole Tauntaun rode across the screen, it was actually a 12-inch puppet with bendable joints, built by Phil Tippett."

Editor Paul Hirsch faced a special challenge on the film because of the large number of special-effects shots—over 700 in all. "We had pencil-animated drawings of the scenes leading up to the battle that would stand in for special-effects shots we would receive later," Hirsch says. "We might have live-action footage of Luke sitting in his cockpit, talking to the other pilots. Then we'd cut to a pencil sketch representing optical effects that ILM was busy producing. Next we'd cut to another pilot. For the scene in the asteroid belt when the monster comes out of the hole, snaps its teeth at the disappearing *Millennium Falcon,* and angrily disappears, we had to take it on faith for a long time that the scene would work and the pacing would be right.

"We got the final sets of special effects in March, 1980, and had to have the picture locked in by the first week of April so that 70 mm release prints could be made. Fortunately, with such a disciplined and professional team, the shots were perfect, even though they'd been extremely difficult and complex to produce. When we finally put the picture together, everything worked."

The techniques we have discussed in this chapter are the tools of film communication. Filmmakers use these tools to communicate messages to us. Just as a painter uses brush strokes, paint, canvas, and colors to communicate a picture—a writer uses paper, ink, words, sentences, paragraphs, styles, moods, and characters to communicate a story—just as a dancer uses body motion and music to communicate the dance—a filmmaker uses cameras, film, long shots, angles, editing, lighting, and actors to communicate the film.

Keep in mind that our descriptions of the techniques in this chapter only scratch the surface. There are many techniques that have no name. Many techniques happen simultaneously.

To visually perceive and understand the message that the filmmaker is communicating, the astute student of film should be able to describe in words what it is that was seen and heard.

Reflections

1. What are some examples of techniques or tools that the filmmaker uses to make films?

2. As you see a film, ask yourself: why is this scene a long shot; why is the sound pulsating or quiet; the lighting shadowy or bright? How do these things establish a film's mood?

3. Try image skimming. Image skimming is recalling as many specific images that you can remember. You might try writing down as many specific images as you can remember. You will find that the more you do this, the better you will be at remembering and understanding film.

4. What does A + B = more than A + B mean? How can the whole scene or film turn out to be more than the sum of its parts? It is very important that you understand this concept.

5. Another way to understand a film better and how the filmmaker uses techniques is to ask yourself, "Why do I feel the way I do about a particular sequence? What did the filmmaker to do make me feel this way?"

Activities

1. Write about a film that you've seen. This will help you really put your thoughts in order.

2. Find a short story or poem and see if you can write a film idea from it. You may want to try to make a film from this film idea. Use the right techniques to describe the idea.

3. Create a storyboard idea for a film from a story or poem. A storyboard looks like a comic strip with the important scenes drawn in the squares.

4. Cut pictures from magazines which illustrate different aspects of film techniques.

5. Bring music to class that might be the new background sound for a film that you've seen in class.

6. Did you know that you can cut stereo or music tape from a reel-to-reel tape recorder? You can edit a tape the way you would like it to be.

7. Listen to some music that you like. Let your imagination go and see if this leads to an idea for a film.

Further Reading: *Check your library.*

Coynik, David. *Film: Reel to Reel,* St. Mary's College Press, 1972.

Grannetti, Louis D. *Understanding Movies,* Prentice-Hall, Inc., 1972.

Knight, Arthur. Mentor, 1957; *The Liveliest Art,* "Special Effects in SciFi Spectacles," *The Smithsonian,* April 1978.

Kuhns, William. *The Moving Picture Book,* Pflaum/Standard, 1975. This book is excellent for the serious film student.

Valdes, Joan and Crow, Jeanne. *The Media Works,* Pflaum/Standard, 1973. This is an excellent book for all of the media.

Vilmos Zsigmond (right). (Universal City Studios, Inc.)

The Director of Photography

Like fellow countryman Laszlo Kovacs, Director of Photography on Ghostbusters, *Vilmos Zsigmond is a graduate of the Hungarian Film School who fled his country in the 1965 revolution. He and Kovacs photographed the Russian invasion, escaped, and sold their film to CBS, providing funds for their start in America. Zsigmond learned English, began photographing low-budget features and commercials, and came to Los Angeles. Academy Award winner for* Close Encounters of the Third Kind *and winner of an award from the British Academy of Film and Television Art, Zsigmond has an impressive list of credits, including* Deliverance, The Rose, The Deer Hunter, Heaven's Gate, Cinderella Liberty, Blowout, *and* The River, *for which he received an Academy nomination.*

The director of photography is like a conductor of an orchestra. My camera operator is part of the orchestra. He frames the action during the filming, following my direction. A first assistant cameraman makes sure the actors are always in focus. The lens must always be set at the right distance to get sharp images. A second assistant cameraman loads and unloads the magazines and sends the film to the lab. Often, on a major film, I supervise a second camera unit, telling them how to photograph scenes and what kinds of lenses and filters to use so shots can be integrated.

I also direct the lighting crew, which includes the gaffer (chief electrician), the best boy, and four to six other electricians. I decide how to light a scene for the best effects. Exteriors are shot in sunlight, but if the sun goes away, I must bring in the arcs and do closeups without the sun. I must be able to match the shots so the audience won't see the difference.

With interiors, the director of photography lights the scene. Suppose you're photographing a room at sunset. You'll place an arc so light comes through the window and makes people and objects appear to be bathed in that sunset glow. You'll use warm colors and filters to get the sunset feeling.

A director of photography learns a lot about lighting by studying paintings in museums, looking at how artists create certain effects and then duplicating that lighting in films.

As director of photography, I also direct my grip crew. The key grip has his best boy and three to six grips. They help get the cameras into the right position. If you have a moving shot, they set a dolly. They build dolly tracks, either from lumber or metal, which may have to be fabricated. If there's a crane shot, the grip crew moves the crane while we film up and down. If we're shooting from a 20-foot tower, the grips build the tower, pull up the camera and tripod, and set it up.

On a major production like *The River,* I became involved nearly three months before filming began. There were many conferences with the director. I went on location and made test footage. I did test photography on costumes to see what kind of filters to use. I participated in actors' rehearsals to have a better idea of what they were going to do—what camera moves were needed.

Just as in painting, composition is extremely important. How do you frame the action to get the effect the director wants?

In *The Rose,* we have a helicopter shot, looking down into the stadium, seeing thousands and thousands of people waiting for Bette Midler to arrive. The spotlights hit the helicopter as it lands. She gets out, walks through the crowd, up to the stage, and starts singing. That was a difficult scene to plan and film.

We needed hundreds of different shots, hundreds of different cuts in *Deliverance,* when the canoes broke in the rapids and the actors had to swim for their lives. The camera crew traveled in rubber boats, and set cameras up with long lenses.

In *The River,* I had to work with the production designer and special effects department to create the lighting effects and smoke of a real steel mill.

My job as director of photography encompasses whatever is connected with the camera. If the actors aren't standing in the right positions, I have to tell the director. If the lighting is wrong, it's my job to fix it. You must see the actors' expressions. If the scene is shot in closeup, you must see their eyes.

A director of photography works closely with the director to make sure the scene is covered. How many closeups? How many over-the-shoulder shots? Do we have the necessary masters? Did we get the actor's expressions?

After filming ends, I am heavily involved in the final phase. By this time, the picture has been cut, and music and sound effects have been added. We must choose the right colors—the right density for each scene—must "time" the final print for the look of the picture.

6

Editing the Film

Opening scenes from *Raiders of the Lost Ark* found Harrison Ford fleeing for his life from temple ruin. Skillful editing made the sequence so real that audiences were spellbound. (Raiders of the Lost Ark ©*Lucasfilm Ltd. (LFL) 1981. All Rights Reserved. Courtesy of Lucasfilm Ltd.*)

Film Editing

Editing—selecting the best of all the angles and shots provided by the director, choosing the best performances, and uniting them into scenes and sequences with appropriate pacing and timing—is one of the most significant steps in the making of a film.

When editing is done well, you will often not be aware of cuts or transitions between scenes: you will be caught up in what is happening to the characters. For instance, in *Breaking Away,* Cynthia Scheider, who edited both the film and a subsequent television pilot, believes you should not be conscious of the editing. "The film is like a story that keeps happening," she says.

In certain films, however, the script, or the way in which the director chooses to interpret it, may dictate a style of editing that is more obvious. *"All That Jazz,"* says editor Alan Heim, who won an Oscar for the picture, "is a flashy film that calls attention to its structure. But *Network* (a film which Heim edited, and brought him an Academy Award nomination) although a strong narrative film, is not visually dazzling."

Film editors try to carry out the director's vision. But editing is far more than merely following a director's orders, or mechanically splicing bits of film together. A good editor tries to place the audience within the film—directing their attention where it *should* be directed, keeping the audience interested throughout the film and holding them so they become emotionally involved with what is happening to the characters. For instance, editor Sheldon Kahn, (*Ghostbusters, One Flew Over the Cuckoo's Nest*) believes deliberate cutting for the dramatic moment is essential for audience belief. "In the *Ghostbusters* temple scene with Gozer and the terror dogs," he recalls, "Gozer puts her hand on one of the dogs and it's growling. Because of our tight shooting schedule, the terror dogs' mouths were not yet operational when we photographed the scene.

"If you watch very closely, in the medium-long shot when Gozer walks toward the dog, its mouth is not open. She puts her hand out toward the dog. Immediately, I cut to her hand landing on the dog's head. The dog snarls and bares its teeth. No one ever notices the mismatch, because the audience is watching the movement of

Gozer's walking. Editing makes the terror of the scene work better."

Before an editor begins work on a film, however, a great deal has happened. Most movies (though not necessarily documentaries) begin with a plan, or screenplay. Most scripts are basically dialogue. The scriptwriter may indicate some sort of stage directions. Nevertheless, it is generally up to the director to block out where each scene takes place and how the actors move.

Just as actors rehearse their performances, a director rehearses how a movie is going to be shot. For each scene, before the cameras begin to roll, the director and the cinematographer usually have planned how many cameras they will use, how far away each camera will be from the actors, at what angle it will be placed, and what it should photograph.

Sometimes this coverage can be extensive. When Kahn edited *Absence of Malice,* there was a long courtroom scene near the end of the picture in which Will Brimley, as the federal attorney, confronted both parties on the movie's issues. Paul Newman, Sally Field, Brimley, and eight or nine other characters were part of the scene. Director Sidney Pollock made sure he covered the scene by ordering two masters (long shots), as well as closeups of the players.

"Most of the people were sitting at a long table, except for Paul Newman, who sat by the door," Kahn recalls. "We made sure we had one establishing shot that included most of the people at the table. Then we went around to the other side of the room and did another establishing shot, so you could see the backs of the people who were in the first scene. We needed extensive closeup coverage of Paul Newman, because for the first five or six minutes of the scene, he doesn't say anything at all. He reacts to what is happening. We had to keep his character alive by cutting to those reaction shots at the important moments of dialogue, so when Paul did start to talk, what he said then became even more important."

At other times, the camera coverage is much tighter; this depends on what is appropriate for a particular scene and film. In the emotionally-tense restaurant scene in *Kramer vs. Kramer,* Meryl Streep (playing Joanna) says to Dustin

Editor Paul Hirsch, shown here on the *Empire* set with 7′ 2″ Chewbacca, grew close to the actors during the making of the *Star Wars* films. Hirsch says one of his biggest editing challenges was the allowing of appropriate footage for special effects he had not seen when he cut many of the live action sequences. (The Empire Strikes Back, *courtesy of Lucasfilm, Ltd.,* ©*Lucasfilm Ltd. (LFL) 1980, All Rights Reserved.*)

Hoffman (her ex-husband), ''I want my son back!'' Only three different camera angles were used.

These decisions, and many others, are made by the director as he or she plans the film, even though the extent of coverage, the camera angles, and the amount and quality of film shot determine the material a film editor has to work with. Sometimes experienced film editors are consulted before shooting actually starts, and have a chance to participate in these decisions. Alan Heim, for instance, was sent one of the earliest scripts of *All That Jazz* a year before production began.

An Editor on the Set

The usual practice, however (and practice required by union rules), is to place an editor on the payroll for the first day of shooting. There is no film ready yet to be edited—the cameras are still rolling, and the negative is still being exposed and must be processed. However, the editor, an assistant, and perhaps an apprentice, will need time to set up their cutting room, where much of the actual mechanical piecing-together of the film will be done.

Bernard Balmuth, whose first editing credit was on the television series, *The Monkees*, has edited many television series, including *Taxi, The Waltons, The Flying Nun,* and *Born Free.* He was a 1981 Emmy nominee for an episode of *Palmerstown.* Balmuth's more recent credits include a feature film, *The Red Fury*, and made-for-television movies: *Flight #90: Disaster on the Potomac,* and Kenny Rogers' *Gambler II.* Despite his years of experience, Balmuth still remembers vividly the first time he stepped into a cutting room.

''There were racks of film cans and reels of film,'' he says. ''Film was hanging from bins, from desks, from everywhere, it seemed—even from the walls and ceiling!

''Numerous clipboards with papers attached were also hanging from an assortment of hooks and nails. Enmeshed in this film jungle were two men. One was winding film from one end of his bench to the other, while the other individual was

To be sure coverage is adequate, the film editor works closely with the director and the director of photography during shooting. *The Natural,* a Robert Redford film about an aging baseball player, received an Academy Award nomination for cinematography. *(The Natural © 1984 Tri-Star Pictures. All Rights Reserved.)*

hunched over a strange contraption, looking at film.

" 'Was this catastrophic mess,' I wondered, 'the way movies were made? Why, for heaven's sake, don't they *organize* the place?'

"Some time later, when I, too, had become a part of this industry, I learned that the appearance of a shambles is the nature of film editing. Despite its appearance, that cutting room *was* organized, and it was indeed making movies."

There is, of course, a reason for the way a cutting room looks. Films are almost never shot in sequence. The events you see happening on the screen were actually filmed in quite a different order. All the scenes that take place in a certain location, for instance, may be shot before scenes that happen somewhere else—regardless of the order in which they will occur in the finished film. Or a director may try to finish shooting all the scenes involving a particular character, particu-

larly if that star playing that character has other contractual obligations.

Much, much more film is shot for a movie than the audience will ever see. Feature films are usually shot in 35 mm. There are 16 frames to a foot of film, which runs 24 seconds when it is projected. Ninety feet of 35 mm film go through the projector for every minute you see on screen. For each hour of a movie, there are 5400 feet of 35 mm film. A picture such as *Breaking Away,* which runs 1 hour, 43 minutes on screen, has 9270 feet of 35 mm film in its release print (the version that is sent to theaters).

A director, however, deliberately shoots this additional film. For each scene, he or she will use a number of angles, and often more than one camera. The director will always want a *master shot* (the full scene shot, which shows the geographical relationship of the actors to the locale). There may be a master two-shot, which will be a closer shot of the two characters who are talking to each other, and there will probably be closeup coverage of each of the main actors in the scene.

Almost certainly it will require a number of *takes* to make sure the editor has enough material to work with and to get the appropriate performances the director wants from the actors.

"I may shoot as many as 20 takes of a particular scene," says Ivan Reitman, producer/director of *Ghostbusters*, "but usually I'll average eight or nine takes, and print three or four. It's essential to cover the scene so the director and editor have choices, so the scene will have a life and rhythm."

"Part of an editor's job is to make sure an actor's performance is seamless," says Alan Heim. "Many people think scenes are shot in long takes, but in reality, they're often put together out of many, many fragments. Maybe we shot an interior scene first, but the exterior scene, which will come before it in the finished film, may not be shot until four or five weeks later. The actor or actress must have a lot of control over the quality of their performance so that they can project just the right level of emotion to lead into the scene they may have done more than a month earlier.

"It requires tremendous discipline and structure to be able to give that kind of consistent, professional performance time and time again throughout a film. For instance, Roy Scheider in *Jazz* had to *be* Joe Gideon, the choreographer, in every movement, every expression. Roy's previous roles in *Jaws I* and *II* and *The French Connection* were straightforward, dramatic performances. Yet in *Jazz*, he not only portrayed an extremely complex character, but he had to project the impression he was a highly skilled, experienced dancer and choreographer. When he demonstrates steps for the show numbers, or when he's dancing with his daughter, every slide, every movement is physically correct, even though he'd never danced on film before. It's a sparkling performance!

"The emotional buildup and development of a character like Roy's Joe Gideon in *Jazz* must be carefully watched by the film editor," Heim says. "You look for the very best of the material, the words and emotions, that the player is projecting. Meanwhile you must keep the entire film in mind.

If you tighten a scene too much, you may find you've left out an essential line or even facial expression that *had* to be there in order for the audience to believe the character. You've got to edit in such a way that you retain the integrity of the performance, and get the effect in the finished film that the director wants."

Most people do not realize how many steps there are between the time a film is photographed and the time they see it in the movie theater.

After the Shooting Stops

Film is shot on a negative. Before it can be viewed, it must be developed and printed by a laboratory. All the film that a camera operator exposes during a particular scene will not be printed. Instead, the director has only certain takes printed in the lab. These will be shots that the editor will use when the film is edited. Even the amount of film that has been printed will be cut to one-tenth or less of its original footage by the time the final version of the picture has been released. Sometimes, however, as much as one-third of the material may be used when shooting has been restricted due to limited time (as in TV), limited funds, or both.

Some films, however, present an extremely difficult challenge to their editors because of the sheer volume of film that must be viewed, considered, remembered, analyzed, and decided on.

For the fight sequence in *Rocky,* shot with six cameras, editor Scott Conrad had 84,000 feet of printed film. Watching all that film from start to finish, just *one* time through, would take 15½ hours if viewed on just one editing machine. Instead, to save time, Conrad used a Kem, a German-made horizontal editing machine, which allowed him to view, simultaneously, the film shot by three of the cameras.

Nevertheless, it took him six weeks of full-time work to edit the fight sequence to its first cut of 27 minutes. In the version of the picture that was finally released, the scene had been trimmed to 16 minutes (or 1,440 feet of the 84,000 feet printed).

Apocalypse Now, Francis Ford Coppola's statement about the Vietnam War, ran approximately

2½ hours in theaters (or 13,500 feet of film). Editor Jerry Greenberg, an Oscar nominee along with fellow editors Richard Marks, Walter Murch, and Lisa Frucktman, says there were *one million feet* of printed film! "The picture was conceived to epic size and epic proportions, and required a huge editing crew," he says. "The best way to approach the film seemed to be to carve it up; each of us had different responsibilities for different portions of the film. We would constantly screen it together with the director, and would constructively criticize each other's work. Because of the breadth of the film, it took many more people than usual to refine it and to hold that picture together."

Greenberg remembers the battle scene as being especially challenging. In that scene, which ran for ten minutes in the film's final version, a native village was decimated by helicopters and superior firepower. "There was more footage shot and printed of that battle than most films have in their entire two hours," he recalls. "Shrinking it down to 10 minutes and attempting to solve the technical problems took a long time."

Clearly, then, because of the high cost of salaries and materials, and the millions of dollars involved in making a movie, an editor of a feature film must be a master of the craft. He or she must know intimately the technical skills required in manipulating the editing tools (machines such as Moviolas or Kems). There are special sound editors, music editors, and specialists in optical effects (film devices created in the lab). The editor on a film must know all the technical details of how the work is accomplished—how it can be best used to blend with how he or she is cutting the picture. A film editor must be able to solve technical problems and make suggestions that may help a director create the desired effect.

In addition, good editors frequently have a "sixth sense," a talent or instinct they find hard to describe, which not only lets them see the picture as a whole, even in its earliest stages, but also enables them to creatively and selectively choose the shots and angles which will hold the audience's interest and control the pacing and rhythm of the finished film.

A "supervising editor" sometimes does not work directly on the film. He or she requests

Veteran film editor Bernard Balmuth, Emmy nominee, teaches a film editing course at UCLA and is author of *The Cutting Room,* a widely used text for students.

changes in a projection room, as do a director and producer, after they have viewed the dailies. Generally, a supervising editor acts as a liaison between the editor and producer/director.

The competition in the film-editing field is intense. A film editor does not need classes in editing or even a college degree in cinema in film to be hired, though many editors do have such a background.

Editors have varying backgrounds. Bernard Balmuth, an English major, took part in theater on campus—first at Youngstown (Ohio) College, and then at U.C.L.A. After graduation, he served in Army Special Services, and then took part in many stock companies and actors' workshops. Balmuth explains, "I finally was able to work my way in after a good many years of fruitlessly trying to crack the stone walls of the motion picture studios."

From the time he was seven years old, spending every weekend in Chicago theaters watching movies and playing with his friends at moviemaking, Sheldon Kahn knew he wanted to be behind the scenes in feature film. A University of Southern California Cinema School graduate, Kahn was first hired by the County of Los Angeles to help start their film program. His picture, *Angel By the Hand,* won a prize for best documentary film in the New York Film Festival.

Kahn asked the Editors' Union in Los Angeles to help him break into the entertainment industry. He looked for jobs all over Los Angeles. Finally CBS hired him to run its shipping department. "How come?" he asked an executive's secretary several months later. "There were an actor's nephew and a writer's son applying for the job. Did the boss really like me that well?"

"C'mon, Shelly," she said. "Don't tell me you have no connections in movies. Isn't your father Irving Kahn who runs Acme Labs?

"That's my dad's name," Kahn told her, "but no labs in the family. Wrong person."

CBS laughed, and promoted him—eventually—to a spot where his job responsibilities permitted him to be eligible for union membership. His second film, for producer Saul Zaentz, was *One Flew Over the Cuckoo's Nest,* which earned him an Oscar nomination.

Alan Heim graduated from City College of New York with a degree in social science and a major in film. Cynthia Scheider, trained as a Shakespearian and classical actress at the prestigious Central Academy in London, England, walked into a New York restaurant in 1969 and announced to friends she was no longer going to be an actress; instead she was going to be a film editor. The next day, the restaurant owner phoned her and said, "I have a friend who is doing documentaries for *Time/Life.* He wants to meet you." She was hired at the first interview.

Retired film editor Fredrick Y. Smith, who studied at Stanford University, began his career in 1928 as a projectionist. He edited "shorts," trail-

ers, music, sound effects, feature films, TV films. Smith also worked as a supervising film editor, editorial supervisor, production assistant, and second unit director, taught editing at Columbia College in Hollywood and served four times as president of A.C.E. (American Cinema Editors), before his retirement in 1978. Smith worked with many famous stars during his career: Spencer Tracy, Joan Crawford, Jean Harlow, Errol Flynn, and James Cagney. His credits include *Babes on Broadway* (the Busby Berkeley musical starring Judy Garland and Mickey Rooney); *Return of the Thin Man* (with William Powell and Myrna Loy); and the original *Misty,* story of the wild horse roundup on Chincoteague Island. This last movie starred David Ladd, then only 16.

Scott Conrad (Oscar winner, along with Richard Halsey, for *Rocky*) started in the mailroom at 20th Century-Fox in 1964, but returned two years later to the University of Southern California as a cinema major while working part-time as an assistant editor.

In 1968, Ron Preisman, a friend of Conrad, was director George Roy Hill's assistant during the on-location shooting of *Butch Cassidy and the Sundance Kid.* Cinematographer Conrad Hall showed Preisman how to use a 16 mm Bolex camera. Preisman photographed the making of the film, interviewed the major stars, and explained how the technical elements blended together to make movie magic. Preisman shipped this footage back to Conrad, who spent nights editing it after his regular job and studies.

The result of Conrad's work, the film, *The Making of Butch Cassidy and the Sundance Kid,* is still shown on college campuses, and won an Emmy award as best documentary of the year. However, it posed a slightly embarrassing situation for Conrad, who says he got his hands slapped by the Editors' Guild for his participation in editing it.

To understand why Conrad could get into trouble for editing a highly-praised and money-making film, you need to know a bit about the importance of unions in the film industry.

Film editors belong to I.A.T.S.E., the International Alliance of Theatrical Stage Employees and Moving Picture Machine Operators of the United States and Canada, an umbrella-type union covering a number of crafts. So do camera operators, sound crews, art directors, set designers, illustrators, cartoonists, makeup artists, wardrobe attendants, story analysts, script supervisors, publicists, grips (stagehands), studio projectionists, lab technicians, laborers, first aid workers, electricians, painters, cinetechnicians (who do camera repair and metal work), and studio teachers (who also act as advocates for child actors, monitoring the length of time and situations in which the young actors can appear before the cameras). Each craft has a separate union local.

The Motion Pictures Editors' Guild makes and enforces contracts for its members, handles members' grievances, administers welfare and benefit plans for its members, and runs seminars and training programs. It also sets rules for its members. Like other unions, it protects seniority. As members progress, they move up in seniority.

When a new, aspiring editor begins the long process to becoming an editor, he or she usually starts as an apprentice. Often, apprentice editors are assigned to shipping and receiving; coding (marking the edges of a synchronized picture and sound-track reel with letters and digits (A-1000, BC-6000, etc.) for easier identification); storing prints and units of the completed films; and carrying film between the editing room and projection booths. Eventually, as an apprentice editor learns, he or she may splice film and even sync up dailies.* (Matching together a separate piece of 35 mm film containing the images and a separate piece of 35 mm film containing the sound for the assistant editor.)

An assistant editor is usually the person who is actually responsible for organizing and managing the cutting room. He or she files all forms, reports, and film. An assistant editor is responsible for syncing up dailies; ordering any necessary film, including opticals; making out reports to the front office and producer; cutting in opticals and relaying instructions to the apprentices in the coding room; and taking notes during the running

of a film. Eventually, an assistant may be given the opportunity to edit a sequence.

Editing is a long, complicated union-covered training process, learned on-the-job from those who are more skilled and experienced in the craft.

In Hollywood at that time, according to Conrad, the Motion Picture Editors' Guild had an eight-year (apprentice and assistant) employment requirement before an editor was allowed to truly cut film on his own. "I was only four years into that when the documentary was released and won an Emmy," Conrad recalls. "So here I was with an award-winning film. Yet, under union rules, I wasn't supposed to be editing for another four years. I was reprimanded, and had to go back and continue as an assistant editor till my required additional four years were up."

In 1980, the *American Film Institute to College Courses in Film and Television* showed that colleges and universities were offering 7648 courses in film, television, or media, to 44,183 students majoring in those areas.

Of 3991 film courses, 2270 were offered to undergraduates, 335 to graduate students, and 886 were open to both undergraduate and graduate students. There were 227 colleges and universities awarding bachelor's degrees in film, 76 with master's degree programs, and 16 schools awarding doctorates.

AFI statistics for 1980 (latest available) showed a total of 44,183 students majoring in film, television, or related areas. And AFI estimated that 200,000 non-majors take a film, television, or media course each semester.

The Cutting Starts

After the editor, director, and other interested production people view the rushes, or dailies, from the first day's shooting, the director decides what pieces of film, or what takes, may work best to achieve the desired effect. Sometimes shots from the rushes are never given further consideration, because of technical flaws or performances that do not fit the director's concept of the total film.

As soon as shooting on a particular scene has been completed (a process that varies according

---

*dailies—film from the previous day's shooting which the director has ordered to be printed. It is usually viewed by the editor with the director and/or producer together before editing starts. Dailies are called "rushes" in England and by some film people here in America.

to the complexity of the scene) and the film has been processed and viewed, the editor can begin work. He or she will continue working in the cutting room while the director is on the set, shooting the rest of the picture.

One very important member of the production crew whose job is crucial to an editor is the script supervisor. As each scene is shot, the supervisor writes it down, keeping track of every single piece of film. For each take, the script supervisor writes down which camera or cameras were used, what lens was used, how the film was loaded, what the shot did, a short description of the shot, and which actors the shot favored. The takes the director wants printed are circled, and the script is lined to reflect exactly what happened on the set. A copy of these detailed script notes is sent to the editor immediately after each

day's shooting, and becomes the editor's working script—the basis on which the first cut will be edited.

The mechanical part of editing film is not difficult. Each piece of printed film is cut apart into different shots. Then the shots are spliced together in such a way as to create the effect the director desires, keeping the total film in mind.

It is precisely because there is a *choice* of shots that editing decisions must be made. An audience can even see images that may have been shot at different times, and may—if taken apart and isolated—have nothing to do with each other. Yet, because they have been spliced together, the editor has evoked a certain reaction from the viewer.

In the film classic *Potemkin,* the camera focused on soldiers shooting, hundreds of people

America's entry and co-winner of the gold medal in the 1985 Moscow Film Festival, *A Soldier's Story* included this scene of Art Evans (seated), William Allen Young, and David Harris (far right) relaxing off duty. (A Soldier's Story © *1984. Thorn EMI Films Finance PLC. All Rights Reserved.)*

running, and a baby carriage rolling down a flight of steps. Yet, when these sequences are joined together, they quickly create for the viewer a sense of the horror and tragedy that took place at the time of the Russian Revolution. Editing, then, can establish the emotion the director decides is necessary for the film.

Let's see how this worked in a contemporary film. In *Kramer vs. Kramer*, Dustin Hoffman and Meryl Streep have not seen each other or spoken to each other in a long time. Streep had walked out on her husband and son. Hoffman who had been granted sole custody, has been raising the child, coping with the day-to-day responsibilities of parenthood, and forming a deep emotional bond with his son. They meet at a restaurant.

"Dustin Hoffman played the scene as if the love the couple once shared was being rekindled and he was falling in love all over again with his ex-wife. Meryl Streep, a very consumate actress, played the part as if she were deliberately using him," recalls editor Jerry Greenberg.

"He comes to her, believing she is about to say, 'I want you back.' Instead, she says, 'I want my son back.' That has to be the all-time hurt in the world, and we had to play the scene with just that emotion. The editing had to take Hoffman from almost abject love to the razor's edge of a man about to hit his ex-wife in a public place.

"Because of the emotional intensity of the scene, we would not have used a long shot," Greenberg says. "We couldn't get away with only closeups of Hoffman and Streep because that's too much like television; you get bored if you see the same camera angle all the time. So we used a master two-shot, showing both their faces, to vary the camera coverage."

Choosing Shots and Sequences

Sometimes editing is deliberately planned for effect, even in the first version of a script, long before production begins. The dazzling opening of *All That Jazz*, a sequence which usually wins applause even from movie professionals, tells the story of hope, rejection, and success at a Broadway tryout; establishes the history of Joe Gide-

on's marriage, divorce, and relationship with his daughter; and drops the audience abruptly into the story of a self-destructing choreographer.

"For the final moments of that sequence when the dancers spin in succession, we used a full-body shot of them and a waist-high shot of them, taken from slightly different angles—a front view, and a three-quarter view, all photographed against the same background, the pipes on the back wall of the theater," recalls editor Alan Heim. "We locked down the camera to give us the technical control needed so the film could later be spliced to show one dancer changing into another.

"We opened the scene with the full shot to begin the turns—then stayed in close to retain the tension and surprise of the dancers' changing. At the end of the sequence, however, we deliberately went back, knowing the audience would relax for a second—only to come to attention again when the last dancer did a double pirouette that ended the scene."

An editor cuts a picture with a rhythm and pacing that's dictated by the particular material. "The film I'm cutting now," says Cynthia Scheider, "is a horror story about murder and love. It certainly will not be cut with the same rhythm in which I did *Breaking Away*. That film had simple people, simple wants, and simple desires. The audience fell in love with the four boys, right from the beginning shot of their walking through on the way to the quarry."

Editing can create illusions, so that what the audience "sees" is not necessarily what really happened. "Half the shots of the last bicycle race couldn't be used because the stands had to *appear* to be filled," says Scheider. "That stadium holds 35,000, and in reality, only 2,000 people showed up for the filming.

"Taking that race down from the thousands of feet of film to the 20 minutes it played on screen was a challenge," she continues. "You go through the entire sequence, and you pull the exciting shots and start from there. We couldn't take the bicycle riders around the track for the full 200 laps, so we used the device of a narrator, a man calling the race who said, 'It's lap so-and-so.' I would cut away to the father, and when I cut back, the audience could see that a certain amount of time had passed.

"In addition to dramatizing the bicycle race, I was trying to tell the story of the boys, because they were more important than the race itself. I still cry when I see Mike's brother come in and grab him, and I'm still moved when the bad college boy looks up and grudgingly starts to applaud. He's not that bad; he *does* recognize the excellence of the other boys. Those are the things you can do with editing that make film interesting."

A skilled, experienced editor can often creatively add to the success of a film . . . can even, perhaps, turn it into a hit.

As the story in the industry goes, *High Noon,* with Gary Cooper and Grace Kelly, was considered a potential disaster when it was first completed. The studio, it is said, was even thinking of not releasing it. Film editor Elmo Williams was given the picture and asked, "Can you do anything with it?"

Williams suggested they film the inserts of the railroad track and a big insert of the clock as it neared high noon. With those additional shots, he was able to revise the tempo of the whole picture, juxtaposing the characters against the clock to heighten the tension. That tension may have been precisely what made the movie a hit.

Scott Conrad was brought in on *Rocky* as co-editor partway through the picture, when the producers were trying to complete it in time for the Cannes Film Festival. Richard Halsey and he decided to split the film in half, so Conrad ended up with the fight sequence.

"Originally *Rocky* had a downbeat ending," Conrad recalls, "where Rocky left the ring a loser, met Talia Shire in the hallway, and walked off together into the locker room. Stallone's original script had much more of an upbeat ending.

"I suggested to the producers that anyone who had gone 15 rounds in a heavyweight fight and nearly won except for a technical decision would be pretty happy and would want his girl friend coming into the ring. Together with the director and with Richard Halsey, we convinced the producers to reshoot a portion of the ending of the fight here in Los Angeles, staging it with close-ups, 2-shots and 3-shots. We had the masters, with Rocky jumping up and down and yelling. We shot Talia Shire and Sylvester Stallone in closeup, Talia coming through the crowd to meet

Rocky and finally reaching him. We ended the film with a high shot of the arena going crazy.

"I had to intercut those inserts with the basic fight footage, which showed the interaction between Stallone, Weathers, and technical consultant Jimmy Gambina, himself a boxer.

"The fight was patterned very closely after the first Muhammad Ali–Fraser heavyweight bout. The choreography moves like a dance number, with six cameras photographing everything the actors did. In addition to their locked-down camera position, there was also a man in the ring for most rounds with a hand-held camera, to give us the subjective point of view over the boxers' shoulders.

"In editing that sequence, I had to organize each section, breaking it down into rounds and finally into individual combinations of punches.

"Realistically, Rocky lost the match on a technical decision. The one line that was really important, that *had* to come across, was when Rocky asked Apollo Creed (Carl Weathers) if there would be a rematch. 'I don't want a rematch,' Apollo answered. That was enough for the audience. They wanted to believe in Rocky . . . believe that he was a winner."

Putting It Back Together

Because the editor has been cutting scenes all during the filming, by the time shooting has been completed, there is enough edited film to put the sequences together in the order in which they will appear in the completed film. However, none of the unused film is thrown away. It's carefully catalogued, in case it's needed.

This first run-through of the completed film is just a starting point. Often a year or more of post-production work lies ahead before the film is ready for distribution.

The objective of a commercial film is to make as much money as possible for its investors by attracting and pleasing as many viewers as possible—both in the theater, and perhaps later, through a sale to television. Therefore, a film will be edited in the way those who make it feel it will be the most successful.

Although the editor cuts the film to try to achieve the effect a director wants, a director does

Because of the complexity of special effects in *The Empire Strikes Back,* they were not completed by the time live action footage was ready for editing. Paul Hirsch had to cut many sequences, including this snow battle, leaving space for the effects, which were added just before the film's release. (The Empire Strikes Back, *Courtesy of Lucasfilm, Ltd.,* ©*Lucasfilm, Ltd. (LFL) 1980. All Rights Reserved.*)

not always control final editing. Some experienced directors—the late Alfred Hitchcock was one of them—have contracts giving them the absolute right to approve and control the film's version released to theaters. At other times, the director may control editing and post-production work for only a specified length of time after shooting has been completed. Perhaps the film is not ready at that point; perhaps there are conflicts or budget problems. Then, depending upon the contract terms for that particular film, a producer may have the legal right to take over, change the editing, and make all decisions on just how that release print will look.

Many things happen to that first run-through of a film before you will see it in a theater.

Adding Final Touches

Perhaps stock inserts are needed. If a production company doesn't want to spend money filming car crashes, burning planes, or exploding buildings, they can order stock footage from film houses—scenes which have already been filmed and are sold by the foot, usually with a ten-foot minimum. An assistant film editor will usually do the ordering and occasionally cut in the footage at the appropriate places. (The editor usually cuts it in. When it is approved by director and/or producer, the assistant editor will order a "dupe" and cut that in, matching it to the original, and replacing it.) Of course the editor will check and review this part of the film.

Credit lines for the film must be decided on, ordered, and cut into the film. (Not everyone who works on a film is named at the end of the picture—credit is usually determined by legal, guild, or union regulations.)

Title shots must be ordered. Some films, like the James Bond series (*Octopussy, Never Say Never Again*) and the *Pink Panther* series have won recognition for their unusually creative title designs, which help get the audience into the mood for the opening scenes.

Opticals (a variety of film devices created in an outside lab, such as blowups and multiple images) will be carefully planned, ordered, and cut

107

One of the reasons for the success of the *Star Wars* trilogy was the skillful integration of special effects and live action footage through precise editing. Scenes like this with C-3PO and R2-D2 were shot on several continents; editing pulled them together, matching them so audiences saw no break in continuity. (The Empire Strikes Back, *Courtesy of Lucasfilm, Ltd.,* ©*Lucasfilm, Ltd. (LFL) 1980. All Rights Reserved.*)

into the film. Other opticals such as fades, dissolves, irises, and wipes serve as transitions in time and space, or are used for dramatic or comedic effect.

For an extraordinarily complex movie, such as *The Empire Strikes 'Back,* months of post-production work in the special effects lab at Industrial Light and Magic were necessary to integrate opticals, miniatures, animation, and other processes with the live-action film. Experimental research was required to solve a technical problem when a white matte,* instead of the usual black, proved necessary for scenes on the Ice Planet Hoth where combat craft were shown against snow. The Rebel Snowspeeders, which were light gray, and which were manuevering against a white snow background, had to match up with the live-action coverage of the battle on Hoth (actually filmed on the Hordangerjokulen Glacier in Norway).

Sound Editing

Many sound effects are added to a film after filming has been completed. Perhaps the sound recorded at the time of shooting was interrupted, or not the consistent quality needed to match the visual action. Actors often are brought back to a sound stage to re-record dialogue *in sync** with their previously-filmed performance (a technique called *looping*).

Background noises often must be added to a film. A scene can originally be shot in a room with an open window. Although the dialogue is perfect, a sound track must be added later with traffic noises of cars and trucks outside the window so the audience will accept the scene as authentic.

Sound effects for a major film can be surprisingly complex. Veteran sound editor Frank Warner, Oscar winner for *Close Encounters of the Third Kind,* says the sound of the "mother ship" in that film was made up of a mixture of grain threshing machines, animals, crowds of people yelling, and earth sounds.

Warner, whose credits for more than 30 years in film include many of Hollywood's top movies, has a personal "sound library" of nearly one million 35 mm feet. He has cataloged each of the sounds in looseleaf notebooks and alphabetized them. A typical entry reads, "Auto, old (dirt road). 1930 Model A. Start, idle for 5 sec., away slow for 15 ft. Return fast with skid stop, off, door open and close, pull on emergency brake."

Warner and other sound editors can layer sound on sound, taking various sound effects and scoring them like music to get the effects needed for a particular film.

Foley is a special process which sound effects editors use. Human or animal footsteps that walk, run, or dance and many other obvious required sounds are re-enacted and re-recorded on a sound stage in sync with the picture to improve the original production track.

"In a Western," explains Bernard Balmuth, "you may see John Wayne walking down one side of a street on wooden boards, and another actor across the street, walking on dirt. Perhaps the sound of the second actor's boots is not heard clearly. You have to go back later and duplicate those footsteps, and get them into the sound track.

"A foley stage has a number of different areas: cobblestones, gravel, brick, boards, dirt, etc., that can be used to walk on. At Burbank Studios, two women who were formerly professional dancers but who now have made careers in foley duplicate any desired footsteps by walking or dancing on the 'right' material. These experts can even combine individual steps to create the sounds of a crowd walking on downtown streets!"

Foley is also used for many other sounds that may be needed and aren't available in the sound effects library . . . anything from a body landing to the scratch of a quill pen.

When a picture is ready to be scored, there's a special music-and-effects showing. The director or producer explains to the composer what kind of background he or she wants for particular scenes. Where should the music start? Where should it end? How should the music enhance the dialogue, the action, or the mood of the

---

*matte—optically photographing a scene with a section of it blanked out or covered so that it might later be filled in with a second shot or painted art work.

*in sync—in synchronization with, in time with, at the same time with.

Veteran sound editor Frank Warner demonstrates the Moviola to his assistants. Over the past 30 years Warner has worked on many of Hollywood's top movies, including *Close Encounters of the Third Kind* for which he won an Oscar.

scene? Then the composer writes the score, based on music cues. It's recorded by an orchestra and rerecorded with all the sound tracks for the composite "release" track.

For dance production numbers, however, the music is composed and recorded first. Then filming of the dancers is done by using a playback system that matches the music.

Editing can deliberately enhance a production number depending on the nature of the film. "I like to make cuts on a music downbeat or upbeat right on the note, so that it accentuates the fact you are changing from one image to another," says Scott Conrad, who worked on *A Star Is Born,* which starred Barbra Streisand and Kris Kristofferson.

After all stock shots, opticals, and special effects have been cut into the film, and after the sound effects, foley, and music tracks have been completed, the picture is dubbed. Dubbing, also called re-recording, is the final editing phase in which everything is mixed, re-recorded, and blended with the work track into one composite track. An answer print (the first print of the completed film) is made that contains both picture and composite track on one film. The producer or director may request certain corrections, such as color. Once a successive print is approved, then release prints are made, usually from a duplicate negative, and distributed to theaters.

Documentary

Some types of film present special editing challenges. Fredrick Y. Smith believes a documentary film makes the most demands on an editor's creative ability. With a background of nearly 50 years as a film editor, Smith should know.

"If it's a big picture, the footage on a documentary can be astounding," he says. In 1947, MGM sent him to Washington D.C. to select footage taken on Admiral Richard E. Byrd's Fourth Antarctic Expedition (Operation Hi-Jump).

"They must have had about 25 different camera crews on the expedition," he recalls. "They shot *everything* they thought we could possibly use and sent back the film. There was so much footage that it took nearly two months just to look at all the film before I could start selecting the material!

"For many documentaries, like this one, you don't start out with a script. A writer is assigned to you. The two of you have to look at all that film and try to build up a story that will hold audience interest by putting together shots that seem to work well.

"I can still remember how beautiful the shots of the Antarctic ice were at dawn and sunset," Smith says, "with their purple, violet, and sunset colors. I edited the film to hold these shots on screen for quite a bit of footage, because we had music going behind them to keep audience interest."

Smith also directed and photographed the re-enacted scenes for the picture. It was released as *The Secret Land,* and won the Motion Picture Academy of Arts and Sciences Feature Documentary award in 1948.

Changing Techniques

Editing is the only art associated with film that's native to film. Every other art—costume or set design, lighting, stagecraft, acting, or directing—has roots in traditions that go back many years. Even photography has its roots in the tradition of painting.

"We don't have a tradition of film editing that goes back hundreds of years," says Paul Hirsch, editor of *Empire* and Oscar winner (with Marcia Lucas and Richard Chew) for *Star Wars.* "Instead, film editing is less than 100 years old. The fascinating thing about it is that we're all still discovering new things!"

Techniques are constantly changing. Fredrick Y. Smith cut the first "Bobby Jones Golf Series" in 1929 and edited a number of musical short subjects in Tehnicolor that year by the sound-on-disk method.

Smith remembers vividly the big production

musicals. "Because the music is recorded before the scene is shot," he says, "the singing and dancing have to be plotted out very carefully to correspond with the length of the musical arrangement. Busby Berkeley took advantage of this and camera cut—that is, to a certain extent, he edited the film in the camera while shooting was going on.

"When Bus made those famous overhead shots of girls, he knew exactly, even as they were being photographed, where he was going to cut in those particular scenes, because he knew to the fraction of a second when the music would change. He knew exactly where each cut would come, and what that cut would do. That's why editing his work was so easy.

"In older-style editing, we always dissolved and faded," Smith says—"techniques you seldom see today. In a dissolve, one scene melts into another, and you don't lose the density of light at all. But in a fade, however, the aperture of the camera (the lens) is actually closed, and the scene goes black.

"When I first started in the business over 50 years ago," Smith remembers, "fades were four feet long. Today, if they're used at all, anything over two feet is considered too long. We've speeded up the action."

Films shot in the forties, such as Hitchcock's *Rebecca,* might use a dissolve to take you from day to night or from one place to another. Let's suppose you were moving from London to the English countryside. A shot of the country landscape would be optically superimposed on top of shots of London.

The same scene, if shot today, because viewers became more sophisticated through watching a great deal of television, might splice the country sequence directly after the London sequence without any optical effects.

Television has speeded the pace of editing. Most of the difference, says Balmuth (who has most of his editing credits in TV), is in time. "A one-hour television show only gives viewers 46 minutes of action footage," he says. "The rest is commercials and station-break material. So everyone involved with the show—writer, producer, director, and especially the editor—must be conscious of limited time. Cuts are sometimes arbitrarily made to speed the action and pace of

Dancing girls and elaborate shots were trademarks of the great film director Busby Berkeley. Fifty years later, in *Indiana Jones and the Temple of Doom,* Spielberg and Lucas used similar shots for Kate Capshaw's opening sequence in a Shanghai nightclub. (*The Museum of Modern Art/Film Stills Archive.*)

the program, so viewers will stay caught up in the story and not switch channels."

How an Editor Feels About Editing

"Years ago, I was watching a sequence with a brilliant editor named Aram Avakian," remembers Alan Heim. "Aram looked over my shoulder at what seemed to me to be a very simple sequence, and said, 'That's a marvelous cut!' He ran it back and forth for me several times, and finally I understood why. From one character to another, there was a flow of the eye . . . a smoothness that kept the audience moving through the frame, across the frame, and into the next shot.

"Editing—*good* editing—" says Heim, "tells the narrative simply and smoothly; it lets the pictures flow into each other, keeping the audience interested in the movement of the story . . . the rhythm and pace of the action.

"Editing helps the audience know where the film is going."

Reflections

1. In film, more than in other art forms, the order in which you view material is preselected for you by the film's editor. What would the effect have been in some of the films you've watched in class if the sequence of events had been changed?

2. Context, in editing, changes audience reaction. A scene of a couple kissing, followed by a shot of the woman's husband silently watching, implies something about the quality of the relationship. Pick a scene from a film that other class members have also seen. By changing the context, how might you change the audience reaction?

3. Can you identify pictures you've seen where the editing seemed to help the film flow smoothly and unobtrusively?

Activities

1. Choose a familiar television commercial. When it plays, turn off the sound and concentrate on the visual image. Learn to become conscious of where editing cuts are made between sequences.

2. Collect a number of photos illustrating contrasts: black vs. white, up vs. down, good vs. evil, etc. Arrange them in different orders. Do you have a stronger effect when you juxtapose opposites?

3. If you have access to a movie camera, film a brief sequence with your classmates or family. Then edit and tighten the sequence. Keep track of the proportion of film you discard to what remains.

Further Reading: *Check your library.*

Balmuth, Bernard. *The Language of the Cutting Room,* North Hollywood, CA: Rosallen Publications, 1981.

The Costume Designer

Stanford University graduate and design major Bill Theiss, whose mother was a custom milliner in Boston during and after World War I, designed costumes for Captain James Kirk, Spock, the Klingons, and the crew of the Starship Enterprise as costume designer for the 78 television episodes of "Star Trek." Theiss, whose training also included four years as a fashion illustration major at California's Art Center College of Design, was hired to design costumes for his first feature film, Blake Edward's The Pink Panther, *while the production was shooting in Italy.*

Academy Award nominee for Bound for Glory, Butch and Sundance: The Early Days, *and* Heart Like a Wheel, *Theiss, who has an extensive television background, credits shows like "Dynasty" with making television audiences more aware of the importance of costume design.*

Ideally, a costume designer uses appropriate color and design to enhance the characterization and the emotional mood of a film.

For example, in a film set in the thirties, you might put a man in browns or dark colors, to imply strength. If he's poor, you might put him in grayed, washed-out colors to imply he's been weathered by life.

A cheap woman might wear gaudy colors. But if she's a secondary character, you might be careful to keep her a bit muted so she doesn't upstage the leads, dressing her in combinations that are strange and a bit garish, like lavender and pale green, but which still keep her relatively subdued in the scene.

In Hollywood's golden years, studios had large costume departments with enormous stocks and workrooms that could make everything from scratch: dresses, suits, hats, shoes, jewelry, and anything you wanted. There were button collections, trimmings, furs, long tables of women doing beading, special dryers, annual trips to Europe each year by top designers such as Adrian to bring back new and antique fabrics, laces, and accessories.

Today, the film business is much more economically controlled. You design and make only what you have to. You do costumes in the cheapest, fastest, most practical, and yet most aesthetically correct way you can.

A costume designer comes on board in pre-production. The shortest time I've ever had before shooting started was 3½ weeks; the longest time was 10 weeks.

Bill Theiss (left).

I try to read the script quickly the first time, making mental notes and thumbnail sketches to get an overall emotional feeling. Then I re-read the script more carefully and do a breakdown. I must determine how many changes each character has, and when they occur. In what scenes? Is it day or night?

In working to determine the budget, I must know how many costumes for characters there are. Can I call any of the actors or extras in their own clothes or must I provide costumes? Because we must fit many different sizes, we'll need from 30 percent to 50 percent more costumes than I'll end up using.

On *Bound for Glory,* (the Woody Guthrie biography), I had 3500 extras to dress and 200 principals' costumes. Finding Depression-era clothes was a problem. For example, you could re-create the design and cut of house dresses, but finding appropriate prints was almost impossible. Therefore, it was a godsend when I discovered over a hundred mid-thirties cotton dresses from a store that had gone out of business years before. We had to age the garments to give them a well-worn, grayed look that was actually and emotionally appropriate for a film about the Dust Bowl. To age costumes properly, you overdye. You can strip colors. You abrade new fabrics with rasps and sandpaper and chemicals to make them look old . . .

For a period film, the costume designer has to do research from then—contemporary sources—from novels, diaries, newspapers, and society pages written at the time—whatever is appropriate for the characters. You have to understand psychology and sociology to know what people would wear. For example, servants probably wouldn't wear bright colors on a day off unless they were cheap and sleezy. Also, their clothes wouldn't be stylish. They'd want to keep their place and have their clothes last longer, instead of being short-lived fashion.

Costume design is even more important on contemporary films. Unconsciously, audiences ascribe personality traits and attitudes to characters from the clothes they wear.

Costume designers need ingenuity and the ability to project themselves into the middle of a film while it's still being planned. You must second-guess the logistics of what a costume might be required to do. If there's a stunt that might damage the costume, how long will it take the wardrobe people to put the costume back into its original condition for the next take? That's how long you have for refurbishing, because you must not hold up production. How long will each take require to shoot? If there's a rain sequence in a comedy, you'd better anticipate the costume may get muddy as well as wet, because it might be funnier that way.

Will a costume be worn throughout the picture and perhaps require progressive aging? If the director shoots "tattered-and-torn sequences" first, and "new" sequences later, how many multiples of the same costume will you need in how many stages of disarray?

A very low-budget film might allow $5000 to $10,000 for costumes; a major feature like The Cotton Club might have a million-dollar costume budget.

You shop second-hand stores. You buy on the open market, using hopefully the same stores the characters in the script might patronize—whatever is appropriate, from thrift shops to couture. You may have to rent some costumes, paying $200 a piece for a "production rental," meaning the costume is "on hold" until the picture is in release.

You need to anticipate accessories. Is there a hat? Will the actress wear gloves? Will she open her purse so she needs a handkerchief? What can you say with her jewelry?

Costumer designers play an important political role behind the scenes, by supporting the actors and the director. I try to include actors in my preliminary planning, asking them how they see the character being played, how they see that character dressing. The director must always be consulted. He or she has the final word.

Ideally, well-designed costumes suggest a mood to actors, putting them in a frame of mind where they can do their best work.

Sheldon Kahn

The Film Editor

Film editor Sheldon Kahn, a graduate of the University of Southern California Cinema School, began his film career with CBS in film shipping. He quickly moved to television news and documentary editing for CBS, as news broadcasts expanded. As soon as he had enough "union time," Kahn began editing television and feature films. Elaine May gave him his first break as a feature film editor on her Mikey and Nicke. *His second feature film,* One Flew Over the Cuckoo's Nest, *for Saul Zaentz and Milos Forman, earned him an Oscar nomination and the British Academy Award. Among the features he has edited is* Ghostbusters, *one of the most successful comedies of all time.*

One of the first things film school tries to instill in you is there are no rules, that editing is an emotional way of telling a story. It comes from inside you. You wonder what will happen if you take scene seven and put it in place of scene two, telling the story in a different sequence in order to get the best emotional reaction from the audience. You try it and it works! . . . The most important thing in editing is to explore all the different possibilities to find what works.

I am a performance editor. Many times, I use shots that aren't necessarily in response to the lines that are being said, but are particularly interesting portions of an actor's performance that fit in other parts of the film. I don't think of film as the words and the picture locked together. Instead, if dialogue is better in a closeup, but a certain visual is better in long shot, I marry the two to get the best overall performance, or the one that works best for the film as a whole.

An editor always has to keep an eye on what an actor is doing, not necessarily on the spot he's doing it in, but possibly for another place to make the perfect moment in a different place in a scene. I look for moments when something happens in his head, where his eyes react, where his expression changes. The day after a shoot, you look at the dailies with the director. He picks certain takes, certain reactions. As an editor, you are also recording in your own mind certain moments that you try to find ways of using. Your memory has to be so good that you can find that tiny piece of film you want and put it in at the "right" spot when you cut the scene several weeks later. I can remember almost all the footage on every movie I've edited in the last ten years.

No two pictures are the same to an editor. You're working with different directors, different moods. You can't invent a formula for editing. Even the way a person opens and closes a door can be cut differently.

As an editor, you're one of the few people who works on the *whole* picture—not just the hair or the make-up or the costumes. You're not just interested in making a scene work, but you are involved in the overall effect of the film on the audience.

An editor works closely with the director. When I did *Electric Horseman* and *Absence of Malice* with Sidney Pollack, he'd tell me, "Make sure I cover" (shoot many angles). Many times on the set, the scene looks and sounds terrific. As a scene, it's wonderful. But when you put 7 scenes ahead of it and 14 scenes afterwards, the scene may not work as well as it did alone. It's important that even though the director has the performance he or she wants in a particular scene, there's enough material to cut around it, if necessary, at a later time if it doesn't work in the overall film.

Many times, the director has been so busy shooting that there's no chance of his looking at anything you've cut during shooting. As the editor, you put the film together the way you see fit. It's usually two weeks after shooting finishes that the director sees the whole movie together—the first cut.

Then the editor and the director sit down in a lonely room to make the decisions on what they feel the film should be. The editor follows the director's vision, but inevitably has a lot of influence over the final outcome. With good directors, there's a chance to suggest, to try the overall effect of the film on the audience and to try different versions of the same scene, possibly cutting down or cutting out material that may be repetitious. Then you preview the film, and emotionally, you psych yourself up to look at the picture the way the audience will see it, so you can see your mistakes.

As an editor, you strive to make the "right" choices so the performances are believable, real, and immediate. The audience must believe a particular scene happened exactly the way you're showing it. Even if it took three days to shoot, it all must "seem" to have occurred within a one-minute time frame. The actors' performance level from the beginning of the scene in the first master you use must be consistent, right to the last closeup. It's like working out a puzzle.

7

From Script to Film: A Case Study

Developing the Special Effects Concept

Every minute of film you watch in a movie theater, on television, on a VCR, or in your film study class represents literally hundreds of hours of preparation time. When you add together the hours of planning, rehearsing, shooting, and technical time spent by all the people who work on the film, they total more than you've realized.

Many film professionals believe that if you are aware of all the components of a film the *first* time you watch it, they have not done their job well. If you are too conscious of camera angles or sound effects, or a particular actor's performance, they say, the film has not blended properly. The total effect they have been trying to get has not been achieved, because you have been too conscious of the hidden details. But when you see a film a *second* time, they suggest, your enjoyment can be heightened by an awareness of the techniques used to create that total effect.

One of the top-grossing comedies of all time is *Ghostbusters,* Ivan Reitman's fast-paced comedy about three New York parapsychologists who go into business for themselves after losing their research grant. "'Ghostbusters' are the guys you call when things go bump in the night," says Ernie Hudson, who plays Winston in the extraordinarily successful film.

Bill Murray, Dan Aykroyd, and Harold Ramis have been finding and trapping unwanted ghosts by removing ectoplasmic material and storing it in their specially designed ghosttrap. When the Environmental Protection Agency orders the trap opened, the ghosts escape. Meanwhile, Murray as Dr. Peter Venkman, has become involved with Sigourney Weaver (Dana), whose ghost-ridden apartment building on Central Park West has turned into a temple for the pagan god Gozer, complete with an altar guarded by terror dogs.

Unless the Ghostbusters can destroy Gozer, New York City will fall. Gozer doesn't attack them with demons from the underworld. Instead, the god forces the boys to choose their own executioner. Whatever invading force their minds create will materialize.

"Don't think of anything!" Murray yells. But Aykroyd is unable to resist the power of sugges-

Ghostbusters was the first comedy to use large-scale special effects on the scale of those from *Star Wars*—not surprising, since Richard Edlund worked on both films. Here, Edlund's experts prepare the Marshmallow Man for filming on his miniature set depicting Central Park West. (Ghostbusters © 1984 Columbia Pictures Industries Inc. All Rights Reserved. Virgil Marino, Photographer, Entertainment Effects Group.)

tion. He tries to imagine the most innocuous figure he can conjure up—the familiar Stay-Puft Marshmallow Man of his childhood television memories.

We hear Something coming up the street . . .

Something over 100 feet tall, coming to get the Ghostbusters. . . .

Here's how Dan Aykroyd and Harold Ramis wrote one of the film's biggest scenes, and how it was translated on screen.

Who you gonna call when things start happening? Bill Murray, Dan Aykroyd, and Harold Ramis star in Ivan Reitman's top-grossing comedy of all time, *Ghostbusters*. (Ghostbusters © *1984 Columbia Pictures Industries, Inc. All Rights Reserved.)*

Script Excerpts—*Ghostbusters*

181 CONTINUED:

*   *

                    VENKMAN
                  (in a panic)
          We didn't choose anything!
                  (to the others)
          I didn't think of an image, did
          you?

                    SPENGLER

          No!

*   They look at Winston.   *

*   WINSTON   *
          My mind's a total void!   *

*   They all look at Stantz.   *

*   STANTZ   *
                  (guilty)
          I couldn't help it! It just
          popped in there!

*   VENKMAN   *
                  (desparately)
          What?   What popped in there?

*   STANTZ   *
                  (pointing)
          Look!

          They all turn and look to the south.

182 <u>OMITTED</u>   182
183   183

184 <u>GHOSTBUSTERS POV</u>   184

          Looking south past Columbus Circle, they see part of
          something big and white moving between the buildings
          accompanied by thunderous footsteps of almost seismic
          proportions.

          <u>VENKMAN</u>

          He doesn't know what it is yet, but he knows it's coming.

                    VENKMAN
                  (desparately)
*   What is it? Ray, what did   *
          you think of?

(Ghostbusters ©1984 Columbia Pictures Industries Inc. All Rights Reserved.)

184   CONTINUED: 184

BROADWAY AND 55TH

The massive white shape passes behind some buildings,
offering a glimpse of what appears to be a fat, white
arm.

*   STANTZ   *

He's about to go into shock.

*   STANTZ   *
                        (babbling)
                  It can't be! It can't be!

COLUMBUS CIRCLE

The thundering footsteps continue to plod as the thing
starts to emerge from behind the buildings. Now we can
see part of a blue garment covering its enormous chest.

STANTZ   *

He recognizes the monster.

*   STANTZ   *
                        STANTZ
                  It's...It's...It's the
                  STAY-PUFT MARSHMALLOW MAN.

Winston, Venkman and Spengler gape.

THEIR POV

They look across the roof tops and see a large, square,
white, bobbing, laughing head atop a massive body of
similar puffed white squares. The being is dressed in
a tiny sailor's hat, red bosun's whistle and lanyard and
a little blue vest with a button undone at the middle
revealing a little white belly. It is the cute, quint-
essential American brand symbol like the Pillsbury Dough-
boy or the Michelin Tire Man, looming as large as Godzilla.

*   STANTZ   (V.O.)   *
                  (desparately apologizing)
                  I tried to think of the most
                  harmless thing...something that
                  could never destroy us...something
                  I loved from my childhood.

THE GHOSTBUSTERS

They watch the Marshmallow Man plodding toward them.

                                          (CONTINUED)

(Ghostbusters © 1984 Columbia Pictures Industries Inc. All Rights Reserved.)

Creating the Effect

What's involved in making the Stay-Puft Marsh-mallow Man come alive on screen? Here's how some of the key people describe their roles.

Production designer John DeCuir (winner of Academy Awards in art direction for *The King and I, Cleopatra,* and *Hello, Dolly!*), first heard of the Stay-Puft Marshmallow Man during 10 hectic weeks of pre-production, before filming actually started. A 40-year film veteran, DeCuir originally had not been enthusiastic about *Ghostbusters*. "At first I thought it was a nice $6 or $7 million comedy," he recalls, "but Ivan Reitman, who produced and directed the film, told me, 'That's not the picture I want to make.'

"'I want the boys to go to the edge of the abyss, but not beyond,' Reitman said. 'It's more exciting drama if they don't cross into the other world. I want *Ghostbusters* to be big and believable. I want real cars, people, subways and skyscrapers. Then, when strange things begin to happen, they'll be more meaningful. This isn't a picture shot on a two-wall flat, with ghosts. I want to feel the bricks, the stone, the monumentality of New York and all the people, and feel this psychic energy break loose. I want the counterpoint of the clash between reality and the supernatural.'

Director Ivan Reitman felt *Ghostbusters* would be more believable if "the boys" went to the edge of the abyss, but not beyond. Harold Ramis, Dan Aykroyd, Bill Murray, and Ernie Hudson battle underworld demons on the temple set. (Ghostbusters © *1984* Columbia Pictures Industries Inc. All Rights Reserved.)

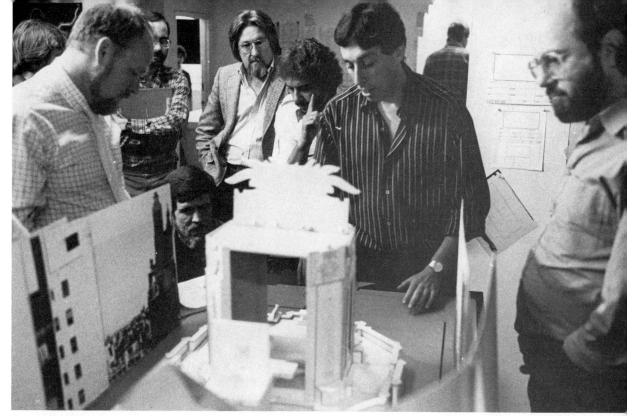

Elaborate special effects like those for Gozer's temple demanded a team effort by veteran professionals. Here, director Ivan Reitman (striped shirt) confers with (l to r) associate producer Michael Gross, Stuart Ziff, Richard Edlund (seated), director of photography Laszlo Kozacs, John Bruno, and associate producer Joe Medjuck. (Ghostbusters © *1984 Columbia Pictures Industries Inc. All Rights Reserved. Virgil Marino, Photographer, Entertainment Effects Group.*)

"That was my kind of picture," DeCuir remembers. "It's no longer a little lightweight piece of stuff. Ivan wanted to stay close to the characters, so the audience would buy the starting premise: that ghosts really existed."

DeCuir began to storyboard the picture, touching on what the sets would be like, how the action would play, and the general look of the production. "I usually make large sketches," he says, "20 x 30 inches, 30 x 40 inches, and some even 40 x 60 inches. I sketched the main building in nine panels—12 feet long and 6 feet high —in order to really feel the building and get to know it. In the case of *Ghostbusters,* we were fortunate to have a crew of skilled key technical people who understood a creative visual climate."

When the script page describing the Stay-Puft Marshmallow Man was shown to DeCuir, he was concerned. "I don't want to do a foolish character," he thought. "There were many questions

we had to answer. Should there be one little Marshmallow Man, various sizes of Marshmallow Men, or one big *feeling* of Marshmallow Man?"

DeCuir began sketching. A fine arts painter who himself painted the entire Sistine Chapel for *The Agony and the Ecstasy,* he was prepared for almost any eventuality. After 40 years in film, if a Marshmallow Man was needed, DeCuir could create one. As was his custom, he started big. "I always exaggerate first, and then pull back," he says. "My first sketches had him 280 feet high —almost as large as the temple building.

"At one point, we considered having the Marshmallow Man come up out of the East River, with boats tipping over. When Ivan and I were in New York, looking at locations, we rode the ferry to the Statue of Liberty. We stood on deck and picked a spot where the Marshmallow Man would surface. I started drawing cliché things—a Godzilla-like figure coming out of the water, and

Integrating shots of live action with Edlund's special effects was challenging for film editor Sheldon Kahn. Although several Marshmallow figures of varying sizes were constructed by Edlund's crew, a real man in a specially constructed suit actually climbed the miniature building. (© 1984 Columbia Pictures Industries Inc. All Rights Reserved. Virgil Marino, Photographer, Entertainment Effects Group.)

all kinds of monsters. Eventually we abandoned the river idea, because Ivan wanted to keep the audience's attention focused on the Ghostbusters on top of the temple.

"He decided to let the Marshmallow Man be seen gradually, just as the boys would discover him. First there's his little sailor cap . . . then a piece of his head, peeking out between the buildings. Then we see more of him. Finally he breaks out into Columbus Circle in his full glory."

The Marshmallow Man became the subject of a special meeting, with associate producers Michael Gross and Joe Medjuck contributing ideas. "So many departments were involved, and meeting production schedules was so crucial that we had to set his size," DeCuir remembers.

"We were beginning to have meetings on the series of storyboards involving the special effects on the picture. By that time, I'd already started building models of the temple. We'd made a number of trips to New York. We knew the dimensions of the little church next door, and had settled the path the Stay-Puft Marshmallow Man would take, coming from Columbus Circle down the street, getting to the temple, and climbing up. At first, I'd sketched him the full height of the building. Ivan decided the scene would work better if he were smaller—half the size of the building, so there could be effort involved in climbing.

"We found the little church on the corner was actually a third of the temple's height, making a good stepping stone for the Marshmallow Man. Then how far did we want him to climb? These decisions helped to dictate his final size.

"Then we had to make a model of the building that would be scaled properly for our miniature work. The building that we photographed wasn't high enough, so we had to add 10 floors, plus my top-level temple. By the time we had constructed our art department study models, we had working drawings at quarter-inch scale. Then we used them to make blueprints and pasted those on cardboard. We had models of the temple and the church next door, and we used these to help define the size of the Stay-Puft Man."

There were still choices to be made. DeCuir's early sketches had the figure much larger. There was a set of smaller sketches, in which the Marshmallow Man was too small to climb the building. But the overriding factor was the need for Richard Edlund's temple to be built at a certain size for effective miniature shooting.

Edlund (Academy Award nominee for *Ghostbusters* special effects, as well as for *2010,* was responsible for the film's 193 special effects shots). In addition to making a complex model for the temple, his company, Boss Film Corporation, with The Entertainment Effects Group, had to build a Stay-Puft Marshmallow Man suit and find a man to wear it.

"We coordinated between the size of a man wearing the suit, and the mechanism to move it, and the restriction that the temple had to be a particular size for miniature photography," DeCuir recalls.

"At the meeting, Ivan made the final decision to take the Marshmallow Man to half the size of the building—about 140 feet. The scale worked out just right.

"It was important to settle his size, because in New York we had built his little sailor cap. In the real size scale, it would have been 24 feet across. We originally thought that after his burning, the hat would symbolically drift down and settle in Central Park West. It was a nice idea, and we actually shot the sequence. But in the editing, Ivan felt at that moment, the action on the street with the EPA agent was more important. The story had to keep moving."

Even though time, money, and material had been spent making the hat, the sequence was eliminated by the director. This is normal in filmmaking, says DeCuir. "We do things that look right, but for the overall look and flow of the picture, something has to give."

By the time the Stay-Puft Man's size and character development had been set, Richard Edlund began to work on him at his Marina del Rey studios. Edlund, a four-time Academy Award winner (*Star Wars, The Empire Strikes Back, Raiders of the Lost Ark,* and *Return of the Jedi*), had been involved with *Ghostbusters* before its final draft. He feels the film is the first major comedy to use the large-scale special effects usually reserved for space or fantasy films. "We didn't want this to be 'Abbott and Costello Meet Some Ghosts,'" says director Reitman, "where you know ghosts are present because you see picture frames move. Instead, the approach was, 'give us ghosts like we've never seen before.'"

Edlund and his crew, which included people who have worked on every important special effects picture in the last 10 years, got busy. They set up shop, including a rubber department, a shooting department, a shooting stage, an optical department, an animation department, and an editorial department. His actual special effects work on *Ghostbusters,* however, began in the machine shop, where Gene Whiteman designed and built the cameras.

"Our field is so rarified that almost everything

Equipped with the latest in ectoplasmic-trapping devices, Dan Aykroyd, as Stantz, is ready to tackle ghosts and demons from the underworld. Directed by Ivan Reitman, *Ghostbusters* is sixth on the list of top-grossing all-time film hits, according to *Variety.* (Ghostbusters © *1984 Columbia Pictures Industries Inc. All Rights Reserved.*)

has to be hot-rodded to some degree," says Edlund. "A lot of the equipment we need is not available off the shelf. We have to find something close, and then modify it to fit our needs."

The Stay-Puft Marshmallow Man sequence created a challenge, even for Edlund. "If it didn't look right," he says, "the whole movie wouldn't have worked. That was a climax scene. If the audience didn't buy the concept from the first peek at the figure between the buildings, they wouldn't have bought the rest of the picture."

Miniatures made the Stay-Puft sequence possible. The foreground buildings were miniature buildings, constructed and shot in miniature. The background buildings were paintings. The Marshmallow Man was shot against a blue background, and towers in the foreground were photographed separately. Edlund and his people composited all these elements on the optical printer, a sophisticated machine that permits each part of a scene to be assembled, re-photographed, and "layered" into the finished shot.

Because live-action sequences for *Ghostbusters* were filmed both in New York and in Burbank, Edlund needed a number of matte shots to re-create New York in his studio, and to enhance the buildings and skyline with the elements of fantasy necessary to create the temple set, so vital to the Stay-Puft sequence. Matte painter Matthew Yuricich added nearly 30 stories onto the building that was actually used in New York. The matte paintings made it possible to match the great temple set DeCuir designed on the Burbank soundstage. Other buildings actually photographed in New York were made shorter through matte painting, so the temple building would dominate . . . would be the one the audience saw on the screen in establishing shots. Mattes were photographed under the supervision of Neil Krepela.

When all the elements were assembled, visual effects editor Conrad Buff synced them and timed the sequences. Black and white prints of each element were superimposed over each other. Next, Mark Vargo, head of optical compositing, re-photographed the layers of elements so they looked right.

"Even 10-year-old moviegoers have seen millions of feet of film," says Edlund. "If it doesn't look right, they'll notice. If the matte is sharper

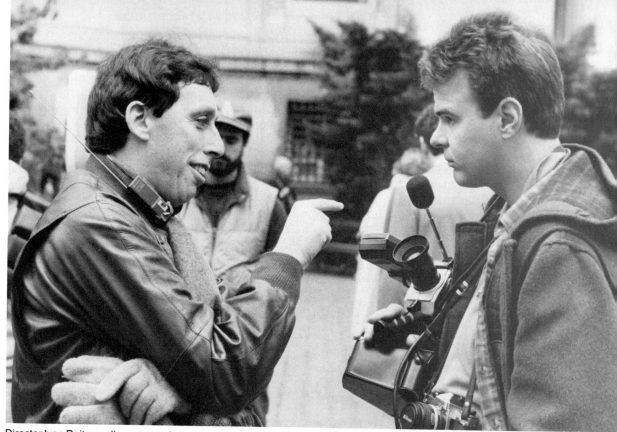

Director Ivan Reitman discusses an important scene with star Dan Aykroyd. Comedy is especially difficult, Reitman feels, because timing is so important. (Ghostbusters © *1984 Columbia Pictures Industries Inc. All Rights Reserved.*)

than the background film, the scene doesn't work, and you've lost the audience."

Matching shots is complicated. "If we have a shot on a Take 1 composite that doesn't work, we massage it," Edlund explains. "Perhaps we have to animate shadows, or darken or lighten areas. Shadows in a scene are what ties the scene together. These subtleties or throwaways make the difference between mediocre effects and great special effects."

Edlund's crew built several marshmallow figures of varying sizes. In addition, a real man in a specially constructed suit actually climbed the miniature building. There was a Stay-Puft man that could actually walk on a piece of street in a 30 x 50-foot miniature.

For the climbing sequence, Edlund constructed and photographed a building 14 feet high, in scale with the Marshmallow Man, who was six feet tall. Lights on the scene and lights on the dark buildings in the background were all painted in through animation.

As *Ghostbusters* production designer, DeCuir was kept up to date on the status of the Stay-Puft Man Edlund was creating. "Color, line, photographing—all these are part of production design," DeCuir explains. "The costume designer, Theoni Aldridge, also had ideas on how he should look. But we're not just free to plan on our own. In every case, these decisions are made and finalized by the director; though we certainly suggest ideas. We are always trying to make the kind of picture the director wants. Through joint discussion, we arrived at the suit and the hat and the whole look. Ivan was in on that, Theoni was in on that, I was in on that, associate producer Michael Gross (who has art training) was close at hand. It was a cooperative decision."

Because the Marshmallow Man melted in great gobs, Edlund faced another responsibility—how to make that sequence believable. At his studio, pyrotechnics expert Thaine Morris worked out the logistics of burning. Meanwhile, DeCuir had storyboarded the figure's skeleton as seen from various camera angles. The art department at the Burbank studio created and built giant melted marshmallow ''droppings'' as large as 12 feet across, and more than 50 smaller droppings of various sizes. Construction was carefully timed so the droppings would be ready for shipment to New York for live photography. ''There was a dropping on the newsstand, one on the opening of the street, and marshmallow gobs every-where,'' DeCuir recalls. ''They had to match the gobs of sticky marshmallow—in reality, shaving cream—falling on William Atherton, the EPA agent.''

Ghostbusters editor Sheldon Kahn (Academy Award nominee for *One Flew Over the Cuckoo's Nest*) had unusual challenges in the Stay-Puft Marshmallow Man sequence. During the first week of shooting, he'd been in New York with Reitman and Edlund; then he'd returned to

When director Ivan Reitman called for ''ghosts like we've never seen before,'' he got the Stay-Puft Marshmallow Man, conjured up by Dan Aykroyd's memories. Here, the Marshmallow Man walks up a forced perspective miniature set of Central Park Avenue. (© 1984 Columbia Pictures Industries Inc. All Rights Reserved. Virgil Marino, Photographer, Entertainment Effects Group.)

Burbank to begin cutting the film. This was Kahn's first picture with special effects. "I'd purposely stayed away from them because I like doing pictures in which I can see performances," he explains. "It's difficult to get performance from things that aren't happening until after you've dubbed the picture and you are putting in the special effects shots. Normally, special effects aren't ready till a picture is almost in the theater, so an editor has to cut to blank leader (film with no photographed images)."

Live action on *Ghostbusters* was photographed in 35 mm film, while Edlund shot special effects in 65 mm, so his images were nearly twice as big. "That's because you can reduce the larger film to 35 mm without losing grain," Kahn says. "Audiences are sophisticated. If they notice in a film that one shot is really sharply focused, while the next one is a little bit fuzzy, they'll say, 'Here comes a special effect. They've gone to another generation in the negative.' You may not consciously realize this, but you've watched so much film that you sense the change.

"When we reduce the special effect shots, you don't notice the cut-ins from the live-action sequences."

Integrating the live-action sequences with Edlund's special effects shots was like fitting together a jigsaw puzzle. On the set in Burbank, Reitman was directing Murray, Aykroyd, and the others in the rooftop scenes, filming in 35 mm. At the same time, Edlund, using a 65 mm camera, also photographed the actors.

Reitman and Kahn had Edlund's 65 mm film developed and printed. They screened it in the main theater at The Burbank Studios—the only theater on the lot equipped to project the giant images—and picked the best takes. Those were reduced to 35 mm and were made available to Kahn within a few days. Then Kahn cut the sequences, using his imagination on where the special effects would go. Meanwhile, Edlund was still creating the Marshmallow Man at his Marina del Rey studios, 20 miles away.

Before Edlund's material arrived, each scene had been worked out and carefully timed. Reitman and Kahn had planned the length of the special effects shots and the order in which they'd appear. "We were right in the way we'd built the scene, even though we built it out of

thin air because we hadn't yet seen the shots of the Marshmallow Man," Kahn says. "Most of Edlund's shots were exactly to the frame. I'd tell him, 'This shot needs to be two feet, three frames long,' and he'd send up two feet, five frames to be on the safe side.

"It was amazing that we had figured out a working formula, since animation and special effects shots are so costly."

It was important for Kahn to have an awareness of Edlund's footage for timing purposes so he could figure out the right rhythm of the scenes. "I looked at the live action on my editing machine, and I imagined it! I cut to the timing I thought it would take to see it. I cut back to the crowd . . . to Bill Murray reacting, to Danny saying, 'It's the Stay-Puft Marshmallow Man' . . . to its turning the corner, when the audience sees it for the first time."

Because of the complexity of *Ghostbusters*, which has 193 special effects shots, there were blank spaces in much of the film shown at the first screening for audiences. Reitman and Kahn recruited about 200 people between 14 and 30 to look at the film. "We have a picture here that's quite different from most films you've seen," Reitman told the preview audience. "Unfortunately, a lot of the important special effect shots aren't in the movie yet. We're really interested in seeing if the comedy works, so we'd like you to see the picture. There are going to be some strange things going on. In Columbus Square in New York City, you're going to see crowds of people running away, but in the background, you're going to see nothing coming toward them. Believe me, though, it's going to be something spectacular!"

When Kahn first edited the Stay-Puft sequence, he had to use his imagination, since Edlund's special effects shots had not been completed. "I didn't know what the Marshmallow Man was going to look like, or how it was going to actually walk and come down the street," Kahn recalls. "But Ivan and I both felt very strongly that we wanted to build the audience suspense. First Bill Murray asks Danny, 'What is it? What did you do?' During the conversation, we hear this 'Clunk, clunk, clunk.' Harold says, 'Look!' and the boys all go over to the edge of the building. There's a closeup of Danny looking.

We go to a figure behind the buildings. We can't make out what it is.

"That's deliberate. We wanted to keep the surprise for a later moment, to release that audience energy later. We needed to keep that scene as tight as possible.

"I cut to Bill Murray looking over to Danny, and another closeup of Danny. All this builds up the tension. Danny says, 'It's the Stay-Puft Marshmallow Man!' We have a long shot of Columbus Circle as the Marshmallow Man turns the corner and comes toward the crowd, which runs from him.

"That's the moment of release. The audience goes insane. They've been wondering what this awful, terrible thing is that's happened—and it's the absurd Marshmallow Man, over a hundred feet high! They love it!"

The whole Stay-Puft sequence lasts only 3½ minutes from the time audiences first see the Marshmallow Man till he melts into gluey blobs. Kahn used editing techniques to help foster the illusion of the 120-foot figure. "I cut back and forth between the Edlund's miniature buildings," he remembers, "and Bill Murray and the boys on top of the temple, and the crowds running away. We kept the Marshmallow Man down to minimum footage so he'd be more believable. The crowds were always looking up, as though he were very, very tall."

Special effects techniques were smoothly integrated with live action to make the sequence believable. "When we blew up the Marshmallow Man," Kahn recalls, "nothing came out of the guys' guns. The ray that destroys him when they cross the streams was all added later—created by Richard Edlund through animation."

Timing, in comedy, is extremely important. Reitman used an old Laurel-and-Hardy trick to set up the gag in which the marshmallow droppings spill on the EPA agent. "The audience is expecting it," says Kahn. "They know it's coming. They say, 'Oh oh, it's coming now!' and then we give them the pleasure of seeing it happen. It brings down the house every time."

Reflection

1. Why do you think director Ivan Reitman felt *Ghostbusters* would be a more exciting drama if "the boys" went to the edge of the abyss but not beyond? What did he mean?

Activities

1. Check *Variety's* list of All-Time Film Rental Champs, usually found in its mid-January issue. Using library reference books or other material that describes films briefly, make a list of 5 or 10 other comedies that rank high as all-time box-office favorites. Talk about these films in class.

2. Choose a brief scene from a short story or novel. Break it down into shots you would need if you were filming the sequence.

Further Reading: *Check your library.*

Finch, Christopher. *The Making of The Dark Crystal,* New York: Holt, Rinehart & Winston, 1983.

Harmetz, Aljean. *The Making of The Wizard of Oz: Movie Magic & Studio Power in the Prime of MGM & The Miracle of Production 1060,* Arcade, NY: Limelight Editions, 1984.

Kael, Pauline. *The Citizen Kane Book,* Arcade, NY: Limelight Editions, 1984.

Debbie Reynolds

The Actress

One unique feature of the big studio system of the 1940s and 1950s was the studio contract. Young performers who were put under contract were, in a way, brought up in the studio, with a combination of school and professional training.

Debbie Reynolds, once a high school student in Burbank, Cal., began as a contract player when she was just 16. She first starred in Singin' in the Rain; *some of her many other films are* The Tender Trap, How the West Was Won, The Unsinkable Molly Brown, *and* The Singing Nun. *She has also played on TV and in nightclubs and, on stage, in* Irene.

Reynolds' daughter, Carrie Fisher (Princess Leia in the Star Wars *trilogy), has followed her mother into films, while Reynolds herself has most recently concentrated on the nightclub circuit, most noticeably in Las Vegas. In her successful workout video,* Do It Debbie's Way, *she uses her years of dancing to demonstrate safe exercise routines for mature women.*

. . . When I first started in films, I was 16. I didn't know which way to face. My back was always to the camera. I didn't know camera angles. I wasn't aware how you positioned yourself to act without being aware of the camera. You've got to be really aware of it, but not seemingly aware. That technique alone takes you three or four years to learn. . . .

After I became Miss Burbank, Warner Brothers studio gave me a screen test. They put me under contract. I studied there for a year and went to school there. . . . It was very difficult to go to school and do films because you have to do three hours of schoolwork a day. That's the law. So you're learning script and you're doing a dance number, and right in the middle of it, the teacher or the social worker can say you have to finish your math. It just tears your mind apart! You're just doing a scene, you're all excited about getting it right, and suddenly you have to go to a textbook. It's very difficult.

. . . Then Warner Brothers dropped my contract, and I went to MGM. I went under contract there. I made a picture called *Three Little Words,* where I did the Helen Kane part, and then I did *Two Weeks of Love* with Janie Powell. I did the ''Abba Dabba'' record in that picture, which started my career going. And then I did *Singin' in the Rain* next, when I was 18.

Gene Kelly was the director, along with Stanley Donen, but Stanley really worked on camera, whereas Gene, I felt, was the true creative power there. He's a perfectionist and a very gifted man in the field of writing and directing, and he really came up with the idea of doing it as camp in 1951. The film has become a classic because of that—all due to Gene.

. . . I lived a long way from the studio. I got up at 5 A.M. every day because I had to take three buses to get to work. I didn't have the money for a car. I'd take breakfast and lunch in a bag. I'd get to the studio at 7 A.M. From 7 to 8:30, we had to do make-up and hair. . . . Then you started shooting at quarter to nine on the set. In those days, they didn't have a union law about when a child had to stop, so we would work until eleven at night—until you collapsed. You worked Saturdays; you had Sunday off. You fainted Sunday, you know—you could barely get rested up so you could go to work on Monday. Now it's different. They have laws so that young people can only work five hours a day, with three hours for schooling, and you're off on Saturdays and Sundays. It's much easier today than it was when I started.

That was our schedule. You just kept doing it until Gene Kelly had that take exactly like he wanted. It didn't matter if your feet were bleeding. It just didn't matter. I was so tired I didn't even go home. I just stayed in my dressing room at the studio. . . .

But I had the advantage of being under contract. You made a salary every week which paid for your eating, and the studio paid for your lessons. You were subsidized. You worked hard, but you also had your training paid for. Really, those studios used to be like universities. . . .

. . . Acting is like playing the violin or piano. You have to study. You have to take lessons for technical training, whether or not you ever use it. . . . One day I'll teach. I'll make young people who don't dance, dance. I'll tell young people who don't sing to sing. I'll tell them if they're bad, to laugh at it and to be better next time. No matter if you're bad, use the experience.

Roy Scheider (as Joe Gideon) and Erzsebet Foldi (as Michelle) his daughter in *All That Jazz*. (All That Jazz © 1979 20th Century-Fox Film Corporation. All Rights Reserved.)

The Actor

Roy Scheider fell in love with acting as a pre-law student at Franklin & Marshall College, where he took part in nearly every play the school produced during his college years. Summer stock was followed by three years in the Air Force, and he started acting professionally in 1960.

Versatile veteran of stage as well as screen, Scheider sees the actor's role as making a situation larger than life. "You deal with self-examination, and the examination of people around you," he says. "In every golden age of civilization, there was a very active theater. Actors have this incredible desire to share the adventure of life with others."

Film—GOOD film—is about emotional experiences. I believe that any material, no matter how staged, photographed, or mounted, is worthless if its content does not move the audience emotionally. Lots of films and plays that are heralded as masterpieces leave me cold. They don't make me angry; they don't make me happy; they don't make me laugh.

What I look for in a role is dramatic conflict. Is there a change in a person's life? Audiences like stories of people going from one point in their lives to another and how they get there. They want to share the emotional experience.

All actors are obsessed with trying to find their next project. No matter how big or famous you are, or how strong your career is, you want to keep going. Every time you reach a level of proficiency in acting, you want to keep that level and to get even better. You're constantly searching for material. You plot and scheme and finagle, trying to find a part that's really worth playing.

I usually read 10 to 12 film scripts a week. In a month's time, maybe only one or two capture me. The first thing I ask myself is, "Would I want to see this?" Next, I want to know what contribution I can make to this project as an actor. Can I use my particular talents to make this idea come alive? If I think I can, my interest in doing the project increases.

I want to know who will direct. How is the picture being financed? What other creative people are involved? I meet with the producer and director to see if my vision as an actor is similar to theirs in interpretation.

Because the film director is the commander-in-chief, in charge of film looks, pacing, cutting, cinematography, and acting, he or she is the leader. If the actor is in sync with the director, together they can march on to an agreed-upon goal.

There are many questions to ask. What can we do with this film that hasn't been done before? How can the actor and director look at some human condition from a different angle? It's rare when all these conditions and creative inputs come together—when a project takes off and elevates itself above "normal" film fare.

The French Connection was that kind of movie. Every one of today's cop shows and movies are all based on what was done in that film. The street philosophy between Gene Hackman and me, sparked by William Friedkin's dynamics, set the standard for those kinds of films. From that point on, the American Western became the city story. The traditional frontier became the city streets.

Jaws was another unusual film. Here was a film about man's battle with an age-old enemy, directed by a very bright and imaginative young man who presented the story—not only from the viewpoint of the character, but also from the viewpoint of the shark. Steven Spielberg equalized the struggle and created this marvelous adventure film.

In *Jaws,* I had the opportunity to play Everyman. I was the character the audience took to heart. I didn't like water. I worried about my family. I constantly questioned my own courage and was the least likely of men to have to finally deal with the shark. It was a wonderful role!

Playing Joe Gideon in *All That Jazz* gave me the chance to examine a workaholic who sacrificed everything in his relationships with people to achieve perfection in his art. Many women, as well as men, were totally affected by that film . . . were so moved by the struggle of this character that they totally identified with him. They went into another profession. They reunited themselves with their families. They took inventory of their lives.

When a film affects the course of your life, it's great art.

Once an actor takes on a role and signs a contract, no one can do your job for you. There is no limit to the amount of times you can reread the script and examine your part. But as an actor, you have to have six choices for every dramatic scene and hundreds of ways to bail yourself out. You can't count on the director to do it.

An actor must adjust to film. The closer the camera comes, the more concentrated and real your performances has to be. Yet you must reduce the energy level, otherwise your close-ups will explode.

Working with the camera requires your highest level of mental and emotional concentration. When you act on stage, you take a journey. But every day in film, you concentrate on taking just one or two steps. You're always shooting a rehearsal—never a finished product.

Diahann Carroll

The Actress

Television, Broadway plays, musical comedy—all these are roads that can lead to a professional actress to a career in films. Diahann Carroll became a star in all these fields early in her career. Despite her success on stage and as the star of the television series "Julia," there seemed to be no place in film for black performers, except in stereotyped musical comedy roles and bit parts.

For her, the breakthrough into film came with Claudine, an inner-city love story in which she played a Harlem woman, mother of six. Her sensitive portrayal won her an Academy Award nomination for Best Actress. Most recently, her work includes major television specials, which highlight her singing talents as well as her skills as a dramatic actress. As Dominique, Blake's half-sister in television's Dynasty, *she became a major character in the saga of the Carrington family.*

. . . It's ridiculous to pretend that we're not aware of color or religious differences. These experiences go into making up a whole human being. Why should we negate them by pretending they don't exist?

. . . I began in this business back in the 1950s. There were no opportunities for Blacks in film. The only things we really had open to us were musicals, and even then, there was an enormous risk in casting a stage play. Therefore, musicals were not integrated. . . .

I used to sustain myself with variety TV shows, which involved flying to the Coast quite often for taping. I'd always ask to be booked out of Los Angeles on the "red-eye" (the 11:00 P.M. flight) on the same night as the taping. Hollywood, Beverly Hills, and that world rejected me. I was not a part of the major industry that was there. I felt so helpless, with so little opportunity to experiment in the areas that fascinated me. All I wanted to do was to get my TV musical job finished and to leave. I still can't believe today that I own a home in California.

Film roles for me weren't even discussed because there was nothing to discuss. I can remember so often, as I became more successful, hearing my own agent say, "Do you want to visit a set and watch so and so?" Ninety percent of the time I'd say no. A film studio was the largest monument to my rejection.

. . . Even with *Porgy and Bess,* the Gershwin film. We all knew we were doing a token film, that tokenism was just about on its way out. We'd all just about had it. Many of us had a personal emotional question as to why we were there, doing this film. Even today, if I see it on television, I am torn between the rich, incredibly beautiful music, and the absolutely one-dimensional, stereotyped characters. . . .

From a performer's viewpoint, we who are Black have much more exposure now than we used to . . . exposure much more quickly than in other areas of daily work. In the past, many of my co-workers have found themselves in a very uncomfortable position. They had to understand what they were as human beings, only in terms of the text of a script. Too often in the past, the text confined itself to what the "government" or any other group would have enjoyed having said about Blacks.

At this particular time, filmmaking is extremely open. It's inventive. It's independent. A big studio has to contend with a creative producer or director who has his hand on the pulse of the populace. The public has seen fit to support fresh, young, stimulating ideas, rather than large movie studios, with their stables of actors and actresses.

. . . Black exploitation films are part of a social phenomenon. They came right on the heels of white exploitation films and followed them to the letter. James Bond was emulated by Shaft.

Even James Bond didn't interest me after the second film. The white community proved that they, too, were bored with that sort of escape. If you have too much of it, what good does it do? You only have to come back to reality. I do think some outlet for emotional frustration, a "Get Whitey" attitude was necessary to relieve hostility, and Black exploitation films attempted to fill that need.

The support for those films primarily came from minority neighborhoods. Now it's time for us to become a little more sophisticated. . . . The feeling that we've got a character just as mean and tough and defiant as anything the white community can offer never really quite lasts. That character is a fairy tale and not the kind of emotional relief that we as Blacks really find fulfilling.

We're realizing this and beginning to demand better quality.

. . . It's a very hard thing to speculate on the future of Black actors and actresses in the motion picture industry. . . . I think new films that will involve Blacks will take on a broader scope, because we are in so many areas of American living. We have really never been seen on the screen in all facets of our lives. I still say there is a long way to go.

8

Motion Pictures-for-Television

Made-for-Television Movies

Seeing a feature film in a motion picture theater provides a certain type of communication experience—one that's colored by the total environment. The giant screen, the larger-than-life images, the Dolby™ stereo all combine with the film itself to enhance your perception of what the filmmaker intended to convey.

Many films have proved so popular in theaters that they have had a built-in audience when shown on television. Whole new generations of audiences thrill to Clark Gable as Rhett Butler telling Scarlett O'Hara, who asks what will become of her, "Frankly, my dear, I don't give a damn." Christmas wouldn't be Christmas for many viewers without Judy Garland telling Margaret O'Brien to "Have Yourself a Merry Little Christmas" in *Meet Me In St. Louis,* without Bing Crosby crooning "White Christmas" in *Christmas in Connecticut,* or without Natalie Wood's childish wistfulness in *Miracle on Thirty-Fourth Street.* Chances are that you and your family have watched *The Wizard of Oz* or *The Sound of Music* together.

Theatrical-released feature films often lose something in the transition to television, however, especially when they are edited so that commercials can be inserted. Also, viewers may be less interested in too-familiar stories.

"Theatrical movies have a life in theaters and on cable prior to coming to broadcast TV," says Steve Mills, CBS vice president for Motion Pictures-for-Television and Mini-series. "By the time *Star Wars* reaches broadcast television, viewers have been saturated with the film, both in the theater, and at home on cable."

Networks like CBS are finding today that theatrical films are no longer their big draw. Motion pictures made for television are. For example, CBS-produced *The Blue and The Gray,* which *The Washington Post* called "the most substantial dramatic treatment of the Civil War ever undertaken," achieved virtually equal delivery in pay TV and non-cable homes. That is, it received essentially the same rating in homes that could receive only broadcast television as it did in homes that could have watched cable if viewers had chosen to.

Numbers of viewers are carefully calculated by television networks, because they form the basis for advertising rates. There are three months per year when all stations are rated: November, February, and May. Local stations usually set their advertising rates according to their performance in these "sweeps" periods. Networks try to help their affiliates by programming special events during those months, such as made-for-television motion pictures or theatrical films.

Yet in contrast to *The Blue and The Gray,* two of the major theatrical films that were shown during the November '82 sweep period, *Kramer vs. Kramer* and *The Blue Lagoon,* did well in non-cable homes but performed poorly in pay-cable homes.

Motion pictures made especially for television, while becoming more popular with viewers, are scripted and produced to take advantage of the medium's intimacy and faster-paced action. But such was not always the case. In the early days of television, when networks first went into movies, they turned to the 'B' filmmakers. Budgets of that day couldn't support television networks hiring filmmakers who were used to working with 60-day shooting schedules, major stars, major writers, and major directors.

"We turned to a certain group of people who were used to never having enough money," remembers industry veteran Bill Self, former vice president in charge of Motion Pictures-for-Television and Mini-series at CBS, one of the most influential forces behind the evolution of the medium.

"As a result, the movies were poor. But as we learned that, we began turning to the 'A' moviemakers, and tried to get them to conform to our problems."

By the late 1970s, the feature film world was slowing down. Writers, directors, and actors began to work in movies-for-television because they could complete a project, walk away from it, and not jeopardize their relationship with the feature film community.

"That's what made the medium so appealing," says Dick Rosetti, former vice president in charge of Motion Pictures-for-Television and Mini-series at 20th Century-Fox. "Actors could do movies for television and still continue doing feature films."

The first crossover from feature films to televi-

140

Mini-series, shown on prime-time television over several nights, attract and hold audiences for networks. *Ellis Island,* shown on CBS, portrayed the lives of four immigrants en route to a new life in America. (*Courtesy of CBS.*)

sion came with the writers then the directors and then the stars. The process was gradual.

"In the early days of movies-for-television, it was almost impossible to get a star," says Self. "They hadn't heard of a particular writer. They didn't like a director because he did commercials."

By 1979, made-for-television movies began to be accepted on an equal footing with theatrical films. Quality writers were writing; quality directors were directing; quality actors were acting.

Today, almost all television movies are being made by people who are quite capable of doing theatrical films. Even *The New York Times* critic John J. O'Connor says that television watching can no longer be considered an afterthought. "In terms of cultural enrichment," he says, "it increasingly demands the time and effort normally given to setting aside an evening for going to the theater or standing in line for a hit film."

O'Connor credits technical improvements in picture and sound transmission as one reason for the maturing of television. Another, he says, is that television has been finding and developing its own special programming territories—including everything from blockbuster "events" to modest TV movies, to controversial films about every conceivable sort of social problem. ABC tackled nuclear Armageddon in *The Day After.* CBS took a long, hard look at the insanity plea in *With Intent to Kill.*

Movies-for-television, it could be argued, may be more serious than some of the super hits in theater release, like *Porky's, Terminator,* and *Beverly Hills Cop.* However, Frank Yablans, president of MGM-UA disagrees. "These TV films are not controversial by themselves," he says. "They are just controversial for television. I don't think the public would pay $5 to see them. Movies have to be bigger than life."

Yet audience repsonse to made-for-television movies has been impressive. Independent pro-

141

ducer Gerry Abrams, president of Cypress Point Productions, doesn't do feature films, because, he says, "The lowest rated made-for-television movie that I have ever done was seen by more people than all the 15 or 20 top-grossing feature films of all time."

Made-for-television movies are often deliberately scripted and edited for television's intimacy. As an enraged father who leads a crusade of vengeance against the boy convicted of his daughter's murder in *With Intent to Kill*, Karl Malden's portrayal brought anguish and emotion into viewers' homes. (*Courtesy of CBS.*)

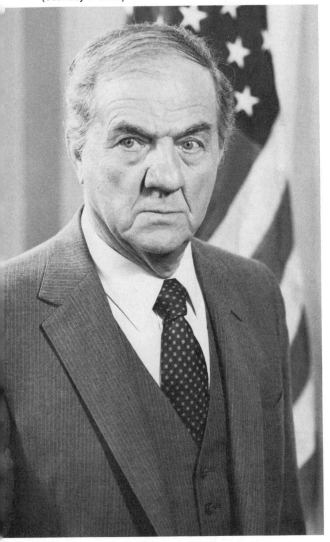

Adam, a powerful NBC made-for-television real-life story about a kidnapped and murdered youngster had such impact on audiences that it ultimately led to the finding of a number of previously missing children. *Something About Amelia,* ABC's drama about child abuse and incest had an audience of 60 million on its first showing. An ABC-sponsored survey after its airing showed that 72 percent of professional psychologists and counselors dealing with incest said clients had mentioned the program. Farrah Fawcett's performance in NBC's *The Burning Bed,* based on a true-life story of a wife who set her husband afire after repeated beatings, won top ratings and praise for her performance. And CBS's acclaimed *Silence of the Heart,* a strong, sensitive film about teen suicide, starred Mariette Hartley and Howard Hesseman as heartbroken parents, struggling to put their lives back together after the suicide of their teenage son. Ironically, Hartley herself had a father who committed suicide.

CBS Made-for-Television Movies

At CBS Studio Center in Studio City, California, Steve Mills, vice president, Motion Pictures-for-Television and Mini-series for the entertainment division of CBS Television Network, heads planning and production for an operation responsible for more films per year than any major motion picture studio. "We now make more original movies for telelvision," he says, "because theatrical pictures do not play as well. We need fresh product that will attract a larger audience."

Mills and his staff have more than 10,000 ideas a year presented to them. Some come as simply as a phone call saying, "Would you like to do a movie about _____?" while others arrive via a completed thousand-page manuscript. Five of his staff members meet directly with writers, producers, directors, and stars every day. Often they read scripts on nights and weekends, or go to off-Broadway shows or local community theater. Mills himself sits in on 8 to 10 meetings a day, listening for possible ideas that may result in made-for-television films.

Staff members have been selected to represent

When a son, convicted of murder and sentenced to a mental institution, returns to his home town, Paul Sorvino (left), as his father faces agonizing choices in a psychological mystery. *With Intent to Kill* was one of 50 CBS projects in 1984—more films than any major studio. (*Courtesy of CBS.*)

a diversity of backgrounds and tastes: urban, rural, young, and old, so Mills doesn't rely solely on his midwestern instincts, he says. Although they propose projects, final approval rests with him. Sometimes a writer or producer will appeal to Mills to personally review an idea that staff members have turned down.

Decisions are often complex. When *Silence of the Heart* was presented to CBS, Mills and his staff knew immediately that they wanted to do the film. At stake, however, was the sobering statistic from the National Institute of Mental Health that the suicide rate for young people is increasing 10 times faster than that for any other age group. What would the impact be if CBS

presented the movie? The final decision to make the film was eventually reached after considerable discussion and input from mental health experts.

Approximately 150 of the 10,000 ideas the CBS unit receives each year are developed into shooting scripts. CBS hires writers and researchers who adapt the books and plays. From those 150 scripts, 45 to 50 a year are chosen and filmed.

"If we shoot it, we know it will make it on to the network," says Mills. "In 10 years of making movies for CBS, we've never made a film we didn't air." The network's aim: to get a balance of programs—true stories, pure escapist entertainment, action comedies or romantic comedies,

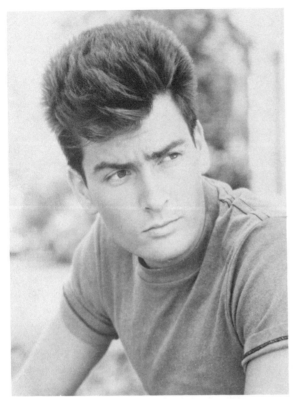 

In recent years, made-for-television films have tackled formerly taboo subjects, such as teen suicide. The widely acclaimed *Silence of the Heart* featured Chad Lowe (right) as a teenager who saw suicide as the only solution to mounting pressures, and Charlie Sheen (left) as his friend who ignored his pal's distress signals. (*Courtesy of CBS.*)

sci-fi or thriller movies. Male appeal movies with cops, detectives, and cowboys are popular; so are movies with strong female appeal. "One year we did the same movie four times," says Mills. "We presented the story of an older woman falling in love with a younger man, but cast it differently and disguised it well. We run the gamut of emotions and issues, from marriage, divorce, and affairs to abortions, diseases, afflictions, triangles, and homosexuality."

At stake for CBS and Mills is the bottom line —the ratings, and what they mean for future sales of time to advertisers. Mills gets a daily report card telling him how well CBS made-for-television films or mini-series did the night before. Nielsen shares tell him how CBS did directly compared with competition on a particular night of the week.

Television shows are ranked by rating points. Each rating point is a percent of the approximately 86 million households which have television sets; therefore, each rating point represents 860,000 homes. "Shares" make up the percentage of Homes Utilizing Television (HUT) at any given time. The total HUT, therefore, is 100 percent. If a program has a 35 percent Nielsen Share, then 35 percent of all homes with their sets turned on at that time were tuned to that program.

In the fourth week of November 1984, for instance, CBS had a 16.8 rating compared to NBC's 16.6 and ABC's 15.2. Each rating point represents millions of dollars in advertising income to the network.

The diversity of films is carefully planned to appeal to various segments of the network's broad demographic audience. In 1985–86, CBS and Mills handled *Blade of Hong Kong,* a detective story, and *North Beach and Rawhide,* a story of San Francisco motorcycle bikers committed to a juvenile detention home on a working ranch. In *First Strike on Sycamore Lane,* a family's lifestyle changed abruptly when the husband married a younger woman, deserting his former wife and two children.

George C. Scott starred in *The Last Days of*

Made-for-television movies deliberately cover a wide variety of subject matter to appeal to different audiences. *He's Not Your Son* told the story of a couple, shocked to learn that their infant son was inadvertently switched in the hospital nursery. (*Courtesy of CBS.*)

Patton, a three-hour movie. *Passion Flower* was set in Singapore. Kenny Rogers starred in *Gambler III,* with Linda Evans as his love interest. Agatha Christie's *Thirteen at Dinner* was shot on location in London.

Costs average out at about $1 million per hour of film, Mills says, and twice that for the mini-series. During the November 1984 sweeps, CBS presented *Ellis Island*, a sprawling seven-hour mini-series based on the best-selling novel by Fred Mustard Stewart about immigrants in melting pot America. The movie featured Richard Burton in a role he completed shortly before his death.

RFK aired in January, 1985; *Space,* the James Michener blockbuster novel, was shown in April, starring James Garner, Blair Brown, and Bruce Dern. An international all-star cast including Faye Dunaway, Max von Sydow, and Virna Lisi was featured in *Christopher Columbus,* with Gabriel Byrne, an Irishman, playing the title role.

Some CBS made-for-television movies are pure escapist entertainment, like *Hedda and Louella,* the film about two 1940s Hollywood gossip columnists. Others are controversial, like *The Atlanta Child Murders.* "We know the murders were committed," Mills says. "We know a man was accused, tried, and convicted. We are not sure justice was done." Written by Abby Mann and directed by John Erman, the project stars Jason Robards, Morgan Freeman, James Earl Jones, Rip Torn, and Martin Sheen.

The CBS Television Reading Program

Working closely with educators, the CBS Television Reading Program, begun in 1977, has involved over 23 million students. The television script-reading project uses students' enthusiasm for television to help improve their reading skills and their motivation for additional reading, learning, and creative thinking. More than 200 affiliated CBS stations are provided with original scripts of programs that have been chosen for use within the Reading Program. Working with local teachers and school systems, the stations then select the programs they'd like to participate in. Stations then either get a local newspaper to print and distribute the scripts, or order scripts from the Reading Program's national supplier. Teacher's Guides are also available.

Many major corporations have underwritten costs of the CBS Television Reading Program in their corporate home towns, including the Hallmark Foundation in Kansas City, the Monsanto

To produce quality made-for-television movies and mini-series, networks like CBS often use top stars and lavish production budgets. Mini-series such as the seven-hour *Ellis Island,* which starred Richard Burton (shown here with his real daughter, Kate), have costs averaging $2 million per hour of broadcast time. (*Courtesy of CBS.*)

Fund in St. Louis, John Hancock in Boston, International Multifoods in Minneapolis, Allstate in Chicago, and United Technologies in Hartford. In a number of cities, local banks have participated; in others, the CBS affiliate station has arranged a consortium of local businesses that share underwriting costs.

Joanne Brokaw, whose background includes 10 years of junior high language arts teaching and development and administration of an alternative junior high school program, heads the CBS Television Reading Program, an educational project of the CBS Television Network. As its vice president, she watches CBS's made-for-television movies throughout their development, and supervises preparation of educational materials for selected scripts.

From Mills' nearly 50 projects a year, The CBS Television Reading Program picks four scripts to develop and promote. Two are made-for-television movies, one is a mini-series, and the fourth is a half-hour program chosen so scripts can be prepared in both English and Spanish.

Past choices have included *Cook and Peary: The Race to the Pole; Jack Dempsey; Bill: On His Own,* which starred film veteran Mickey Rooney as a retarded man, institutionalized for 46 years, who struggles to make a life for himself with the help of others who care about him; and *Anatomy of an Illness,* the story of *Saturday Review* editor Norman Cousins' unique self-treatment of a degenerative spinal condition and his affirmation of the power of positive thinking.

The 1984–85 season included *Silence of the Heart;* Dickens' *A Christmas Carol,* featuring George C. Scott as Scrooge; and a Charlie Brown half-hour special, with scripts prepared in English and Spanish.

Brokaw and her staff monitor the made-for-television movies and mini-series throughout their production, evaluating them as possible candidates for the Reading Program. "We start looking at brief synopses from production people," she says. "We can begin speculating about certain scripts as they move along. We watch their development. When we find a promising film has been shot and is in post-production, we begin making calls. 'Can we get a rough cut?' 'Can we see a shooting script?' Then our work really starts."

A made-for-television movie or mini-series such as *Ellis Island* provides teachers and students with many opportunities for discussion. The story of American-bound immigrants can spark classroom consideration of historical issues. (*Courtesy of CBS.*)

Staff members work with production companies to prepare shooting scripts as close to final version as possible, with consultants on writing Teacher's Guides for selected scripts, with CBS affiliates to explain the Reading Program, and with writers and editors to develop promotional materials.

For instance, Brokaw worked closely with Charlotte P. Ross, a leader in the field of youth suicide prevention for 19 years, on developing the Teacher's Guide for *Silence of the Heart*. Director of the Suicide Prevention and Crisis Center of San Mateo County, California, Mrs. Ross, who served as technical consultant during the filming of this made-for-television movie, is co-chair of the recently established National Committee on Youth Suicide Prevention. She developed, for the state of California, the nation's first statewide youth suicide prevention program, consisting of

training for school personnel, students, and parents.

Also involved were the office of New York Lt. Gov. Alfred B. DeBello and the Bergen Regional Counseling Center in Hackensack, N.J.

Many teachers chose to have students read the script aloud in class for one or two weeks before the broadcast, assigning parts to various students. An explanation of how to read a television script, as well as an explanation of all technical terms used in the format, helped students to imagine how the action would be presented.

Suggested activities gave students insight into film techniques. They were asked to consider the action sequence in which the suicidal teen floors the accelerator and drives his car off the bluff. "List the times the camera shifts," the Guide asked. "What is shown with each shift? Why are these shifts without voice? How is cohesiveness achieved? What other dramatic effect is achieved by splicing this scene with shots of the Circus Pizza, of Ken, and of the Lewis's backyard?''

Other sections of the Guide made teachers aware of contributing factors to depression, of behaviors that might indicate depression, and of suggested educational intervention programs that encouraged teenagers to understand problems that could arise in their lives. Vocabulary and Language activities for enrichment; plot, character, setting, and theme analysis exercises; and creative activities involving outside-classroom work were suggested.

For instance, students were asked to work with a small group of other students to create slogans for a Suicide Prevention Center's Rap Group Sessions. ''Share a Secret, Save a Friend'' is one such slogan alread in use. Slogans could be turned into bumper stickers and distributed throughout the school.

Books and audiovisual materials for teachers and students, including film, television, and drama references were included in the Guide.

Brokaw and her staff also work with the Library of Congress to help disseminate book lists based on CBS programs to libraries and to put together a 30-second on-air promotion in which someone connected with a particular made-for-television movie suggests viewers read more about the topic.

''Viewing and reading can be complimentary activities,'' she says. ''They're two different ways of learning about a topic. Each has strengths and weaknesses. Using them together gives you the best available from both.''

Reflections

1. In Chapter 6 (the editing chapter), television veteran Bernard Balmuth discusses the difference between editing for television and for films in theatrical release. As you watch made-for-television movies, which technique do you think the editor used primarily?

2. Frank Yablans, president of MGM-UA, says he does not think the public would pay $5 to see movies-for-television. Do you agree or disagree? Why?

3. Following a rerun of *Adam*, NBC's powerful made-for-television movie about a kidnapped and murdered youngster, several missing children whose pictures were shown on television were reunited with their families. On the other hand, a man who set his estranged wife on fire pleaded he had been influenced by *The Burning Bed*. Do you think made-for-television movies are a ''good'' or ''bad'' influence on behavior? Should there be prior censorship by the networks on subject matter?

4. Theatrical motion picture hits like *Raiders of the Lost Ark, Gone With the Wind*, and Sylvester Stallone's *First Blood* are proving popular in videocassette form for rental or sale. Do you feel made-for-television movies have a future in video?

Activities

1. Check television schedules in your local newspaper. Often, critics will preview movies-for-television. Keep a file of the clippings. Ask friends who saw the movies whether or not they agreed with the critics' recommendations.

2. CBS executive Steve Mills and his staff screen more than 10,000 ideas a year. Using sources like *Time, Newsweek*, or wire service stories in newspapers, clip articles about events that you feel are dramatic enough to be turned into made-for-television movies. At the end of a month, pick the most interesting three ideas, and summarize them in a memo recommending their production that you would send to Mills if you were on his staff.

Further Reading: *Check your library.*

Breyer, Richard and Moller, Peter. *Making Television Productions*, New York, Longman, Inc., 1984.

Goodman, Ellen. *Writing Television and Motion Picture Scripts That Sell*, Chicago, Contemporary Books, 1982.

Marill, Alvin H. *Movies Made for Television: The Telefeature and the Mini-Series: 1964-1984*, rev. edition, New York, Zoetrope, 1984.

Vale, Eugene. *The Technique of Screen & Television Writing*, Englewood Cliffs, NJ, Prentice Hall, 1983.

James Earl Jones

The Actor

Versatile actor James Earl Jones, Oscar nominee for his starring role in The Great White Hope *and Tony award winner for his starring role in the stage play from which the film was made, has a long and distinguished career. A former member of the Advisory Board of the National Council on the Arts, Mr. Jones here discusses his feelings about screen, stage, and television acting. Known also for his recordings and narration of films and filmstrips, Mr. Jones will long be remembered for the sinister voice of Darth Vader in* Star Wars *(1977),* The Empire Strikes Back *(1980) and* Return of the Jedi *(1984). His versatility ranges from playing King Lear to a significant role in CBS's made-for-television's* The Atlanta Child Murders, *a controversial docu-drama.*

On *Star Wars,* Lucas's people called me and asked if I wanted to do a voice-over. I'm not shy about doing voices, because then your face is not overexposed.

Dubbing Darth Vader in *Star Wars* only took half a day! On *The Empire Strikes Back,* I worked a full day.

The usual method of doing voice-overs in America is that they project the film. You hear three beeps, and begin to speak on the fourth beep. You see a line that runs from right to left on the screen. When the line goes to the right, you're supposed to start speaking.

It's all very mechanical, and it's difficult to sustain a character. When I'm counting beeps and looking at lines and looking at Vader's mouth, it's hard to keep contact with what the character is trying to say. . . .

When I dubbed Darth Vader, I was able to see the loops, because I was not familiar with the story. They project the piece of film where the dark line starts on the left and ends on the right, when you start speaking. The amount of film that follows the right edge line is the loop. Usually it's a burst of dialogue that takes a few seconds to read. It's enough so that you can get a good feeling of what the character is saying—usually a line or two—but not so much that you get bogged down in timing and pauses.

I often find myself not fitting into trends. For example, in 1970, when I played in *The Great White Hope,* I was playing a very assertive Black American male at a time when the assertive Black male trend had not yet started.

Then they came out with *Shaft* and *Superfly.* Once that started, I did not participate. I didn't want to be part of the Black exploitation wave of films. In order to make those films work, to create a Black, assertive character, you had to exploit the same things that made white, assertive characters work—at the expense of the Blacks, the Indians, the females. At that time, I thought there was more value in characters who cried than in characters who dodged bullets. . . .

What I look for when I'm selecting a role is the vulnerability of the character—the common thread that links him with all of us, whether he's a villain or a good guy, whether he's tough or weak. The few mistakes I've made have been with characters where there wasn't sufficient time on the screen to explain how they tick. . . . Vulnerability is important if it leads to universal behavior—if I get the chance to project on screen *why* people do what they do.

Characters that show vulnerability are more valuable to watch. If you think that drama is socially or psychologically relevant, there's no point in showing characters who glory in their strength. Instead, it means far more to show characters who are vulnerable, characters who are in jeopardy, who are terrified—who are learning how to cope with trouble in a very real way.

I majored in drama because that's what I wanted to do with my life. It's far more than pleasure. There's a contentment I feel when I know I'm using my time creatively and constructively in my career.

Each actor has his own way of preparing for a role. The key factors for me are concentration and relaxation. Both are important to me, from the first time I read the script, to the first time I walk on the set or cross the stage. . . .

At times, I think of myself as a mercenary jobber, taking a day's work here, a day's work there, rather than an actor. Unless you're a signed, contracted member over a period of years in a company like the great repertory companies which they have in Europe, and which we don't have in America, you're basically a free-lancer.

I'm not totally satisfied yet with anything I've done in film. So far in film, I don't feel I've achieved what I know I can. . . .

Acting is a craft . . . a skill . . . a profession . . . a job—it's all these, plus being an art. And I want to bring it together in film, when the project is right. . . .

Ruth Warrick

The Actress

Few performers—especially those who have never before acted in films—would expect their first film to become the greatest classic of American filmmaking. Yet Ruth Warrick, who had worked with Orson Welles in the Mercury Theater radio productions, played her first film role opposite Welles in the now-classic Citizen Kane.

Since then, Ruth Warrick has become known as a dramatic and character actress in many films, radio and television dramas, and stage productions such as The King and I, Who's Afraid of Virginia Woolf? *and* Irene.

Millions of television viewers know her as Phoebe Tyler Wallingford on All My Children, *a role she has played since the soap opera first aired, over 15 years ago. Her 1980 autobiography,* The Confessions of Phoebe Tyler, *and her record album,* Phoebe Tyler Sings and Tells, *as well as her popular* Phoebe Tells All *lectures on the college circuit have shared her behind-scenes experiences.*

Still, for her, the making of Citizen Kane *remains an unforgettable experience.*

Citizen Kane . . . a long time ago, but it seems like yesterday. I think any time you work with somebody that engages you completely, time really doesn't have any meaning.

I always remember Orson's quote. He said, "The only point of making a movie is to have the eye of a poet behind the lens." Film is a very poetic medium. I think it's best used that way. For me, the strangest thing about doing film work is that if you yourself experience too much emotion in the film, you stop the audience's emotion. You have to suggest enough of the emotion, but still leave room for them to complete it. . . . If you put something on a film, many more people are going to see and hear it. It's permanent. You have no idea of the number of lives that are going to be touched by it. Like the breakfast scene in *Citizen Kane.* Of course, I admired it at time I did it, and knew that it was brilliantly done, but I had no idea naturally. . . .

Everybody wonders. They say, "Did you know you were making a classic?" Of course we didn't. We knew we were making a different kind of movie, and we believed in it. But success was not a prerequisite to anything we did as far as we were concerned.

. . . I think the brilliance of *Citizen Kane* is far more evident now than it was then, because people didn't really know what Orson was talking about at that time. His point was that people whom America honored—the tycoons who people felt were the makers of America—he felt were the unmakers, the defilers, the ones who were really raping America and changing it and putting it on a track that was going to be disastrous. I think that events since we made the film have borne that out. It's like a Shakesperean tragedy.

And for myself? I guess I would like people to realize how incredibly fortunate I was. It's like the old soap operas—can a young girl from a little mining town in Colorado find love and romance? How could I as a young girl have taken part in what is generally considered to be the definitive American film? When I made the test, I was 23. When I did the film, I was 24.

When I wanted to go to New York to be an actress, people said, "Think of all the unemployed actors and actresses. What do you think you have that they haven't got?"

I said, "I don't know. I'm sure that there are more that have more talent than I do, but not one of them is me." That was always the knowledge that I carried about me. There was nobody else who was me. What I had to contribute was individual.

Well, that's true of every person. I try to say, "You are unique. If you're not you, the world is less than it could have been. Everyone has their own special quality."

But to think that in my first film I could play opposite Orson—a man with such genius—and be able to play with him on a more or less equal level and to be able to understand! I remember thinking that he absolutely did not direct me at all in that breakfast scene. I was given the assignment, and I thought how unique it was. I had seen the feeling before. I had watched other couples. That's how I got to be an actress, just watching and observing. I'm very curious, and I always analyze: why do people do that? why do they say that? why? what's happening? what's the interaction between them? In *Citizen Kane,* I just felt it was as if Orson and I were living the roles. . . . You had the tragedy of people growing apart because they have different values, ambitions, and backgrounds. I knew then that it was a remarkable scene. I didn't know how successful the film was going to be.

Jack Lemmon. (Save the Tiger © *1972 by Paramount Pictures Corporation, Filmways, Inc., Jalem Productions, Inc., and Cirandinha Productions, Inc.)*

The Actor

Professional performers come from many backgrounds, but most are star struck from childhood, convinced that acting is the only way of life. Jack Lemmon, whose background includes prep school and a degree from Harvard, knew he had to become an actor. From radio, television, and stock company roles, Lemmon went on to make his first film, It Should Happen to You, *in 1954.*

In more than twenty years, Lemmon has been in such memorable films as Mister Roberts, *for which he won an Academy Award as best supporting actor;* Some Like It Hot, The Apartment, *and* Days of Wine and Roses *(all of which brought him Oscar nominations).* Save the Tiger *brought him a second Academy Award in 1974.* Missing *(with Sissy Spacek) and* Mass Appeal, *in which he played a Roman Catholic priest, were recently challenging roles, and he co-hosted the 1985 Academy Awards.*

I think an actor's main obligation is to play a part as well as he possibly can, and to hope that others agree. He can't let other things influence him. He can't say, "This way will make it more appealing." He must play his part as legitimately and honestly and excitingly as possible. There's only one excuse for acting—to get the highest level of dramatic conflict. The secret of acting and directing lies in what you choose. There might be thirty legitimate ways to do a scene, but only one will be the most exciting. In the process of elimination, you hope you pick it.

An actor can hope that, in his selection of parts, he not only can entertain, but also can enlighten people. He may be part of the new awareness. Like *The Apartment.* You might say we grew a rose in a garbage pail. Billy Wilder, the director, was smart enough not to hit the theme too hard. If you have social comment, as we did in that film, keep it in the background. Basically, it was a love story, with people you care about. But it had tremendous comments about a certain segment of society and the business world—where values lay and what people will do to get ahead.

. . . Film is emotionally exhausting. We often have an eight to ten week schedule, more if we're shooting on location. Most actors are exhausted after it's over. After a major part, I've got to have one to two months' rest. I feel as if I never want to work again. It's not so much physical as emotional exhaustion. . . .

On the way to work, I start running the scene in my mind, preparing myself. I come on the set, and greet people rather mechanically. I do my hellos, but I'm not really with it. I'm thinking of the scene coming up. . . . Then we're into it. I try to cut everything else out of my awareness except the scene. Even when we're in between scenes, while they're doing lighting, setting the cameras, working on props, I'm working on the scene. It's right in front of my mind.

I find it difficult to lie down and take a rest. My energy level drops. It's hard to get it back up when they suddenly say they're ready. I keep myself occupied. I play the piano, read a book, or work on a crossword puzzle.

When it's magic time—when they call you—you have to be way up, wide-eyed and alert. Other actors can catnap and feel refreshed, but I try to psych myself up. . . .

The most difficult thing is to make your audience feel that, in each and every take, you've never said the words before—no matter how often you've had to do retakes. When you're saying the lines for the fifteenth or twentieth time, it's very difficult for an actor to make it seem like it's happening for the first time, and to keep it fresh. The real pros are the actors who, once they have the performance, are able to turn the key in the lock and to repeat that performance 80 to 90 percent, over and over, without making it seem as if it's the twentieth time.

. . . All my life, I've wanted to be an actor. The main satisfaction I've had is not the good fortune, it's the fact that I am doing something that I love to do. I love acting! The luckiest thing about it is that I've worked enough to be successful. Acting excites me. I love it! I never wanted to be a star. I wanted to be the best actor I could possibly be. If that remains my intent, in no way can I be unhappy. I want to keep on doing the best work I can. I hope I continue to improve. I should do my best work in the next ten years. My horizons should be broader. I've seen and absorbed more, and I should be able to really bring something to my characterization.

9

Evaluating Film: Does It Work?

Learning to "See"

In *Understanding the Film,* we are trying to help you see film better, to more closely observe the images and sounds. We have discussed why film is so popular here and around the world. And we described ways to see the moving image better; and why how we see the film is influenced by our environment, experience, and the person we are.

These areas concern how we perceive it. They are a first step in looking closely at the film and taking it apart so we can see and understand it better. The next steps describe the language of film, and film editing; what it is that filmmakers do to communicate their messages. Filmmakers use various techniques to communicate to us and make us feel or perceive the image. We have followed a movie from the script into film: how a film is created, put into words, produced,

"Art is the power to express oneself fully."
—Henry Sendejas

"Art is the expression of beauty in life."
— Bill Zondea

"ART is like a budding ROSE; it unfolds a deep SENSE of truth and creates an illusion of loveliness."
— Susan McGown

directed, acted, filmed, edited, promoted, seen, and other aspects of its creation.

Now it is time to understand if the filmmaker did it very well or not. Does the film work? Is the film art?

We are asking you to criticize—criticize means to evaluate, that is, to express a judgment which takes into account the merits of the film, a work of art. You will need to judge the filmmakers' degrees of success in achieving their purpose. Criticism requires the ability to evaluate, analyze, observe, and understand the process of making films. It is true that experience, life experience and film experience, is another aspect, or part, of effective criticism. We have frequently referred to the filmmaker as an artist. It is fairly easy to describe what a filmmaker is: he or she is someone involved in creating what we know as a film. However, it is much more difficult to describe what an artist is. A filmmaker always creates films, but a filmmaker doesn't always create art.

Perhaps the following definitions of art may help. They come from students at Lillis High School in Kansas City, Missouri.

Perhaps you can think of your own definition of art. Yet there probably isn't any definition, including the one in the dictionary, on which everyone would agree. Art involves individual opinion, past experience, age, and all the other factors influencing perceptions. Each of you should try to describe your own definition of art, recognizing that this definition will change and grow with experience.

Good art is often pleasing. You feel a sense of satisfaction in your experience. Movies that are art often give you pleasure: "I like it." "It was a great movie." "It was good." With such comments, you are attempting to tell others about your experience with the art of a particular film. This is an excellent beginning for understanding art. When you like a work of art, you begin to comprehend more of its aesthetic qualities.

But simply liking a particular work of art, or a film, is not enough for a serious student. You should go further. You should discover *why* you like it, or why you *don't* like it. Your teacher can help you express your feelings. But it is hard for a teacher, or for anyone, to help others grow and change in their experience with an art form.

It is possible to tell or teach someone about

mathematics. In just about every instance in our experience, the statement 7 x 4 = 28 will be true. Science, too, is another area in which it is possible to be very precise. "Right" and "wrong" are more difficult in other subjects. How you perceive history, or psychology, or social change depends on the point of view from which you're looking at it.

But it is many times more difficult for a teacher to show students a film and have them learn to look at it aesthetically. What the teacher considers "art" will not always be what you find "art." One teacher may feel a particular film is outstanding; another may disagree strongly (even the authors of this book have different opinions about a number of films). The teacher of a film class may be in constant emotional conflict with many of you as he or she helps you grow and change your experience with film. In many cases, there are no "right" or "best" answers.

Many times, teachers of an art form such as film are criticized (and sometimes this criticism is valid) as being artistic and aesthetic snobs. That is, they are accused of having a list of "good" films and another list of "bad" films ("bad" in the technical and artistic sense). Such teachers often consider the popular films that students like as "bad" films. They may feel that most Hollywood-made films fall into this category, while most European films are "art films" and therefore "good." They may think that certain film directors are noble, exceptional, and "in," while other directors are dull, abdominable, and "out"—until they are very old or dead. Then they become "in."

As a student of film, you should constantly challenge the answers that are given, by critics or teachers or friends, in describing the aesthetics of an art form. You should also be challenging this book. You have a right to ask a teacher *why* he or she makes a certain statement about a particular film. The teacher has the same right to ask you the reasons behind your opinion and statements.

You are probably a beginning student in the serious study of film. Therefore, you need to develop your *own* criteria, list of standards, for evaluating film.

In this chapter, you will be looking at stills from various films. From these, and from the films you have seen in class on your own, try to evaluate the ones you consider "good."

How is it possible to evaluate the "good" and the "not so good" films? What are some of the criteria you can use?

Here is a list of possibilities for you to consider. As you, your class, and your teacher discuss various criteria, you will probably add to the list.

Citizen Kane, said by some critics to be based on the life of newspaper publisher William Randolph Hearst, has been called an American classic, and is frequently shown on television. What elements of the film do you feel have contributed to its being a favorite for so many years? (Citizen Kane ©*RKO General Incorporated.*)

The Elements of Film

There are at least nine component parts that make up most story-line films: theme; plot; script; acting; setting, costumes, and makeup; sound; photography; directions; and editing. You can look at each of them separately and ask specific questions about how well they work.

Theme

The theme is the basic idea of a film. It may touch on any aspect of life. It may concern itself with vengeance, vindication, dehumanization, love, courage, the triumph of good over evil, murder, greed, and hundreds more thematic ideas. Usually, the better the theme, the better the film. (On the other hand, even a great theme can be badly handled in a film.) A film need not have a vibrant and important theme to be entertaining. However, films that do are usually remembered as great films, even though they may not have been the most popular, then or now.

Popularity has very little to do with art. If a film considered to be a great work of art is also popular with the general mass of society, it is probably coincidental. There are, of course, many people who do not agree with this point of view. They believe the general public has better taste. Perhaps most people go to see films because they want to be entertained, rather than to learn a great truth.

Many times the theme of a film will be expressed through a single repeated or recurring motif. A motif is a device, like the clocks used in *High Noon* and *Time Piece* to show that time is running out.

A filmmaker also uses metaphors or symbols to convey the theme. As in writing, a metaphor in film *expresses* a feeling or intent by comparing similar things. For example, in *Bless the Beasts and Children*, director Stanley Kramer used the captive buffalo as a metaphor for the boys, who were "captives" of the system and of their parents' expectations for them. The images of Christian symbolism in *Cool Hand Luke* and *On the Waterfront* describe a "crucified" man.

Planet of the Apes was one continuous metaphor—a comparison between human civilization and the civilization of the apes.

In *The Music Man*, a visual metaphor is created with several close-ups of women gossiping, with one quick cut to a scene of a group of chickens, heads close together, pecking and clucking.

A symbol *stimulates* a feeling or intent. The Statue of Liberty at the end of *Planet of the Apes* may stimulate a feeling of hopelessness or forgotten dreams of a once-great country. The monolith in *2001* stimulates a feeling of wondrous and unknown power. In *The Blue Angel*, the bird symbol was used both as a continuing motif and as a symbol of tragic romance.

Many times characters become symbols—perhaps of qualities such as innocence, steadfastness, evil, or greed. The man in the black hat in older westerns was an instant symbol of the "bad guy." Certain actors and actresses may become symbols of certain qualities—for instance, we almost instantly recognize John Wayne, Clint Eastwood, and other superheroes as symbols of masculinity and stubborn strength.

Some questions you might ask in an attempt to define the theme would be:

What is the basic idea of the film? What is the film about or concerned with? Is the theme of the film honest and sincere? Is it treated honestly? In what way does the theme relate to the plot? How were metaphors used? Symbols? Motifs?

Plot

The plot is the story line. It is what is happening. The plot may appear to be extremely simple, as in a Japanese film called *Ikiru*, which means "to live." The film is about a man who works as the director of public works in a large city. One day he decides to see a doctor about the pains in his stomach and discovers he has stomach cancer, with only about a year to live. The rest of the film is about his discovery of life.

The plot of *Ikiru* is very simple, but the theme is profound. Although this film was never a box-office hit, its theme reveals something about the nature of human beings and the human spirit. Many great dramatic films rest on a very simple plot line expressing a profound theme.

By contrast, many lighter, "entertainment" films, especially mysteries and spy or suspense

Early films by foreign directors were responsible for the introduction to American audiences of foreign stars. Marlene Dietrich portrayed Lola in the original German version of *The Blue Angel,* a dramatization of the complete degeneration of a man (Emil Jennings). (The Blue Angel, *The Museum of Modern Art/Film Stills Archive.*)

stories, depend mainly on their ingenious and exciting plots, as in *Three Days of the Condor* and *The Falcon and the Snowman.* Alfred Hitchcock's complicated, suspenseful plots in films such as *Rear Window, North by Northwest, The Birds,* and *Psycho*, are famous.

The plots of many films are very much like each other, but changes in how the story is told make them seem different. Most crime or detective stories, for instance, have basically the same plot: a crime is committed. Sooner or later the detective figures out who the criminal is. The crime is solved. Thousands of films, stories, novels, and TV shows have been written with this plot. But the hero or heroine may be a private detective, a police officer, an amateur sleuth—or even the criminal. The story may take place on a train, in a cornfield, on the streets of San Francisco, or in the slums of New York. The characters, the setting, the way the crime is solved, the crime itself—all these change to create a new story.

Sometimes the writers rearrange the sequence of events in the basic plot. Perhaps the whole film is about someone trying to *prevent* a crime from being committed (as in *Day of the Jackal*). Sometimes a crime occurs before the film begins.

Questions you'll want to consider in describing the plot include these:

How does the plot develop the story? Are there sub-plots? Who does what—where, when, and how? What influences the characters in their actions? How does the plot relate to the theme? Is the plot interesting? Is it believable? Is it too complicated?

Script

The script is the plot in detail. It describes the scenes in detail, specifies who and what the characters are, how they appear, and what they do and say. The script arranges events in a logical order and in progressive intensity so that

A successful film frequently has sequels. *The Empire Strikes Back,* which had Billy Dee Williams playing Lando Calrissian, governor of Cloud City, was part of a trilogy that included *Star Wars* and *Return of the Jedi. (Courtesy of Lucasfilm, Ltd. ©Lucasfilm, Ltd. (LFL) 1980. All Rights Reserved.)*

lesser climaxes lead up to important ones. The characterization of the persons in the story and the dialogue they speak are interesting not only in themselves, but also because they enhance and advance the story. The script should be clear and logical. Digressions (tendencies to stray from the plot) and irrelevancies (events that don't seem to belong in the story) should be avoided, unless they have a special purpose.

Sometimes it is difficult to distinguish between the script and the plot or other components, such as the acting. However, you should remember that nearly all films are written and planned out in great detail before filming begins. Good film directors can, and do, improve on the original script, because a film script is seldom a finished product. However, the script must still contain enough substance for the director to create a film.

These are some of the questions to ask in trying to discover the value of the script:

Does the dialogue the characters say seem real? Does the continuity of the film hold together? Does the script bring out the theme fully? Does it help the plot? Is the idea of the film clear to you?

Acting

Some of the greatest actors and actresses perform in films. Many people have a special feeling about the performers in films and look up to them as someone wonderful. There is no doubt that many of these special men, women, and children have great talent and ability in creating characters who will catch our interest and sympathy.

However, some directors consider the performers in a film as mere puppets who go through various scenes and sequences, saying lines that have no real meaning to them. Other directors explain the film in great detail to the performers, so that they can play their parts better. But whatever method the director uses, it is the actors and actresses in the film who are most likely to be remembered by the audience.

During the past twenty years, the "star system" that was prevalent in Hollywood in the 1930s and 1940s faded away, though many people think it is making a comeback. Your parents may remember their reactions to Clark Gable, Claudette Colbert, Spencer Tracy, Errol Flynn, Bette Davis, Katharine Hepburn, Greta Garbo, Fred Astaire, Ginger Rogers, Humphrey Bogart, Vivien Leigh, Peter Lawford, Van Johnson, Shirley Temple, Marilyn Monroe, Betty Grable, Judy Garland, and other special favorites. Even today, some of these stars still have a following. During the height of the star system, many of the major studios held a near death-grip on their particular group of stars. Today many actors and actresses are not affiliated with one particular studio. Instead, their agents contract with various film production companies for specific films.

Some names still stand out and will help the film to do a better business. The late John Wayne and Katharine Hepburn, over 65, both veteran pros with long years of experience, filmed *Rooster Cogburn*, a western continuing the exploits of the one-eyed, whiskey-wallowing marshal Wayne portrayed in *True Grit*. Robert Redford, Clint Eastwood, Paul Newman, Elizabeth Taylor, Barbra Streisand, Olivia Newton-John, John Travolta, Robert DeNiro, Burt Reynolds, Diane Keaton, Jack Nicholson, and many, many more all have their own special attraction. Certain stars of the past—Bogart or Garbo, for instance—almost assure the success of a revival of their films.

Acting for films is extremely difficult, because most films are shot out of sequence. Various scenes are shot on many different days in any kind of order—not necessarily convenient for the actors. For example, if the beginning and end of a film take place in New York City and the rest of the film happens in the middle of the Rocky

Mountains, it would be expensive to shoot on location in New York, fly to the mountains, shoot the next part of the plot, and then fly back to New York. It is more likely that all the shots in each location will be done at one time—it's less expensive to do it that way.

Disasters and spectacles, though, are often shot in sequence. After the tidal wave hit the ocean liner in *The Poseidon Adventure,* most scenes from there on were shot in the order they happened in the script. If you're going to burn down a building, blow up a ship, or set fire to Atlanta (as in *Gone with the Wind*), you'd better have your cast finished with the set before you destroy it.

Still another complication can affect shooting sequence. Sometimes an actress or actor who costs the studio a lot of money has a contract for

F. Murray Abraham's outstanding portrayal of Antonio Salieri in *Amadeus* won recognition from peers when he was named Best Actor. Tom Hulce, who played Mozart, was also an Academy Award nominee for Best Actor. (*Amadeus* ©*1984 The Saul Zaentz Company. All Rights Reserved.*)

another film. This arrangement conflicts with the shooting schedule of a film in progress. The star wants to be in both pictures. And both producers and directors want that star. The answer: shoot all the scenes with that star first; then complete the rest of the film. Meanwhile, the star can go on to make the second picture.

You can imagine the tremendous ability a performer must have to be able to act in such confusion. Often performers are called upon to show changing emotional responses in the same film.

For instance, F. Murray Abraham, Academy Award nominee for his role as Antonio Salieri, eighteenth-century composer and Mozart rival in *Amadeus*, is called upon to age 40 years in the film. Abraham must make his characterization of Salieri believable, progressing in emotional depth and response from the young, ambitious composer at the court of Emperor Joseph II to the half-crazed hospital inmate who babbles his confession of having murdered Mozart.

There are other major difficulties for film performers. In an emotional scene, an actor or actress must "turn on and off" many times to get the responses the director wants. And, unlike stage acting, they cannot play to an audience—their audience will not see the performance for perhaps more than a year.

Actors and actresses should be able to play their parts so well that they almost become the characters they are portraying.

Some questions you should consider when attempting to evaluate acting performances:

Did I identify with the actress or actor? Did they cause me to respond emotionally to the film? What did they do that caused me to become caught up in the film? Was I conscious of who was playing the part, or did I feel that the performers had submerged their "normal" personalities in the characters? Were small roles played as well as big ones?

Setting, Costumes, and Makeup

These three aspects of filmmaking aid actors and actresses in creating effective performances. They help create atmosphere and define character. They help make the film seem real.

In films set in a time other than the present, setting, costumes, and makeup can be extremely important in making the picture "believable." They must be so authentic that they do not distract the audience from the story. Most viewers don't realize how difficult and expensive this can be.

For instance, Patrizia Von Brandenstein, production designer for *Amadeus*, used 20 sets and 75 locations in Prague to recreate the world of Mozart in the eighteenth century. Josef, Svoboda, chief designer and technical director of the National Theater of Prague and National Artist of Czechoslovakia, designed 11 different sets for the five opera sequences.

A complete 700-seat eighteenth-century theater was constructed on Czechoslovakia's largest sound stage, 330 feet long, as a faithful reproduction of the "Volkstheater" used and built by Mozart's friend, composer Emanuel Schikaneder. It required a crew of over 100 workers six weeks to build. The theater was used for the filming of sequences from Mozart's opera *The Magic Flute.*

Another theater used for *Amadeus* filming was Prague's Tyl Theater, the very same location in which Mozart conducted the premiere of *Don Giovanni* two centuries ago.

Producer Saul Zaentz and director Milos Forman re-created the theater's period lighting with candles mounted in 11 chandeliers, each burning 40 to 60 candles. The chandeliers, which weighed over 700 pounds each, could not be hung directly from the ceiling. Instead, the grips, gaffers, and special effects crew devised an aluminum and steel grid that rested on the theater's roof and extended through the windows of the dome.

Over 1500 wigs were worn in *Amadeus* to achieve the authentic period look of Mozart's Vienna. Research showed that all members of the aristocracy, their servants and functionaries, and shopkeepers wore wigs; in fact, the richer you were, the more wigs you had.

Wig designer Paul LeBlanc was responsible for the custom-made wigs all principal actors in *Amadeus* wore. He needed a staff of 21 for wig fitting and care. Zaentz says a half million dollars was spent on the design and creation of wigs, giving *Amadeus* one of the largest wig budgets in movie history.

Wolfgang Amadeus Mozart (Tom Hulce) conducts in a scene from *Amadeus*. The film's painstaking attention to detail and its superb craftsmanship contributed to its being named Best Picture, and to the eight Academy Awards it won. (Amadeus ©*1984 The Saul Zaentz Company. All Rights Reserved.*)

Questions you might ask here are these:

Did the settings, costumes, and makeup help to make the film better? Did they create the right atmosphere? Did they blend in unobtrusively with the plot and theme? How did the costumes help us to understand the characters better? Were settings, costumes, and makeup appropriate and accurate in "period" films? ("Period" films are set in a previous historical time or in the future. Films that apparently take place today are called "contemporary" films.)

Sound

There are three basic kinds of sound for film: natural sounds, music, and dialogue. All three help create an atmosphere of reality.

Natural sounds are the sounds that give the scene a feeling of authenticity. Many of them are added after the scene has been filmed, because it is difficult to control all the sounds during filming. Also, the recording machines used in professional filmmaking do not pick up the sounds as the human ear does. When you watch scenes of a car moving down a city street, you hear car horns tooting, the sound of passing cars, people talking, perhaps the clanging of an elevated train—all these sounds may have been added later to bring realism to the film.

If dialogue and music are added to this street scene, it becomes more interesting. In this particular case, the director may have planned to add the dialogue later, as well as the music. Perhaps two people inside the car are exchanging comments. The actors may record the sound later in a special sound room. However, they will also have said the lines during shooting, and the dubbed-in sound must match the movements of their lips. This type of film creation is called *sound-sync* (short for *synchronization*), meaning that the film and the sound go together in perfect synchronization.

When music is added to films, a paradox occurs—the music is both real and unreal. It adds to the realism because it affects our emotions, involving us more deeply. But it is unreal, because life isn't like that. We don't hear music

163

during most of our daily experiences. Full orchestras are not hiding behind every tree. Music, especially in older films, often seems artificial. In an old film called *Monte Carlo*, Jeanette MacDonald sings "Beyond the Blue Horizon" in her compartment on a train. Not only does she suddenly get a full-orchestra accompaniment, but farm workers stop their tasks as the train passes, wave to the train, and sing along in a chorus! Musical spectaculars of the thirties, teenage romantic pictures made during the World War II years, and films deliberately designed to show off the talents of the studios' top singing stars like Deanna Durbin, Judy Garland, or Mario Lanza used song-and-dance numbers wherever possible, whether or not they fit into a logical plot.

Questions you'll want to consider in evaluating sound and music are:

Did the sound and music add to or detract from the film? Did they make the film seem more real? Or did they interrupt it? Were they effective?

Photography

The photographer of a film—the cinematographer—faces many challenges. Usually there is not just one photographer, but several working on any one film, often under the leadership of a director of photography.

A high degree of technical skill is demanded of directors of photography, who must be sure the quality of light of scenes shot at different times is consistent with the look of the film the director wishes to achieve. Here, a production shot of a Terror Dog in *Ghostbusters* calls for the camera to be mounted on a dolly. (Ghostbusters © *1984 Columbia Pictures Inc. All Rights Reserved.*)

Many cinematographers are true artists. A number of great films are remembered primarily for their photography. *Apocalypse Now, Days of Heaven, Gone with the Wind, Walkabout, Paper Moon* (in black and white), *Dr. Zhivago*, and the classic western *Shane* are just a few of the films in which the photography was exceptionally beautiful.

When you look at the credits for a film, you may see the letters *A.S.C.* after the cinematographer's name. This stands for the American Society of Cinematographers, a by-invitation-only professional organization of directors of photography. Your film teacher may have copies of the their monthly magazine, *American Cinematographer,* an international journal of motion picture photography and production techniques. You will enjoy reading behind-the-scenes stories of the making of such films as *Ghostbusters; The River; Paris, Texas;* and others.

Reading *American Cinematographer* gives you an idea of the technical challenges that directors of photography and their colleagues had to surmount. For instance, for *Ghostbusters*, Laszlo Kovacs had to overcome lighting differences between New York and California. As he explains, ''Shooting at night is no trouble, because you create your own atmospheric conditions with smoke and backlight. But, during the daytime, the light looks different. New York, first of all, is very far north, and during wintertime the arc of the sun is much lower, so you have a much more pleasing light, as opposed to even winter light in California.''

For *The River*, director of photography Vilmos Zsigmond spent four weeks of the production schedule with scenes involving rain. Many of those were photographed at night. The rain was all created by rain towers, with sometimes as many as 10 or 12 towers working in a single shot. In the shanty town sequence, telephone poles held the rain spouts so the entire set could be covered with rain and filmed without the audience's seeing the towers. In order to photograph the rain, it had to be backlit. Zsigmond often used construction cranes to hold the backlights.

For *Irreconcilable Differences*, director of photography William Fraker needed to light a large driveway and four-story mansion quickly for a moonlight effect. His crew built a ''moon rig'' from a 20-square-foot tent-like translucent cloth and frame that lit the huge area and only showed one shadow.

Many camera techniques that filmmakers use were discussed earlier. The suggestions and questions for evaluating aspects of the photographic element should help you understand film language better.

In addition to the earlier terms, here are two others you will find useful when you analyze cinematography:

Composition refers to the way in which the cinematographer decides to frame the subject in the rectangle of the screen to create a pleasing effect.

Texture is the surface area, which appears rough or smooth, soft or hard, appealing to our sense of touch. Film is a visual medium. You'd think you could not perceive texture. Yet you can tell when a surface that's being photographed is rough, hard, sandy, slippery, smooth, or slimy by the way the light reflects and creates shadows.

Textures are created by the subject itself, by the way the light strikes the surface, by the use of various kinds of lenses, and by different types of raw film.

Black-and-white or color film can be used to create various kinds of moods, feelings, and experiences. Each can be used in beautiful and creative ways.

In *Irreconcilable Differences*, a 1984 film about a marriage breakup in which the couple's 8-year-old daughter receives a divorce from her parents, cinematographer William Franker, ASC, and production designer Ida Random use a change in colors to show the marriage falling apart.

The romantic mood of courtship was emphasized by the warm lights of fireplaces and sunsets. A family scene in the kitchen of a small Los Angeles house, showing the couple together, is shot with daylight coming through the windows and warm, yellow kitchen walls.

As Ryan O'Neal and Shelly Long move to a larger, colder house, Fraker removes much of the golden glow. Subsequent bedroom scenes are deliberately photographed in progressively cooler, grayer colors to give viewers a sense of the deterioration of the relationship. Finally, the apartment that Lucy (Shelly Long) moves into is devoid of color, with stark, flat white walls.

Another instance of color's being used to signify emotional mood comes in *Rumble Fish* (1983) shot by Francis Ford Coppola in an intense monochrome. The film has two sequences, however, in which color was used—"as a visual pen stroke to communicate an emotional feeling," says director of photography Stephen H. Burum, ASC.

In the pet shop interior scene, the brothers were photographed in black and white; and that footage was projected on a rear projection screen. The fish tank with brightly colored Siamese fighting fish was placed in front of the screen, and the scene was rephotographed with color film.

The vivid color is Coppola's way of letting you know that the Motorcycle Boy is getting near the edge psychologically. To him, normality means that everything is in black and white. Previous dialogue has explained that although Motorcycle Boy saw color as a child, after his mother deserted the family, he could only see black and white. The color of the fighting fish—and later, the flashing red lights when his brother is killed by Patterson—represents an emotional schism.

Although the techniques of color photography were known as early as 1908, when Charles Urban invented a process called Kinemacolor that required a special projector, making movies in color presented special difficult technical problems. An important breakthrough in solving them came in 1939, when Technicolor was able to offer negative material at least twice as fast as those previously available. *Gone with the Wind* was the first major feature to use this new process, which offered greater flexibility in photographing closeups. It is said that more Technicolor prints have been made from this film than from any other picture.

Today more pictures are probably shot in color than in black-and-white. Yet director Peter Bogdanovich deliberately chose black-and-white for *The Last Picture Show* and *Paper Moon* to create the special mood he wanted for the films.

Sometimes color and black-and-white are used together. If you remember *The Wizard of Oz*, you'll recall the film opened in a sepia-toned mood. Kansas was bleak, the unfriendly neighbor pedaled rapidly on her bicycle against a brown and gray background, and even the approaching twister looked monochromatic.

Carried up inside the swirling winds, the farmhouse and Judy Garland were photographed in black and white. The house landed. Judy picked up Toto, opened the door, and stepped out into Munchkin Land, photographed in brilliant Technicolor.

Victor Fleming, who directed *The Wizard of Oz*, used color for the main body of the story, emphasizing the fantasy and dreams in a world "Over the Rainbow." Essentially, the absence of color in the drab opening sequences became a lead-in to Dorothy's adventures, separating the film into before and after.

When you evaluate photography in a film, you should often ask "why." Why was this camera put in a high place, a low place, at this angle? Why was a telephoto lens used? Why did the director of photography use a wide-angle lens in a particular shot? Why did the camera follow the subject the way it did?

You'll want to evaluate the lighting. Why was the girl's face partially in the shadow? Why was the lighting placed low?

When you evaluate the composition, ask yourself, "Why was the subject framed that way?" There's a classic scene in *Shane* in which Brandon deWilde, the young farm boy, and Alan Ladd, the mysterious stranger, carry on a conversation in the foreground while a rider on horseback gallops closer and closer, moving from a far-off cloud of dust until he rides into the scene with deWilde and Ladd, bringing the news of the murder of one of the settlers. The cinematographer deliberately holds the shot, prolonging it till the rider arrives, creating suspense and curiosity through his composition.

We can ask questions about the texture of a film: did the effects seem soft or harsh? Brittle and stark? Misty and dreamlike? What shots in the film showed varying textures? Why do you think they were planned this way?

We can ask if a film would have been more effective in black-and-white or in color.

In general: Did the photography add to the film? Did it seem to blend with all the other components? How did the camera move? Was the photography effective?

And, finally, did the photography achieve the specific images that would best tell the story?

Direction

The director of the film puts it all together. He or she is the creator of the film. The director is the person who says "Cut!" and everything stops.

Until recently, the director of the film was overshadowed by the stars in the film. But now many directors are almost as well known as the stars. Certain directors' names will pull an audience into a theater as much as the cast of stars. Directors and their role in film history will be discussed in Chapter 12.

It is difficult to determine the role of the director in a film. But as you view a film, it is possible to identify some functions. For example, some directors exercise too much control. Perhaps the camera movement will appear obvious. Maybe the actors will seem to be controlled and directed by someone off camera.

Perhaps the best course in attempting to discern the director's role in a film is to evaluate each of the components of the film. We can do this because every aspect of the film is ultimately the director's responsiblity.

As the director–artist creates a film, he or she is always aware of its aesthetic quailities. A good artist will strive for artistic perfection. If the director knows the skills of the craft well, he or she will usually produce quality works of art. But at the same time, there are innate psychological and culturally induced elements in the director's own personality that will inevitably affect the film.

For example, a good director *knows* when a specific camera position is right for a particular scene. This feeling comes not just from skill in the craft, but from an internal sense that says what is right and what is not right.

These factors have great influence on the results of the work of art. They put the director's "signature" on each film.

You may try these questions:

Did all of the components of the film work well together? Did any parts of the film seem to be controlled? Did the film succeed in its original purpose?

Editing

The editing of the film should not be noticeable, at least not to the point where we notice the scenes changing more than the overall film. The editing should help the audience to see the contents better: a close-up scene to show a hand turning a doorknob; a series of scenes to enable a man to move from one side of town to the other in four seconds; a high-angle scene, after a series of close scenes, to establish the location again. Some films are known for their excellent editing: *Citizen Kane, North by Northwest, Psycho, One Flew Over the Cuckoo's Nest, Breaking Away, Star Wars* and its sequels, *Amadeus, The Cotton Club, A Passage to India* (edited by David Lean who also wrote the screenplay and directed the film), and *Romancing the Stone.*

Questions: Was there a smooth flow in the film from beginning to end? Did the editing help you to see and understand the film better? Did the editing help you discover and understand the theme, the plot, and the other components?

All these questions that are suggested for you to use in evaluating the good and the not-so-good films are just that—suggestions. You can use all of them in discussing the films that you see, but they are just a starting point. As you and your friends discuss films, you will begin to think of more questions.

No film can make a perfect score on all these criteria. Your job is to attempt to measure the film's effectiveness *for you.* Certainly you can't do it for anyone alse. You must learn to evaluate a film not in terms "good" or "bad," but in terms of how successful the film was *for you.* No film you ever see will be completely "good." Few will be completely "bad." If you pin labels like these onto a film, you are adopting a black-and-white attitude and forgetting that there are all shades of gray in between. When you evaluate a film, you break it down into its different components and consider each part separately. Then you decide how you reacted—to each part and to the whole film. What "works" for you may not "work" for your best friend or for your teacher. But, at least, when you discuss the film together, you have a number of specific points you can consider, rather than just vague, top-of-your-head value judgements.

After you have considered all of the elements

of the film, you should put it all together and see if the film works for you. Does it hold together? Do all the parts of the film seem to go together? Or are there some parts which are strong and other parts which are weak?

Then consider the entertainment, learning, and artistic value of the film.

Entertainment Value

The entertainment value of a film is very important. If a film doesn't hold your attention, it accomplishes nothing. You can't appreciate its other qualities. Sometimes entertainment can be *amusing, intellectual,* or *emotional.* An entertaining film is dramatic and suspenseful. It has human interest, mystery, and ingenious plotting. It is these elements of entertainment that make film dynamic, exciting, and interesting. Think of some recent films you have seen, and the interest the film created in you—*Breaking Away, The Killing Fields, Ghostbusters, Tootsie, Raiders of the Lost Ark* and its sequel, *Indiana Jones and the Temple of Doom, The Karate Kid, Star Trek III: The Search for Spock, Flashdance, Gremlins, Witness, Micki & Maude,* and *Beverly Hills Cop.*

Perhaps you were surprised that entertainment was included in a list of suggested criteria. Many people associate "entertainment" more closely with "amusement," with unserious, "fun" movies. However, entertainment exists on many levels. Some people have come to accept entertainment only as a diversion from learning, but actually it is a most necessary part of learning.

Learning Value

Film is a kind of education, just as all other aspects of our environment are. We can learn something from any film. Even films made primarily for entertainment teach us something. Many of them deal with social, psychological, or emotional problems in thoughtful and provocative ways. Some deal with the past seriously and creatively.

Breaking Away and *Rich Kids,* for instance, show us what it means to be human. Some of the films of past years also have done this: *The Yearling, The Human Comedy, With a Song in My Heart.* Other films, such as *Treasure of Sierra Madre, King Solomon's Mines,* and *Kelly's Heroes,* show us the effects of greed. Still others explore the results of courage, jealousy, unselfishness (and selfishness), and other human emotions.

Others are *One Flew Over the Cuckoo's Nest, The Killing Fields, A Passage to India, A Soldier's Story, Witness, The Verdict,* and *On Golden Pond. A Soldier's Story* (Norman Jewison) the American entry in the Moscow Film Festival, explores the changing social attitudes, both black and white, at the end of World War II as the Department of the Army, under pressure to investigate the murder of the leader of an all-black company, dispatches Captain Richard Davenport (Howard E. Rollins, Jr.), a very polished, black, Howard University-trained military attorney—much to the dismay and initial distrust of the white base commander, who assumes his findings are a foregone conclusion.

Nearly every film instructs, teaches, or shows us about something.

It takes a strong actress to play opposite Harrison Ford's performance as archaeologist Indiana Jones. Karen Allen, as Marian, in *Raiders of the Lost Ark* combined sweetness with gutsy determination. (Raiders of the Lost Ark © *Lucasfilm Ltd. (LFL) 1981. All Rights Reserved. Courtesy of Lucasfilm Ltd.*)

Films interpret life and illuminate human destiny. They can strengthen people's approach to living. The subject matter is not important, so long as it says something to the audience.

Artistic Value

When all these integral parts of a film are done well, the film has artistic value.

Science fiction and western films can have as much artistic value as dramatic films. Low-budget films can be as artistic as expensive supercolossal spectacles. But superiority in one or two areas doesn't necessarily mean that the entire film can be considered artistic. Superior acting or scriptwriting doesn't make the entire film a work of art. For a film to have artistic value, artistry must be found in all its parts.

As you may have noticed, we are no longer investigating the factual and technical elements of film (such as shots, dissolves, or editing techniques). Instead, we are beginning to examine the elements of film that are related to value judgments. We are suggesting ways in which you can evaluate and appraise various elements of film to develop your own aesthetic judgment. You can use qualifying terms: "I believe . . ." "It seems to me that . . ." "I felt . . ." "Perhaps . . ." "Apparently . . ." "In my opinion . . ." These phrases should help and encourage you to stick your neck out and speculate creatively on some aspect of film about which you feel strongly.

A word often used to help in the discussion of any art form is "work": "Does it work?" Looking at art in this light helps you evaluate how effective different variables are. For example, in these short descriptions of film elements, the word "work" helps clarify the meaning:

Twyla Tharp's choreography and staging of Mozart operas in *Amadeus* work especially well in the three selections from *The Marriage of Figaro.*

The climatic crater sequence with 16 helicopters airborne over Meteor Crater works in *Starman.*

Using an austere Japanese dwelling with mats, screens, and a pond complete with koi and hundred-year-old bonsai works, as it conveys the essence of Miyagi's inner calm in *The Karate Kid.*

Evaluating Other Films

Some films cannot be evaluated using the criteria that we have suggested, and some of these films will have no actors, no plot, no script, and may even be silent. If you have seen documentary, experimental, certain types of animation, or information films, you will soon discover that we need a different set of criteria.

A filmmaker, as any artist may do, will often set up an artistic obstacle to present a challenge to overcome. In other words, the filmmaker/artist may find an idea which he or she wishes to communicate and then will go about finding a way to communicate the idea on film. For example, Charles Braverman probably wanted to communicate the excitement of the Beatles during the sixties before he decided *how* he would communicate it.

Sometimes, rather than concentrating on the subject, the filmmaker will try to focus on a technique. Using the technique, the filmmaker will convey a message. Perhaps the message is no more than movement, or editing techniques, of the use of color, slow motion, fast motion, relationships between the shapes, colors, kinds of movements and sound.

How do we evaluate films like this? Sometimes we can't—except to consider if the film is pleasant or not. Or maybe we can "feel" a sense of visual beauty in the movement (as in *Dream of Wild Horses*) or the sound in relation to the image (in certain scenes in *The Sixties*) or the color (as in *Omega*), the editing rhythm (in *The House* and *Vivre.*)

You should understand that art is often beautiful for its own value. We do not have to ask if a sunset or a flower is beautiful (even though we might). They are beautiful in their color or their symmetry. They were created by nature. But when human beings create art, we seem to need to consider, to evaluate, to appraise—rather than to let the art stand on its own to be exalted for its own values.

The questions we can ask are these:

Does the film make me feel in harmony? Can I feel a rhythm? Is the film beautiful, even if the subject is ugly and obscene as in *Night and Fog*? Does the film make me feel as if I am

The powerful film, *A Soldier's Story,* nominated for an Academy Award as Best Picture, was a searing drama of murder and mystery. Howard E. Rollins, Jr. (left) and Adolph Caesar starred in the film, based on Charles Fuller's award-winning play. (A Soldier's Story ©1984. *Thorn EMI Films Finance PLC. All Rights Reserved.*)

seeing something in balance? Is the film pleasing to my senses, even if the subject is not to my liking? Can I find artistic purpose for the film?

Perhaps the most important suggestion is to try to consider the film/art aesthetically or artistically and to *not* consider the film/art rationally. A common mistake among many people is that art is not worth considering art if it doesn't have a purpose—if it doesn't have a meaning.

Finally, try not to be influenced by your friends in what to like and what not to like. The influence of friends in this area of film criticism (concerning artistic appreciation) is one of the biggest problems among young people. Even when you really think you're *not* being influenced by anyone, that you are your own person, you are often influenced by your friends.

Reflections

1. What is art? What is an artist? Are you an artist?

2. How do you go about "measuring" the value of a film? How do you decide if the film was worthwhile or not?

3. Do you understand the kind of questions you can ask after each of the component parts of a movie?

4. How would you consider a film that had no story? How would you decide if it was art?

5. Are *you* influenced by what films your friends like and dislike?

Activities

1. If you have made a film as suggested in the earlier chapters, see if you can evaluate your own film, using some of the techniques outlined in this chapter. Ask your friends or classmates to evaluate your film.

2. Write critical reviews of some films you have seen. This will sharpen your awareness of the artistic merits of films.

3. Clip a bad movie review from your local newspaper. See the movie and write your own review, either agreeing or disagreeing on different aspects of the film.

Further Reading: *Check Your Library.*

Faulkner, Robert R. *Music on Demand: Composers & Careers in the Hollywood Film Industry,* New Brunswick, NJ: Transaction Books, 1982.

Leigh, Janet. *There Really Was a Hollywood,* New York: Doubleday, 1984.

Lenburg, Jeff. *Dustin Hoffman: Hollywood's Anti-Hero,* New York: St. Martin's, 1983.

Mordden, Ethan. *Movie Star: A Look at the Women Who Made Hollywood,* New York: St. Martin's, 1983.

Rissik, Andrew. *The James Bond Man: The Films of Sean Connery,* North Pomfret, VT: David & Charles, 1984.

Stacy, Jan and Syvertsen, Ryder. *The Great Book of Movie Villains: A Guide to the Meanies, Tough Guys, and Bullies,* Chicago: Contemporary Books, 1984.

Patrick Williams

The Film Composer

Veteran film composer Patrick Williams whose 50 movies include The Slugger's Wife, The Best Little Whorehouse in Texas, Breaking Away, *and* Butch and Sundance: the Early Days, *knew at a young age that he'd be a musician. "When you're hot in kindergarten rhythm band," he says, "you know you've got something going."*

After seven years in New York, working as arranger for Broadway shows while attending graduate school at Columbia University, Williams headed for Hollywood to compose his first film, How Sweet It Is *(James Garner, Debbie Reynolds). Today, he composes four films a year, interspersing them with television shows, made-for-TV movies, his own recordings, and teaching.*

The film composer needs a multifaceted ability. He or she must deal with the fantasy of what a particular film is trying to say, must use music to help the audience understand the film's emotional subtleties.

Music works best when it deals with people's feelings. It can tell the audience something they are already seeing, or can lead the audience to insights by enhancing the story line and filling in the gaps. Movies can be a choppy

172

medium, and music can help sustain the emotional thrust, providing pace and tempo.

Music helps provide emotional consistency for characters. Usually, music is added in post-production, as the film gets solidified and release dates firm up. Although a director might talk to you a year ahead, you're usually called from two to six weeks before you begin work. You may think you'll start on a certain date, but projects jam up because of release schedules and money commitments. Film composing, then, becomes a deadline business, since composing the score generally takes four to eight weeks.

I don't usually read the script for a film. It's better to see the movie. Your instincts as an experienced composer will tell you things about the film you'll never get from the printed page. I want to be alone when I see the rough cut of the film for the first time. I look at it three or four times, organizing my thinking. I spend several days "cooking by myself," getting my mental fix on the type and style and overall musical approach. The approach is crucial. A film composer can be forgiven sins in detail work, but if the approach is wrong, you can get into terrible trouble.

You write your main themes, usually two or three, which are varied, and used in different ways. It's a game of theme and variations. You're trying to link the audience constantly to certain characters, giving the viewer kind of a home base feeling.

Next you write the music for the various scenes in the film that you've decided to score. If the performances are strong, silence is an extremely effective tool. Some scenes play better without music, which would sentimentalize them, or push the film over the edge.

In a normal theatrical 90-minute feature film, there's approximately 30 minutes of music. It's written to precise timing, down to the tenth-of-a-second.

The director is the creative head of the film. He or she tells you what's wanted for the feelings of a particular scene. A director may decide the scene needs some pacing, because it's a little slow. Maybe the audience should feel that the hero is in jeopardy at a particular point, even though it's not life-threatening danger. It's up to the film composer to translate those instructions into music, working closely with the music editor and the film editor.

Technology has made the life of a film composer much easier. Years ago, I had to drive to the studio every time I wanted to see the film. Today, my office in back of my home has a piano, a large screen television, five speakers, a compact disc player, and a synthesizer. I can see the film there on my video-cassette player.

Most film composers can work at pianos, but the orchestra is not a piano. You can play something on a piano and say, "This is a trumpet," but it doesn't sound like a trumpet. You must fantasize about how the instruments will sound, organizing in your mind what you want to hear. I write all my music down by hand. I start by 6:15 A.M., writing for six to eight hours. By the end of the day, on the average, I've composed 2 to 2½ minutes of music.

When we record the music, the picture is projected at the studio, and the composer conducts his own score with a full orchestra of highly-trained studio musicians. You're part of the live process as the music is fitted to the movie. It's magic! You make adjustments on the spot if the timing isn't quite right, or the melody needs to come through more clearly.

I sit in on dubbing, when music, dialogue, and sound effects are put together. Then I sign off on the film.

Michael Westmore

The Make-Up Artist

Probably 80 percent of all films made in the period from the 1930s through the 1950s carried the famous Westmore name for make-up credits. The family tradition started when George Westmore, formerly a wigmaker in England, came to California at the time movies were still being shot in barns, and actors were making themselves up.

Continuing the family tradition, Michael Westmore began with a three-year apprenticeship at Universal, eventually becoming assistant department head of make-up effects there before leaving in 1971 to free-lance. Today, he's president of his own company, which specializes in rubber masks and special make-up effects for motion pictures and television. Recent films include Rocky I, II and III, New York, New York, Raging Bull, Escape to Victory, *and Peter Bogdanovich's* Mask. *He was nominated for an Academy Award for both* 2010 *and* The Iceman, *and won a 1984 Emmy for make-up on television's* Why Me?

Make-up is a practical art that's done with hand–eye coordination. To learn how to do a black eye and to do it once is not enough. You have to do it 200 times, and even then, you still keep practicing. As a Universal apprentice, when I learned how to make beards, they locked me away with a false rubber head and a couple pounds of hair. I did nothing but make beards over and over again for months . . .

It took 5½ hours a day and four persons to do make-up for Keir Dullea in *2010,* though that's halved from the 11 hours it took years ago when he was made up for *2001.*

I constructed his entire head in a mold, making the bald part of his head with sculpted blood veins. Then I developed a series of multi-overlapping pieces for his nose, upper eyes, forehead, and ears.

Make-up today is much thinner than it was 10 years ago. For a man, you might put a very thin base on his face to balance out under the lights so he looks healthy. It's a simple matter of a base to normalize his skin tones and then bringing out his eyes a little bit with a little pencil and mascara. Normal make-up might take from 5 to 20 minutes for a man. But with women, make-up can take as much as an hour.

The fight sequences for *Rocky* and *Rocky II* were challenging. Stallone was involved in all the production details, including make-up. We used special pieces applied to the face. Stallone left it up to me to decide how far the pieces were going to swell, but he would tell me that he was going to get hit in the nose . . . that he would be hit in the right eye first, and then the left eye, so it meant that I had to make his right eye swell before his left eye. We'd stop filming and change the make-up for each shot. In each of the 15 rounds, Rocky's right and left eye swelled differently. I had to keep track of just which eyepieces I'd used on the top or bottom of each eye.

Once the director has chosen a master take, you get Polaroid photographs of that particular make-up and glue them into your script. In *New York, New York,* we spent 10 days shooting a scene where Robert DeNiro had confetti in his hair. Every day I had to put the right tiny pieces in the right places—one pink and one green stuck on his forehead, three yellows on the left side, and so on.

In *Escape to Victory,* Stallone, as goalie in a soccer game between Nazi and Allied prisoners of war, gets kicked in the face. He runs off the field holding a towel, goes to the locker room, and cleans up. Blood, mixed with sweat, runs down his face, forming lines. Even though some of those scenes were shot several weeks later on inside stages, the make-up had to match exactly in color, texture, and even the angle of the lines.

When you go on location, you have to take everything with you. I carried two quarts of artificial blood to Budapest. The blood, which I buy from a special effects house, is made with honey that has been colored. It has clarity and stickiness, and looks like real blood when it dries. . . .

For *Mask,* Peter Bogdanovich's film about a boy with the rare "Lion's Disease," in which the body shrinks and the head continues to grow, it took me three months to design and develop the latex face mask the actor wore. I made one very large head, with separate upper lip and chin pieces, but we tested eight different models till it was right. I had to design the mask in such a way that when it was applied to his face, it could work with his own muscle structure. He could smile. He could wrinkle his forehead. And he used all his natural muscles. . . .

The professional make-up artist is always learning. For the picture *True Confessions,* there's a body found in a vacant lot. I had to take a cast of the actress, build a wax body with glass eyes, and put a wig on it. To be sure the shots of the body and autopsy sutures in the morgue looked authentic, they sent me to the Los Angeles County Morgue with my camera to take photographs and match needles and thread. I spent half a day there, getting a Disneyland tour of all different types of stitches and accidents, watching the morgue attendants sew up the bodies. . . .

Make-up's changed since the old days. When my uncle Frank did *The Ten Commandments* for Cecil B. DeMille, they lined up thousands of extras. They turned the people in a circle, loaded the make-up in spray guns, zapped the bodies, and away they went. . . .

10

Evaluating Film: Talking About Your Reactions

Critiquing Films

Dinner starts out routinely. A father and his son, eating together at a kitchen table. The man, tired from work, is trying to be reasonable. Billy looks at his plate, pushing it aside.

"Eat your dinner." Ted Kramer is only mildly annoyed at first. Billy stubbornly shakes his head. "You eat that dinner first before you get ice cream."

A close-up of Billy's rebellious face. The scene cuts back to Ted's rising anger. We see Ted's irritation grow as Billy climbs down, drags his chair to the refrigerator, brings out the ice cream carton, and heaps ice cream on his plate. Ted watches incredulously. As Billy starts to eat the ice cream, Ted explodes, striking the child, and then hugging him. Both are nearly in tears.

Many filmmakers believe the best thing they can do for an audience is to make them laugh or cry or both. Emotions play an important part in seeing a film. Perhaps we could even suggest

Dramatic lighting creates a mood of terror, as Alan Arkin tries to frighten "blind" Audrey Hepburn into revealing the whereabouts of a doll packed with heroin in *Wait Until Dark.*

that a person who could see the scenes from *Kramer vs. Kramer* described above without at least being deeply moved has difficulty handling his or her emotions.

In our society, we are taught to hide our emotions and not display them publicly. Nevertheless having a concern for others is the beginning of understanding other people better. Film helps this to happen. Film helps us see what it is to be a human being.

Perhaps only in determining justice, in looking for facts, and in scientific investigation should we prevent our emotions from becoming a part of the event. When you investigate the nature of film, emotions *are* important. You should examine film with your emotions naked before the world—not to show the world that you know how to feel, but to allow you the chance to discover yourself as you discover the film. It is probably impossible to see a film without giving part of yourself away. You should take advantage of this opportunity to examine why you feel the way to do as you see films.

Sometimes seeing a film is like seeing a mirror—a mirror that reflects only images we want to see. It takes insight, perceptiveness, and understanding to discover all the images, even those we don't necessarily want to see. For some people, a major problem begins when they start to talk about what they see.

Talking about Film

Talking about or discussing film is an integral part of learning about film. Discussing the film helps you to:

- Understand the film better by hearing the views of other people.

- Understand how and why other people have different viewpoints.

- Exercise your own opinions and feelings about film and its relationship to life.

- Become more articulate about your reactions.

- Grow and become more proficient in your perceptive, intellectual, and emotional skills.

- Enjoy the film more.

In addition to the adventure—some plot, the strong emotional relationship that develops between Princess Leia (Carrie Fisher) and Han Solo (Harrison Ford) heightens audience interest. From *Star Wars* through *Empire* to *Return of the Jedi*, the pair has been one of the most popular couples in film. (*The Empire Strikes Back, courtesy of Lucasfilm, Ltd.,* ©*Lucasfilm, Ltd. (LFL) 1980. All Rights Reserved.*)

What to Say

You've seen the film. You liked it. Or maybe you didn't like it. Now what?

The first thing you do is open your mouth, being polite, of course, and not interrupting anyone else. Then you simply begin to talk about anything that you believe relates to the film you've just seen.

Sometimes a film is so good that you think words just can't describe it. This, in fact, may be true. It is very difficult to put into words the excitement of the battle sequence in *Star Wars* or the creepy-crawly feeling of the bugs in *Indiana Jones and the Temple of Doom,* the impact of the

Sally Field's dramatic performance as young widow Edna Spalding in *Places In The Heart* won her a second Academy Award as Best Actress. Her determination to hold her family together despite lack of money is evident in this shot of her in the cotton fields of West Texas. (Places in the Heart ©1984 Tri-Star Pictures.)

labor room nurse's testimony in the courtroom scene of *The Verdict*, the explosions of fire and devils flying down from the ceiling in the flamboyant "Don Giovanni" staging in *Amadeus*.

What are your emotional feelings when Harrison Ford shows Amish widow Kelly McGillis how to dance in *Witness* while listening to his car radio in the deserted barn? Her life and heart become entwined with Ford, who plays a tough Philadelphia cop on the run. And how do you feel when the pair is discovered and she is threatened with shunning, the Amish custom which, if imposed, forbids others of the sect even to talk with her?

How do you feel about *A Passage to India* when Victor Banerjee as the young Indian doctor is accused of rape? about *The Karate Kid* when Ralph Macchio learns karate from Noriyki "Pat" Morita for revenge on his tormentors? about *A Soldier's Story* when Adolph Caesar, as Master Sergeant Vernon C. Waters, humiliates and manipulates his segregated troops into line? about *Places in the Heart* when Sally Field, as a young widow struggling to keep her family together, picks cotton till her hands are scratched and bleeding?

Some teachers will expect immediate responses to questions like these. But ask the teacher to wait for a few minutes or even until the next day. Many times our emotions respond instantly to the film, while our minds and bodies take longer to absorb and react to it.

However, don't let this be an escape from taxing your thought process. Try to find the words to describe these "hard to discuss" films. The more you talk about the films you see, the more you will understand and find the right words to use.

A discussion of a film should not be a critical review of it. Unless you have a lot of background in studying film, leave the reviews to the film critics for now. Discuss the merits of the film. Decide for yourself and with your class whether the film succeeded or not, but don't make a definite final decision concerning the film's worth. It could be that you are right, that a film you have just seen has flaws. But the reverse could be true, too. Maybe you simply didn't understand or didn't perceive the film very well.

When you see a film that seems difficult to understand, try to look for components that have meaning. In *Mindscape* the emotional appeal and symbolic use of visual images such as this mind maze can lead to interesting discussions. (Mindscape, *courtesy of Pyramid Films.*)

Film, like theater or dance, is a *time art*, and the passage of time is needed to play out its statement or expression. Sometimes our memory of what we might have seen only minutes earlier fails us. You will find, though, that the more films you see and discuss, the better your memory of these films will become, because what you remember is related to your skill in perceiving it in the first place. Another advantage to a discussion of a film is that what one person doesn't remember, someone else usually does.

It is important that your discussions *be* discussions. No one person, not even your teacher, should lecture on the film or try to be an "authority." Perhaps your teacher will guide the discussion, or perhaps there will be student leaders.

Approaches to Studying Films

There are many ways you can approach studying and discussing film: to relate ideas and concepts presented in groups of films; to study individual films in great detail; to study certain kinds or categories of films; to study films historically; to study films by certain filmmakers; to study films made in other countries; to study films in relationship to society.

Investigating Film Thematically

You may have noticed that some ideas are used over and over again in many different films that you see. These thematic ideas may be con-

Non-theatrical films have much to offer, since often they have been made with a particular theme. When you see films such as *Two Men and a Wardrobe,* you will want to talk about its historical and cultural implications. (*Courtesy of Janus Films, Inc., NYC.*)

cerned with freedom, death, love, friendship, dehumanization, inhumanity, brotherly love, and many hundreds, perhaps even thousands, of "big ideas." The themes become even more sophisticated when we begin to discuss relationships and conflicts between various thematic ideas.

One method used in investigating film is to study it thematically. Usually the teacher has grouped together films expressing a similar theme. Often films have many possible thematic ideas, but can usually be grouped together under a particular theme. As each of the films is viewed and discussed, the common or similar themes become apparent.

Investigating Film Analytically

As you become more proficient, you may begin to draw out new thematic ideas and to relate these ideas to other films you have seen and to life itself. Studying the film analytically usually means that you spend time going into much more detail about many aspects of the theme, film techniques, and how the film brings out responses within people.

Investigating Film Historically

There are at least three ways to investigate films historically:

1. A film made in a specific year is studied in the light of the events that might have caused or influenced its creation: for example, films made during the 1950s in the light of the Cold War and people's fears about Communists.

2. Some films can be studied that describe certain periods of time in history. *The Happy Years* is a film set at the turn of the century. *Bon-*

nie and Clyde, though not historically accurate, was set during the 1930s. So were *The Sting, Paper Moon,* and *Places in the Heart.*

3. Another way to study films is to investigate particular films in historical order by viewing representative films, perhaps from successive decades.

Investigating Film Genres

A film *genre* is a certain style of film, depending largely on the background setting but also on subject matter and form. There are many genres, and most of them are probably familiar to you. The western is perhaps the most popular genre. Other genres are science fiction; detective, police, and mystery films; comedies; family dramas; social dramas; documentaries; war films; suspense and adventure films; musicals; and animated films. Many of the genres overlap. A film about war can be a drama like *All Quiet on the Western Front.* Or it can be a comedy-drama like *M*A*S*H.*

Investigating Foreign Films

Another exciting way to study film is to investigate foreign films. You can examine films from only one country or select films from all over the world. You may want to compare films from various countries for their style, techniques, stories, etc. Or you could compare them thematically, historically, and by genre.

There is one drawback, but it isn't serious. Films from non-English-speaking countries are either subtitled or dubbed in English. A subtitled film has the words the performers say printed at the bottom of the screen. Most people adjust to this situation fairly rapidly, and many people can think back to a foreign film, after it is over, in English.

When a film is dubbed, usually the entire soundtrack must be remade. English speakers (sometimes, not always, actors and actresses) say the lines of the actors in the film and attempt to match the lip synchronization. Many times this is done quite poorly, so many people prefer to see a film with subtitles.

Investigating Film as a Reflection of Society

Many people believe that the art a society creates reflects that society in numerous ways. On the other hand, other people believe that an art form simply imitates the environment seen by the artist. Probably there are elements of truth in both viewpoints.

It is, however, very interesting to investigate film by studying its relationship to society. For instance, if you discuss the dehumanizing spirit that underscores the film *Midnight Express,* you will surely discuss other dehumanizing qualities of any society.

Violence is used often in films for excitement, for fast action, and sometimes even for artistic and aesthetic effects. Questions like "Are films too violent?" and "Does film reflect the violence of our society?" are all relevant.

Investigating Short Films

The short film (usually any film under about 50 minutes), like the short story in literature, is a separate genre.

Short films are most often used in classrooms because they are usually less expensive and because instructors can show them in one classroom period. Sometimes, too, these films are more available to teachers.

However, there are better reasons for investigating short films. There are literally thousands of short films that are interesting, exciting, and well made. Most of the other suggestions for investigating films apply to short films, too.

Other Approaches

There are many other ways film can be studied and investigated. Perhaps you can search out the mood, the feeling, the intent of the filmmaker and make the comparisons between the various films by the same filmmaker.

You might try to concentrate on various techniques, how they are used, and in what way they influence the subject matter.

Perhaps the best way to investigate film is to

work with a combination of all these ways. Certainly you don't want to get so bogged down in study and investigation that you lose sight of the entertaining and original reasons for enjoying film. At the same time, knowing and understanding various ways to investigate film should increase your enjoyment of the art.

"Why investigate any film?" you may ask. The answer to this question is extremely important, but not recognized by many people. At no time in history have human beings been so innundated with images and sound. In the past, people had time—time to reflect, to digest, to grasp the information which came their way. But today, with the influence of television, and perhaps to only a slighter extent, movies, our minds are constantly flooded with images and sounds. Experts in the area of media communication, and many social thinkers, including psychologists and sociologists, believe that people watching television day after day need time to think about what they have seen. The media authorities and others believe that critical thinking, which allows us to evaluate the media, must be taught in both elementary and high schools to prepare students to function in the fast expanding communications world.

A study of film should have this as one of its most important objectives. Your class should have ample opportunity to discuss the films you see in class, the films and programs you see on television, and the films you see in the theater.

Expressing Your Reactions: Eight Film Case Studies

Thousands of feature films and many thousands more short films have been produced over the past 75 years. Out of these films, we have picked four feature films and four short films to use as detailed examples of ways to talk and write about film. It was very difficult to choose these films, for there are so many different genres of films that is was impossible to give an example from each genre. Further, it is almost impossible to select certain film directors as "typical."

We feel that it is important that you know why we chose these films to discuss in more detail.

1. We wanted films that would be interesting for you to see. Ideally, your class will be able to watch several of these films, so you can compare what is said here with what you see in the film itself.

2. The films were all chosen without considering who directed them or from what genre they came. We did it this way because we want to emphasize the *discussion* of the film. We felt that almost any film would serve this purpose.

3. Be sure to understand that these discussions are not critical reviews. Their purpose is to give you an example of how one of the authors of this book perceived these films. You should consider these examples as *examples only,* not as the "right" way or only way to discuss film.

As you read and study the film case studies, look for examples from the film that the writer has used to support his or her opinions. The writers have used the correct terms to describe various techniques used by the filmmaker to create a film. Try to observe how each writer uses these terms to make his or her views clearer.

Case Study One: Little Big Man

(1)   Dustin Hoffman plays the part of 121-year-old Jack Crabb, sole white survivor of the Battle of the Little Big Horn. I began to believe that Jack Crabb was a real person telling a story.

(2)   The film begins in a nursing home: Jack Crabb is being interviewed by a younger man. Crabb looks very, very old. He has wrinkles, dried-up skin, and moves and talks very slowly. There are many close-up shots of Crabb's face.

(3)   The film is narrated by Crabb, but not all the time. The narration interrupts the flow of the film only at points where narration helps the audience follow the story better.

(4)   Crabb begins his story by telling the interviewer that when he was 10 years old, 111 years ago, he and his family were crossing

the plains. A band of Indians attacked their wagon, killing his mother and father. Only Crabb and his sister, Caroline, survived.

(5)   The scene cuts from Jack Crabb and the interviewer to a long shot of a smoldering wagon and bodies—even dead animals lying nearby. The scene establishes death and destruction and communicates to me the violent life of Jack Crabb. The title of the film and the credits begin. A young boy and an older girl, about 17, crawl out of the wagon, but quickly dash back to the safety of the wagon. Soon, a lone Indian brave rides up to survey the carnage.

(6)   We see the brave riding around the destruction in long shots and we get a subjective point of view of the children hiding under the overturned wagon. This point of view made me identify with the children. I became hidden in the wagon, too—and was surprised and scared when the Indian brave ripped the cover back. This interesting shot is framed, with the wagon canvas forming an "A" shape up the center of the screen. When the brave opens the flap and stares at the children, Caroline starts praying.

(7)   The Indian brave is a Cheyenne warrior who takes Jack Crabb and his sister, Caroline, to the Indian's camp.

(8)   Caroline very soon escapes because she thinks she's going to be raped and treated badly by the Indians. But the Indians are friendly. In fact, they call themselves the human beings. Crabb becomes a member of the tribe and is raised by Old Lodge Skin, "Grandfather," as Crabb calls him. He learns to hunt, to ride a pony, and to do all the things Indians do.

(9)   Soon he becomes a young man, but he is small for his years, a runt, and is teased by the other young braves. Crabb makes an enemy first by hitting Younger Bear, *and then apologizing*. One never apologizes in this culture. Later Crabb saves Younger Bear's life, which also is seen as an insult.

(10)   Grandfather tells Crabb, "Little Man was small, but his bravery was big. You are Little Big Man."

(11)   Soon after this the Indians attack the "bluecoats" the battle goes well for the Indi-

ans. They are able to get many coups; that is, they are able to touch the enemy. This is considered more important than killing the enemy, but the soldiers do not understand. Soon the tide turns. One soldier starts after Little Big Man. Each man is on a horse. The soldier catches up and slashes out at Little Big Man with his sword. Little Big Man literally jumps off the horse as it runs, dashing between its legs and around the horse as an attempt to get away from the soldier. Finally the soldier catches him. There is a wild fight. Suddenly Little Big Man has a knife at the soldier's throat. Crabb explains to the startled soldier that he is white.

(12)   Jack Crabb is taken into town and given to the Rev. Silas Pendrake and his wife (played by Faye Dunaway) so they can care for him.

(13)   Then a series of adventures begins that allow the director of the movie, Arthur Penn, to tell an exciting story with humor and wit. Penn establishes a provocative and interesting character. During the course of what must be many years, Jack Crabb becomes an adopted Indian brave, then a gun fighter (the Sodey Pop kid), muleskinner, scout, and town drunk. He works with a medicine man-con artist, discovers the evils of sex, becomes religious, and is loved by a minister's wife. He is friends with Wild Bill Hickok and knew General George Armstrong Custer! While living with the Indians, he becomes a father and enjoys the sexual company of his wife's three sisters. He is a store owner, but goes broke when his partner cheats on him. He is also married to Ulga, a Swedish woman who speaks no English, and he is later kidnapped by Indians.

(14)   Jack Crabb lives a very full and exciting life. However, I remember that the entire story is told from the point of view of a very old Jack Crabb. I think Jack Crabb tells a very good yarn about his life. How much is true and how much is tall tales is not known, nor is it important. Arthur Penn's *Little Big Man* is probably one of the most authentic and realistic westerns ever made. I realize that through the life of Jack Crabb, I am seeing an Old West, perhaps exaggerated,

but nevertheless, realistic because I see through the stories and see the real West. I especially see the relationship between the whites and the Indians.

(15)   At another time, Old Lodge Skin tells Jack, ''There's an endless supply of white men, but a limited supply of human beings.'' I take this to mean that the white man wasn't human. It was true in this movie.

(16)   I especially liked the way the film takes me on the adventure, and as I think about it, I don't remember why. I don't remember too well, because the transition from one scene to the next and from one sequence to the next is done so smoothly that I don't realize the implied passage of time until I am well into the next part. For example, the change from Crabb's boyhood to a teenager and then a young man is so smooth that I don't even notice the transition.

(17)   When Crabb is living with the Indians again, the transition from one sequence to the next is not easy to see. We see Crabb in front of the tepee during the winter, the scene of his baby's birth, the scene when Crabb believes the soldiers are coming, the discussion of this belief with Old Lodge Skin, the battle and the aftermath without any dissolve (which usually shows the passage of time) or any other technique, just the straight cut from one scene to the next.

It must be the arrangement and editing of each scene and the plot itself which made me unaware of the passage of time.

(18)   I see Arthur Penn's film as the real West when Jack Crabb becomes the Sodey Pop Kid, a gunfighter. He is sitting in a tavern attempting to make his legs reach the table like Wild Bill Hickok is doing next to him. Finally he makes it, but looks very uncomfortable. Then they trade lies of how many men they have shot. Both men are very nervous. When a man at a nearby table gives a loud yell because of a good hand at cards, both men nervously but rapidly draw their guns. Everyone is startled and fearful.

(19)   The relationship between Crabb and Hickok, though exaggerated and archetypal western movie, is real because of the truth it tells about the nineteenth century in the im-age of aspects of today and the westerns we enjoy. For example, Crabb's view of the homosexual Indian, the dialogue of Old Lodge Skin, the values and beliefs of the characters, and the entire spoof of the American western is evident in these images of twentieth-century America in a nineteenth-century setting.

Explanation:

I attempted to describe the film as I saw it. I made various interpretations of what I believed to be the reality of the film. I used examples from the film to substantiate my composition.

Keep in mind that the writing is not a criticism of the film as a professional film critic would write it. It may seem very similar, sometimes, but rather it is a written description of my perceptions. By writing down my feelings and perceptions immediately after seeing the film, I have an opportunity to think more about the film.

My immediate reactions on seeing *Little Big Man* are described in the first paragraph (1). I was caught up in the story immediately. I believed that Jack Crabb was an old man telling a story.

Paragraphs (4) through (12) describe the plot at the beginning of the film. The plot is the action in this film. Around the action revolves the entire story and its theme. Sometimes the plot is not vitally important in a film, but the theme becomes the most important. In *Little Big Man,* the plot is very important because it really is the story that Jack Crabb is telling. Nevertheless we should be careful not to concentrate on the plot so that we fail to see a deeper, perhaps more profound theme.

In some paragraphs, I described the techniques the filmmaker used to advance the story and to influence my perception of the film: in paragraphs (3) and (4), I describe how the narration is used. In (5), I describe the long shot and what the long shot communicated to me.

The subjective view in paragraph (6) is another technique used by the filmmaker to get us involved with the characters and see what they see. I have described what I felt at this point, how the filmmaker involved me in the story.

Describing what one perceives in a film is opinion. When opinion is supported with evidence in the form of examples, the credibility of the writer (in this case, the "seer" of the film) is helped. I begin to descirbe some of the purposes of the film in paragraph (13): "That allows the director of the movie, Arthur Penn, to tell an exciting story with humor and wit. Penn establishes a provocative and interesting character." Then I continue by giving examples of the roles Crabb played during his life.

In paragraph (14), I continue to describe the purpose . . . "tells a very good yarn about his life." I am seeing an Old West, perhaps exaggerated . . . I see through these stories and see the real West." Perhaps some of the purposes of the film suggest a main idea or theme.

Paragraph (15) describes Old Lodge Skin, somewhat, and his feelings toward the white man. Even though the development of the characters in this film is very important and adds much to the film, I guess I was more impressed with the plot and important themes than with each of the characters. That is why I describe what Old Lodge Skin says about the white man, rather than describing the old chief himself.

I admit in paragraphs (16) and (17) that I didn't see how the filmmaker crossed time and space. I was so caught up in the story that I didn't even notice the technique. I even remember thinking during the film, "How is the filmmaker making me believe the rapid passage of time and the transitions from one place to another?—and then I'd forget to watch for the technique."

Again in paragraphs (18) and (19), I describe further the purpose and theme of the film. "I see in Arthur Penn's film the real West." Then I support this opinion by suggesting examples from the film. "The relationship between Crabb and Hickok, though exaggerated and archetypal western movie, is real because of the truth it tells about the nineteenth century and our world today. . . . We have recreated the nineteenth century . . ." Then I suggest examples from the film to support my opinions.

Case Study Two: **Walkabout**

Various sentences have been underlined in the discussion of the second film. The underlined

One of the most beautiful and haunting films ever made, *Walkabout,* the tale of two children lost in the Australian desert who learn survival techniques from an aborigine has been popular the world over. Audiences understand and react to the cultural differences between the children, and the attempts each makes to bridge the cultural gap. (Walkabout © *Twentieth Century-Fox. All Rights Reserved.*)

sentences are examples given to support the statements that have been made about the film. Can you discover why these statements were used and find a relationship between the underlined sentences and the opinions?

Walkabout has some of the most beautifully photographed scenes and sequences I've ever seen in a film. There are many imaginative shots of beautiful Australian landscapes and wild animals. But the unusual photography is merged into the content of the film without being distracting.

A "walkabout" is a primitive coming-of-manhood ordeal undertaken by aborigine boys. The boy walks about the general area of his tribe's location for some time, experiencing the environment and surviving on his own. On one such walkabout, the young aborigine male discovers two white city-bred youngsters, a boy about 8 years old and a teenage girl about 15, lost in the Australian desert. We see the story action, however, through the eyes of the little boy and the teenage girl, who are brother and sister.

The film begins with a montage of the city, of people walking to work or shopping. Most of these shots are taken with a telephoto lens that compresses the images, creating feelings of overcrowded conditions and the monotony of everyday life. These shots are soon contrasted with shots of the Australian desert wildlife and landscapes. Then there are various shots of the small boy at school, the girl walking home, and their father at work. To me, most of these interrelated shots are somewhat vague in meaning. Perhaps the filmmaker is attempting to establish a contrast between the tensions and anxieties of the city and between modern technology and the orderliness of nature.

Evidently the father has been fired from his job and has lost control of himself and of his grasp on reality. He takes his children on a picnic into the desert and is soon taking potshots at them with a high-powered rifle. He misses. Then he sets the car on fire and shoots himself.

He is sitting down when he shoots himself. The fall backward is repeated and overlapped several times to emphasize the agony of the moment. Perhaps this bit of fancy editing was done

on purpose to illustrate the agony, but the children do not seem to be bothered at all. In fact, the girl and boy take off for points unknown, without a glance back at their dead father and burnt car, and promptly get lost in the desert. Why they simply didn't follow the road back to the city is beyond me.

The sound throughout this sequence is very abstract, with the music of the aborigines in the background. It establishes the mood and the sound for the rest of the film.

The teenager and her brother continue to plod over rocks and up and down mountains, trying to find their way out. The girl has a transistor radio, which serves as an audible symbol to me of their ever-present relationship to the world of automobiles, TV dinners, tall buildings, and modern society.

There are many wide-angle shots of small reptiles, snakes, rodents, and other Australian wildlife in the foreground as the children pass by. Throughout the entire film, the girl does not come to grips with the reality of the desert. The boy does, partially, and then only through the aborigine boy, because neither of the city youngsters ever notices the animals and the surrounding beauty. To them, the desert is simply an obstacle in their attempt to get home.

They experience great difficulty traversing the sand without water. The boy is nearly exhausted, and the girl carries him. Finally they come to an oasis. The brother and sister both sponge up the water and bathe. It is interesting again to see the city-bred youngsters and the neatness and modesty they display while bathing. The boy and girl are perhaps 75 miles from the nearest human being, but both are concerned about looking nice and not getting dirty. At one point, she says to her brother, "Don't walk in the water. You'll ruin your nice shoes."

In the morning, they awake, to discover that the water they drank and bathed in has dried up. They decided to wait where they are and hope the water will return. While the girl is resting, the boy begins to play. Suddenly he notices a figure off in the distance. He yells, and his sister sits up. They both look in amazement as a teenage aborigine boy comes closer. He is nearly naked and has a number of dead animals hanging at his side, with a swarm of flies flying around. He stares at the boy and girl.

The girl asks the aborigine boy for water, but he doesn't understand until her brother pantomimes the drinking of water. This beginning communication with the aborigine boy is a continuation of the girl's inability to understand the environment. Her relationship with the aborigine is exactly the same relationship she has to the rest of the environment.

Together the three begin to trek across the Australian terrain. The girl hopes that the aborigine boy will lead them to civilization. She has asked the aborigine, but he doesn't understand.

The aborigine provides food for the party by hunting. There is a beautiful sequence of the boy hunting down and killing a kangaroo. The actor who plays the part of the aborigine boy is a real aborigine and isn't so much acting for a film as playing out something he has done many times. His stalking movements are truly graceful. I became very aware of my ancient ancestral heritage as I watched the boy carefully stalk his kill. The filmmaker also used another interesting technique. He edited the film to intersperse quick scenes of meat being chopped in a butcher shop with scenes of the aborigine boy's beating the kangaroo and killing it. These sequences suggested to me our own "civilized" way of pouring meat, prewrapped in neat little packages in the supermarket. Perhaps we forget that the meat we eat was once alive and also had to be killed.

The filmmaker uses this concept of the aborigine way of hunting and obtaining food several times again in the film. In one beautifully done sequence, the director creates a metaphor of the raw naked meat of the animals the aborigine boy has killed, with the naked body of the girl swimming innocently in a pool.

In another sequence, the director suggests the encroachment of civilization when the aborigine boy witnesses two men in a jeep killing buffalo with high-powered rifles. The aborigine simply doesn't understand when the men drive away, leaving the meat to rot and taking the horns as a

trophy. There are several close shots of his face and quick short scenes of his tribe cooking and eating.

Perhaps the most significant part of the film happens when the aborigine boy believes the girl likes him. To the aborigine, her kindness is a sign of romantic interest. So he begins to perform a ceremonial mating dance. The girl is terrified. She doesn't understand his intentions or how to respond. Because she doesn't know what to do, the young aborigine continues in vain.

The next day, they discover his dead body hanging in the fork of a tree. She never realizes that he died because he believed he had been rejected.

The whole treatment of the sexual relationship, though overt, is done extremely well. Her view, of course, is a sophisticated concept conditioned by her modern environment. His concepts come from a primitive view. But because we view the film through the perspective of the girl and her brother, the images of sexual symbolism are suggested by what the aborigine boy perceives and what she thinks. For example, the brother playfully jumps on the aborigine, who grabs the younger boy and puts him in a nearby tree. Soon they are all playing in the tree. The editing of short scenes is used again. When the girl is hanging from a limb, we see in quick order a scene of an aborigine girl's buttocks, a scene of the girl's lower anatomy, a selected composition of tree limbs suggesting naked thighs, and a closeup of the aborigine boy's face. This sequence is repeated several times when suddenly the girl seems to partially understand. She runs away and begins combing her hair.

Soon after the girl and her brother find the aborigine's body, they discover a road that eventually leads them to civilization.

I believe the film should have ended here, but the filmmaker adds a final sequence of the girl, now perhaps married. She is in a kitchen. A young man comes in and begins to caress her. She looks wistfully off in the distance. There is a cut to a pool in the Australian forest. The girl, her brother, and the aborigine boy are swimming and playing naked and innocently in the pool. A narrator's voice is heard. I remember the part which says, ... "those happy highways that went and cannot come again."

I didn't like this ending because I'd rather believe that she never did understand the aborigine boy and his environment. The last sequence suggested to me that she did.

I especially liked the photography and the thematic ideas in *Walkabout*. However, there are parts of the film that seemed unreal and superficial. Questions about the unexplained relationship between the children and their father are not answered successfully for me. I needed to know why the children did not have affection toward their father and why the father wanted to kill his children and himself. I was not satisfied with the lack of explanation about why they left a road and took to the rugged terrain.

Even though I got a lot of enjoyment from the film, and though I learned and profitted emotionally from the experience of watching it, I felt somewhat empty and unfulfilled at the film's end. I think it may be that I never got very close to any of the characters in *Walkabout*.

Explanation:

Notice that this time I incorporated the plot throughout the composition as I described the plot, the theme, and the filmmaker's use of techniques to tell the story and influence the way we see the film.

Case Study Three: The African Queen

Various sentences have been underlined in my discussion of the third film. As in the second case study, the underlined sentences are examples given to support statements made about the film. Can you find the relationships between the underlined sentences and the opinions?

I like the film *The African Queen* very much. It is an adventure story and at the same time it is the story of a developing relationship and a love story between two people who need each other to survive.

Humphrey Bogart plays Charley, the dissolute skipper of *The African Queen,* a 30-foot river steamboat. Katharine Hepburn is Rose, an old maid type of thirty or so, who is in Africa with her missionary brother (played by Robert Morley).

Charley and Rose are forced to flee from World War I German troops down an uncharted river of central Africa to a lake after the troops set fire to a Congo village. Charley wants to wait for the war to end by hiding in the backwaters, but Rose wants to take the *African Queen* down the river to the large lake and there destroy a German gunboat that guards a route open to a British invasion force.

The two characters meet in combat. Charley thinks the idea is ridiculous; Rose is a very strong-willed person, and insists. Charley agrees to push off, finally, but very unwillingly.

The director, John Huston, establishes the characters. Their conflicts seem real because they become real, ordinary people.

Charley is a rather hard-boiled, bitter, hard-working man who knows and understands machinery and the river. He is practical. He knows enough to bury a body. For example, while waiting for dinner with Rose and her missionary brother, Charley's stomach begins to growl "something fierce." At another time, he sticks a screwdriver in the boiler to repair it temporarily. When Rose asks why he doesn't fix it, Charley replies by saying he likes to kick it. He drinks, which is revolting to the puritanical Rose. So she pours all of the alcohol in the river. This certainly upsets Charley—who calls her a "song-singing skinny old maid."

Rose is straight-laced, slightly prudish, and certainly morally upright and elegant; she is amost foolish in her ambitions. When Charley becomes drunk, she ignores him. Later she leaves him in a downpour while she is safely under a canopy. When Charley attempts to enter to avoid the rain, Rose is shocked and orders him out.

Huston fills the screen with many shots of the river and the *African Queen*. They seem to epitomize the shots of Rose and Charley, who are

One of the all-time film classics, *The African Queen,* still delights audiences when it is shown on television. Humphrey Bogart plays Charley and Katharine Hepburn is Rose. They plan to use his boat to blow up the German steamer *Luisa. (From the Horizon presentation* The African Queen ©*1951 Horizon Enterprises, Inc. Copyright renewed 1979 by Horizon Management, Inc.)*

constantly at each other's throats (and are later in love). After some particularly hazardous river rapids are navigated successfully, Charley and Rose are exuberant, hug and then kiss, and slowly begin to fall in love. She fixes him breakfast and he comforts her. The filmmaker makes a comparison between the beauty of their jungle surroundings and their love for each other.

Rose and Charley reinforce each other. Where Rose is courageous and daring, Charley is fearful and apprehensive. But Charley has the boat and the ability to keep it running. He has the strength, where she is somewhat frail. Together they make a team which daringly challenges the Germans and the forces of nature.

The adventure down the river, through the rapids, under the fire of the Germans, battling the insects and leeches and the river itself, brings Rose and Charley together. At first they have battled each other verbally, but as they meet and conquer each new obstacle to their ultimate fate, they grow to love each other more.

The film is uplifting. Two people can fall in love amid the turmoil of the struggle against the forces of nature. Even when all hope is gone, a benevolent force seems to help them after all their struggles causing a torrential downpour to raise the river. This allows the *African Queen* to float away from the river that has held the boat in its grip of the jungle growth and mud.

The African Queen is an exciting adventure and love story from the beginning to the very end. After they discover the *African Queen* has floated out into the lake and away from the grip of the mud, Rose and Charley see the German gunboat heading their way. Quickly they head the boat for the cover of the jungle. Here they fix a makeshift torpedo to the side of the *African Queen.*

The actual gunboat attack continues the adventure and excitement. Rose and Charley encounter a storm which destroys the *African Queen,* but they are rescued by the crew of the German gunboat.

They are questioned by the Germans and sentenced to hang. But again, a seemingly benevolent force reenters and saves them from certain doom. The German captain has bowed to their last request and married them. As the ropes are placed around their necks, the German boat runs into the remains of the *African Queen* and strikes the torpedo trigger. The gunboat is destroyed and sinks, but not before Rose and Charley jump to safety. The last scene is of Rose and Charley clinging to part of the *African Queen,* clearly still in love and thrilled with the adventure which they encountered together.

Case Study Four: **Places in the Heart**

Places in the Heart is a wonderful, tender, and deeply moving film about a young family that meets tragedy and adversity with dignity and courage. It is about love that endures.

The Spalding family has just sat down to a late afternoon Sunday supper, when the father, the local sheriff, is called away to look after a black drunk who is making threatening gestures with a gun. The drunk takes a few pot shots at a bottle he has thrown into the air, a few more shots at random, turns and fires one more shot. The shot hits the sheriff, killing him almost instantly.

Edna Spalding (Sally Field) is now a widow with two small children, a boy about nine and a girl about six. They live on a small farm near Waxahachie, Texas. Now that her husband is dead, she has to manage for her family and the farm. The time is the middle of the Depression in the 1930s. She hasn't any experience in the responsibilities which have befallen her. She doesn't even know how much money her husband made as sheriff.

Frank, the representative from the bank that holds the mortgage on the farm, suggests that she sell her property, farm the children out to relatives, and move in with her sister in town. Edna will have none of this idea because she wants to hold her family together and keep the farm. So she hires a black man named Moses (Danny Glover) to help her raise cotton.

The banker thinks this idea is ridiculous because, as he points out, many local farms have gone under with much better help trying to grow cotton at falling prices. However, she insists and with the help of Moses, they begin. The banker, feeling sorry for her, brings his brother-in-law to live as a boarder and help to pay the expenses. The brother-in-law, Mr. Will (John Malkovich) is blind, as a result of injuries suffered in World War I.

They struggle together in order to grow the cotton and to save the farm. Each member of the "family" needs the other. Mrs. Spalding needs the others in order to make the payment on the mortgage. Moses needs a job. Mr. Will needs a place to live, and the children need a loving parent.

There is a subplot, a love affair between Edna's brother-in-law and a married woman. Eventually, Edna's sister finds out and tells her husband that she can't love him any more.

I especially like the setting in this film. I really believed it happened during the Depression. Not only was the thirties'-style clothing, vintage automobiles, the town businesses, Depression programs and news on the radio and the farm itself right out of the thirties', but I found the dialogue, the mannerisms, the way the characters talked, and the thirties subdued color and dusty down-home background scenes to be very reminiscent of this period in American history. The elements were all put together to communicate a real sense of life in a small Texas town and on a farm fifty years ago.

The film communicated the enduring power of love. Her new "family" worked and cooperated together in order to harvest the cotton. The scenes of the people picking the cotton stand out in my mind. The sun bears down on the workers in the huge fields of cotton. There are many close shots of hands picking the cotton. It is quite evident that it is back-breaking hard work to pick the cotton. Yet there are also smiles and mutual assistance to get the job done. When high winds and a tornado threaten, each of the members struggle to help and save each other as they race to reach cover in a cellar.

I remember two scenes between Edna and Mr.

The worry and anguish of getting their cotton crop in on time is evident in the faces of Sally Field and Danny Glover, but the urgency of completing the picking is not understood by young Yankton Hatton and Gennie James. Writer-director Robert Benton set *Places in the Heart* in West Texas, close to his boyhood home. (©*1984 Tri-Star Pictures. All Rights Reserved.*)

Will. She is taking a bath in a big old metal tub in the kitchen after an exhausting day. Mr. Will comes bumping and bumbling into the kitchen because he has found that a record has been scratched by the children. Since he is blind, he doesn't realize until he accidently touches the water that she is in the tub. The close look on his face is priceless as he realizes this fact.

In another especially beautiful scene, Mr. Will asks Edna what she looks like. Love and sympathy are communicated through close shots, tender words, and excellent acting. The scene is especially moving because of Mr. Will's blindness. The widow responds with sympathy, love, and empathy for her blind boarder.

In a scene with Moses, Edna has returned from a dance and finds that Moses has been beaten by five members of the Ku Klux Klan. Moses is getting ready to move on because he fears they will return. The scene is dark. It is just light enough to see Moses' swollen face. Edna is con-

soling. She says they will miss him but understands why he has to leave. As Moses heads for the door, she tells him that he is the one that brought in the cotton harvest, that he did it better than any white man.

When her son, Frank, has been caught smoking behind a building at school, Edna is forced to give him a licking as his father would have. After the licking, she says, "God, I miss my husband," to Mr. Will.

In the last sequence in the film, the camera pans over the central people in the film as they sit in the pews in church. The pastor is preaching from 1 Corinthians :13. As he reads the holy definitions of love from the Bible, there is a closeup of the hands of the brother-in-law and his estranged wife. She slowly moves her hand and grasps his hand, holding it tight. The camera continues to pan, past Moses (who in reality has already left), past the children, to Edna and then to her husband (who had been killed) and her husband's killer (who, earlier, had been killed by mob action). When the camera pans to her husband and the killer, the church music swells, ". . . and He walks with me and talks with me and tells me that I am His own," from the classic hymn, "In the Garden."

I believe the director made this ending sequence to sum up the theme of enduring love, to say that, even though her husband is dead, he really lives on in their love.

Case Study Five: The String Bean

Edmond Sechan, the filmmaker of The String Bean, uses an interesting technique to contrast the difference between the drab, dark apartment of an old lady and the outside world. When the scenes are interior, the filmmaker uses black and white. When the scenes are outside, he uses color.

An old lady lives alone in an upstairs apartment. She seems very lonely. Everything in her apartment seems to reflect the loneliness. She makes purses. Most of the film centers around her work as she quickly sews up and down each purse.

One day she plants a bean seed in a flower pot and puts the pot on her window sill. The filmmaker shows the rapid passing of time as the old lady checks the progress of the bean plant through a series of scenes from different camera positions, showing her looking at and touching the plant.

The woman cares for the plant almost like we would care for a pet. One day, when she is sitting on a park bench with the plant, a child comes too close, and she moves the plant closer to her.

Perhaps at first impression, some viewers of this film would scoff at the care she gives the plant. But I believe she is very lonely, and any other life form is something for a lonely old lady to care for.

Soon the plant is too big for the pot, and she takes it to a nearby park. She plants the bean plant behind some cultivated flowers and shrubs.

Each day, she stops by to see how her plant is doing, keeping a wary eye on the park caretakers. Then, one day, as the old lady is sitting

The problems of the elderly can be highlighted by their actions. In the short film The String Bean, an old lady with nothing else to do concentrates on growing beans as her attempt to withstand the relentless advance of time. (The String Bean, courtesy of Contemporary Films/McGraw-Hill.)

on the park bench, she notices two caretakers weeding their way toward her plant. One of the men pulls out her plant and tosses it aside.

When the caretakers leave, the old lady goes to the bean plant and picks it up. She then picks off several pods.

Later we see her planting the new bean seeds in the pot again. I believe this ending tells me that life continues, even when one life is gone. Perhaps, in some way, the old lady sees her own life in the life of the bean plant.

I was particularly impressed by one scene. The filmmaker placed the camera directly above a spiral staircase. As the old lady climbs the seemingly endless flight of stairs, I could not help but notice her age and her living conditions.

Case Study Six: Toys

Toys of war seen in a department store window by small children become almost like the real monsters of destruction. Tanks and jeeps are blown up, and men are shot and burned.

The filmmaker, Grant Munro, has ingeniously created the action by using the technique of pixilation to make it appear as if a dramatic battle is taking place before the eyes of innocent children.

It is really a horrifying film. Some people may believe it is a film about the evils of war toys for children. I believe it goes further than this. I think it is a film about war and how inhumane it is for children and all living creatures. One scene stands out in my mind above all to illustrate this idea. A soldier suddenly goes up in flames. Cer-

tainly we know that the soldier is made of plastic, and the fire is simply causing the plastic to melt. However, the grotesque figure of the contorted toy is almost too near a realistic reminder of a real man.

I like the sound of cheerful music at the beginning and end of the film that is juxtaposed with the battle throughout the film.

Case Study Seven: Mountain Music

Mountain Music was made by Will Vinton, who also made *Closed Mondays* (an Academy Award winning short film) and *Rip Van Winkle.*

Mountain Music starts with pans of beautiful mountain landscapes and country background music. But shortly I discovered that the scenes of mountains, trees, and waterfalls that I was seeing were not real. The various scenes were completely made of clay! There were literally hundreds of evergreen trees made of clay covering

Filmmakers often use short films to convey powerful themes. As the toys of war come to life through the "magic" of pixillation, a form of animation, they begin to attack each other brutally. (Toys, *Courtesy of Contemporary Films/McGraw-Hill.*)

the mountains. Even the waterfall was gracefully moving globs of clay. It was done beautifully and realistically.

Then I saw various animals; a wolf, owl and other birds, frogs, and squirrels. They were all reacting to the country music. The animals appeared very human-like. I first noticed their eyes, which seemed to embody human qualities.

The scene moved upward and in the distance I saw a mountainous and forested landscape. Several people were playing simple, plain, harmonious musical instruments. The camera moved in a dolly shot to the people. One of the individuals looked like Roy Clark.

The scene changed as the camera moved from one individual to another. Then one of the characters moved a lever, and more instruments appeared and then amplifiers appeared. The music became progressively more abstract and louder.

As the film continued, the characters added more sophisticated parts to their instruments, and the level and volume of music increased. Several times, the scene would cut to the various animals shown earlier. Each of the animals was affected by this new, loud music. The birds flew away, the frogs jumped in the pond, the squirrels scurried off, and the wolf covered his ears with his paws!

Suddenly the ground and the whole landscape began to tremble when the music seemed to reach a peak. One of the mountains began to erupt in a volcano with lava pouring down the side into the forest and raising much tumult.

The characters playing the instruments seemed to fly out of the scene, and earthquakes shook the land as the lava covered the entire countryside.

Slowly the forests and mountains came to rest. Steam and smoke fell away, and the camera panned the countryside and ended with a fade.

I liked this film very much. The technique of clay and the bringing to life of the clay was done exceedingly well.

I think the filmmaker was showing me the beauty and harmony of nature as juxtaposed with the disruption and intrusion of human beings. I even "read" or saw further into the message of the filmmaker. He was saying that man's technology may often conflict with the natural world, but nature will triumph.

Case Study Eight: Kelly's Heroes

Following are two film case studies for *Kelly's Heroes*. Each study was written by a student in a film study class.

Note the emphasis each case study takes. Different perceptions and different specific scenes influenced each student.

It is important to remember there is a difference between the way in which these students describe a film and the way a professional film critic would write. The students writing about this film are simply identifying what they perceived. A film critic would be trying to sway the readers to a certain viewpoint.

Even though there are many errors in writing techniques and some of the film is misunderstood, Meghan (the first example) was able to describe many examples of techniques used by the filmmaker to influence the way she saw and understood the film.

She begins in paragraph (1) by listing various techniques used by the filmmaker to keep us interested and excited. In paragraph (2), she doesn't explain why she says the movie is a fantasy. She explains how the weather influenced how she felt about the characters.

A filmmaker really doesn't use comedy, sadness, and happiness to communiate (as Meghan states in paragraph (3). Rather the filmmaker uses the various techniques that Meghan describes in the paragraph to communiate these feelings.

In paragraph (4), Meghan begins to discuss the music—but doesn't continue with this idea. In the same paragraph, she starts describing the use of closeups of expressions—but only describes the expression of Clint Eastwood and what it meant to her. Then she jumps to another thought concerning a long shot and how it was used to communicate the scene involving the men walking toward the German tank.

It would be better when discussing or writing about a film, to stay on a single subject. Don't jump from one thought to another.

Paragraph (5) describes the use of rection shots and how she understood what was happening visually. Unfortunately Meghan doesn't go into enough detail in describing the use of intercutting. She only describes the scene with

Eastwood and the scene with the soldiers hiding in the church chapel (actually a tower atop the church).

Paragraph (7) was done well, but could have had more detail.

In paragraph (9), Meghan describes how much the men depend upon Kelly, but then doesn't give examples from the film to support this statement. She doesn't explain why, in her opinion, nor does she give any examples, to support the statement that the film is farfetched.

She attempts to point this idea of how the film is farfetched and a fantasy (as in paragraph (2)), but she doesn't really describe enough of her perceptions to give us an idea of what she means in paragraph (9).

Both of these film case studies written by students are excellent examples of what to do and what not to do. Even though writing excellence is important in good communications, it should be noted here that both students are merely exercising their skills in visual perceptions rather than attempting to write well.

Meghan could try to explain her opinions better by giving examples from the film as Alicia does.

Kelly's Heroes

(1)   The filmmaker used techniques like character conflict, controlling the weather, bombings, and torn-up buildings. He kept us interested in the film because it was full of excitement like when they were going through the minefield and one of them stepped on a bomb.

(2)   The actors were very convincing and, even though the movie was a fantasy, it made me think that it did happen. When one of the soldiers was killed, the filmmaker had it rain, but when they were fighting, it was sunny. By controlling the weather, the filmmaker communicated to us how they felt and what they were going through.

(3)   The filmmaker used comedy, sadness, and happiness. He communicated comedy, when Kelly had gotten a German drunk so he could find out where the gold was. A scene that showed happiness was when they had escaped the Germans with the gold. There was a lot of sadness when soldiers were killed and when their plans didn't work out.

(4)   The filmmaker played the same marching music when the Americans started off to steal the gold. The filmmaker used closeups of expressions. Clint Eastwood (Kelly), never changed his expression through the whole movie. He had an expression that communicated to us that he was always planning a strategy. The filmmaker used a lot of long shots. He used one in a courageous scene when Kelly and two other soldiers started walking towards a German tank.

(5)   When the American soldiers found the gold, the filmmaker showed each of them and their reaction when they saw all of the gold. When Kelly was sitting under a tree, the filmmaker used a soft focus shot. Because of the expression Kelly had, we knew that he wasn't sure if they were going to get away with stealing the gold.

(6)   When they were separating and hiding around the town, the filmmaker used a lot of cuts. He would go from Kelly to a soldier that was hiding in the church chapel, watching the German guards.

(7)   Before the soldiers left to get the gold, the filmmaker used juxtaposition showing a peaceful, quiet farm with lots of land, and then went to a scene of fighting and buildings being blown up.

(8)   The filmmaker communicated to us that all the soldiers depended on Kelly to get them through. When they had gotten across the German lines, it was a little farfetched, because the Germans would have been there. They didn't even know they had gotten across.

(9)   It was the kind of movie that you know couldn't really occur, but it's the kind of movie you can watch, relax, and enjoy. The filmmaker used a lot of war scenes to try to communicate to us that the movie was really true. When the filmmaker used extreme long shots, he communicated to us that the war was a major event.

—Meghan Kelly

In the next study about the same film, see how Alicia describes personal opinions, which are underlined; techniques, which are in bold type; and examples, which are in parentheses.

Kelly's Heroes

The filmmaker of *Kelly's Heroes* used a variety of techniques to communicate his ideas to the audience.

The filmmaker showed us a war in Germany. But unlike many other war films, he did not use very many long shots to show us a big war. He kept the ordeal rather personal with a lot of close-ups. With these shots, we saw each man's feelings of anguish, sorrow, and triumph. These close shots promoted personal involvement of the audience with the action.

The setting of the first scene was a good indication of the way these men had been living. **It was cold, raining, and rather unsanitary.** The filmmaker made me think that these men were tired of living like animals and would love to get out of the situation. (One soldier even commented on how unfair the situation was. He was complaining about the living conditions and the low pay—$60 a month.)

The men were then presented with a little something to make the war a worthwhile trip—a chance for $16 million in gold bars. (Their enthusiasm and amazement) for this chance was shown a great deal through **closeup shots. They showed closeups of various men** looking at the single gold bar (with their eyes almost popping out of their heads.) This showed a very basic theme—greed.

The closeness of this particular battalion was shown particularly when they were crossing the mine field. (When one man was blown up in a mine field,) the majority of the men—**in close shots**—looked as if the would cry. They were hesitant to get his identification from his body. But leadership is needed to guide these hesitant men. Here, Telly Savalas as Big Joe, told them to keep moving. This showed us that in a war, there isn't much room for emotion.

In the brief battle scene that followed, there were **many close-ups.** These shots showed us the personal feelings of each man. The sorrow of the loss of a friend was shown to us after (all the Germans were dead and the men looked into the mine field to find two more dead). **The shot of the three dead men** looked very distant. The other men felt helpless about their loss.

The character played by Carroll O'Connor was put in the film to show us what a joke the idea of war is. (He was all gung ho about hearing the radio communications from Kelly, Big Joe and all the rest.) But if he really knew their purpose, he would absolutely die! I think the filmmaker really make him look like a fool.

Triumph was another important element in the film. One example of this was (Oddball's facial expressions as he rode off in his newly-purchased tank. **His head was held high** and he looked as if the world was his own.) Another example of triumph, as well as the way Kelly's men felt about serving their country, was demonstrated by (the graffiti on the bank wall.) The message told the army what to do.

—Alicia Hammond

Reflections

1. Is it possible to react emotionally to film while —at the same time—analyzing film critically?

2. *Places in the Heart, The River,* and *Country* were three strong save-the-farm films released at the same time by different studios. Try to see at least two of them. What similarities or differences do you find?

3. *The African Queen,* frequently shown on television, has been termed a "film classic." Why? What makes a film a classic?

Activities

1. Take a notebook or a pack of 3 x 5 index cards to the movies. Jot down your immediate reactions to the film you see. Then look at the cards a few days later. Try to remember the film. Do you feel your reactions are still valid?

2. Your class will probably watch several short films. Look at them carefully. Discuss in class any differences in pacing you notice between the short films and a feature-length film.

3. One technique for evaluating film is to identify your perceptions and give examples supporting your statements. For each of the films you see in the next two weeks, list three statements, along with specific examples that illustrate your points.

Further Reading: *Check your library.*

MacKinnon, Kenneth. *Hollywood's Small-towns: An Introduction to the American Small-Town Movie*, Metuchen NJ, ScareCrow Press, 1984.

Sinyard, Neil. *Classic Movies*, Salem NH, Merrimack Publishers' Circle, 1984.

Gene Kelly

The Choreographer

Dancing in films—and the modern musical itself—reminds most filmgoers of Gene Kelly, the dancer–actor–choreographer whose vigorous style changed film dancing. Beginning on Broadway as a dancer and choreographer, Kelly moved to films and starred in many of the great movie musicals of the 1940s and 1950s, including For Me and My Gal *and* The Pirate *(with Judy Garland) and the memorable* On the Town, Singin' in the Rain, *and* An American in Paris.

Kelly has also played dramatic roles and has directed and produced many films and TV specials. His experimental film Invitation to the Dance *received several international awards, and Kelly was given a special Academy Award for his contributions to film choreography.*

Kelly's awards are many: the Jean Renoir Humanities award from the Los Angeles film Teachers Association; the Medaille de Vermeil award of the city of Paris; the Charles Chaplin award from UCLA; and the American Film Institute Life Achievement Award. As producer and host of the MGM feature film That's Dancing, *Kelly selected and narrated film clips to accompany the visual history of dance in motion pictures.*

When I first started dancing for motion pictures, I was shocked at the difference between dancing for the stage and dancing for the screen. It took me a long time to learn to change series of steps so they could be shot effectively for the camera.

All choreographers for films still have this problem. . . . Cinema is a two-dimensional medium, like painting. But dance is a three-dimensional art form, like sculpture. That is why so much attention has to be paid to the look of the dance as it's photographed. In the theater, when a number is finished, it's finished. In movies, when a number is choreographed, it still must be put on film. . . .

All dances for film should be choreographed with the camera in mind. The choreographer needs to consider all possible movements of the camera—its positions, its heights—so that each move of the performer is seen from the best possible angle.

A commonly done technique is just to photograph the dance straight on, as if it were being performed on a theater stage. While you can handle dance that way, you still have just a photographed stage dance and less of a cinematic number.

I often choose to shoot a dance out of doors. Immediately I've taken the dance number away from the limitations of the proscenium arch. I can see things from a different point of view. So can the camera.

Musicals have changed over the years. In the beginning, there were a lot of variety shows—musical films where style and characterization made no difference to the plot. Later on, there were films which featured exhibition-type dancing. The Fred Astaire–Ginger Rogers work portrayed that type quite successfully and took it up several notches. And still later, audiences began to accept dance as important in helping the story line to progress.

. . . While there were a lot of musicals later on in which dance helped to advance the story, *On the Town* was the first film to take the musical outside on a real location. Before that time, the usual thing was to shoot on studio backlots. We started at Brooklyn Navy Yard with three sailor coming down the streets of New York, singing and dancing and cutting all over. *On the Town* broke the standard mold of shooting musicals. . . . From that day, they were never quite the same.

. . . Ideally, a dance is part of the story that we tell, part of the plot of the film. The dance or dances should fit in as naturally as possible. They should help the story progress. A dance should be compatible with the style of the character who's doing it. . . . "Singin' in the Rain" was an easy number to work out. The music just naturally helped to dictate the dance. We knew we were using the song. Obviously it was going to be raining, and I was going to be singing. That number was worked out in many ways before we ever started to film. I was happy. I was in love. It was a joyous number. The dance had a certain simplicity of style, and it had to show happiness and joy.

Some numbers are a lot more complicated. They can become very intricate when one starts mentally setting them up to be photographed. The most difficult dance number I've ever done was my alter ego in *Cover Girl,* where I danced with myself. . . .

There can always be exceptions, but mostly I believe screen dances should be happy events. . . . I think that's the main reason for doing musicals. I want to create joy.

Milt Tatelman

The Creative Consultant

Creative consultant Milt Tatelman, who invented the slogan, "Yahoo, Mountain Dew. It will tickle your innards," as an advertising copywriter, continues his brand of hype and humor by manipulating potential film audiences.

From fourth grade to this day, Tatelman has kept a log of every movie he's seen, grading the films on acting and technique. After graduating from Case Western Reserve University as an English major, he entered the advertising curriculum at Bernard Baruch College of City University. His academic background didn't impress Madison Avenue agencies, but his film log did. They hired him.

His first movie campaign (for MGM'S Day of the Evil Gun, starring Glenn Ford and Arthur Kennedy), taught him ad-writing for films. "They had one enemy even more deadly than the Apache . . . each other!" he wrote, and audiences flocked to see the picture. Later, at Paramount Pictures, he rose to the position of creative director—then left to freelance.

I get paid to go to the movies.

I'm the person the studios and their agencies hire to dream up many of the ad campaigns that convince you and folks all over the world to see films.

I won't work on hard-core porno movies, or films that are excessively violent. My favorites are either horror movies or wild comedies—movies that I can have some fun with. I don't like westerns. I've worked for every major studio and a lot of the independents.

I've created campaigns for the best and the worst films, from those rated PG to R or X.

Some films I've worked on include *Little Big Man, Love Story, 2001: A Space Odyssey, Kramer vs. Kramer, The Blue Lagoon, Rocky I* and *II, The Godfather* and *Godfather II, Where Were You When the Lights Went Out?,* and *Star Wars.* I did early work on *Gandhi.* I handled some of the Elvis Presley pictures, including *Speedway.*

I prefer working on lousy movies because the challenge is greater. It's easy to make a good movie look super. It's more challenging to make a stinker a success.

I deal in paid-for-media advertising. It's a totally different field than publicity or public relations.

My job encompasses print, radio, in-theater promotions, and television.

For print, I create a basic selling strategy with the mood . . . the graphic look, and the copy I write, as well as creating press books for exhibitors.

Radio is the easiest medium to write for, because I can let listeners use their imagination. We can conjure up images . . . write copy we might not get away with on television.

In-theater promotions include teasers that describe movies you'll be seeing, maybe months in advance. Trailers are coming attractions or previews. That's my most difficult work. I must turn a 90-minute movie into a 3-minute trailer, choosing the scenes I want to show. I work closely with film editors, whom I con- sider true geniuses of the movie business.

Television ads sometimes make or break a film. The original copy for *Buster and Billie* was, "There's a girl like Billie in every school. All the guys knew about her, but Buster loved her, and nobody understood. Buster and Billie . . . It should have been a love story."

This copy had been submitted by another writer. I felt it was good but needed more emotion, so we showed the same film clips in the ad. But now we said, "He's the guy all the girls wanted. She's the girl who wanted all the guys. 1948—when everybody knew they were never meant for each other, but nobody knew what they meant to each other. If you've ever laughed and cried at the same time, you know how it feels to be Buster and Billie."

Variety said the picture became a hit because of the television campaign.

I'm usually brought into a picture after shooting stops. An ad agency calls me. I look at the entire movie or am shown a few of the better scenes. If I'm doing radio or television promotion, I'll write those scripts. If I'm doing a trailer, I'll write the script for that, breaking it down into columns labeled "video," "audio," and "billboarded on screen."

Studios hire me because I have a reputation for fast thinking and can usually solve a crisis quickly. Sometimes I fix what another creative consultant started, and, in the process, earn twice as much money as if I'd been hired in the first place.

It's a pleasure business. I've submitted the script for a trailer on a Monday. The film editor worked for the next two days, putting the trailer together. Then we finalized the presentation. On Friday, less than a week after I was first called, I presented the trailer to the studio. Often I'll work through the night. I work in New York, because that's where I want to live.

Every day is different for me. Some days I work with film editors. Yesterday, I gave a lecture. Tomorrow I may write a radio script. When I write an audio spot, I hear certain voices. Usually I suggest a particular announcer. One of my favorites is Adolph Caesar, who was nominated for an Oscar for his performance in *A Soldier's Story*. I use him for horror movies, because he can have a scary voice.

You exaggerate, because that's what the public wants. In the campaign for *Captain Kronos, Vampire Hunger,* I wrote, "For dear life, hold on to your blood, because your blood is *their* life—because your nightmare is *their* reality. They are history's deadliest vampires, creating a panic only one man can stop: Captain Kronos, Vampire Hunter! With death at every doorway, with trembling in every heart, now the terror must be challenged! Who lives to destroy the curse? Who duels to battle the undead? Who dares to bleed the bloodthirsty? At last, horror has met its match! *Captain Kronos, Vampire Hunter.* Rated PG—Parental guidance suggested."

Probably the most truthful lines I ever wrote came with this teaser for *Friday the 13th, Part IV.*

"Part I grabbed you . . . Part II shocked you . . . Part III hooked you. Now, the first suspense series that dares to go this far! *Friday the 13th, Part IV.* Because the worst is yet to come."

Recently I created a product reel, which is shown to the exhibitors to tell them about upcoming films. By the time those films get to theaters, however, I'll be working on many other movies.

Sometimes I never see the films I write about until they turn up on the late show or HBO.

I like manipulating audiences, because they realize that quite often they are being ripped off. I am giving the public something to look forward to . . . something new, coming next week. And, just as in life itself, the anticipation is usually much greater than the event.

11

Evaluating Film: You Be the Judge

We have looked at ways in which viewers can evaluate and discuss film. You can review the plot, describe the characters, mention a theme briefly, and discuss any unusual film techniques you've noticed. Often you mention how you reacted to a particular scene, giving the reason for these reactions.

This kind of evaluation works well in classroom discussion, but it is quite different from a critical review. How does a professional film critic look at a movie? Is he or she watching for the same points as a student seeing a film in class? What topics does a critic choose to write about in the film review? How does he or she express them?

The Critics—What Do They Do?

Most critics inject their own feelings into their reviews. Should they write more descriptive copy about the film? Is it their job to get people to see a film or at least to provide readers with enough information to make a decision? What should a critic be doing?

First of all, a critic on a newspaper or magazine usually does a number of other things besides going to movies and writing about them. "It's a hard field in which to find full-time employment," says Roger Ebert, Pulitzer Prize-winning film critic for the *Chicago Sun-Times.* "There are a lot of people interested in films, but most of them suppport themselves by doing something else than writing about movies. They teach. They are reporters. They hold other jobs. I don't think there are more than 100 people in the whole country who make a full-time living doing nothing but writing about film. I belong to the National Society of Film Critics, and I believe there are only 28 members."

Most of the critics who are writing about film did not start out intending to be film critics. "Once someone did a study of critics," says Gene Siskel, a Chicago film critic for both TV and newspaper. "By and large, the overwhelming pattern of how they got their jobs was happenstance. Being a critic was not their life-long goal. . . . Most of the critics felt they'd learned by doing—that is, they'd been trained on the job, rather than studying specifically for it."

Together, Ebert and Siskel have been co-hosting a hit television program, "At the Movies." Ebert also reviews films for WLS-TV Chicago, while Siskel's reviews are seen on WBBM-TV, another Chicago station. Ebert's "Movienews" commentaries are heard daily on the ABC radio network, and he is a lecturer on film in the University of Chicago's Fine Arts Program.

Self-trained in film appreciation, for the most part, and probably combining other activities with film review work, the average critic may well inject his or her own personality and reactions into film reviews. In fact, the above-average critics feel it's their duty to do so.

"I go to the movies," says Ebert, "with every experience I can muster—not only in terms of knowing what a particular movie is, or could be, but also with my experiences of life. Once I start watching a film, I let the movie happen to me. Then I try to combine myself and the movie into my review.

"I vary my reviews about describing film on various levels. One level is pure reporting. What was the film about? What kind of characters did it have? What was the story about? Was it a particular kind of movie, such as a western? Did it raise any issues that are interesting in the current context of events?

"On another level, you can discuss the movie in terms of the craft of film—the mechanical shark in *Jaws,* the color in *Moulin Rouge.*

"On still another level, in a more subjective view, you can just try to report what happened to you as you watched that movie. Were you representative of the movie audience? Were you moved and, if so, how and why?"

Let's see how all these factors combine in professional critics' reviews.

The Critic's Review: A Case Study

One of the top 10 films of all time, in terms of box-office receipts, is *Indiana Jones and the Temple of Doom,* a Lucasfilm Ltd. production. The movie was directed by Steven Spielberg and starred Harrison Ford as the macho archeologist whose breathtaking scrapes offer a mile-a-

As intrepid archaeologist Indiana Jones, Harrison Ford faces death in a remote Asian jungle at the hands of believers in a thugee cult. Audiences and critics had mixed reviews for the film, citing excessive violence. (Indiana Jones and the Temple of Doom ©Lucasfilm Ltd. (LFL) 1984. All Rights Reserved. Courtesy of Lucasfilm Ltd.)

minute thrills. By May 30, 1984, only three weeks after *Variety* critic "Cart." reviewed the film, *Variety* was reporting that *Indiana Jones and the Temple of Doom* had achieved the largest first week gross in the history of motion pictures: $45,709,328.

Make no mistake—Lucas, Spielberg, and Ford are a bankable combination. Between them, George Lucas and Steven Spielberg have made 6 of the 10 top-grossing movies of all time, and Harrison Ford has starred in five of them: three *Star Wars* films and two Raidersland epics.

Their astounding popularity translates into healthy dollars beyond theatrical receipts. Licensing royalties from *Star Wars* saga characters and *Indiana* spin-off merchandise have been substantial.

When *Star Wars* was first shown on cable television, ratings zoomed. *Time* magazine reports that *Raiders of the Lost Ark* has already become the largest-selling video cassette of all time.

Clearly Ford's low-key approach to acting and his personal magnetism are hits with viewers. But what about the critics? How did they react to this "prequel," as Lucas calls it—a film about Indiana Jones set in a time period (1935) before *Raiders of the Lost Ark* (1981) supposedly took place?

Library Resources

There are several library sources to help you locate movie reviews. You'll find them indexed—first by "motion picture reviews" and then by the title of each film—in the *Readers' Guide to Periodical Literature*, a reference index universally available.

Another source of movie review listings is a reference tool called *The Magazine Index*, first available in 1976. This handy listing on microfilm is updated monthly and includes reviews from a wide variety of periodicals. Unlike the *Readers'*

Guide, The Magazine Index assigns a rating to each review, rather like a report card. By using *The Magazine Index,* you can tell quickly whether critics loved or hated the film. You can find the actual texts of favorable or unfavorable reviews by checking back issues of the magazines your library has available. Many libraries, especially those in major metropolitan areas, also subscribe to a service that can get you copies of articles from periodicals your own library doesn't carry. Check with your reference librarian. Usually this service is available without charge, though there may be a delay until your library can get the periodicals for you.

Major metropolitan newspapers like *The New York Times,* the *Los Angeles Times,* and the *Chicago Tribune* regularly review films. These reviews are listed in the annual index for that newspaper.

Movie Violence

George Lucas wrote the basic story for *Indiana Jones and the Temple of Doom,* and Willard Huyck and Gloria Katz did the screenplay (or shooting script). The film was expensive to make. In addition to elaborate technical and special effects (by Industrial Light & Magic, the Lucasfilm-created complex north of San Francisco that brought together top technicians who developed complex technology), film production units shot at Thorn EMI-Elstree Studios (near London, England); in California, in Macau, and in Sri Lanka. A separate unit did aerial photography.

Indiana Jones and the Temple of Doom won praise from critics for its visual and technical effects, especially for an underground rail chase featuring Ford, Kate Capshaw, and Ke Huy Quan that was actually created by integrating stop-motion animation techniques involving hundreds of photographs of elaborately constructed models

This mine chase from *Indiana Jones and the Temple of Doom* earned an Academy Award for its special effects. Miniature models were photographed in stop-motion animation, then integrated with live action footage for a hair-raising sequence. (Indiana Jones and the Temple of Doom ©*Lucasfilm Ltd. (LFL) 1984. All Rights Reserved. Courtesy of Lucasfilm Ltd.)*

with live action sequences. But critics generally had considerable reservations about parts of the story.

Newsweek's Jack Kroll called the sacrificial sequence in the temple of doom "a careening juggernaut of beatings, gougings, and crunchings." Gene Siskel, *Chicago Tribune* and local CBS-TV film critic, described it as "endless human melting pot," and said, "When we see Willie (Kate Capshaw) dangling over molten lava, frankly we wish she would fall in." David Denby, critic for *New York* magazine, called the film "the best-sustained idiot-adventure movie in film history," and the magazine headlined his review, "Lost in the Thrill Machine."

Singled out for unfavorable mention by several critics was the progression of—as they saw it—unnecessary violence in a film youngsters were sure to watch. Chicago's Gene Siskel put it this way: "Good luck on keeping your little ones away from this movie, but you just might want to be there to help cover their eyes."

The *Los Angeles Times* carried a sidebar next to Sheila Benson's review describing the reaction of Los Angeles television critic Gary Franklin, quoted as saying, "*Indiana Jones* is no different from the *Halloweens* of the film world in the way that it desensitizes young viewers to violence." Franklin, whom the *Times* reported gave *Scarface* a rating of 9 (of a possible 10), reportedly defended that rating by arguing that the violence in *Scarface* carried a weighty message.

"I think the people who produce films should have a social responsibility," the *Times* reported Franklin as saying, "and I'm in a position where I can speak out and be heard. One of the beauties of working in this town is that you have an effect, even subconsciously, on the people who decide what movies get made."

Role of the Critic

Franklin's comments raise interesting questions about the role of a movie critic. *Should* the critic's function be to influence moviemakers who produce future films, or should the critic's aim be to review and describe films so prospective viewers can decide whether or not to see them? To what extent should a critic's *personal* philoso-

phies on social questions influence his or her reviews?

How did critics handle *Indiana Jones and the Temple of Doom?* At the end of the chapter, you'll find three reviews: Sheila Benson's *Los Angeles Times* review; Ralph Novak's look at *Indiana* in the "Picks and Pans" section of *People Weekly;* and *Variety's* review.

Sheila Benson

Benson's review, published just as *Indiana Jones* was released in Los Angeles, assumes right from the beginning that everyone reading it has already seen *Raiders of the Lost Ark.* Her tip-off comes with the phrase, "Bring the intrepid Indy back to us." She says Harrison Ford is "better than ever," and reminds us "we know ol' Indy better than to imagine he's on the trail for crass reasons."

Throughout her review, Benson uses a psychological technique called projection—defined as attributing your own ideas, feelings, and attitudes to other people. She tells us what she assumes Lucas and Spielberg were thinking: that stunts were behind the box-office success of *Raiders,* and that *Indiana Jones* had to have bigger and better exploits in order to succeed financially.

Benson asserts that Lucas and Spielberg remembered the cliff-hanging thrills and suspense of early Saturday-matinee movie serials and tried to recreate that terror/delight combination in *Indiana Jones.*

But is she right?

Serials like *Tom Mix* and *The Lone Ranger* were the mainstay of movie theaters in the thirties, when admission cost a nickel and youngsters had to wait a whole week to find out what would happen in the next episode of their favorite thriller. Lucas was born in 1944; Spielberg, in 1947. George was 10 years old before his father agreed to buy a television set. Even though he watched serials like *Flash Gordon Conquers the Universe* and *Don Winslow of the Coast Guard,* broadcast nightly over a San Francisco channel, there was a big difference between seeing them on the wide screen in a packed movie house, as Depression youngsters did, and catching them at dinner on the small black and white TV the Lucas family owned.

One biography of Lucas, at least, seems to disprove Benson's claim. In *Skywalking—The Life and Films of George Lucas,* author Dale Pollock says, "When Lucas decided to do a high-adventure children's film *(Star Wars),* he went back and looked at the original serials like *Flash Gordon.* 'I was appalled at how I could have been so enthralled with something so bad,' he recalls."

Benson asserts the 1940 film, *The Thief of Bagdad,* starring native boy Sabu in an Arabian Nights-like tale, triggered Indiana, Willie, and Short Round's bout with roaches and stuffed beetles at the Maharajah's palace in the Lucas/Spielberg film. She claims that the two men have reworked the movie myths of their childhood, making them unforgettable in the memories of today's youngsters.

Is Benson projecting her own concerns, rather than Lucas' and Spielberg's actual working processes? Perhaps. Or perhaps she's using these statements to suggest to readers that she's widely acquainted with film and film history, making us more ready to acknowledge her expertise and qualifications as a film reviewer. Such a conclusion is strengthened by her use of the phrase, "in those old films," suggesting to readers she's a veteran moviegoer.

Her allusion to Children's Crusade overtones also establishes her as knowledgable in the way most of us are not. For many people who read her review, "Children's Crusade" will not have a specific meaning, though most people know that a crusade is a fight for a belief against strong opponents.

But Benson's mention of the Children's Crusade means more. In the thirteenth century, there was a real Children's Crusade. Bands of youngsters from northern Europe set out to walk across the Alps to fight the Moslems in the Holy Land. They struggled on without food, clothing, or equipment. The fate of most of these children is uncertain, but many were sold into slavery in North Africa.

Benson, then, is suggesting that the slave children in *Indiana Jones and the Temple of Doom* were intended to remind viewers of the real Children's Crusade—a debatable point, since the youngsters in the mines were kidnapped from their impoverished village, rather than voluntarily following a cause.

Finally, is Benson's opinion of Kate Capshaw's performance as Willie Scott biased because she's a women reviewer? Not necessarily; other reviewers have found fault with the character. Gene Siskel *(Chicago Tribune)* describes Willie bluntly: "a whining deadhead. Karen Allen (Ford's love interest in *Raiders),* please come back; Indiana needs you." Benson blames the screenwriters for Willie's deficiencies, rather than Capshaw's acting. Yet she calls Harrison Ford, as Indiana Jones, "the master of pure male charm."

Benson's verdict? Indy's *Temple of Doom* is desecrated by the film's problems, despite superior effects, direction that makes the characters real, and a brilliantly shot and edited opening sequence.

Ralph Novak

Ralph Novak's review of *Indiana Jones* for *People Weekly* is less kind to Spielberg and Lucas. Novak likes the opening sequence and first half of the film, and praises the makers for their "happily cartoonist imagination."

Though Novak obviously enjoyed *Raiders,* calling it a megasmash and a triumph, he not only feels *Indiana Jones* doesn't measure up to the earlier film but also pans the picture.

To prove his contention that the film is "a relentless, tedious stream of graphic brutality," Novak lists the ways in which violence occurs: "People are chained, shot, ground up, crushed, stabbed, poisoned, thrown to crocodiles, clubbed, attacked using voodoo dolls, bounced off rocks, and drowned." Novak himself gives us a relentless, tedious stream of action verbs, hoping we'll react as he feels viewers do in the film—by turning off.

In fact, though all the episodes Novak mentions do occurs in *Indiana Jones,* the poisoning episode (Harrison Ford vs. a Shanghai gangster) comes before the grinding up, and the voodoo dolls (Short Round vs. the boy Maharajah) before the crocodiles. Could Novak have written his review as an appeal against violence, amassing evidence out of sequence to make it sound more impressive?

The shooting, stabbing, and poisoning, in fact, are part of the same wild, colorful, nightclub brawl that Novak praises. They take place in the film's first hour, the same hour that Novak calls "a worthy sequel" to *Raiders*.

Novak makes the assumption that Spielberg and Lucas intended *Indiana Jones and the Temple of Doom* primarily for children. Consequently, he looks at his review as a warning to parents of young children, whom he urges to keep from seeing the movie.

That approach—as moral guardian, protecting youngsters—doesn't jibe, however, with his wish that Capshaw (as Willie Scott) would match *Raiders'* Karen Allen in sexy spunk.

A comparison of Novak's review with that of Benson's brings out important differences. Novak accused Spielberg and Lucas, whom he calls villains, of *not caring,* of deliberately violating the trust parents have for their good-natured approach to movies. Benson, on the other hand, puts herself inside the minds of the filmmakers, and she blames them for the effect she feels the thuggee rites will have on young children seeing the film.

Variety

Finally, the fast-paced review of *Indiana Jones* from the daily issue of *Variety* provides still another look at how professional critics review a film.

"Cart.,"—*Variety* doesn't identify reviewers by full names—writes for an audience that's film-knowledgable; most readers are in the entertainment industry. Consequently, the review is top-heavy with technical credits, since a listing indicating someone worked on a Lucas/Spielberg major hit may bring that person job offers on future projects. Many readers are show business professionals looking for a capsule tag on which they may base future casting or hiring technicians and production people for their own films.

Variety's review also assumes familiarity with *Raiders.* It compares the two productions in pace, amount of incidents, noise level, budget, close calls, and violence. *Indiana Jones,* it says, is a letdown, but that won't matter to box-office receipts.

We can learn much from the *Variety* review

about the complexities of making a blockbuster film. There are 14 lines listing credits for special visual effects; though you may not be as conscious of special effects in *Indiana Jones* as you were in the *Star Wars* trilogy, a great deal of time, effort, and money was spent in producing and integrating those shots, and in fact, they won an Academy Award.

Technical crews are listed for shooting in the United Kingdom (including a second unit in London), for California, for Macau, and for Sri Lanka. The difficulties in planning, financing, and overseeing such a complex production as *Indiana Jones* become apparent as you read the credits. A special aerial unit was needed for the shots of the trimotor plane in which Indy, Willie, and Short Round make their getaway, only to find that the treacherous pilots have bailed out and they must escape before the plane crashes into a mountainside.

It's possible to say that this listing of professional talent by the reviewer is an attempt to give credit for technical achievement. Because *Variety* is the trade paper for show business, its readers have a special interest in the behind-scenes accomplishments of films. Usually, giving such professional credit is omitted by newspaper and magazine critics who write for a general audience, because their readers are not interested.

The *Variety* reviewer spends the most space recapping Indiana's story rather than critiquing the film. "Cart." doesn't care whether readers think he or she is an expert or not; he or she tells us the plot, blames director Spielberg for Capshaw's "manic, frenzied performance," and says kids from 10 years old on up will eat up the film.

There's less philosophizing in this review than in Benson's or Novak's, though the *Variety* writer warns that younger children may be frightened by the banquet menu of live snakes, eyeball soup, and monkey brains, and by the vividness of the sacrificial ceremony.

Still, he feels, the film will be a box-office smash, not only because any sequel to *Raiders* had a ready-and-waiting audience, but also because technical achievements like the runaway mine car sequence, Ford's performance, and the Spielberg/Lucas formula make *Indiana Jones* a sure-fire hit.

Indy's 'Temple of Doom' Desecrated by
Too Much Worship of Special Effects*

Sheila Benson

As they plotted the best way to bring the intrepid Indy back to us, the makers of *Indiana Jones and the Temple of Doom* (selected theaters) listened to the wrong pulse-takers. They got it into their heads that the charm of their first film was its stunts, and if something wasn't whizzing past Indiana every second—or vice versa—it would be all over for the movie.

So what we have is an endurance test of breakneck action—wall-to-wall, mind-contracting and finally numbing perils for Harrison Ford's Indiana, for his new sidekick, Ke Huy Quan as 12-year-old Short Round, and for Kate Capshaw as blond Willie Scott, a Shanghai nightclub singer penciled in for this ride.

Director Steven Spielberg and George Lucas, who wrote the original story and co-produced the picture, remember acutely the combination of delight and shivery terror that the Saturday-matinee movie serials produced. But, ironically, with *The Temple of Doom* they've outdone themselves, and it's the kids who are the losers. Someone has misread the voltage on state-of-the-art effects, and they're going to have to scrape youngsters out from under the seats like old chewing gum with this one. If there ever was a film to point up the need for a stringently policed PG rating, this is it.

What's particularly sad is that Ford is even better than before. He's now the master of pure male charm with a minimum of obvious effort, and his Indiana is a lovely character. His scenes with the enchanting Short Round strike strong father-and-son chords for the youngsters in the audience. About his scenes with Willie, more in a minute.

But it's because the effects are as superior as they are, and the direction has made all these characters so real, that problems set in. The film has Children's Crusade overtones, and plaintive little kidnapped children are at the heart of the story (improbably, but no matter). There is the greatest

encouragement for kids to identify with both the derring-do of Short Round and the ghastly condition of the young beaten prisoners.

Opening in the Shanghai nightclub (the Obi-Wan, with a tip of a top hat to Mr. Lucas) for a sequence of diamonds, poison and antidotes that is brilliantly shot and edited, we move to India and a famine-plagued village whose children have all been taken away, along with the stone from their local shrine. Indiana, accompanied by Short Round and Willie, sets out to remedy all that.

The stone will supposedly bring fortune and glory, but we know ol' Indy better than to imagine he's on the trail for such crass reasons, no matter what he growls. The precipitous journey brings Indiana et al. to the palace of a child maharajah (Raj Singh) with dire hints about the forbidden cult of thuggee.

At the palace there is one of every sort of danger. Remember Sabu and his duel with the hairy-legged spider in *Thief of Badgdad*? The film makers do, with a vengeance. Mr. Spielberg's thing is bugs. He faces his fears by having his actors ankle-deep in roaches, wearing living roach brooches, eating stuffed beetle banquets. But in those old films there was a sequence of press and release that gave us breathing time. And I can't remember sequences involving sacrificial victims in which you felt terror so horribly.

You will here. We must see a thuggee rite, headed by Mola Ram (Amish Puri, straight from four awards as Best Villian in Hindu films—I'll say), to appreciate that these are vicious fellows. We would have taken their word for it, like the olden days. Instead, the new realism follows a hysterical native to his death by incineration, strapped to a huge wire basket, his living heart having been plucked out of him at the height of a hypnotic rite. (Like the Philippine faith healers, Mola Ram's ''surgery'' is magical. His victim's chest closes up again and he has minutes more to writhe, in absolute terror and agony, before he dies in the flames.)

There are scenes with the little kidnapped chil-

*Copyright, 1984, Los Angeles Times. *Reprinted by permission.*

dren and threats to Short Round (not to mention Willie) that are haunting. (Put out of your mind the question of why anyone wanting strong laborers in their mines would impress a frail batch of half-starved Indian children.) And even if you had no concern for the children in the audience, is this anyone's notion of a good time at the movies? The bravura parts—dives into rapids, a no-brakes ride through a mine shaft, a repeat of the race against a crushing stone, but with a wall of water taking the place of the stone—are somehow more exhausting than exciting.

And there's one last problem: Indiana's lady of the moment. Screenwriters Willard Huyck and Gloria Katz may have seen Willie Scott's constant complaints as adorable, but it's not a charm that travels well. Between her anguish over a split nail and her nastiness about what she will not eat (the meager best a starving village can provide), her appeal is minimal. Actress Capshaw may have other, signal qualities to be revealed in later films; here she seems to have been hired for her shriek in a film perhaps better called *Indiana Jones and the Beverly Hills Princess*.

One of the greatest assets Spielberg and Lucas have had was their ability to go straight to the movie myths of their childhoods and, in reworking them, enrich a new generation of moviegoers. This time it feels as though they could never erase these movies from their memories, and now no one else will be able to either.

As Indiana's sidekick, Short Round, the appealing Ke Huy Quan captured favorable reviews, though the film itself was not universally accepted by critics. Box office receipts soared, however, putting *Indiana Jones and the Temple of Doom* firmly in the list of Top 10 pictures of all time. (©*Lucasfilm Ltd. (LFL) 1984. All Rights Reserved. Courtesy of Lucasfilm Ltd.*)

Reminiscent of Busby Berkeley's lavish production numbers, the opening sequence of *Indiana Jones and the Temple of Doom* features Kate Capshaw as a Shanghai nightclub entertainer, singing *Anything Goes* in Chinese. The stacatto tapdancing and brisk pace of the tune provide an introduction to the gunfire that follows, sending viewers off with Indy on another razzle-dazzle adventure. (Indiana Jones and the Temple of Doom ©*Lucasfilm Ltd. (LFL) 1984. All Rights Reserved. Courtesy of Lucasfilm Ltd.*)

*Indiana Jones and the Temple of Doom**
Ralph Novak

For its first hour this much-anticipated film, directed by Steven Spielberg from a story by George Lucas, is a worthy sequel to 1981's megasmash, *Raiders of the Lost Ark*. It opens with Kate *(A Little Sex)* Capshaw singing *Anything Goes,* mostly in Chinese, at a Shanghai nightclub in 1935. Harrison Ford—returning as the superintrepid archaeologist Indiana Jones—is among the listeners. Soon a wild, colorful brawl ensues. Capshaw, Ford and their henchboy—played charmingly by Ke Huy Quan, 12, the son of Vietnamese refugees—flee via roadster, trimotor plane, life raft and elephant. By this time, they're a drought-stricken Indian valley, embroiled in a search for a sacred stone. All the verve, wit and happily cartoonish imagination that made *Raiders* such a triumph seem to be back. But what then follows may be the most unconscionable 45 minutes in movie history, a relentless, tedious stream of a graphic brutality. Children are whipped and kicked. One sacrifice victim's heart is torn out of his chest and then—somehow still alive—he is very slowly deep-fried in a pit of molten something-or-other. People are chained, shot, ground up, crushed, stabbed, poisoned, thrown to crocodiles, clubbed, attacked using voodoo dolls, bounced off rocks, drowned. This is all depicted in the most detailed, sadistic way. It is an astonishing violation of the trust people have in Spielberg and Lucas' essentially good-natured approach to movies intended primarily for kids. If they had set out to prove that they could get away with anything— insult the intelligence of viewers and literally make them sick— they couldn't have done it more effectively. Ford is his usual laconic self. When he drinks a trance-inducing drug, it's all but impossible to tell if it's working, since there's so much trance in his basic acting style. While Capshaw is attractive, her character is almost all helpless-dumb-blonde; she isn't allowed to develop any of the sexy spunk Karen Allen showed in *Raiders*. Weak acting and undeveloped characters are the least of this film's problems, though. The ads that say "this film may be too intense for younger children" are fraudulent. No parent should allow a young child to see this traumatizing movie; it would be a cinematic form of child abuse. Even Ford is required to slap Quan and abuse Capshaw. But then there are no heroes connected with this film, only two villians; their names are Spielberg and Lucas. (PG)

Reprinted from PEOPLE WEEKLY, *June 4, 1984,* © Time Inc.

Indiana Jones and the Temple of Doom*
Cart.

(Color)

Noisy, overkill prequel headed for smash b.o.

Hollywood, May 7

A Paramount Pictures release of a Lucasfilm Ltd. production. Executive producers, George Lucas, Frank Marshall. Produced by Robert Watts. Directed by Steven Spielberg. Stars Harrison Ford. Screenplay, Willard Huyck, Gloria Katz, from a story by Lucas. Camera (Rank color; prints by DeLuxe), Douglas Slocombe; editor, Michael Kahn; music, John Williams; sound design (Dolby), Ben Burtt; production design, Elliot Scott; chief art director, Alan Cassie, set decoration, Peter Howitt; special visual effects supervisor, Dennis Muren at Industrial Light & Magic; costume design, Anthony Powell; mechanical effects supervisor, George Biggs; second unit director, Michael Moore; choreography, Danny Daniels; associate producer, Kathleen Kennedy. Reviewed at MGM Studios, Culver City, Calif., May 7, 1984.

(MPAA Rating: PG). Running Time: 118 MINS.
Indiana Jones .... Harrison Ford
Willie Scott .... Kate Capshaw
Short Round .... Ke Huy Quan
Mola Ram .... Amrish Puri
Chattar Lal .... Roshan Seth
Capt. Blumburtt .... Philip Stone
Also with: Roy Chiao, David Yip, Ric Young, Chua Kah Joo, Rex Ngui, Philip Tann, Dan Aykroyd, Pat Roach.

Special Visual Effects Unit Credits

Industrial Light & Magic; visual effects supervisor, Dennis Muren; chief cameraman, Mike McAlister; optical photography supervisor, Bruce Nicholson; ILM general manager, Tom Smith; production supervisor, Warren Franklin; matte painting supervisor, Michael Pangrazio; modelshop supervisor, Lorne Peterson; stop-motion animation, Tom St. Amand; supervising stage technician, Patrick Fitzsimmons; animation supervisor, Charles Mullen; supervising editor, Howard Stein, production coordinator, Arthur Repola; creative consultant,

Phil Tippet. Additional optical effects, Modern Film Effects.

Additional Technical Credits

U.K. crew: assistant director, David Tomblin; production supervisor, John Davis; production manager, Patricia Carr. U.S. Crew: production manager, Robert Latham Brown; assistant director, Louis Race. First unit: stunt arrangers, Vic Armstrong (studio) and Glenn Randall (location); additional photography, Paul Beeson; sound mixer, Simon Kaye; chief modeller, Derik Howarth; chief special effects technician, Richard Conway; floor effects supervisor, David Watkins; research, Deborah Fine; post-production services, Sprocket Systems.

London second unit: second unit director, Frank Marshall; assistant directors, David Bracknell, Michael Hook; cameraman, Wally Byatt; floor effects supervisor, David Harris.

California unit: second unit director, Glenn Randall; director of photography, Allen Daviau; art direction, Joe Johnston; stunt coordinator, Dean Raphael Ferrandini; special effects supervisor, Kevin Pike; sound mixer, David McMillan; production coordinator, Lata Ryan.

Asian unit: assistant director, Carlos Gil. Macau: production supervisor, Vincent Winter; production manager, Pay Ling Wang; assistant director, Patty Chan. Sri Lanka: production supervisor, Chandran Rutnam; production manager, Willie de Silva; assistant director, Ranjit H. Peiris; steadicam photography, Garret Brown; art direction, Errol Kelly; sound mixer, Colin Charles.

Aerial unit: second unit director, Kevin Donnelly; director of photography, Jack Cooperman.

Just as *Return of the Jedi* seemed disappointing after the first two *Star Wars* entries, so does *Indiana Jones and the Temple of Doom* come as a letdown after *Raiders of the Lost Ark*. This is ironic, because director Steven Spielberg has packed even more thrills and chills into this

*©1984, Variety. *Used with permission.*

follow-up than he did into the earlier pic, but to exhausting and numbing effect.

End result is like the proverbial Chinese meal, where heaps of food can still leave one hungry shortly thereafter. Will any of this make any difference at the box office? Not a chance, as a sequel to *Raiders,* which racked up $112,000,000 in domestic film rentals, has more built-in want-see than any imaginable film aside from *E.T. II.*

Spielberg scenarists Willard Huyck and Gloria Katz, and George Lucas, who penned the story as well as exec producing with Frank Marshall, have not tampered with the formula which made *Raiders* so popular. To the contrary, they have noticeably stepped up the pace, amount of incidents, noise level, budget, close calls, violence and everything else, to the point where more is decidedly less.

Prequel finds dapper Harrison Ford as Indiana Jones in a Shanghai nightclub in 1935, and title sequence, which features Kate Capshaw chirping Cole Porter's *Anything Goes,* looks like something out of Spielberg's *1941.*

Ford escapes from an enormous melee with the chanteuse in tow and, joined by Oriental moppet Ke Huy Quan, they head by plane to the mountains of Asia, where they are forced to jump out in an inflatable raft, skid down slopes, vault over a cliff and navigate some rapids before coming to rest in an impoverished Indian village.

Community's leader implores the ace archaeologist to retrieve a sacred, magical stone which has been stolen by malevolent neighbors, so the trio makes its way by elephant to the domain of a prepubescent Maharajah, who lords it over an empire reeking of evil.

Remainder of the yarn is set in this labyrinth of horrors, where untold dangers await the heroes. Much of the action unfolds in a stupendous cavern, where dozens of natives chant wildly as a sacrificial victim has his heart removed before being lowered into a pit of fire.

Ford is temporarily converted to the nefarious cause. Ke Huy Quan is sent to join child slaves in an underground quarry, and Capshaw is lowered time and again into the pit until the day is saved.

What with John Williams' incessant score and the library full of sound effects, there isn't a quiet moment in the entire picture, and the filmmakers have piled one giant setpiece on top of another to the point where one never knows where it will all end.

Film's one genuinely amazing action sequence, not unlike the airborne sleigh chase in *Jedi* (the best scene in that film), has the three leads in a chase on board an underground railway car on tracks resembling those of a rollercoaster.

Sequence represents a stunning display of design, lensing and editing, and will have viewers gaping. A "Raidersland" amusement park could be opened profitably on the basis of this ride alone.

Overall, however, pic comes on like a sledgehammer, and there's even a taste of vulgarity and senseless excess not apparent in *Raiders.*

Kids 10-12 upwards will eat it all up, of course, but many of the images, particularly those involving a gruesome feast of live snakes, fried beetles, eyeball soup and monkey brains, and those in the sacrificial ceremony might prove extraordinarily frightening to younger children who, indeed, are being catered to in this film by the presence of the adorable 12-year-old Ke Huy Quan.

Compared to the open-air breeziness of *Raiders, Indiana Jones,* after the first reel or so, possesses a heavily studio-bound look, with garish reds often illuminating the dark backgrounds.

As could be expected, however, huge production crew at Thorn EMI-Elstree Studios, as well as those on locations in Sri Lanka, Macao and California, and in visual effects phase at Industrial Light & Magic, have done a tremendous job in rendering this land of high adventure and fantasy.

Ford seems effortlessly to have picked up where he left off when Indiana Jones was last heard from (though tale is set in an earlier period), although Capshaw, who looks fetching in native attire, has unfortunately been asked to react hysterically to everything that happens to her, resulting in a manic, frenzied performance which never locates a center of gravity. Villains are all larger-than-life nasties.

Critical opinion is undoubtedly irrelevant for such a surefire commercial attraction as *Indiana Jones*, except that Spielberg is such a talented director it's a shame to see him lose all sense of subtlety and nuance.

In one quick step, the *Raiders* films have gone the way the James Bond opuses went at certain points, away from nifty stories in favor of one big effect after another. But that won't prevent Spielberg and Lucas from notching another mark high on the list of all-time b.o. winners.

Reflections

1. Los Angeles Times film critic Sheila Benson uses her review of *Indiana Jones* to tell us what she assumes Lucas and Spielberg were thinking during production. Do you feel this is an appropriate role for a critic? Why, or why not? Do you think she's correct?

2. Despite mixed reviews, *Indiana Jones* is firmly on the top ten list of all-time box-office hits. Do you feel that Spielberg and Lucas will take critics' reactions into account when planning sequels? Should they?

3. Do you feel film critics should have special training or education so they can do a better job of reviewing and recommending films? If so, what background or experiences do you feel would be desirable?

Activities

1. You'll appreciate the reviews more if you fully understand the meaning the reviewers intended to convey. Look up the definitions of the following words: desecrated, ironically, plaintive, derring-do, crass, precipitous, writhe, intrepid, bravura, anguish, crass (*Los Angeles Times* review); sadistic, laconic, fraudulent (*People* review); dapper, labyrinth, nefarious, incessant, garish, nuance, manic, opus (*Variety* review). For each of these words the reviewers used, find a simpler, more common synonym.

2. In the title sequence of *Indiana Jones and the Temple of Doom*, Kate Capshaw as Willie is singing the Cole Porter tune *Anything Goes*. What can you find out about Cole Porter and the Broadway show in which the song originally was used? You may need to use library reference books. Why do you think Lucas and Spielberg selected this particular song to kick off the film? After you've seen the film, do you think the song was an appropriate choice?

3. The finale of the nightclub act features Capshaw and the dancers in a production number reminiscent of Busby Berkeley's choreography or the Radio City Music Hall Rockettes (a famous New York precision dancing team of high-kicking chorus girls). Since the film is set in Shanghai in 1935, why would these two models be good choices to establish the period?

4. Each of the reviewers has mentioned his or her concern for young children who see the movie. Sheila Benson (*Los Angeles Times* review) says, ''If there ever was a film to point up the need for a stringently policed PG rating, this is it.'' Check back in Chapter 1 to learn more about the controversy when this film and Spielberg's *Gremlins* were given PG ratings. If you had been a member of the MPAA Screening Board, what rating would you have given this film? Why? You may want to review the definitions for each rating category. Discuss several other films you have seen. In your opinion, were they rated properly?

5. Check year-end lists by major cities of the 10 top films. Choose a film you yourself have seen. Then check *Readers' Guide to Periodical Literature* or *The Magazine Index* for a listing of reviews of the film. Look up and read several of the reviews. Write a report explaining why you agree or disagree with what the critics said about the film. (Be sure to include the names of the reviewers and the newspapers or magazines in your report.)

6. Each reviewer quoted in this chapter discusses *Indiana Jones and the Temple of Doom* against the earlier movie, *Raiders of the Lost Ark*. Pick another set of films: *The Godfather* and *The Godfather: Part II*; *Rocky, Rocky II, Rocky III*, and *Rocky IV*; *Jaws, Jaws II*, and *Jaws III*; *Superman, Superman II*, and *Superman III*. Write a review in which you use the techniques of comparison and contrast to bring out the strengths and weaknesses of each film.

7. Do newspaper film critics, magazine reviewers, and television reviewers look for the same things? Check your local library for reviews from out-of-town major papers like *The New York Times* or the *Washington Post*. Look up reviews in magazines like *McCall's*, used by many parents as a guide to films they let their children see. Try to watch a television show in which films are discussed: the Public Broadcasting System show or Cable News Network's *Show Biz*. Do you see any pattern in the criteria reviewers from the different media are using?

8. Are movies-for-television evaluated differently than theatrical films? Watch newspapers (your local paper plus two or three major metropolitan newspapers) for reviews of a recent made-for-television film. Compare the points these critics make with the criteria they seem to use to review a theatrical release.

9. With the increasing popularity of VCRs and video rentals, a theatrical film may be available on video cassette shortly after its theater debut. Check your video store for a review of a new video. Then look up the review of the same film when it was released in a theater. Do critics see it the same way? Can you write a review of a recent film you've seen in a theater that would be suitable for a video publication?

10. Imagine you are a critic on a major newspaper. Pick a film you've seen recently—one that may still be showing in your city. Write three separate reviews. In one, discuss mainly the plot and stars. In the second review, describe some of the technical strengths and weaknesses of the film. In the third review, compare the film with other films that may be part of a trend or may make similar comments about society. Which review was the hardest to write? Show each of the reviews to a few friends, parents, and teachers. Ask them which review would prompt them to see the movie and why.

11. The *Variety* review says the *Raiders* films have gone the way the James Bond films went: away from nifty stories in favor of one big effect after another. Check a reference book for the list of Bond films and release dates. Then look up reviews for two or three Bond films. Did critics say anything at the time to support the *Variety* contention? Do you agree with the *Variety* reviewer?

12. Offer to be film critic for a month for your school newspaper or radio station, or to write film reviews for your community newspaper.

13. Talk with your local theater managers. Do they feel reviews help or hurt box-office receipts? Ask them for specific examples. Look up the reviews of the films they mention and discuss the review in class.

Further Reading: *Check Your Library.*

Dosne, Mary A. et al, eds. *Re-Vision: Essays in Feminist Film Criticism,* Frederick, MD: University Publications of America, Inc., 1983.

Ebert, Roger. *A Kiss Is Still a Kiss*, Fairway, KS: Andrews McMeel & Parker, Inc., 1984.

Elley, Derek. *The Epic Film: Myth & History*, Boston, MA: Routledge & Kegan, 1984.

Giannetti, Louis. *Understanding Movies*, 3rd edition, Englewood Cliffs, NJ: Prentice-Hall, 1982.

Grierson, John, *John Grierson on the Movies,* Hardy, H. Forsyth, ed., Winchester, MA: Faber & Faber, 1981.

Kaminsky, Stuart M. *Before My Eyes: Film Criticism*, New York: Da Capo, 1982.

Pollock, Dale. *Skywalking: The Life and Films of George Lucas*, New York: Crown Publishers, Inc., 1983.

Variety Film Reviews: 1907–1980 (15 volumes, more than 40,000 reviews, including American and foreign films), New York: Garland Publishing, Inc., 1982.

Gene Siskel. *(Courtesy of the Chicago Tribune.)*

The Critic

For many moviegoers, the opinions of film critics play an important part in guiding their attitudes and thoughts about which films to see or not to see—perhaps even influencing what they think about films they have seen themselves.

According to Gene Siskel, who reviews films for both a daily newspaper and a TV station in Chicago, most film critics come to the job by "happenstance." They learn to review films by—reviewing films. Siskel himself began as a reporter and still thinks of himself as a journalist, though his style of reviewing is different for TV and for newspaper. In this interview, Siskel tells something about the work and thinking that go into his reviews.

. . . I think there are a lot of people who have a much better acquaintance with film than I do. Film scholarship is not my long suit. I'm not one of these guys who has seen all these films and remembers all the actors, and so on. My long suit lies elsewhere, probably in terms of being able to break something like this down, to stay with very specific things. The thing I want to be able to do is always to have the person I'm talking to know exactly what I'm talking about and stay with it very hard for a long period of time. . . .

I sometimes try to write reviews right after I see a film—to get something down on paper. I take notes every time. Then I go home or to the office and write a rough draft in some way. Sometimes I can let this sit, and then I can go back at it and write it a couple more times. . . . It varies anywhere from writing it right that night, because it has to be done then if I go to a movie theater, to about 2 weeks, if I get a preview screening.

I look at the words I write very carefully. Each word that is there is put there for a very specific purpose. Some reviews are more challenging than others—not enough of them—you get the challenge out of your sense of pride.

For instance, I started writing the review for *Lenny* right after I saw the film. I came back to the paper and wrote a four-page review. It stayed on my desk, and then I began to reread Lenny's autobiography, which involved maybe another six hours of work. Then I began to read all the *Tribune* clips on Lenny Bruce, and I talked to our nightclub critic, who knew him pretty well, and I read other things about him. And then I wrote a couple more drafts of the review. There were about four different days in a ten-day period where I spent time writing about it. . . . the words there are pretty well-chosen. They could still be improved, but what I'm saying is that you try to get it right. And getting it right does not mean writing the one correct answer in a multiple-choice test. But I do have these particular reactions; I think I know what I'm feeling, and I try to get them down the way I really felt them. And that's the point of it all.

In other words, anybody who thinks about these things—you know, "What qualifies you to be a film critic?"—I think the one answer is, you see all the movies that are made and think about it hard, and that's enough. Then you can be pretty good. . . .

This issue of the "right review"—it's very important that kids don't believe that there is *one* answer to these films. What you should demand of kids, or anybody, is to try to know what they're feeling while they're feeling it. That's tough—that's stage one—perception of themselves, of what they're thinking when they're watching the movie. What are they thinking about? The guy or girl sitting next to them? I mean, acknowledge that in some way. I have a note pad with me, and on more than one occasion I've written down a grocery list while I'm watching a movie because the film's so dull. Or I've planned my day for the next day, or what I'm going to write, or I've written a letter to a friend. . . .

But be aware of what you're thinking about. And then if you're a film critic, try to get it across in very specific language. My thinking is that there isn't an idea that's too complex for somebody to understand. If it's in your head and you understand it, you can get it across to someone else, unless you're not a good enough writer to figure out how to say it clearly enough. . . . All the ideas that we've talked about, I want to believe that an 11- or 12- or 15-year-old kid could understand every one of them, if we take the time and figure out the right mechanism to have them understand it.

You have to believe that, whether it's true of not. That's almost one of the prerequisites for doing what we do, which is called "communication."

Larry Dieckhaus. *(Photo: Susanne Havlic.)*

The Publicity Director

Why do you go to a particular film? Because you have heard about it somewhere—advertising on radio and TV, interviews with performers, "word of mouth" from your friends. The job of making sure you hear about a film is that of the promotion and publicity manager. He or she decides how best to reach the audiences that each film will appeal to.

Larry Dieckhaus handles publicity in the Midwest for 20th-Century Fox. He has done the same job for Metro-Goldwyn-Mayer and has also learned more of the film business as manager of several theaters in shopping centers. In this interview, he tells what his job involves.

Mostly I'm responsible for how a film is promoted. Our sales department actually sells the film to groups of theaters. We get advertising material produced in California, including television "trailers" and radio spots. When a film comes into Chicago, I'm responsible for screening it to the widest audience. I sell it so that people will know that it's been released.

I had a challenging job promoting *Romancing the Stone,* because the picture was finished close to the release date, and there hadn't been much pre-publicity. Kathleen Turner, Michael Douglas, Danny DeVito, and director Robert Zemeckis came to Chicago for interviews. They did an hour-long personal appearance at

Marshall Field's, and we ran a full-page newspaper ad to co-promote the film. I brought in critics and reviewers from every town in the Midwest that had a television station: Rockford, Decatur, Peoria, Ann Arbor, Kalamazoo, Lansing, Saginaw, Grand Rapids, Flint, South Bend, Omaha, and others. They interviewed the stars. Actor Alfonso Arau did interviews with the Spanish press from Chicago and Milwaukee.

I set up a radio-promoted screening the Sunday before the picture opened. The station gave every fifth or tenth caller a seat. We got $20,000 worth of free air time, and they had 1200 seats to give away to listeners. The blitz of radio, television, and print stories appearing at the same time the film opened helped make *Romancing the Stone* a hit.

For *Cocoon,* the Ron Howard film starring Steve Guttenberg (of *Police Academy* films) and Tahnee Welch, I arranged four screenings before the film officially opened. One was a radio promotion for WGN listeners. The next day, I had my press showing for editors and writers of daily papers, plus television and radio personalities. I also invited airline and restaurant people. Another screening was held for record dealers,. record distribution and promotion people, and book dealers and bookstores, since there was a novelization in paperback. Finally I held a screening for ad agencies, and contacts for *People* magazine. *People* screened for their clients in exchange for a full-page ad in their regional edition.

Publicity's harder now, with more competition from other films. There's no longer a downtown run, followed by a neighborhood run. I have to create a subtle awareness . . . have to make our *films* stand out and seem important so people will see them rather than pictures from other studios. There's always a tug-of-war between what I know I can do if I have the money, and the limit on funds available for promotion. . . .

Monday's the day we get our grosses. We have to know not only how our pictures did, but also other people's pictures. Very often, another film may open against you, and they've spent more money than you have on television saturation ads. What was the weather like in the towns where we played the film? What else was going on? A parade? A football game? When things like that occur, the grosses just tumble.

Timing's important, too. Maybe it's the third or fourth week of a picture. Perhaps it's smart to consider spending some additional money to boost the film. On the other hand, maybe the picture is dying, and it's not going to do us any good to boost it further. . . .

On Tuesdays, we figure out what we are going to be spending for new films opening around the territory. We generally have at least three new films per month. I've got to stay with the whole thing while the films are playing. And once they play, we have all the book work. . . .

At least one week of the month I'm tied up with some star, producer, or director. Out of Chicago I hire an agency to set up an itinerary. In Chicago we handle itineraries ourselves. . . . Personalities are usually interviewed by either film critics or feature writers.

. . . I handle correspondence. I get requests for stills from fans and from newspapers. I send out press kits to major papers—these are made up by the studios and carry news and features about particular films that newspapers and magazines can reprint. I meet with editors as closely as possible to the opening of the picture.

Publicity . . . It's a busy job.

Paul Kalas

The Theater Manager

Theater manager Paul Kalas, who holds a degree in commercial recreation management from Southern Illinois University, heads Barrington Square 6 Theaters, part of the 160-location American Multi-Cinema, Inc. (AMC) Theaters. His six screens, each in a separate auditorium, total approximately 2000 seats. Two screens are equipped with Dolby Surround Stereo.

Like most recently built movie houses, Barrington Square 6 Theaters are located in a shopping mall, this one, about 40 miles northwest of Chicago. Kalas, who has 10 years experience as a manager, chose his career because he's always been a movie fan.

As a theater manager, I don't select the films our theaters will play. Films are booked and contracts are arranged by our chain's regional film buyer, who takes regional preferences and differences among audiences into account. You'd probably not expect a film such as *Desperately Seeking Susan,* which stars young favorites Rosanna Arquette and Madonna, to have an extended run in the retirement communities of Phoenix or St. Petersburg.

We show G, PG, PG-13, and R-rates movies at $1.25 for all seats at all times. Because competing theatre chains in Chicagoland have been able to obtain first-run film bookings, our chain has lowered the price to attract audiences, and we show films that have played elsewhere first. During September to May, when schools are in session, we offer two or three evening performances, and no matinees. On Saturdays and Sundays, summertime and holidays, we're generally open noon to midnight, seven days a week.

My main job is the operation of the physical plant and facility. Much of my work is administrative. Every hour the theaters are open, one or more of our management team is there, greeting patrons, helping box-office cashiers make change, being sure there's plenty of popcorn, directing patrons in the lobby, and overseeing the cleanup.

Here in metropolitan Chicago, we have union projectionists, but in nonunion areas, like Carbondale, Illinois, I've run the projectors myself, in addition to my other duties.

As general manager, I handle weekly payroll for our 35 employees. I do the weekly concession inventory, counting popcorn, cups, candy items, and order appropriate merchandise after evaluating what we can sell for better profit.

Each week, I make out a profit and loss statement. I pay rent, bills, and payroll, repairs, and supplies. I keep track of gross revenue from each film and send the appropriate film rentals to the distributors, as required by the individual contracts that AMC signs for each film we play.

I hire and train new people and evaluate employee performances each week. We have staff meetings regularly to help us work well together as a team and to talk about motivation.

Our company adheres strictly to its policy on R-rated films. When we show an R-rated movie, we don't allow anyone to see it unless they're at least 17, or their mother or father accompanies them. We ask for a current state driver's license with a photo before we allow a teen to purchase a ticket, and we don't accept school IDs. I assign an extra usher to stand at the auditorium door, making sure everyone who enters has purchased a ticket for that particular film.

One of the biggest and most important jobs is cleanup. I assign an usher, and often, two, to clean up the lobby, restrooms, the sidewalk, and the parking lot. We clean the auditorium and pick up all debris between every performance. Our basic goal is to try to have the theaters as clean for the patron who sees a show at 9 P.M. as one who came in at noon. After we close at midnight, a janitorial crew thoroughly cleans and mops everything.

As theater manager, I'm responsible for my weekly performance schedule. Usually I get film bookings on Mondays or Tuesdays for all six screens. Then I have to make out a performance schedule, so we don't have one huge ticket line. I stagger starting times to give us one movie beginning every 15 minutes for each hour and a half. Next, I make an employee schedule so we have the right number of staff available to serve patrons.

In the Chicago area, a theater manager doesn't place display advertising, but in many cities, such as Columbus, Ohio, the theater manager usually places the individual ads in local papers.

It's also the theater manager's job to get the theater's individual show times listed in directory ads. I have the ads typeset and delivered to newspapers. Usually there's a 5 P.M. Tuesday deadline for the following Friday and Sunday editions.

Promotional activities are an important part of my job. I get the word out that a particular film is playing at our theaters. For one of the recent Muppet movies, I arranged a promotional activity at a nearby restaurant. With every children's meal they sold, customers got a coupon good for a discount on the Muppet movie shown at our location.

Recently, I arranged a promotion for *The Cotton Club.* Nearby record stores offered a discount on the record album with customers who had their ticket receipt from the film. I worked out a special screening of the film for listeners of a big band radio station because the film featured bands of the 30s. The station helped us promote our movie by making announcements. Usually, I'll tie in with local or regional merchants: an auto dealer, a record store, whatever seems appropriate.

The theater manager is on the edge of what's happening in American culture. The films we play are what people are talking about. The stars we show on our screen make headlines.

Theater managers are in the entertainment business, acting as hosts or hostesses to make sure our patrons have a good time. When people enjoy your movies and the popcorn tastes great, when people applaude at the end of a film, you feel good that you helped to achieve this.

12

The Moviemakers: Great Directors and Their Films

Film Directors

Most people have heard of John Wayne, Charlton Heston, Clint Eastwood, Katharine Hepburn, Spencer Tracy, Ingrid Bergman, Marilyn Monroe, Clark Gable, Bette Davis, and Joan Crawford. But most people would probably have trouble identifying Fritz Lang, John Ford, Howard Hawks, John Huston, Billy Wilder, Federico Fellini, Vittorio de Sica, and Akira Kurosawa. Some people would recognize the names of Mack Sennett, Alfred Hitchcock, Stanley Kubrick, Franklin Schaffner, George Roy Hill, and Ivan Reitman. However, on the whole, most people recognize films by the stars who are in them rather than by the directors who direct them.

The director's influence on a film is probably only second to that of the producer or the motion picture production company. In some cases, the director is *the* most influential person in creating the film. The director's role in many short films is most important. In some instances, several people take credit for the direction of a film.

". . . Movies are a collaborative medium. It is impossible to consider one man the absolute creator of a film, be he John Ford or Ingmar Bergman. Innumerable hands touch and affect the finished product, and no matter how much a director is in control, he does not make every decision on every aspect of the work as would a painter, writer, or composer." This would seem to indicate that we cannot discuss the films of various directors, but quite the opposite is true. "When, in chaotic circumstances such as the making of a movie, one man's vision emerges to such an extent that the films in which he has been involved bear his artistic imprint, one must assume that they are his films."[1]

In major motion picture productions, the director is usually assigned or asked to create a film by the production company. Some directors have reached a level where they seek out people to help them create a film. This situation has only recently been accepted among the motion picture production companies. For most of the history of commercial film production, MGM (Metro-Goldwyn-Mayer), 20th-Century Fox, Paramount, and other large studios have insisted on final artistic and economic control. This demand upon the artistic freedom of the director has often strained the economic and artistic merits of the film.

In this chapter, we will discuss a number of film directors. We have chosen these directors for their profound historical, almost legendary, influences on film and/or for their artistic contributions.

Some of the directors and their films may be unfamiliar to you, even though you may have seen some of their pictures on television. However, you should realize that there are a number of films that, in a visually oriented world, should, but never do, reach your eyes and ears.

Griffith and Eisenstein

In the early years of film, two directors of film, one in America and one in Russia, had a profound influence on the new art. In America, **David Wark Griffith** took (as Arthur Knight describes in *The Liveliest Art*) "the raw elements of moviemaking as they had evolved up to that time and, single-handedly, wrought from them a medium more intimate than theater, more vivid than literature, more affecting than poetry. He created the art of the film, its language, its syntax.

"It has often been said that Griffith 'invented' the closeup, that he 'invented' cutting, the camera angle, or even the last-minute rescue. This, of course, is nonsense. What he did was far more important. He refined these elements, already present in motion pictures, mastered them and made them serve his purpose. He discovered ways to use his camera functionally, and developed editing from the crude assembly of unrelated shots into a conscious, artistic device."[2]

Until D. W. Griffith, films were really an imitation of the theater. Griffith, more than any other single person, transformed film into an eloquent art. He changed the camera's position in midscene, which was unheard of then. Then he had the actors repeat their motions. Later he edited the two scenes together. The result was a smooth transition from one scene to the next.

Griffith continued to move the camera closer and closer to the actor, even though studio officials told him, "The public will never buy only half an actor."

But the public understood what Griffith was doing. He almost instinctively understood that film was a form that was very different from theater, that what worked on stage did not work in front of a camera.

Griffith did not invent new techniques, but he did understand how to use techniques in a new and exciting way. He started his scenes when the action started and ended when the action was complete, instead of waiting for the actor to come to the center of the "stage." He discovered that a scene shot from an angle seemed more realistic than a head-on view. He became interested in mood lighting and in composing each scene. He edited his own films and discovered that psychological and emotional tension could be created by editing and timing bits and pieces of film in different ways.

Griffith worked directly with actors who were not from the theater. He found that by training new people he could get away from the exaggerated gestures and expressions used by stage performers.

He discovered new ways to use extreme close-ups dramatically—of an actor's hands or eyes, even of objects. When the camera moved in close and lingered on a telephone, a letter, or a revolver, the object would seem all-important. Griffith could force his audience to see just what he wanted them to see.

Griffith summed up his objective: "The task I'm trying to achieve is, above all, to make you see."

D. W. Griffith is best known today for his film *The Birth of a Nation* (1915). More than any other film up to that time, this picture established film as an art form. Woodrow Wilson called it "like writing history in lightning." Even though the film contains bigotry and racism that caused race riots and mob action even in 1919, it is still powerful drama. Today its many strengths are still apparent. Broad long shots of Civil War battles, emotional closeups, melodrama, and beautiful composition make this a truly remarkable achievement by a great artist.

The following films are some of the many short and feature films made and directed by D. W. Griffith:

> *The Birth of a Nation*—1915
> *Intolerance*—1916
> *Hearts of the World*—1918
> *True Heart Susie*—1919
> *Way Down East*—1920
> *Orphans of the Storm*—1922
> *The White Rose*—1923
> *Abraham Lincoln*—1930

Film history, especially of the early days, is recounted in Arthur Knight's *The Liveliest Art.* Knight describes director D.W. Griffith, shown here, as the man who single-handedly created a medium more intimate than the theater and more vivid than literature. (*The Museum of Modern Art/Film Stills Archive.*)

The rise of the Klu Klux Klan was chronicled by Griffith in the epic *Birth of a Nation*. Woodrow Wilson described the film as ''writing history in lightning,'' even though it contained bigotry and racism. (*The Museum of Modern Art/Film Stills Archive.*)

The other great early director was the Russian **Sergei M. Eisenstein**. Eisenstein was to Russia what Griffith was to America. Both men influenced each other and the art of film. Even though Eisenstein differed with Griffith on the use of the closeup, describing closeups as isolated units independent from the rest of the film, his theories of editing remain firmly established in filmmaking today. His greatest accomplishment, *Potemkin* (1925), a film symbolizing czarist tyranny in pre-revolutionary Russia, remains today not only a classic work of art, but virtually a lesson in film-editing technique.

Eisenstein's greatest discovery was the discrepancy between real time and film time. He found that by overlapping pieces of movement from different camera angles, he could distort time. In the film *Potemkin*, the people of the city of Odessa have gathered at the Odessa steps, a fairly long and wide gradation leading to the bay where the battleship *Potemkin* is berthed. They have come to see and cheer the sailors who have revolted against their hated officers.

. . . Suddenly, from behind, comes a fusillade of bullets. The Cossacks have been ordered to put an end to this demonstration, to clear the steps. They march slowly, deliberately downward, firing as they go. The crowd immediately breaks in panic, leaping, running, jumping to the foot of the stairs and safety. Now as one look at the steps would show, any reasonably able-bodied citizen could run down the entire flight in a minute or two—particularly if his life depended on it. But Eisenstein realized that for the people trapped on the steps these would be the most terrifying (and for many, the final) moments of their lives. Obviously the scene should not be simply recorded, newsreel fashion, reproducing the atrocity exactly as it happened in time and in incident. To provide a proper psychological expansion and dramatic weight, Eisenstein broke up the mass into its component parts: the Cossacks moving ruthlessly downward and the crowd fleeing in terror before them, providing the main motifs. Against them, he set a group that crawls up the steps cringing, begging for mercy; another that huddles together in prayer; and a woman whose child has been shot, defiantly carrying the bleeding body in her arms back to the very barrels of the Cossack rifles. Others are picked out as individuals: a legless cripple who scrambles down the embankment on his hands, the mother with the baby carriage, the horrified student. Each character, each incident provides not only an interruption but a counter-rhythm to the steady, measured tread of the Cossacks. Each action extends the scene upon the steps just a little bit longer until, ultimately, each of these knots of resistance has been broken. The final moments of the sequence capture the sense of headlong flight, of panic and disaster in a rapidly accelerating series of shots of the baby carriage, the student, a praying woman and—in an incredible shot just four frames long—the frenzied face of a Cossack slashing with his saber, cutting off the retreat at the foot of the stairs.[3]

Eisenstein wrote about film theory, and his suggestions are still studied as a guide to excellent filmmaking. He continued to make a number of films that glorified the Russian Revolution and the past history of Russia. He even came to America and attempted to make films for Paramount Studios. However, just as in Russia he continued to have difficulties pleasing a tyrannical government, in the United States he had troubles pleasing a studio whose number-one goal was profit, not works from a genius. Eisenstein was also eyed suspiciously by people afraid of the new Communist objectives.

The following are some of the films made by Sergei Eisenstein:

Strike—1924

Potemkin—1925

Ten Days That Shook the World—1928

Old and New—1929

Alexander Nevsky—1938

Ivan the Terrible, Part I—1944

The Early Directors: The Teens to the Thirties

When we begin to examine the creative careers of most film directors, we discover that, as in other creative fields, many film directors have been influenced by directors of an earlier period. William Friedkin (*The Exorcist*) was influenced by Alfred Hitchcock's handling of suspense, especially in the film *Psycho*. Friedkin has seen Orson Welles' *Citizen Kane* about fifty times and studied it on a Moviola.* He says: "There's a kind of muscular, visceral, story-telling sense to the American cinema that I feel is best embodied in the work of Raoul Walsh, D. W. Griffith . . . Hawks, Wellman. This is the American cinema. It's what the American people and people all over the world expect from the American cinema."[4]

Another young American director, Peter Bogdanovich, says: "I don't care how famous or individualistic the director—he's influenced by others, Hitchcock was influenced by Lang and Lubitsch; Lubitsch was influenced by Chaplin, Hawks was influenced by von Sternberg, everybody was influenced by Griffith, and Griffith was influenced by Belasco."*

The early directors—Charlie Chaplin, D. W. Griffith, Mack Sennett, Robert Flaherty, John Ford, and others—didn't set out to create new methods of making films. They certainly did not purposely create a star system. They were explorers, who felt their way, sometimes gropingly and hesitantly, but always with courage and a sense of adventure, along paths of creativity. They had a sense of what the public wanted to see, and they gave the public just that.

Mack Sennett, of Keystone Kop fame, worked for Griffith at the Biograph Studios. He was an actor, a straight man who wanted to be a funny cop.

Sennett learned to direct from Griffith and began turning out an average of two movies a week. Sometimes he acted in his own movies.

---

*Moviola: a machine used in editing films which allows the director to control and manipulate the film.

*David Belasco was a famous theatrical producer of the early 1900s.

Mack Sennett's Keystone Kops became household fixtures, first because they made people laugh; second because they never let audiences forget about society's inability to cope with itself. (*The Museum of Modern Art/Film Stills Archive.*)

Sennett said of D. W. Griffith, ''He was my day school, my adult education program, my university.'' But Sennett soon began to develop his own ideas about comedy in film. They came from circus clowns and from the popular, fast-paced French chase films. Sennett began to feel that the French humor style of gags, tricks, and chase scenes could be done in America, too.

In 1922 Mack Sennett began making pictures in his own studio, the Keystone. Finally he could create his own world of madness. Most of his pictures were created on the spot—while he and his camera crew rushed to film a parade or automobile race, thinking up the situation on the way.

Mack Sennett is remembered best for slapstick, custard pie-throwing, and the Keystone Kops. In his first year, he turned out more than 140 comedies featuring the Keystone Kops. Soon Sennett was joined by all sorts of characters, including ''Fatty'' Arbuckle, Edgar Kennedy, Mabel Normand, Chester Conklin, Ben Turpin, Charley Chase, Mack Swain, and Charlie Chaplin.

Arthur Knight, author of *The Liveliest Art,* says of Sennett: ''In his hands slapstick became sud-

denly, indigenously filmic. He used the camera to exploit the absurd, the impossible, the fantastic. Reason was blurred by the speed of his action and editing . . . and a swift kick in the pants could settle the most abstruse problems.''[6]

Sennett not only discovered and created hundreds of short comedies, but also developed top comedians like Charlie Chaplin and the Keystone Kops and actresses and actors like Gloria Swanson, Carole Lombard, Marie Dressler, Buster Keaton, Harry Langdon, Harold Lloyd, Wallace Beery, W. C. Fields, and Bing Crosby. He also gave training to Frank Capra, George Stevens, and other directors who were to later become outstanding film artists.

Everyone knows **Charlie Chaplin,** the funny little tramp with the baggy pants and the derby hat, walking as if his feet hurt. But not everyone knows that he also directed his own films.

When Chaplin was with Mack Sennett and the Keystone group, he felt uncomfortable about the Sennett kind of comedy. It was too fast and didn't leave him time for the kind of pantomime he had perfected. But Chaplin's character of The Tramp was immensely popular: where before

The comedies of Charlie Chaplin, who became famous for his role as *The Tramp,* delighted audiences and made Chaplin a star. Years later, IBM used a take-off on Chaplin's costume and exaggerated mannerisms to create a series of television commercials advertising personal computers. (*The Museum of Modern Art/Film Stills Archive.*)

1910 he was earning about $5 to $15 a day, by 1914 he was getting $2000 a week, and in 1917 was paid one million dollars to deliver eight films in eighteen months with a bonus of $15,000.

Because The Tramp was so popular, Sennett decided to let Chaplin be his own director. But the Keystone production schedule of two films a week was too fast for Chaplin. Soon he left Keystone for Essanay, assured that he could have more time for the creation of his films and his own direction in production.

At Essanay, Chaplin rounded out the character of the little tramp: "Pathos, irony, satire and, above all, a more conscious identification of the character with 'the little fellow' everywhere . . ."[7]

Chaplin created an intimate style. The camera was placed in a position for a specific reason and the scene held for a longer period of time. He had a feeling for framing, and the props in each scene were there for a specific purpose.

The following are some of the short films and features of Charlie Chaplin:

Making a Living—1914

The Tramp—1915

The Vagabond—1916

One A.M.—1916

The Pawnshop—1916

The Immigrant—1917

The Kid—1920

The Gold Rush—1925

City Lights—1931

Modern Times—1936

The Great Dictator—1940

Limelight—1952

A King in New York—1957

The Countess From Hong Kong—1967

In 1972, Charlie Chaplin was at last honored by the Academy of Motion Picture Arts and Sciences. He "had created one immortal screen figure and in so doing he had refined the art of projecting character upon the screen far beyond any of his contemporaries."[8] "The essence of his cinematic comedy lay in the pathos that tripped into absurdity, the laughter that died into tragedy, the recognition that comic elements are present in life's profoundest moments."[9]

Robert Flaherty was a film poet and, even though he didn't know it at the time, created the genre of documentary films. Hollywood discovered Flaherty when his internationally successful first film, Nanook of the North (1922), was released. It carefully recorded Eskimo life as Flaherty had seen it while exploring northern Canada.

Paramount Studios then sent Flaherty to the South Seas. What the Paramount executives hoped for was an island romance with typhoons, sharks, and girls in grass skirts. What Flaherty produced, in his slow and patient way, was a poetic film about the real South Seas—Moana (1926). To make the film, he had spent two years simply learning the island ways.

Understandably, Flaherty soon left Hollywood to work in the new documentary movement forming in England around John Grierson.

Robert Flaherty's influence on film was his creation of lyrical, factual documentaries. He continued to make such distinctive films as Man of Aran (1934), about existence on a barren Irish island, and Louisiana Story (1948), the story of a Cajun family in the Louisiana bayous.

In 1914, **John Ford** graduated from high school and went to Hollywood to make movies. He started as a laborer, an assistant prop man, and worked his way up to directing shorts. None of the short films survive today.

John Ford's films come largely from his personal vision of American history expressed in the genre of the western film. Even though many of Ford's films are not westerns, this personal vision of American values is still evident.

In his westerns, Ford uses universal patterns of human experience—dances, weddings, births, funerals, honor, and above all, sacrifice. We respond to these rituals with emotion as we see the sacrifice in the death of the general in Drums Along the Mohawk (1939); the ritual of death in the burial of the Southern general in She Wore a Yellow Ribbon (1949); and the wedding and funeral interruptions of the brother in The Searchers (1956).

Ford created his most existential films in portraying the character outside of society, who sacrifices values for that society to continue.

John Ford's *Stagecoach* takes its place as a classic Western, along with films like George Stevens' *Shane* and Clint Eastwood's *The Outlaw Josey Wales* and *Pale Rider*. Many actors and actresses in this film went on to much greater fame. (Stagecoach. *The Museum of Modern Art/Film Stills Archive.*)

His first feature film was *Straight Shooting* (1917). He made about sixty silent films; only three of the silent westerns exist today. *The Iron Horse* (1924) was his first popular film.

Some films by John Ford are these:

Straight Shooting—1917

The Iron Horse—1924

Three Bad Men—1926

The Black Watch—1929

The Informer—1935

Stagecoach—1939

The Grapes of Wrath—1939

My Darling Clementine—1946

The Quiet Man—1952

Mister Roberts—1955

The Last Hurrah—1958

*The Man Who Shot Liberty
  Valance*—1962

Cheyenne Autumn—1964

In 1973, not long before his death, Ford received the first Life Achievement Award from the American Film Institute.

Certainly one of the most colorful early film directors, known for his big pictures with "casts of thousands," was **Cecil B. DeMille.** DeMille is closely identified with his 1956 biblical extravaganza, *The Ten Commandments.* However, he began making films with the other great directors back in 1913 with a western, *The Squaw Man,* one of the first features produced in Hollywood.

DeMille seemed to sense what the public wanted. As America became caught up in World War I, he gave audiences films of super-patriotism like *Joan the Woman* (1917) and *The Little American* (1917). But he also knew that when the war was over, people would want to see something else. He released a series of film comedies set in sophisticated "high society": *Male and female* (1919), *For Better, For Worse* (1919), *Adam's Rib* (1923).

Such films were *too* sophisticated for many

people. So in 1923 DeMille released his first version of *The Ten Commandments*. As Arthur Knight describes it:

> DeMille climbed the mountain with Moses and thundered forth his 'Thou shalt not's.' The reformers' chorus had reached his ears; the Hays Office had been formed;* the women's clubs throughout the land were making known their dissatisfaction with the amount of sex and sin they found in their theaters. The time had come for a change—of sorts. Sex would still sell tickets, but flagrant immorality would not. DeMille solved this dilemma in *The Ten Commandments* by simply masking the kind of sex melodrama that was typical of the era . . . behind a biblical facade. . . . And who would dare to protest against a picture that included Moses and the Ten Commandments?[10]

The public believed it and the DeMille spectaculars were extremely successful. Many of his biblical films are shown on TV around Christmas and Easter to large audiences from home viewers.

DeMille's spectaculars were indeed spectacular. "In Egypt, his cast of 20,000 all had to be costumed and assembled at eight different locations. Engineers built probably the largest movie set in history to simulate the gates of biblical PerRameses, and a 16-sphinx avenue, which drew more tourists than Giza's single sphinx. Technicians rounded up hundreds of horses, innumerable sheep, camels, water buffalo and geese."[11]

DeMille continued to make spectacular films for more than 40 years, becoming one of the best-known directors.

Some films by Cecil B. DeMille are these:

The Squaw Man—1913
The Call of the North—1914
The Ten Commandments—1923
The King of Kings—1927
The Squaw Man—1931
Cleopatra—1934
The Plainsman—1937

Union Pacific—1939
Samson and Deliah—1949
The Greatest Show on Earth—1952
The Ten Commandments—1956

Howard Hawks is one of those people whose films you have seen and liked because of their action and adventure—yet you may have been told by your parents or teachers that they were frivolity and rubbish. But Hawks gave the audience what they wanted to see.

Gary Cooper won fame in *Sergeant York,* the screen biography of the Tennessee mountaineer who became a World War I hero. Cooper excelled in nice guy, underdog roles. (*Sergeant York* ©*Copyright 1941 Warner Bros. Pictures Inc., renewed 1969.*)

---

*The Hays Office was formed to convince the public that the filmmakers were censoring themselves.

His career began in the silent era with *The Road to Glory,* made in 1926, and he made over 25 films before he retired after his last feature, *El Dorado,* in 1967.

Howard Hawks' films are not considered to have great artistic merit. Hawks himself describes them as entertainment and doesn't take them seriously. Their aesthetic merits will probably be debated for a long time, but the popularity of *The Air Circus* (1928), *The Dawn Patrol* (1930), *Scarface* (1932), *Bringing Up Baby* (1938), *Only Angels Have Wings* (1939), *Sergeant York* (1941), *Gentlemen Prefer Blondes* (1953), and *Rio Bravo* (1959) will never be debated.

He discovered quickly, when *The Road to Glory* wasn't very popular, how to make films people would want to see: ". . . so I went home and wrote a story about Adam and Eve waking up in the Garden of Eden and called it *Fig Leaves* (1926). It got its cost back in one theater."

Hawks' films are concerned with motifs of death, responsibility, self-respect, masculinity, accomplishment, and a sense of humor. In *The Dawn Patrol* (1930), the main character is in a command position on the front lines. He must send his men out each day in inferior planes, undermanned and outnumbered. He knows that few will return.

In *Scarface* (1932), Paul Muni plays Tony, a killer who tries to assert his will over others. *Scarface* is the bloodiest and most brutal of the early thirties gangster films and is an example of Hawks' uncluttered technique and stark story line.

Hawks has influenced several generations of moviegoers, more through entertainment than profound statements of social concern. This is how he describes his way of making films: "Life is very simple for most people. It becomes so routine that everybody wants to escape his environment. Adventure stories reveal how people behave in the face of death—what they do, say, feel and even think."

Fritz Lang began making popular films in Germany in 1919. In 1926 he released *Metropolis,* a first-rate science fiction classic. Like many of Lang's films, it becomes both a nightmare and a philosophical dissertation. American director-film writer Peter Bogdanovich calls Lang "a creator of nightmares."

In 1932 Lang made his first sound film, *M,* which is critically acclaimed as a classic. *M* starred Peter Lorre as a murderer of children (his first film role). Even though the theme was horrid, the film was very successful. *Dr. Mabuse* (1932) is a horror story, of sorts, about a mad doctor. In the early thirties, promoters convinced Lang to make another *Mabuse* film. This one was subtly anti-Hitler, and its reception by Nazi officials made Lang decide to leave Germany in 1933.

Lang's first American film, *Fury* (1936), was about an innocent man who is sought for murder. He continued to create films such as *You Only Live Once* (1937), *The Return of Frank James* (1940), *Manhunt* (1941), *Big Heat* (1953), and *The Thousand Eyes of Dr. Mabuse* (1961).

Even though Fritz Lang was new to America, he was able to make the creative transition easily. Maybe the reason for Lang's success in America was because he recognized that film language and theme were universal. Lang's American films were more realistic than his German expressionist horror stories, but they still contained the familiar theme of the pathetic victim's struggle with himself. In Germany, *M* was about the child murderer who cannot help what he does; in America, Spencer Tracy in *Fury* also struggles against a half-hostile, half-indifferent universe.

Alfred Hitchcock established a unique and immediately recognizable style of suspense film. He worked in film since 1922 as assistant director, art director, and director. His ability to touch people's primal instincts and fears and to control almost completely, his audience, is the trademark of all his films.

Hitchcock's use of all the elements of film to create suspense is a lesson in filmmaking. He described how he created the tension and suspense in *North by Northwest* (1959):

. . . not a nook or a cranny or a corner of refuge for our victim. Now we have a situation where the audience is wondering. A mad tension. And it's not going to come out of a dark corner. So, not only do you give them suspense, but you give them mystery as well. He's alone and then a man arrives across the other side of the road, and he crosses to talk to him and this man suddenly says, 'Look, there's a crop duster over there dusting the field where there are no crops.' Now, that's the first thing that you give to the audience: this sinister, mysterious comment. But, before it can be discussed, you put the man on the bus and he drives off, so you and Cary Grant are now—because you are identified with him—left alone. And then suddenly the airplane comes down and shoots at him all over the place.[12]

Hitchcock also explained:

The delineation of suspense covers a very, very wide field. Basically it is providing the audience with information that the characters do not have. The most

A far cry from the lavish Hitchcock thrillers of the 1970s, *The 39 Steps* is still considered among his best. Hitchcock is one of the few film directors who successfully made the transition to television; mystery shows he hosted and produced are still being broadcast on cable television. (The 39 Steps, *courtesy of Janus Films*.)

simple example, the elementary example, is if four men are seated around a table and they're having a discussion about baseball, or anything you like. Suddenly a bomb goes off and blows everyone to smithereens. Now, the audience gets from that scene about fifteen seconds of shock. But up to that time you've spent five minutes on a conversation about baseball; the audience is without any knowledge that that bomb is under the table. Now let's take it the other way around. We show the bomb under the table, and let the audience know it's going to go off in five minutes. Now you go on with your conversation. Now the conversation becomes very potent, with the audience saying, 'Stop talking about baseball, there's a bomb under there.' Just as in *Rear Window*, people were anxious about Grace Kelly being in the room and the man coming along the corridor. You're giving them information that neither of the characters have. So now you know there's a bomb under there and at the end of five minutes it's about to go off. You've driven the audience to the point of anxiety. Now a foot must touch the bomb and someone must look under, discover there's a bomb, pick it up, and throw it out the window. But it mustn't go off under the table. Because if you create suspense in the audience, it needs to be relieved of that suspense.[13]

Many directors study the Hitchcock style of filmmaking and incorporate the visual and editing techniques into their own films. Andrew Sarris, film critic, says, "Hitchcock was the supreme technician of American cinema."

The following are some of the films made by Alfred Hitchcock:

The Farmer's Wife—1928
Blackmail—1929
Murder—1930
The Man Who Knew Too Much—1935
The 39 Steps—1935
Secret Agent—1936
The Lady Vanishes—1938
Rebecca—1940
Suspicion—1941
Spellbound—1945
Notorious—1946
Dial M for Murder—1954

Rear Window—1954

To Catch a Thief—1955

The Trouble with Harry—1955

Vertigo—1958

North by Northwest—1959

Psycho—1960

The Birds—1963

Torn Curtain—1966

Frenzy—1972

The Next Generation of Directors

Sometimes high school students of film are given the impression that all the great films appeared before sound was added or, at the latest, when their parents were teenagers. Nothing could be further from the truth. There have been great films made by outstanding directors all through the history of film. Other influences, such as television and changing social values, certainly have caused changes in the types of films being made today.

Art seems to generate more art. Directors, writers, producers, and others involved in the creative process of making films rarely come up with a brand-new original idea. Generally, creative ideas are usually discovered in the works of previous films. This doesn't mean that the same idea is stolen or plagiarized (even though it often is), but that ideas are combined with other ideas and they in turn create new ideas. Films beget films. Not only do we get *Frankenstein,* but we get *The Bride of Frankenstein, The Son of Frankenstein,* and even *Young Frankenstein.* But the concept is more sophisticated. The total output of films from the beginning until now relates to what the public will accept and purchase. That is why there are "pot-boilers" mixed with "works of art."

These directors of the 1930s, 1940s, and 1950s were largely influenced by the first generation directors. They, in turn, have influenced at least one—perhaps two—more generations of filmmakers.

Busby Berkeley is a name synonymous with dance musicals of the thirties. During the De-pression, audiences were treated to beautiful fantasies of choreography from every conceivable camera angle. Berkeley began with *Gold Diggers of 1935* and continued to make many musicals. He made Fred Astaire and Ginger Rogers famous in early films and can be given some of the credit for the spectacular rise of both Judy Garland and Gene Kelly.

Berkeley couldn't see simply filming the Broadway musicals just as they had been performed on stage. He had cameras that could photograph scenes from any angle and any position. He shot straight down on the choreography from high in the rafters. He shot from below. He zoomed the camera (not lens, because the zoom lens hadn't been invented yet) in from a distance to extreme closeups. He devised trick shots of all kinds. He even tilted the camera at a 90-degree angle to the floor.

Critics argued that the dance spectaculars of Berkeley could never have taken place on any stage. It made no difference. Berkeley was producing the best combinations of visuals and sound yet to come from a film. He was experimenting with the abstract.

The following are some of the films made by Busby Berkeley:

Gold Diggers of 1935—1935

The Go-Getter—1937

Gold Diggers of 1937—1937

Comet Over Broadway—1938

Strike Up the Band—1940

For Me and My Gal—1942

Take Me Out to the Ball Game—1949

Otto Preminger began making feature films in Vienna with *Die Grosse Liebe* (1931), his only film made abroad. He came to the United States in 1935 and made a string of films beginning with *Under Your Spell* (1936). Almost all of Preminger's films have been very popular. They have also been controversial: *The Man With the Golden Arm* (1955) was concerned with illicit drug taking and peddling, a subject that was then strictly taboo and against the rules of the Motion

Picture Producers and Distributors of America. His *Anatomy of a Murder* (1959) was about a man accused of murdering the man who had raped his wife. Because of its theme, this film went through several legal battles.

Preminger himself is controversial and seems to enjoy the effect he creates with his outrageous personality. He even looks like the stereotype of a Hollywood film director—bald and large-featured, with a commanding appearance. His famous rages are known throughout the movie industry and he has become personally involved in such films as *Exodus* (1960) and *The Cardinal* (1963).

Preminger has dealt boldly with themes of social concern: drugs in *The Man With the Golden Arm* (1955); the issues of Israel and the Middle East in *Exodus* (1960); and the American system of government in *Advise and Consent* (1962). His contributions to the motion picture art include films with exciting and stimulating thematic approaches to the human condition.

Orson Welles should perhaps have finished his career as a film director with his first film, *Citizen Kane* (1941). Nearly every critic and connoisseur of film will agree that *Citizen Kane* has influenced the making of American films more profoundly than any other film since *Birth of a Nation.* But after *Citizen Kane,* there was less enthusiasm for Welles' films. Some people believe his film directing declined—on the other hand, his career started on such a high level of promise that nothing could really affect his place as a true giant among film directors.

Welles was well known in radio before becoming a film director. Many people knew about him after a famous and disastrous 1938 radio broadcast of *The War of the Worlds.* At least one million people heard, and believed, that Earth was being invaded by Martians. Orson Welles was the young genius behind this broadcast.

Orson Welles is an artist, a great film artist, who should be allowed to create. But his career illustrates one of the sad facts about Hollywood. As the studios became more industrialized and commercial in marketing and producing their films, they had less room for the creative person. Orson Welles, as well as some other filmmakers like Robert Flaherty *(Nanook of the North),* Mack Sennett, and Erich von Stroheim *(Greed,* 1925),

never were able to succeed in this Hollywood atmosphere. Creativity does exist in Hollywood, but it also helps if pictures are profitable. Welles' problem, as well as that of the other directors mentioned, and unmentioned, is that he did not conform.

The following are some of the films made by Orson Welles:

> *Citizen Kane*—1941
> *The Magnificent Ambersons*—1942
> *Journey into Fear*—1942
> *The Stranger*—1946
> *Lady From Shanghai*—1948
> *Macbeth*—1950
> *Othello*—1955
> *Touch of Evil*—1958
> *Mr. Arkadin*—1962
> *The Trail*—1963
> *Falstaff*—1967
> *The Immortal Story*—1968
> *Question Mark*—1973

Arthur Knight describes the creative problem this way:

The vitality of the film grows out of the daring, the experiments, the originality of the individual artist. Whenever purely commercial considerations are permitted to check that growth, the loss is incalculable—to the art, to the filmgoers, and to the industry itself. It is a shocking waste of the movies' greatest single natural resource, the man of talent.[14]

Orson Welles has described himself as the tormented artist, unable to exercise his craft:

I feel more bitter than ever. Worse than ever. Very difficult. I have already said that I do not work enough. I am frustrated, do you understand? And I believe that my work shows that I do not do enough filming. My cinema is perhaps too explosive, because I wait too long before I speak. It's terrible. I have bought little cameras in order to make film if I can find the money. I will shoot it in 16 mm. The cinema is a métier . . . nothing can compare to the cinema. The cinema belongs to our times. It is 'the thing' to do. During the shooting of *The Trial* (1963), I spent marvelous days. It was an amusement, happiness. You cannot imagine what I felt.

Orson Welles is also an actor and has appeared in most of his own films. He has financed his own new projects by taking on acting roles in other people's films.

A film that deals with greed, *The Treasure of the Sierra Madre* starred Humphrey Bogart (center) and Tim Holt (right). John Huston (left), who directed, has a long string of hits, from *The Maltese Falcon* in 1941 to *Prizzi's Honor* in 1985. (The Treasure of the Sierra Madre © *1948 Warner Brothers Inc., renewed 1975.*)

Orson Welles was recognized and honored for his contributions to the art of film in 1975, when the American Film Institute presented him the Life Achievement Award. (John Ford and James Cagney also received this honor for their contributions to film.)

During Welles' acceptance speech, he expressed his feelings about the freedom to create:

> A maverick may go his own way, but he doesn't think that it's the only way, or even claim that it's the best one—except maybe for himself. And don't imagine that *this* raggle-taggle gypsy is claiming to be free. It's just that some of the necessities to which I am a slave are different from yours.
>
> As a director, for instance, I pay myself out of my acting jobs. I use my own work to subsidize my work. In other words, I'm crazy. But not crazy enough to pretend to be free. But it's a fact that many of the films you've seen tonight could never have been made otherwise. Or if otherwise—well, they might have been better. But certainly they would have been mine. The truth is I don't believe that this great evening would ever have brightened my life if it weren't for this—my own particular contrariety.

Their "own particular contrariety" is the element within all directors and artists that sets them apart. Some seem to have more than others, but all must have some to be able to create.

John Huston has been directing films, and appearing in some *(The Bible*—1966; *Chinatown*—1974), for a long time. Some of his films are the great movies of our time. *The African Queen* (1951) with Katharine Hepburn and Humphrey Bogart who ride the boat, "The African Queen," down an uncharted river evading World War I German bullets, crocodiles, and nasty bugs, makes a great adventure and love story. He made *Reflections in a Golden Eye* (1967), *The Asphalt Jungle* (1950), *Key Largo* (1948), *The Kremlin Letter* (1970), and *The Maltese Falcon* (1941), a very popular detective film starring Bogart as Sam Spade. *The Maltese Falcon* was Huston's first movie. *The Man Who Would Be King* (1975) and *The Red Badge of Courage* (1951) were popular with audiences. The *Misfits* (1961) starred Clark Gable as divorcee Marilyn Monroe's brooding cowboy friend. *The Treasure of the Sierra Madre* (1948) looks at greed as three prospectors look for gold. One of the men is played by Huston's father, Walter. More recent films include: *Wise Blood* (1979); *Annie* (1983), his only musical; and *Under the Volcano* (1984), based on the novel by Malcolm Lowry, about an Englishman struggling with alcoholism. The entire film is set in Mexico with lush visual symbols, music, children in ghoulish garb, and peasants selling grinning skulls made of bread and sugar. It is the Day of the Dead, a festival which celebrates departed souls.

As did many directors, including John Ford, George Stevens, William Wyler, and Frank Capra, John Huston helped the World War II effort. He made several films on the front that recorded actual battles. His film, *Let There Be Light,* showed the effects of the war on soldiers who were hospitalized for shell shock. The War Department banned the film, which was finally released in 1980. Huston's wartime film experiences influenced him later.

Huston made *Prizzi's Honor* (1985) based on the novel by Richard Condon. The film is about the mafia and love, an unusual combination, but nothing new for John Huston.

Several other directors of the 1940s, 1950s, and 1960s, similar to Huston in style and technique, created dramatic films of adventure, rugged individualism, and clashes with overwhelming odds.

William Wellman created many exciting adventure films, particularly westerns, crime, and war films. *The Ox-Bow Incident* (1943) was about the hanging of three innocent men. *Young Eagles* (1930) dealt with a pilot who suspects a girl of being a spy. James Cagney was the *Public Enemy* (1931), a sadistic bully and criminal.

Raoul Walsh was the creator of many adventurous social commentaries like *They Drive By Night* (1940), with Humphrey Bogart and George Raft as long-haul truck drivers. *They Died with Their Boots On* (1941) is about the life of General George Custer. *White Heat* (1949) is concerned with a deranged criminal, again portrayed by James Cagney.

George Stevens also probably falls into the list of "rugged" directors. He is most remembered for *Shane* (1953), about a bold, stubborn homesteader who holds onto his land against the cattlemen, while competing for his young son's admiration with the romantic "drifter" Shane. Stevens also made *Gunga Din* (1939), *The Diary of Anne Frank* (1959), and *Giant* (1956).

Billy Wilder began directing film in 1933. Before this time he was basically a scriptwriter.

Wilder had directed some very important films during his career and has influenced the creative direction of the art. His first few films were successful *Mauvaise Graine* (1933), *The Major and the Minor* (1942), but his first important film is considered to be *Lost Weekend* (1945). Ray Milland plays the alcoholic trying to kick the habit.

Wilder continued to make social documentaries like *The Big Carnival* (1951), an absorbing satire on the dollar and its influence on a reporter who deliberately delays the rescue operation for a man trapped in a cave so the story will gain him fame and wealth.

But Wilder also directed witty, biting comedies such as *The Apartment* (1960), *Irma La Douce* (1963), *The Fortune Cookie* (1966), and *Some Like It Hot* (1959). Even his comedies usually have an underlying social comentary. *Avanti* (1972), *Front Page* (1974) and *Buddy, Buddy* (1981) are Wilder's most recent films.

Stanley Kramer has been directing films of consistently important, strong social commentary since the 1950s. *The Defiant Ones* (1958) were two escaped convicts who hate each other and are chained together. One (Sidney Poiter) is black, the other (Tony Curtis) white. *Guess Who's Coming to Dinner* (1967) concerns an interracial marriage and its effect on the parents. In 1971, Kramer directed *Bless the Beasts and Children,* about a group of misfit teenagers at a summer camp, who attempt to save some buffalo who have been trapped for hunters to kill.

In 1977, Kramer made *The Domino Principle* starring Gene Hackman and Candice Bergen. Hackman plays a man who refuses to comply with a powerful organization that obtains his release from prison.

Kramer made *The Runner Stumbles* (1979), based on an actual incident about a priest accused of murdering a young nun whose religious faith is slowly eroding.

Stanley Kubrick is the film director who sent us on a journey into deep space and, in doing so, created a film that continues to be one of the

As the hard-boiled detective with a beautiful, but deceitful client, Humphrey Bogart started a trend with *The Maltese Falcon*. Years later, Roman Polanski would echo the theme with Jack Nicholson and Faye Dunaway in *Chinatown*. (The Maltese Falcon ©Copyright 1941 Warner Bros. Pictures Inc., renewed 1969.)

best science fiction film stories: *2001: A Space Odyssey* (1968). Science fiction purists believe that films like *Star Wars* (1977) and *Return of the Jedi* (1983) are really fantasy stories not science fiction.

Stanley Kubrick's film themes, at least in his later work, are mostly satirical comments on modern society. He began working for *Look* magazine and at age 21 made a documentary film. His first feature film was *Fear and Desire* (1953). *Paths of Glory* (1957), a pacifist story set during World War I, is considered one of the best antiwar films.

Kubrick directs films with various amounts of black comedy and wit to convey his satirical message. *Dr. Strangelove* (1963) is a frightening, funny film which the President of the United States and the Premier of the U.S.S.R. bumblingly try to save the world from nuclear war.

In 1968 Kubrick collaborated with science fiction writer Arthur C. Clarke to create the classic science fiction film, *2001: A Space Odyssey*. Even though many people admit they didn't understand the film, especially the ending, most people found the photography and effects outstanding.

In 1971, Kubrick did an about-face and made *A Clockwork Orange,* an outrageous and satirical film about a young man who is conditioned by society to abhor violence. Some people insist that this violent film is really the "other side" of *2001*—what is happening back on earth in *2001.*

Full Metal Jacket (1985), starring Michael Hall, is a Vietnam War epic about nurses caring for the soldiers.

Martin Ritt, like Stanley Kramer, has directed some important films which comment about human nature and social conditions. *The Molly Maguires* (1970) is about unrest among early coal miners at the turn of the century. *The Great White Hope* (1971) starred James Earl Jones as the first Black boxer to become a world champion. In *Sounder* (1972), a poor Black family in Louisiana during the Depression is torn apart when the father steals some meat for his family.

Ritt directed Paul Newman in three films that resembled the style of John Huston's character misfits: *Hombre* (1967), *Hudd* (1963), and *The Outrage* (1964).

Martin Ritt also directed *Pete 'N' Tillie* (1972),

Conrack (1974), and *Casey's Shadow* (1977). *Norma Rae* (1978), one of the best films of the year, starred Sally Field and was concerned with unions and women's rights in a textile factory. He made *Back Roads* in 1981 with Sally Field once again as the star. She plays a woman looking for the good life, not realizing it is right next to her. *Cross Creek* (1983) is based on Marjorie Kinnan Rawlings' life *(The Yearling)* and her novel of the same name. In 1985, Columbia Pictures planned to release *Murphy's Romance,* starring Sally Field and James Garner. This modern-day western romance, written by the writers who created *Norma Rae,* was produced by Sally Field and Laura Zisken.

Blake Edwards, husband of actress Julie Andrews *(The Sound of Music,* 1965) is an actor, writer, producer, and a director of some of the best comedies on film, including *The Pink Panther* (1965), *The Great Race* (1964), *A Shot in the Dark* (1964), *What Did You Do In the War, Daddy?* (1966), and all of the sequels to the Pink Panther. But there is a socially-conscious Blake Edwards as well. In 1962, he directed one of the best films of the year, *Days of Wine and Roses.* This film, starring Jack Lemmon and Lee Remick, is concerned with the problems of alcoholism.

Edwards is also adept at mystery, with *The Carey Treatment* (1972), a who-done-it concerned with murder and adventure, and with *The Wild Rovers* (1971) about two cowpokes who rob a bank on a whim. He has been involved in dozens of films since 1948. In 1979, he made *10,* one of the funniest and sexiest films of the year. *Victor/Victoria* (1982) is about a woman, played by Julie Andrews, who portrays a man portraying a woman. Burt Reynolds is a womanizer in *The Man Who Loved Women* (1983). *Micki and Maude* (1985) features Dudley Moore who wants a child so badly that he engages another woman to have one for him.

Woody Allen was a standup comic in the early 1960s and didn't begin to make films until 1969 with *Take the Money and Run.* Most of Allen's humor is cynical and bittersweet about failed love, ineptness, and concerned with a hero who can never do anything right but wins anyway. Allen presented an image in his early comedy and films as a self-deprecatory, gag-spouting Brooklynite. In his later films, especially in *Love* and Death (1975), The Front (1976), Annie Hall (1977), Interiors (1978) and Manhattan (1979), Woody Allen refines the earlier image.

Allen describes his film Manhattan and indirectly himself:

It's my own feeling—my subjective, romantic view of comtemporary life in Manhattan. I'd like to think that a hundred years from now, if people see the picture, they will learn something about what life in the city was like in the 1970s. They'll get some sense of what it looked like, and an accurate feeling about how some people lived, what they cared about.

Again in Annie Hall, Woody Allen explores his themes, and perhaps his own life style, as a "teacher, an introspective, semi-confessional story of failed relationships" and "the stumbling, bumbling speech that expresses witty befuddlement." He made Stardust Memories (1980), A Mid-Summer Night's Sex Comedy (1982), Zelig (1983) about a man who becomes like the character of others, and Broadway Danny Rose (1984) about a theatrical manager. In 1985, The Purple Rose of Cairo was released. It is about a silent screen star who literally comes out of the screen to romance a member of the audience. Allen starred Mia Farrow and her mother, Maureen Sullivan, in Hannah's Daughter, his 1986 film.

Robert Wise was an editor for Orson Welles' Citizen Kane (1941). He has made over 40 feature films, including several Academy Award winning films. His list of credits includes some films considered to be classics: The Day the Earth Stood Still (1951); Executive Suite (1954); I Want to Live (1958), based on a true story of a woman condemned to die in the electric chair; and The Sound of Music (1965).

The following are some of the other films made by Robert Wise:

Mademoiselle Fifi—1944

Born to Kill—1947

Blood on the Moon—1948

The House on Telegraph Hill—1951

Desert Rats—1952

So Big—1953

This Could Be the Night—1957

Run Silent Run Deep—1958

West Side Story—1961

Two for the Seesaw—1962

The Haunting—1963

The Sand Pebbles—1966

Star—1968

The Andromeda Strain—1970

Audrey Rose—1977

Star Trek: The Movie—1979

Joseph L. Mankiewicz is a director of long standing. He has written, produced, and directed films since the late 1920s, including: The Mysterious Dr. Fu Manchu (1929); Fury (1936) about a wronged man, Spencer Tracy, who becomes a hardened criminal; Huckleberry Finn (1939); The Ghost and Mrs. Muir (1947) about a zany woman's romance with a ghostly sea captain; All About Eve (1950) which Mankiewicz recieved an Academy Award for writing and directing; Guys and Dolls (1955); Suddenly Last Summer (1959); Cleopatra (1963); There was a Crooked Man (1970); and Sleuth (1972).

Robert Aldrich makes socially relevant films such as Apache (1954) and The Big Knife (1955), but he also fashions exciting adventure and psychological films: Ten Seconds to Hell (1958), Whatever Happened to Baby Jane? (1962), Hush . . . Hush Sweet Charlotte (1964), The Dirty Dozen (1967) and Too Late The Hero (1969), The Longest Yard (1975), and Hustle (1976).

Aldrich is a director who can be counted on to bring in the buck and entertain the audiences as well. He has made and directed over 40 films since 1945. In 1976, he made Hustle starring Burt Reynolds and Catherine Deneuve; and in 1980, he made The Frisco Kid, a comedy with Gene Wilder and Harrison Ford. Wilder plays a young Polish rabbi who is sent to America to become the spiritual leader of a congregation in San Francisco. He is befriended by a bank robber, Ford, after becoming lost in the untamed West. Aldrich made All the Marbles (1981) with Peter Falk as manager of a women's wrestling team.

George Pal is the most important film director responsible for many of the science fiction films of the fifties, including: Destination Moon (1950), When Worlds Collide (1951), War of the Worlds

(1953), *The Conquest of Space* (1955), and *The Time Machine* (1960). He both directed and produced many of these films.

Pal, who was a puppeteer in the Netherlands and Britian, came to the United States in 1940 and made sci-fi films combining live action, animation, and trick photography. Even after the multimillion dollar special effects in *Star Wars, Superman, Black Hole, Star Trek: The Movie* and other more recent films, many of the effects created on a much smaller budget by Pal stand the test of time.

Pal also created fantasy films like *Tom Thumb* (1958), *Atlantis, The Lost Continent* (1961), *The Wonderful World of the Brothers Grimm* (1962), and *Seven Faces of Dr. Lao* (1964).

Sam Peckinpah, who died in 1984, said about his films:

> Most of my work has been concerned one way or another with outsiders, losers, lovers, misfits, rounders—individuals looking for something besides security . . . [Pretentiousness] is what I really resent in a picture more than anything else, that fatal weakness of so many astonishingly good directors.

Peckinpah has been criticized, not only for this viewpoint because he doesn't always follow this philosophy in all of his films, but also for excessive violence as in *Straw Dogs* (1971) and his most successful film *The Wild Bunch* (1969).

Sam Peckinpah was the first director to illustrate action sequences of violence in slow motion. One source describes this technique as a symphony of violence. Many directors since Peckinpah have used this technique perhaps to the extent that now when it is used in a movie, it is a stereotype.

Some of Peckinpah's other films are these:

The Ballad of Cable Hogue—1957

The Deadly Companions—1961

Ride the High Country—1962

Mayor Dundee—1965 (re-edited
    by the producers)

The Getaway—1972

*Bring Me the Head of Alfredo
    Garcia*—1974

The Killer Elite—1976

Cross of Iron—1977

Convoy—1978

Osterman Weekend—1983

Fred Zinnemann is a filmmaker of considerable importance. Some of his films are some of America's best: *High Noon* (1952), a classic western film starring Gary Cooper, concerning one man who defends an uncaring town against outlaws; *Member of the Wedding* (1952); *From Here to Eternity* (1953), about army life in Hawaii at the beginning of World War II; the musical *Oklahoma!* (1953); *A Hat Full of Rain* (1957), about the hell of a narcotic addict; *The Nun's Story* (1959); *A Man for All Seasons* (1966); *The Day of the Jackal* (1973), about a plot to assassinate Charles DeGaulle; and *Julia* (1977), one of the best films of that year. *Five Days in Summer* (1982) involves a Scottish doctor, a niece, and their mountain guide, Sean Connery.

William Wyler directed *Ben-Hur* (1959), the colossal biblical epic with Charlton Heston. Wyler also directed perhaps one of the finest American films, *The Best Years of Our Lives* (1946). It is about the return of three servicemen from World War II and their frustrations and adjustments. William Wyler directed some of the most important films in film history: *Jezebel* (1938) starring a fiery Bette Davis: *Mrs. Minniver,* an Academy Award winning film in 1942; *Roman Holiday* (1953); *The Desperate Hours* (1955), in which Humphrey Bogart holds a family captive in their house; *The Friendly Persuasion* (1956); *The Collector* (1965), about a man, Terence Stamp, who kidnaps a woman, Samantha Eggar, and keeps her prisoner in a basement in hopes she will love him; *Funny Girl* (1968), starring Barbra Streisand and Omar Sharif; *The Liberation of L. B. Jones* (1970).

Robert Altman was one of the most exciting directors of the seventies. Not all his films since *M*A*S*H* (1970) have been popular, but all of them have been controversial. Perhaps no other director causes more disagreement among moviegoers and the critics.

Altman began in the film business by writing, producing films, and directing a TV movie, *Nightmare* in Chicago (1964) and a documentary film, *The James Dean Story* (1957). His first major commercial film, *That Cold Day in the Park,* (1968) was not very successful. But in 1970 came *M*A*S*H,* a tremendously popular film, later made into a popular TV series. Then came *Brewster McCloud* (1971), about a boy whose ambition is to take wings and fly in the Houston Astrodome. *McCabe and Mrs. Miller* (1971), a western drama, was quite successful and popular. *Images* (1972), *Long Goodbye* (1972), *Thieves Like Us* (1973), and *California Split* (1974) met with success also. *Nashville* (1975) was received well among most of the major critics, but general audiences had trouble with this film. Perhaps the film was hard to understand. At any rate, most critics considered *Nashville* to be one of the best films of the decade. The film followed the lives of some people in Nashville, Tennessee, for several days. The film touched on numerous subjects, including politics, race relations, country music, public relations, violence and assassination, the media, high school cheerleaders, and human vanity. The film emphasized various characters and their relationships.

Buffalo Bill and the Indians (1976) followed, but was not a hit. His next film was *Three Women* (1977), a strange, haunting drama. It concerned the lives of three young women in a small town. Essentially, it was a fantasy, a dream. In fact, Altman has said the film idea came to him in a dream. Again, many people had trouble with this film. Roger Ebert of the Chicago *Sun-Times* suggests that "it was our own fault if we didn't follow along." The next film was *A Wedding* (1976), which was fairly successful. His next film, *Quintet* (1979) was popular with neither the public nor the critics. *A Perfect Couple* was released later the same year.

Altman directed *Health* (1980), *Popeye* (1980), and *Streamers* (1983), about four young Army recruits in 1965. In 1984, he directed *Secret Honor: The Last Testament of Richard Nixon.* Altman directed Roy Scheider in a new version of *Across the River and Into the Trees,* to be shot in Venice and released in 1986.

A director of offbeat comedy is **Mel Brooks.** Most young people have seen one or more of his films: *The Producers* (1968), *The Twelve Chairs* (1970), *Blazing Saddles* (1974), *Young Frankenstein* (1975), *Silent Movie* (1976), *High Anxiety* (1977), *History of the World, Part 1* (1981). Brooks

Bette Davis starred in *Jezebel* (1938), as a vamp who created a scandal at a 19th-century ball by appearing in a bright red gown, rather than traditional white. In 1985, she played an important role in the made-for-television film, *The Mirror Cracked*, with Helen Hayes as Miss Marple in an adaptation of Agatha Christie's novel. *(Jezebel © 1938 Warner Bros. Pictures Inc., renewed 1965.)*

wrote, produced, and directed most of these films, as with most directors, in collaboration with others.

Brooks helped to launch the careers of Gene Wilder and Marty Feldman.

Another director of stature with dependability to make sure winners is **Don Siegel.** You are sure to have seen one or more of Siegel's films. Some of these films include: *Invasion of the Body Snatchers* (1956 and the original version); *Coogan's Bluff* (1968); *Two Mules for Sister Sara* (1969), an interesting western about a young drifter, Clint Eastwood, who helps a "nun" across the desert; *Dirty Harry* (1972); *Charley Varrick* (1973); and *The Shootist* (1976), a story about an aged gunfighter who discovers he has cancer. Ironically, it was John Wayne's last moving picture. The actor died of cancer in 1979. Don Siegel again directed Clint Eastwood in *Escape from Alcatraz* (1979). In 1980, Siegel made *Rough Cut* and *Jinxed* (1982), which starred Bette Midler as an aspiring lounge singer.

Arthur Hiller has directed many interesting movies including *The Inlaws* (1979); *The Last of the Red Hot Lovers* (1972); *Love Story* (1970); from the best selling book; *The Man in the Glass Booth* (1973); and *Popi* (1969) is about a father, Alan Arkin, who wants to get his two boys out of the slums of New York. So he concocts a wild scheme: he teaches them about life in Cuba, then takes them to Florida, puts them adrift in a rowboat in hopes they will be rescued by a passing ship in the belief they are children escaping from Cuba. They would then be adopted by a wealthy family and enjoy the good life.

Hiller made *Silver Streak* (1976) with the famous scene of a train crashing into a railroad station, *Romantic Comedy* (1983) about young love, *The Lonely Guy* (1984) with Steve Martin, and *Teachers* (1984).

Environment Affects Directors

Sometimes it is difficult to determine whether a good film is the result of a good director's exercising creativity, or whether both the director and the film were influenced by the director's environment.

In either case, certain events that have taken place since the beginnings of filmmaking have dramatically changed the direction of the film art.

The first most important event was the coming of the talking picture in 1929. This separated the artists who could handle the new medium from those who could not. But most importantly, a whole new dichotomy of artistic relationships between the visual image and sound had to be explored and discovered. Film would never be the same again.

It may seem strange, if not impossible, for us to believe, but some people thought that sound was just a novelty that would never last. They thought the "pure" film was visual. Perhaps some people would think that the second major event that changed the direction of film art was the introduction of color or the wide lens. Certainly color and Cinemascope lenses were important, but it was the use of television in homes that drastically changed the audience patterns for the motion picture industry: the older generation stopped going to see the movies as much, while the younger generation began to see movies even more.

Another factor related to television is the great influence of all the mass media on society. A youth-oriented society began to develop after World War II as a result of the mass media and its ability to reach and communicate to larger audiences. Big business discovered that kids had more money to spend. Combinations of closely related events—including rock music, changing values, adoption of film production codes, radio as background sound, and new technological inventions in tape, records, and sound—led to a "tuned-in," electronic society.

Filmmakers changed with the times. In the mid-fifties, *Rebel Without a Cause* (1955) and *The Wild One* (1954) vividly expressed the feelings of rebellious youth, and the youth-oriented film began to be important. This is not to say that things changed overnight. Even in the fifties, many films were aimed at an older audience. But a trend began to be established. Films were beginning to be made for selected audiences—and usually the audiences were composed of younger people.

Today's films are made to be seen by a younger audience, and the audience expects to be pleased by what it sees. With stiff competition from television, both commercial and cable, and

Faye Dunaway and Warren Beatty starred in *Bonnie and Clyde,* a film which many critics consider both ''good'' and ''popular.''
A strong story line and excellent acting were factors in the picture's success. (Bonnie and Clyde © *Warner Bros. Inc.*)

especially from video cassettes, films must above all entertain today's young audience. Most films are oriented toward young people's themes: first love, sexually oriented material, violence, fast action, big-screen action. Science fiction and fantasies have also been popular, as well as horror and fright films.

A number of young filmmakers are setting the style of today's films.

Contemporary American Directors

Arthur Penn began his career in television and stage directing; however, he quickly became interested in film. His early films were *The Left-handed Gun* (1958), a film starring Paul Newman as Billy the Kid; *The Miracle Worker* (1962), the story of the blind and deaf Helen Keller and her teacher Anne Sullivan; and, in 1965, *Mickey One,* with Warren Beatty, who later played Clyde in *Bonnie and Clyde.* (This film is now receiving more attention, as earlier films of famous directors often do.) *Bonnie and Clyde* was released in 1967 amid uncertain reviews by the critics. Regardless of what the critics had to say, the public liked it immediately, though most people were shocked by the violence, especially the violent slow motion ending. At any rate, the film became one of the most popular films in a decade. Penn went on to direct *Alice's Restaurant* (1968), *Little Big Man* (1970), *Night Moves* (1975), and *The Missouri Breaks* (1976), a film many considered overblown because of its two big stars: Marlon Brando and Jack Nicholson. Penn directed *Four Friends* (1981) about friends in the turbulent sixties.

Today many critics of film are beginning to recognize *Bonnie and Clyde, The Graduate* (1967), and maybe even *Easy Rider* (1969) as films that were pivotal. They seem to have finally brought about a recognition of new directions in the growth of film as an art form. They were apparently the fulfillment of the cultural expectations we began to have for film with a few films in the mid-1950s. Many of these films are more open and free. It's almost as if the art of film had been given its freedom.

Mike Nichols, who directed *The Graduate* (1967), started out in the 1950s as an avant-garde entertainer and satirist. His films typically take a sharp, merciless look at the characters. *Who's Afraid of Virginia Woolf* (1966), his first film, was controversial for both its language and its subject matter. Nichols followed *The Graduate* with *Catch 22* (1970) and *Carnal Knowledge* (1971), another controversial film that also seemed to suggest that films were maturing both in approach and subject matter. Nichols made *The Day of the Dolphin* (1973) and *The Fortune* (1976). His film *Silkwood* (1983) is about a woman who is accidently exposed to radiation.

Francis Ford Coppola, known for the two Academy Award winners, *The Godfather* (1972) and *Godfather II* (1974), is the first recognized graduate of a film school to make it big as a director. Both *Godfather* films are filled with the stark, violent realism that seems to be a part of contemporary films. They seem to confirm that freedom of the director to do what he believes is right for his film.

Coppola began directing films with *You're a Big Boy Now*, about a zany, rollerskating stacks boy at the New York Public Library who dreams of better things and beautiful girls. Then came the musical comedy *Finian's Rainbow* (1968) and *The Rain People*, based on his own short story (1969). Working in several areas of film, Coppola also produced *American Graffiti* (1973), the nostalgic yet beautiful portrayal of American youth in 1962; wrote the screenplay for *The Great Gatsby* (1974); and wrote and directed *The Conversation* (1974) and the epic *Apocalypse Now* (1979).

Coppola made *One from the Heart* (1982), *Rumble Fish* (1983), and *The Outsiders* (1983) from the book of the same name about wayward youth in the fifties. In 1984, *The Cotton Club* about prohibition-era nightclub life was released to mixed reviews.

Film director Roger Corman *(The Pit and the Pendulum,* 1961; *The Raven,* 1963; *The Man with X-Ray Eyes,* 1963; and many other films) allowed Coppola and later other young filmmakers to work for him for little or no pay in order to gain experience. Coppola, in turn, was instrumental in getting a contract for George Lucas (*Star Wars* —1977) from Warner Brothers. George Lucas, Francis Coppola, and other young filmmakers,

The distinguished team of director Irvin Kershner, producer Gary Kurtz, executive producer George Lucas, and screenwriter Lawrence Kasdan created *The Empire Strikes Back*. Lucas founded Industrial Light & Magic (ILM), a production house that has been responsible for special effects in many films, including those from other directors. (The Empire Strikes Back, *courtesy of Lucasfilm, Ltd., ©Lucasfilm, Ltd. (LFL) 1980, All Rights Reserved.*)

including Steven Spielberg, John Milius, Martin Scorsese, and Brian DePalma. All are close friends who often trade scripts and ideas.

George Lucas, who wanted to be an artist, couldn't get his parents to help him through art school. While at Modesto Junior College in California, he became interested in cinematography and began making short 8 mm films.

He was encouraged by Haskell Wexler, a well-known cinematographer, to pursue his filmmaking interests. Later Lucas enrolled at the University of Southern California.

His first film, titled *THX-1138:4EB,* was a first-prize winner at the National Student Film Festival. Coppola took an interest in Lucas, and allowed him to sit in on the filming of *Finian's Rainbow,* and to shoot a short documentary of Coppola filming *The Rain People* (1969).

American Graffiti (1973) was a film about Lucas' own coming of age in Modesto, California. "It all happened to me, but I sort of glamorized it . . ." he told Judy Klemesrud for *The New York Times.*

With the success of *American Graffiti,* 20th Century-Fox contracted with Lucas to go ahead with *Star Wars,* which was just an idea in his head at that time. (Lucas wrote eight hours a day for three years before he came up with a script,

set "a long time ago in a galaxy far, far away.") *The Empire Strikes Back,* sequel to *Star Wars,* opened in May 1980. It was produced by Lucas and directed by Irvin Kershner.

Lucas has put together the most successful film factory of all time—Lucasfilm Ltd. Of the ten box-office champions between 1903 and 1985, Lucas has a share in five: *Star Wars* (1977) directed by Lucas; *The Empire Strikes Back* (1980); *Raiders of the Lost Ark* (1982); *Return of the Jedi* (1983) produced by Lucas; and *Indiana Jones and the Temple of Doom* (1984).

Of film and other visual entertainment, George Lucas believes it is ". . . a pervasively important part of our culture, an extremely significant influence on the way our society operates. People in the film industry don't want to accept the responsibility that they had a hand in the way the world is loused up. But, for better or worse, the influence of the church, which used to be all-powerful, has been usurped by film. Films and television tell us the way we conduct our lives, what is right or wrong."*

Steven Spielberg has been making films since he was 12 years old. He always knew he wanted

---

*Quote by George Lucas from *American Film* in the article, "Burden of Dreams: George Lucas," June 1983.

to be involved in making movies. The first film he ever saw was C. B. DeMille's film *The Greatest Show on Earth* (1952). He began to wonder, how do filmmakers do these things? He wanted to make films like that some day.

After making a 2½-hour film similar to *Close Encounters* costing $500 and later recouping the costs by playing it at a theater in Phoenix, Arizona, he was ready for the big time. But he had to wait for a little while. He was only 16. But only 10 years later, at age 26, Spielberg's film, *Jaws,* was the box-office triumph.

Next came *Sugarland Express,* which didn't do too well at the box office, but was praised by critics. The rest is history: *Jaws* (1975), *Close Encounters of the Third Kind* (1978), and *1941* (1979).

Then came a phenomenal series of films: *Raiders of the Lost Ark* (1981), *E.T.: The Extra-Terrestrial* (1982), *Poltergeist* (1983), *Indiana Jones and the Temple of Doom* (1984), and *Gremlins* (1984).

Brian DePalma attempts to develop the motifs of exploitation, sexual repression, and guilt in his films. *Carrie* (1976) is a striking example. Carrie is a young lady with the power of telekinesis, or the ability to move objects without physical contact. Her mother preaches ''salvation through the blood of Christ.'' She views her daughter's emerging womanhood as the beginnings of sin and misery.

Brian DePalma also made *Sisters* (1973), *Phantom of the Paradise* (1974), *Obsession* (1976), *The Fury* (1977), and *Dressed to Kill* (1980).

Brian DePalma continued with the themes mentioned earlier with *Scarface* (1983) about the American dream gone awry. *Body Double* (1984) is another familiar DePalma theme; a man's harmless glance at a beautiful woman in a window becomes, eventually, murder. DePalma has been compared to Hitchcock and with good reason. Many of his films contain excellent examples of suspense, as did the films of the master.

Martin Scorsese, another of the new young filmmakers in Hollywood, is perhaps the most personal. He explores social problems in most violent, shocking, and outrageous ways. *Taxi Driver* (1974) is a psychological film about a disturbed man who has a personal vision to rid the world of the scum of life. Jody Foster plays a child prostitute and in a drive to save her from the evils of the world, the taxi driver (Robert DeNiro) commits gruesome acts of violence himself.

The Last Waltz (1978) was fairly popular. It was about The Band, a rock concert starring, among many rock stars, Eric Clapton and Joni Mitchell. *New York, New York* (1979) was not too successful at the box office. *The Raging Bull* (1980) with Robert DeNiro as the boxer Jake LaMotta was a powerful film portraying violent rages of jealousy and a great character study. A recent film is *The King of Comedy* (1983), featuring Jerry Lewis as a talk show host. Robert DeNiro would like to become a great comedian and kidnaps Jerry Lewis to achieve his goal. DeNiro has a passion to be near, or even become, the famous.

Other young filmmakers are also making new and exciting films in America.

Peter Bogdanovich is a filmmaker who likes to see films. Interested in film history, he has studied many films on a Moviola, including *Citizen Kane.* And he has developed a style in his films that seems authentic for the life and times of each period represented. *Paper Moon* (1973), set in the thirties, was about a con man and his ''partnership'' with a remarkable little girl whom he is taking to live with her aunt. *The Last Picture Show* (1971), which took place in the early fifties in a small town in Texas, was about the closing of the picture show in town and the suffocating existence of some of the townspeople.

Bogdanovich began his feature film career in 1968 with *Targets.* The film is about two monsters, a screen monster (portrayed by Boris Karloff in his last role) and a clean-cut kid who succumbs to psychological acts. *What's Up, Doc* (1972) is a zany 1930s-style comedy full of chases and a frenetic plot. He has also made a documentary film, *Directed by John Ford* (1971), a study of the late director's long career.

Peter Bogdanovich has several films which were not too successful at the box office: *Daisy Miller* (1974) and *At Long Last Love* (1975). Bogdanovich has not had recent successful films compared to his earlier triumphs. He made *They All Laughed* in 1982. *Mask,* a story of a youngster with ''lion's disease,'' received excellent reviews in 1985.

Milos Forman comes from Czechoslovakia. He

graduated from the Prague Film School in 1956, and then wrote scripts, directed stage plays, and began directing films. Audio Brandon Films, a distributor, says of Forman's films, "His films offer a fresh, cinema verité approach dealing with the conflict of the generations and the idiosyncracies of provincial socialist life, and its very funny situations. Often he uses non-actors."

Forman made several films in Czechoslovakia, including *Loves of a Blonde* (1965) and *Fireman's Ball* (1968). The later film is about the stupidity and awkwardness of a firefighters' ball. As a result of this film, 40,000 firemen in Czechoslovakia walked off their jobs.

With the Russian invasion of Czechoslovakia in 1969, Forman emigrated to the United States. *One Flew Over the Cuckoo's Nest* (1976) was very popular. Forman also directed the rock musical *Hair* (1979). In 1981, he directed James Cagney (out of retirement) in *Ragtime,* taking over the directorship from Robert Altman.

Forman's most successful film and winner of the Academy Award, *Amadeus* (1984), tells the story of Wolfgang Amadeus Mozart. The account from Peter Shaffer's successful play concerns the last ten years of Mozart's short, turbulent life. The music is superb; and Mozart, as played by Tom Hulce *(Animal House)* is portrayed as a sort of early punk rocker. The real story is about deceit, jealousy, and murder. The film should be seen by all.

Peter Yates made a film with an exciting chase scene that led to numerous imitations: *Bullitt* (1969) starring Steve McQueen. The chase sequence in *Bullitt* is not new. Peter Yates just did it in a new and interesting way. Mack Sennett and the Keystone cops did it more than fifty years ago. In fact, it has been said that in some way *all* movies are just one long chase scene.

Yates started in filmmaking as a dubbing manager and then became an editor of documentary films. Later he assisted film directors, including the British director, Tony Richardson.

Yates also made *John and Mary* (1969); *The Friends of Eddie Coyle* (1973), one of the best films of that year; *For Pete's Sake* (1974); *Mother Jugs and Speed* (1976); and *The Deep* (1977). In 1979, Peter Yates made what is known in the movie business as a "little picture." *Breaking Away* is about a young man's coming of age in

the small Indiana city of Bloomington. The film is considered one of the best films of the year. Yates made *Eyewitness* (1981) with William Hurt, who, after finding a murdered body, talks too much and makes everyone believe that he knows more than he does, all to impress a girl. This arouses the interest of the female reporter covering the news story—and the murderer. *The Dresser* (1983) with Tom Courtenay and Albert Finney is about a fading Shakespearean actor (he's dying) and his valet (Courtenay), who tries to coax just one more performance of King Lear from his master.

Eleni (1985) is based on the novel by Nicholas Gage about the author's mother who was unjustly put to death during the Greek Civil War of the 1940s. It stars Kate Milligan, Linda Hunt, and John Malkovich.

Paul Mazursky's films often reflect the sexual mores of our time. *Bob and Carol and Ted and Alice* (1970) centered about ultrasophisticated couples who try "modern" thinking about sexual freedom. *Blume in Love* (1973) concerns a divorce lawyer whose wife leaves him. Most film critics consider *An Unmarried Woman* (1978) one of the best films of that year. The film is concerned with feminism as well as with the personal choices one can make and may well be a "turning point" film of the 1970s. After a sudden divorce, Jill Clayburgh finds she is now free, her own person.

Mazursky made *Willie and Phil* (1980). It concerns the relationship between two men who love the same woman over a 10-year period. In the *Tempest* (1982), John Cassavetes, with his daughter, leaves his wife to move with another woman to a lush Aegean Island. An island native makes a pass at his daughter. Then Cassavettes discovers he has supernatural powers. *Moscow on the Hudson* (1984) is a comedy that stars Robin Williams as a Russian who defects to the United States.

Universal Pictures wanted **Phillip Kaufman** to make another *Butch Cassidy* when he finally got the go-ahead to direct *The Great Northfield Minnesota Raid* (1972). Unfortunately, the studio and the director did not agree on the film's final version. Kaufman's next film, *The White Dawn* (1973), about three young whale hunters at the turn of the century who are saved by Eskimos, also failed at the box office. Both *The White Dawn* and *Northfield* are cult films, popular at campuses and small screen film showings.

Kaufman was given the opportunity to direct Clint Eastwood in *The Outlaw Josey Wales*—and was preparing to direct *Star Trek—The Motion Picture*. Because of studio, star, and director conflicts, Kaufman did not direct either of these movies.

Nevertheless, United Artists gave Kaufman the go-ahead for a new version of *Invasion of the Body Snatchers* (1978) and later for *The Wanderers* (1978). Kaufman made *The Right Stuff* (1984) about the astronauts in the early space program.

Sidney Lumet was a child actor who, as an adult, began in the industry as a TV producer. His first, and very good, film was *Twelve Angry Men* (1957). He also has made *Long Day's Journey into Night* (1962), a "four-star" film about a family in 1910; *Failsafe* (1964), about an accidental nuclear war; and *The Pawnbroker* (1965), in which Rod Steiger plays a Jewish pawnbroker with haunting memories of Nazi prison camps.

Some of his more recent films are *Murder on the Orient Express* (1974), *Dog Day Afternoon* (1975), and *Network* (1976).

He made *The Anderson Tapes* (1971); *Serpico* (1974), about a copy who resists corruption; *Equus* (1977); the musical *Wiz* (1978); *Prince of the City* (1981), another policeman who challenges the system; and *The Verdict* (1982), starring Paul Newman as the broken-down, alcoholic lawyer who goes against the Catholic Church in a medical malpractice law suit. *Deathtrap* (1982) was a real psychological thriller with Michael Caine and Christopher Reeve. *Daniel* (1983) was based on the children of Julius and Ethel Rosenberg who were executed in 1953 for giving A-bomb secrets to the Russians.

Most of the following American directors, described very briefly, have only directed one or two films of significance so far. Maybe they have just begun their creative journey, with exciting films to come, or perhaps their one or two films were creative flukes, never again to appear. It is also possible, very probable, that we have failed to describe someone who may become one of the all-time great directors.

Michael Cimino directed *The Deer Hunter* (1978) and *Silent Running* (1972). He wrote or co-authored several other films, including *Magnum Force* (1973) and *Thunderbolt and Lightfoot* (1974). In 1980, he directed one of the most expensive films ever made, *Heaven's Gate.*

Alan J. Pakula was originally a producer of such films as *To Kill a Mockingbird* (1963) and *Up the Down Staircase* (1967). He began directing with *The Sterile Cuckoo* (1969) and *Klute* (1971) with Jane Fonda and Donald Sutherland. He also made *All the President's Men* (1977), about two reporters and their investigation of the Watergate break-in and coverup; *Starting Over* (1979), with Burt Reynolds, Jill Clayburgh, and Candice Bergen; *Rollover* (1981); and *Sophie's Choice* (1983), about a Polish refugee and her struggle to come to terms with the past.

You've heard of **Michael Ritchie's** films: *Downhill Racer* (1969), *The Candidate* (1972), and one of the funniest films of 1976, *The Bad News Bears. The Island* (1980), based on a Peter Benchley (of *Jaws* fame) novel, starred Michael Caine. In 1979, he released *An Almost Perfect Affair.* Robin Williams and Walter Matthau were *The Survivors* (1983) playing two losers being overworked by the system.

Herbert Ross made such hit films as *The Goodby Girl* (1978), *California Suite* (1978), *The Last of Sheila* (1973), *The Turning Point* (1979), and *The Seven Per Cent Solution* (1976). He also directed *The Sunshine Boys* (1975) and *Goodby Mr. Chips* (1969).

Ross made *Max Dugan Returns* (1983), a comedy about a dying ex-con who suddenly drops back into the lives of his daughter and grandson. Steve Martin plays the part of a sheet-music salesman in *Pennies From Heaven* (1981). One of the favorite movies of 1984, *Footloose*, was directed by Ross.

Of course you've heard of the great director of disaster movies, **Irwin Allen**: *The Poseidon Adventure* (1972), *The Towering Inferno* (1974), and *The Swarm* (1978). Allen began making semi-instructional films like *The Sun Around Us* way back in 1950. He showed us what happened *When The World Ended* (1980).

Franco Zeffirelli gave us the beautiful *Romeo and Juliet* (1968)—the 13th film version, *Jesus of Nazareth* on television in 1977. Also in 1979, he made *The Champ*, with Jon Voight. Franco Zeffirelli made *Endless Love* (1981). In 1983, he made *La Traviata* for everyone. It is the screen version of Verdi's opera.

James Bridges directed *The China Syndrome* (1979), *The Paper Chase* (1973), and has written and directed other films like *The Baby Maker* (1973). He made *Urban Cowboy* with John Travolta in 1980. *Mike's Murder* (1984) is about a boy who is attracted to a girl. They are just beginning their relationship when he is murdered. The girl tries to find out why.

Robert Benton made one of the best films of 1979, *Kramer vs. Kramer*. He also made *The Late Show* (1977). He continued with *Still of the Night* (1982), a thriller. *Places in the Heart* (1984) was one of the best films of the year. The film, set in the 1930s, tells the story of a young widow (Sally Field) and her family who try to survive after her husband, the local sheriff, is killed. Benton received an Academy Award for writing the film.

Hal Ashby directed *The Last Detail* (1974) and then won an Academy Award for the best picture in 1979 for *Coming Home*.

In 1976, he made *Bound for Glory* with David Carradine as the folksinger Woody Guthrie.* Peter Sellers portrayed a man obsessed by television in *Being There*, released in 1979. *Second Hand Heart* (1981) is about a drunken drifter who gets married to a singer at a local diner. The next day he begs for an annulment, but she talks him into taking her to Texas to pick up her three children. *Looking to Get Out* (1982) is about two gamblers on the run from loan sharks. *Let's Spend the Night Together* (1983) is a beautiful and searing rock study of the Rolling Stones on their 1981 U.S. tour.

Robert Rafelson made *Five Easy Pieces* (1970), a film considered by many as one of the best films of the seventies. However, his *The King of Marvin Gardens* (1972) and *Stay Hungry* (1976) were not successful at the box office.

A turning point film of 1970, *Midnight Cowboy* established **John Schlesinger** as a serious filmmaker. Since then he has made *Sunday, Bloody Sunday* (1972), *Marathon Man* (1976), *Yanks* (1979), *Honky Tonk Freeway* (1981), *An Englishman Abroad* (1983), and in 1985 *The Falcon and the Snowman* with Timothy Hutton and Sean Penn. They play Christopher Boyce and Daulton Lee who sold government secrets to the Russian KGB. The story is based on fact.

Franklin Schaffner has directed films like *The Stripper* (1963) and *Planet of the Apes* (1968). "Apes" is a well-done film and was very popular. He directed *Nicholas and Alexander* (1971), *Papillon* (1973), and *The Boys from Brazil* (1978) which concerned a Nazi conspiracy to resurrect the Third Reich genetically. Continuing with his ability to direct a wide variety of film genres, Schaffner made *Yes, Giorgio* (1982) with Luciano Pavarotti, the famous opera tenor. But his best film, and an Academy Award winning best picture, was *Patton: A Salute to a Rebel* (1970).

Sidney Pollack has made *They Shoot Horses, Don't They?* (1969) with Jane Fonda, Michael Sarrazin and Gig Young; *Jeremiah Johnson* (1972) with Robert Redford; *The Way We Were* (1973); *Three Days of the Condor* (1976); *The Electric Horseman* (1979), is a recent film, again with Robert Redford and Jane Fonda.

In 1981, he directed *Absence of Malice* with Paul Newman as the son of a mobster who is thought by reporter Sally Field to be connected to the disappearance of a union official. Pollack directed Dustin Hoffman in the highly popular *Tootsie* (1982) about a down-and-out actor who dresses as a woman to obtain an acting role in a soap opera. In 1985, he directed Robert Redford and Meryl Streep in *Out of Africa*, based on the life and writings of Isak Dinesen.

Gordon Parks is a musician, composer, filmmaker, director, photographer, writer, and a most remarkable human being. He is one of the first Black film directors in Hollywood.

Among Park's numerous achievements, his work as a photographer for *Life* magazine from 1948 to 1968 stands out. His subjects have almost always been people living in oppressed conditions.

Parks has created several short films, including *The Weapons of Gordon Parks* (his weapons being cameras). In 1968 he released *The Learning Tree,* a semiautobiographical film based on his own book. While filming *The Learning Tree,* Parks was quoted in an interview in *Life* (Nov. 15, 1968):

I know I have to keep the audience involved with camera movement even when there is dialogue. But

---

*Costume designer Bill Theiss talks about the challenges of dressing the huge cast. See page 114.

more important to me is to make each camera movement begin with a beautiful still picture and to end each scene with a beautiful still picture. But I have to worry what goes on each one of those frames as they move through the camera.

Parks next directed *Shaft* (1971) and *Shaft's Big Score* (1972), featuring a Black private detective hired to find the daughter of a Black underworld leader. All Parks' films have shown his exceptional photographic ability. Recently, Parks has been spending most of his time writing.

John Landis directed those great movies everyone has seen! *The Blues Brothers* (1980); *Animal House* (1981); *An American Werewolf in London* (1981); *Trading Places* (1983), about a Black man and a white man who trade places, and *Twilight Zone: The Movie* (1983), a series of short films that capture the essence of the television series. A helicopter crash during filming caused the death of actor Vic Morrow and two children. *Into the Night* (1985) with Jeff Goldblum and Michelle Pfeiffer is a thriller/comedy with cameos of many, many of John's friends. The film is about an aerospace engineer, an insomniac, who gets involved in a life-and-death game of adventure and intrigue.

Landis directed Michael Jackson in the rock video, *Thriller* (1983).

Carroll Ballard has only directed two movies at this point but both are works of art. The first was the *Black Stallion* (1979), a beautiful film of great visual quality based on Walter Farley's novel about a boy and a horse. The second was *Never Cry Wolf* (1984), a film about a man who learns about wolves by living with them in the wilderness of the North.

John Badham made one of one of the most popular films of 1983, *War Games*, a chilling story about the potential of nuclear war starting accidently. He also directed *The Bingo Long Traveling All-Star and Motor Kings* (1976) and the most popular film of 1977, *Saturday Night Fever*, with John Travolta. Badham made another version of *Dracula* (1979), *Whose Life Is It Anyway?* (1981) about a man (Richard Dreyfuss) who wants to end it all because he is in pain and paralyzed, and *Blue Thunder* (1983) with Roy Scheider who tests a new secret helicopter.

Jim Henson is the creator of the muppets on Sesame Street and the muppet movies. He, along with Frank Oz, directed *The Dark Crystal* (1983). Jim is also the director and the star of a famous short film, *Time Piece*. Together with Oz, he created the *Muppets Take Manhattan* (1984).

John Sayles came on the movie scene with *The Return of the Secaucus Seven* (1980) after writing many screen plays, two novels, and a number of short stories. The film is a bittersweet look at life in the sixties. *Baby, It's You* (1983) is as much a film as rock music. It concerns the changing life styles of a young college student (Rosanna Arquette). In *A Brother from Another Planet* (1984), Sayles explores the reactions to New York City by a Black extraterrestrial fleeing from two interplanetary bounty hunters. (Shades of E.T.) He is currently working on a movie adaptation of Jean Auel's best-selling novels *Clan of the Cave Bear* and *Valley of the Horses*.

John Carpenter made one of the scariest movies of all time, *Halloween* (1978). But he hasn't stopped with this genre. He also made *Somebody Is Watching Me* (1978), a made-for-TV movie; *The Fog* (1980); *Escape from New York* (1981); *The Thing*, a remake of the Howard Hawks' film in 1982; and *Starman* (1984), about an alien, a blue light, who takes over the body of actress Karen Allen's late husband.

George Roy Hill has been making films for many years, but the films are still fresh and energetic. One of his earliest films that demonstrated his talent was *The World of Henry Orient* (1964). It is a comedy about two teenage girls who are in love with a quiet musician, Peter Sellers, who doesn't appreciate the attention. Hill also made *The Sting* (1973); *Butch Cassidy and the Sundance Kid* (1969); *A Little Romance* (1979); about two young teenagers in love; and *Slapshot* (1977), with Paul Newman involved with hockey. He made *Cannery Row* (1982) and *The World According to Garp* (1982) with Robin Williams. In 1984, he directed *The Little Drummer Girl*. This film is about a young repertory actress who is recruited by Israeli agents to penetrate a Palestinian terrorist organization.

Alan Parker gave us *Fame* (1980), about the talented young dancers and entertainers at the High School for Performing Arts in New York. Earlier, Parker made *Buggsy Malone* (1976), a musical comedy set in 1929 and composed of showgirls, hoodlums, and all sorts of hot shots—all played by children. He directed *Midnight Express* (1977), about Billy Hayes (Brad Davis) who was caught trying to smuggle hashish out of Turkey. *Pink Floyd: The Wall* (1982) was Parker's story film of the rock group's 1979 award-winning album. He made *Shoot the Moon* (1982) about a troubled family trying to find itself. In 1985, Parker directed *Birdy*, the tale of a lad (Matthew Modine) who wants to fly. The film is about madness, innocence, and friendship. Nicolas Cage plays the friend, Birdy's counterpoint, who tries to save him.

Mark Rydell began his career directing television programs: *Ben Casey, I Spy,* and *Gunsmoke.* His first movie was *The Fox* (1968), based on a D. H. Lawrence novel. Then he directed Steve McQueen in *The Reivers* (1969), from the novel by William Faulkner about a young boy's first trip to the big city. Then came *The Cowboys* (1972) with John Wayne and *Cinderella Liberty* (1973), about a sailor (James Caan) on liberty. When *Harry and Walter Go To New York* (1976) they (Elliott Gould and James Caan) find more than they bargain for when they team up with a suave safecracker (Michael Caine). Next was *The Rose* (1979) starring Bette Midler. *On Golden Pond* (1981) was the last film starring the late Henry Fonda (who won an Academy Award), Katharine Hepburn, and Jane Fonda. Rydell made *The River* (1985), the story of a family trying to save their farm.

Foreign Film Directors

America has dominated the world of films for nearly the entire history of films. However, many exciting and important developments in film have taken place in other countries—in Europe since the time of Eisenstein, in Asia more recently. The films produced in Britain, France, Italy, Germany, Russia, Japan, and Sweden have been known for years as examples of outstanding films.

Foreign film producers, like the American film industry, produce their share of "potboilers." However, except for "spaghetti westerns," the foreign films that we are able to see in America are usually carefully chosen examples of works of art.

The foreign film directors who will be discussed in this chapter are filmmakers who have directed films of outstanding quality and have worldwide reputations. Most of these directors have been directing films within the past twenty to thirty years, up to the present.

Roberto Rossellini is known as the filmmaker who began the neorealist tradition in Italy at the close of World War II. He didn't actually start a new style of filmmaking, because neorealism can be dated as far back as 1914, but his film *Open City* (1945) was the first film of the neorealist school to make an international impact. Neorealism is a style of filmmaking that uses realistic situations, such as scenes shot in the street where they happened and nonprofessional actors, to convey a feeling of realism. *Open City* was an expression of the whole neorealist movement. Rossellini tried to re-create the tensions of the people of Rome during their resistance to the German occupation.

Rossellini has continued to create films, right up to his recent *Socrate* (1970), that express his view, "This is the way things are." His best film *Paisan* (1946) also was inspired by the suffering of the Italian people during World War II.

Some films by Roberto Rossellini are these:

> *Open City*—1945
> *Paisan*—1946
> *The Miracle*—1948
> *Stromboli*—1949
> *The Seven Deadly Sins*—1952
> *Europa '51*—1952
> *The Lonely Woman*—1953
> *India*—1958
> *The Betrayer*—1961
> *Anima Nera*—1962
> *The Rise of Louis XIV*—1966
> *Socrate*—1970

The late **Vittorio de Sica** continued the neorealistic school with *Shoe Shine* (1946), about young juvenile delinquents in postwar Italy. The story centers on two friends who become the victims of the adult system of crime and punishment.

One of the most poignant Italian films of the post-World War II era, *The Bicycle Thief* was directed by the late Vitorio de Sica. His last film was *A Brief Vacation*. (The Bicycle Thief, *The Museum of Modern Art/Film Stills Archive.*)

De Sica made beautiful dramatic statements about the human condition. When you watch *Umberto D* (1952), de Sica makes you wait until an entire train goes by before you find out if Umberto's little dog, his only possession, is still alive. Nearly all his films show the humanity of a director who had a keen sense and understanding of what it is to be human.

De Sica's most famous film is the simple story of a man whose bicycle has been stolen. Perhaps it is hard for us to imagine the agony that the hero of *The Bicycle Thief* (1949) suffers as he sits on a curb with his little boy, not knowing what to do. His bicycle has been stolen, and he needs it desperately for him and his family to survive. Suddenly dozens of cycles returning from a sporting event flash before him. The irony is overwhelming as he looks up at all those expensive bikes used for pleasure.

The Reverend Robt. E. Lauder, writing about de Sica soon after his death, said, "The depth of his vision of humanity and his skill at recording that vision on film have won de Sica a lasting place in cinema history."[16]

Though other directors have had influence in the neorealistic tradition, Rossellini and de Sica made the largest contribution to world cinema.

The following are some of the films made by Vittorio de Sica:

The Bicycle Thief—1949
Miracle in Milan—1950
Bread, Love and Dreams—1953
Two Women—1961
Marriage, Italian Style—1964
Woman Times Seven—1967
The Garden of the Finzi-Continis—1971
A Brief Vacation—1974

In the next generation of Italian filmmakers, Federico Fellini and Michelangelo Antonioni are perhaps the best known and most respected.

Federico Fellini began as a writer for films, including Rossellini's *Open City*. He is the only director of feature films who has so far dared to include his name in a film title—*Fellini Satyricon* (1969). He has put much of his personality into films such as *Amarcord* (1974), which includes autobiographical material. His films belong very much to Fellini. Once you have seen several, it becomes very easy to identify a Fellini film.

Fellini films are bright and colorful, though they often consider symbolic thematic ideas that border on the abstract. His tragicomic *La Strada* (1954) is about a woman, symbolic of the soul; a man, symbolic of the body; and another man, symbolic of the mind. Though the theme is abstract, the story is told very simply.

Fellini has made several internationally popular films, many of them controversial in interpretation and meaning.

La Dolce Vita (1961) is a portrait of Rome. The first scene in the film is a helicopter towing a statue of Christ over the city of Rome. The film depicts Rome as a dark, corrupt, and ugly place seen through the eyes of a disillusioned journalist. Many critics believe this is Fellini's world, with everything exaggerated.

8½ (1963) is a sort of visual diary, in which Fellini shows a movie director's difficulties in making the film we are seeing. To make it even more complicated, the director shown in the film is making a film about his own life. Again, it appears that Fellini is making a personal statement about his own life.

Juliet of the Spirits (1965) is said by some critics to be "the female *8½*." It seems that Fellini is exploring the mind of someone else, perhaps his wife, Giulietta Masina, who starred in this film.

A number of his films have received Academy Awards for best foreign film: *8½*, *Nights of Cabiria* (1957), *La Strada*, and *Amarcord*.

The following are some of the films made by Federico Fellini:

> *The White Sheik*—1952
> *I Vitelloni*—1953
> *Love in the City*—1953
> *La Strada*—1954
> *Il Bidone*—1955
> *Nights of Cabiria*—1957
> *La Dolce Vita*—1959
> *8½*—1962

> *Juliet of the Spirits*—1965
> *Fellini Satyricon*—1969
> *The Clowns*—1971
> *Amarcord*—1974
> *Casanova*—1977
> *And the Ship Sails On*—1984

Michelangelo Antonioni became well known in the United States in 1966 when his American film *Blow-up* became an attraction at the box office. Actually Antonioni was recognized earlier it Italy for his documentary films and for his early feature film, *Cronaca di un amore* (1950). He made several more features in Italy before *L'avventura* (1960) made him known abroad. *L'avventura*, like Fellini films, is highly personal, though more abstract. The film is concerned with the fragility and instability of the basic human sentiments in a modern society. Antonioni's most recent film is *The Passenger.* (1975).

Swedish director **Ingmar Bergman** has created many allegorical and symbolic masterpieces. His films have become fashionable among intellectuals, giving rise to "cults" that admire his profound messages and symbolism. Still, there is no question as to the dimensions of the extraordinary thematic concepts that come from this artist. Bergman has consistently created magnificent works of art. He is one of the greatest directors of actors in the history of film. His films have no equal.

The Seventh Seal (1956) is considered by many to be his greatest film. Set in the fourteenth century during the plague and the Crusades, it is a medieval morality play about a man in search of the meaning of life. The central figure is a knight who returns from the Crusades to find Death waiting to claim him. Bergman films often are not easy to perceive. It takes a lot of background in visual studies to understand the many symbolic and metaphoric ideas that Bergman creates in his films.

Jan Dawson wrote in *The Sunday Times* (Sept. 20, 1970) that Bergman's skill as a great film director, "lies in his ability to express the obsessions of his age in the language of that age." Some writers of film compare Bergman's narrative skill with the greats of literature.

The following are some of the films made by Ingmar Bergman:

Kris—1945

Port of Call—1948

Prison—1948

Monika—1952

The Naked Night—1953

Smiles of a Summer Night—1955

The Seventh Seal—1956

Wild Strawberries—1957

The Magician—1958

The Virgin Spring—1959

Through a Glass Darkly—1961

Winter Light—1962

The Silence—1963

Persona—1966

The Touch—1971

Cries and Whispers—1972

Scenes from a Marriage—1974

The Magic Flute—1975 (for TV)

Face to Face—1976 (for TV)

The Serpent's Egg—1978

Autumn Sonata—1979

Fanny and Alexander—1983

After the Rehearsal—1984 (for TV)

Luis Buñuel, another of the best-known foreign directors, was also one of the outstanding early filmmakers. He began making films as early as 1928 with *The Fall of the House of Usher.* In the same year, he wrote a script for a short experimental film with Salvador Dali, the surrealist artist.* Buñuel then directed and produced the film, *Un Chien Andalou.* The film is very popular today in studying the experimental film, especially surrealist art in film.

Buñuel has had a very long filmmaking career (he was born in 1900). His most recent efforts are *The Discreet Charm of the Bourgeoisie* (1972)

and *Phantom of Liberty* (1974). However, it hasn't always been easy for Buñuel to make films. For many years, he has been a victim of the world's repressions and inhibitions, encountering French censorship, Spanish fascism, Hollywood commercialism, and Mexican film mediocrity. When he released his film *Viridiana* in 1961, it suprised many people by becoming a commercial success. Even Buñuel was probably suprised because he believes there are two kinds of cinema, the "commercial" and the "artistic." He states:

> There are always some men who will try to express their inner world, to convey it to others through the medium of the film, which is above all a marvelous tool for artistic creation. At the same time, films are made to please the culturally inferior masses, who are so either for social or economic reasons. Thus such films are apt to be superficial, stereotyped, easy to understand, and kowtow to the morals and politics of different governments. This could be a good definition of the "commercial" film. Sometimes, very seldom, a creative film is also commercial, but then this quality of commerciality is the predicate whereas the subject is art.

It hasn't been easy for Buñuel to create because of various restrictions. One of the most controversial of film directors, he takes an almost personal triumph in creating films that will offend someone. Many things in his films have offended Catholic and other religious leaders. In *Viridiana,* for instance, the household servants circle around behind a long table in their wild orgy as the camera moves parallel to the table. When the camera stops, the servants form the image of the Last Supper for a few seconds, and then the scene continues on to something else.

He deliberately assaults his audiences for surrendering their emotions. In *Simon of the Desert* (1965), we become very involved with Simon, who is having great difficulty in battling his temptations. Then Buñuel seems to say to the audience, "To hell with your emotions"—and has Simon give in to temptation.

Film critic Pauline Kael remarks: "Buñuel makes the charitable the butt of the humor and shows the lechery and mendacity of the poor and misbegotten. . . . his jokes are perverse and irratioinal and blasphemous. . . . as a movie-making comedian, he is a critic of mankind."[17]

*A surrealist artist is a person who creates art based on the expression of imagination uncontrolled by reason, suggesting the activities of the subconscious mind, in dreams or waking.

In *The Virgin Spring,* another Bergman film, a father discovers his young daughter has been raped by young men and determines to avenge her honor. Bergman films have never been Hollywood blockbusters, but have a steady following among more discerning filmgoers. (The Virgin Spring, *Courtesy of Janus Films.*)

The following are some of the films made by Luis Buñuel:

Land Without Bread—1932

Gran Casino—1947

Los Olvidados "The Young and the Damned"—1950

Daughter of Deceit—1951

Robinson Crusoe—1952

El—1952

Nazarin—1958

The Young One—1960

The Exterminating Angel—1962

Belle du Jour—1967

The Discreet Charm of the Bourgoisie—1972

Phantom of Liberty—1974

That Obscure Object of Desire—1978

In the 1950s in France **François Truffaut** and other young directors began making films in somewhat the same style as the neorealists, though perhaps more understated and symbolic. They used hand-held cameras, employed improvisational acting, and worked cheaply. Critics began calling this style the "new wave" *(nouvelle vague).*

Truffaut was a young director, once a film critic, who has been making films only since the middle 1950s. Truffaut attempted to create films with an emphasis upon reality, but not all his films have achieved this self-imposed goal.

Many of Truffaut's films have become fairly popular at the box office, and all of them are known well by connoisseurs of artistic films. Film teachers sometimes emphasize a disparity between "entertaining" films and "art" films. Most people would agree that all of Truffaut's work succeeds in being both.

Truffaut created comedies, dramatic films, and

historical films. One of his best-known films is *The 400 Blows* (1959), about a young boy who becomes a delinquent because of his parents' ineffectiveness and lack of concern.

Then in 1960 and 1961, Truffaut made two dramas, *Shoot the Piano Player* and *Jules and Jim*. *Jules and Jim* is a beautiful film about the emotionally tangled relationship between two men and a woman.

In 1966, Truffaut released his first and only film in English, *Fahrenheit 451*. Perhaps you have seen this film, taken from the book by Ray Bradbury, about a time in the future when books are banned. One man decides to go against the norm and attempts to save some of the books.

One of his most interesting films is *The Wild Child* (1971). Truffaut became interested in historical accounts of a wild boy found in the south of France in the late 1700s. According to the historical records and the writings of an early French psychologist, a boy about 11 or 12 years old was discovered in the forest by some peasants. He was naked and dirty and apparently walked and ran about using his arms as well as his legs. Eventually the psychologist obtained custody of the child and attempted to make a human being out of the savage boy. He succeeded only partially.

Truffaut decided to make a film from this account. The result is an interesting and moving film in which Truffaut himself plays the psychologist.

Small Change (1976) is simple vignettes of children going about their daily lives. But all of the children are acting; it is not considered a documentary. Some critics consider it one of the best films of the seventies. In 1984, Truffaut, at the age of 52, died of a brain tumor. The world lost one of the great filmmakers.

The following are some of the films by François Truffaut:

In *The 400 Blows*, Truffaut vividly demonstrates the emotions of a rebellious youth. The film ends with a freeze-frame shot of the boy running, symbolic of his flight from authority. (*The 400 Blows, courtesy of Janus Films.*)

The 400 Blows—1959
Shoot the Piano Player—1960
Jules and Jim—1961
The Soft Skin—1966
Fahrenheit 451—1966
The Bride Wore Black—1968
Stolen Kisses—1968
The Siren of Mississippi—1968
Mississippi Mermaid—1969
The Wild Child—1971
Day for Night—1974
The Story of Adele II—1975
Small Change—1976

In *Jules and Jim,* French director Francois Truffaut examines the fascinating relationship between two young men and a girl who cannot make up her mind. Truffaut's *Fahrenheit 451* is frequently shown on cable television. (Jules and Jim, *courtesy of Janus Films.*)

The Man Who Loved Women—1978
Love on the Run—1979
The Green Room—1979
The Last Metro—1980
The Man Who Loved Women—1983
Confidentially Yours—1984

The French filmmaker **Alain Resnais** was a part of the new wave. He began by making short films, including *Night and Fog* (1955), about the horrors of the Nazi concentration camps.

He became known with *Last Year at Marienbad* and then *Hiroshima Mon Amour* (1959), which concerns a young French woman who meets a Japanese man while visiting Japan. The relationship is tragic and frustrating as the theme is developed. Its Romeo-and-Juliet theme takes on

global proportions as we discover the traumas inflicted on the woman during the war. Resnais' *Stavisky* was released in 1975.

Resnais' *Providence* (1976) is beautiful, but like his other films is complex and often troubling. It's set in an indefinite time: a time when the aged are hunted down and put into stadiums to await their execution.

Resnais made *Mon Oncle d' Amerique* (1981), about a man who is visiting in America; *Muriel* (1981); and *Life Is a Bed of Roses* (1984). *Life* is about a man's attempt to restore people's creative innocence, symbolized by placing his friends in the hands of his Oriental staff at the Temple of Happiness. It is a strange tale.

Jean Renoir, perhaps the greatest French film director, certainly rates among the great directors of the world. (His father, Auguste Renoir, was the great nineteenth-century painter.)

Renoir, born in 1894, began making films in the mid-1920s with *Nana* (1926). His best films are many:

The Crime of Monsieur Lange (1926) suggests that man, united with others, can overcome tyranny. François Truffaut has said: "Of all Renoir's films, *The Crime of Monsieur Lange* is the most spontaneous, the richest in miracles of camera work, the most full of pure beauty and truth. In short, it is a film touched by divine grace."

La Grande Illusion (1937) is about World War I and a prison escape. Although the film is comparable in excitement to American films like *Stalag 17* and *The Great Escape,* its theme is actually the end of a way of life that the war destroyed.

The Rules of the Game (1939), some critics say, was Renoir's greatest failure. But it only took several years before it was considered one of his great films. Sometimes great works of art are not recognized for their value until much later. This probably was the case with this film.

In 1941, Renoir left France because of the war and came to America. During the war he made several films in America, from *Swamp Water* (1941), an adventure story set in the swamps of Georgia, to *The Diary of a Chambermaid* (1946). It borders between being a slapstick tragedy and burlesque.

Then Renoir made a triology of great films: *The Woman on the Beach* (1946), *The River* (1950), and *The Golden Coach* (1952). His most recent film is *Le Petit Theatre par Jean Renoir* (1969).

Perhaps of all directors, Jean Renoir has the best control and understanding of the medium and of humanity. According to Truffaut, "Renoir has succeeded in creating the most alive films in the history of the cinema, films which still breathe forty years after they were made."[18]

Halfway around the world, in Japan, another film director has been creating films since World War II.

Akira Kurosawa once was asked about the meaning of one of his films. He said, "If I could have said it in words, I would have—then I wouldn't have needed to make the picture."

Kurosawa is a film director with extreme talent in all areas of filmmaking. He directs the actors in such a way that they seem completely free of control. The movement of the camera is so subtle that it is easy to forget it is even present. But above all, the dramatic thematic ideas of Kurosawa stand out as examples of film at its best and most varied.

Ikiru (1952), which means "to live," is a perfect example of Kurosawa's ability. The theme, which was described elsewhere in this book, is one of great beauty and human truth.

The Seven Samuari (1954) is about a poor farmer's village that is constantly being robbed by bandits. Some villagers seek the help of a Samurai (a sort of professional warrior) to save them. The villagers finally obtain not one, but seven Samurai, who come to the village and help them destroy the bandits.

If the plot of this film sounds familiar, then you saw *The Magnificent Seven.* American filmmakers copied this film, changing the Samurai warriors into gunfighters. The same thing was done with another Kurosawa film, *Yojimbo* (1961), made into the American film *A Fistful of Dollars.* In 1964, the Americans copied still another Kurosawa film, *Rashomon* (1950) and made *The Outrage.*

Kurosawa in turn was interested in the Shakespearean play *Macbeth.* Adapting the play to medieval Japan, he created *Throne of Blood* (1957).

Nearly all of the Kurosawa's films have been received with much excitement in Japan and throughout the world. *Dersu Uzala* (1978) is about a colorful mountain man who saves the lives of some engineers on several occasions. The film won an Academy Award for best foreign film in 1978. *Kagemusha* (1980) is an epic film of sixteenth-century Japan. "Kagemusha" means shadow warrior. The film deals with the warlord of the Takeda clan who is replaced after his death by a nameless thief who looks exactly like him. The story is based on a real incident in early Japanese history.

The following are some of the films made by Akira Kurosawa:

Sanshiro Sugata—1944

Drunken Angel—1948

Stray Dog—1949

Rashomon—1950

The Idiot—1951

Ikiru—1952

The Seven Samurai—1954

Throne of Blood—1957
The Hidden Fortress—1960
Yojimbo—1961
Red Beard—1965
Dersu Uzala—1978
Kagemusha—1980

Satyajit Ray is a director of films from India. His filmmaking is in the tradition of Kurosawa. All of Ray's films tell stories in human terms with comedy and pathos intermingled. We recognize the characters in his films as ordinary people.

In the *Magnificent Seven* (bottom), a 1960 version of Kurosawa's 1954 classic, *Seven Samurai* (right), Mexican villagers hire American gunmen to defend them.

Of Ray's films, the "Apu" triology stands out. The three films follow the life of the boy, Apu, through his early years in *Pather Panchali* (1954), followed by *Aparajito* (1957), and *The World of Apu* (1959), later in his adolescence and young manhood.

Claude Chabrol is another French director who provides audiences with interesting films. Chabrol seems happiest behind a camera and has made over nineteen features since the late fifties. During the early sixties, he did not make artistic films, but commercial thrillers. *Les Biches* (1968) and *Le Boucher* (1970) are both well-known Chabrol films. He has become a master at thrillers and has been compared to Hitchcock.

Werner Herzog is one of the best German directors. His *Fitzcarraldo* (1982) took five years to make and was based on a true story. It is about a man who had an obsession to bring classical music to the Indians of the Peruvian jungles. So he sailed a steamboat up a jungle river and floated it back down another. The cross from one river to the next meant dragging the steamboat up the side of a mountain. Now you have some idea why the film took so long to make. Herzog went through several main actors and many crew members before the film was finally finished. It is considered a masterpiece.

The director Les Blank made a documentary called *Burden of Dreams* which recorded Herzog's filmmaking problems: crossfire between Ecuador and Peru over a boundary dispute, war of neighboring tribes, accusations by Amnesty International that he (Herzog) conspired to imprison four Indians, and the longest drought in this region's history.

Diane Kurys is one of only a handful of women directors. She made *Peppermint Soda* (1979) about two happy-go-lucky adolescents looking for love in France. *Cocktail Molotov* (1981) takes the opposite view and tells the story of troubled teens. *Entré Nous* (1983) concerns women who had been interned in prison camps during World War II and who are trying to escape the emotional claustrophobia of their daily lives.

Lina Wertmulier, an Italian filmmaker of the thirties has begun to direct films again. She has completed four features since 1976 and her *Seven Beauties* (1976) won an Academy Award for the Best Foreign Film.

In many of Wertmulier's films she explores the relationship between women and men, political concerns, and class struggles. *Swept Away by an Unusual Destiny* (1976) is another example of a complex film involving many levels of relationships between characters and perceptions by the audience. It is a contemporary *Taming of the Shrew*.

Costa-Gravas usually makes political thrillers in a documentary style. *Z* (1968) is about a revolution in a third-world country. *State of Siege* (1972) concerns an American kidnapped by terrorists. Costa-Gravas turned away from his usual theme to a study of an ill-fated romance with *Claire de Femme* (1979), but returned with *Missing* (1982) featuring Jack Lemon and Sissy Spacek looking for his son and her husband in revolutionary-torn Argentina. *Hanna K.* (1983) with Jill Clayburgh is about a woman whose relatives suffered in the Holocaust and who now moves from one relationship and problem to another.

The most famous of his films include:

> *The Sleeping Car*
> *Murders*—1965
> *Z*—1968
> *L'Aveu*—1970
> *State of Siege*—1972
> *Missing*—1982

One of **Louis Malle's** early films is *Spirit of the Dead* (1969). *Murmurs of the Heart* (1971) was about a boy who was attracted to his mother. *Lacombe, Lucien* (1974) is a semi-autobiographical film about growing up. *Pretty Baby* (1978), with Brooke Shields and Keith Carradine, is a controversial film because of the theme about prostitution, Shields' tender years, and her unclothed body in a few scenes.

Atlantic City (1981) won much aclaim. In addition, Burt Lancaster's role as an aged mobster was acclaimed by the critics and movie industry, earning him an Academy Award nomination for best actor. *My Dinner with Andre* (1981), a filmed dialogue between two friends, was also well received by the critics and much of the public as well. *Crackers* (1983) is about an inept group of losers and their attempt to rob a pawnbroker.

Peter Weir is an Australian film director who recently has joined the ranks of directors making films in the United States. His first film in Australia was *The Cars That Ate Paris* (1976), a surreal comedy based on his own unpublished short story. It is about an enterprising man who lures unwary motorists into carefully staged accidents and then uses their wrecked cars for parts that he can sell. *Picnic at Hanging Rock* (1975) was a critical and commercial success. It is a breathtaking beautiful film about a mysterious Valentine's Day picnic from which three girls and their chaperone never return. Next came *The Last Wave* (1977), also very successsful as a film and with the public. Weir became interested in the tribal lore and traditions of the aborigines. The main character is called upon to defend a group of aborigines accused of murdering a member of their tribe.

Gallipoli (1981) played in America and around the world to sizable audiences. *Gallipoli* is an antiwar film about two young soldiers who, along with hundreds of other soldiers in World War I, throw their lives away in a useless conflict. *The Year of Living Dangerously* (1983), Weir's next film, received many honors, including the Academy Award for best supporting actress to Billy Kwan who plays a dwarf cameraman. The film is set in 1965 at time of the ouster of president Sukarno. Reporter Hamilton (Mel Gibson) is covering the events in this Cambodian nation.

In the United States, Peter Weir made *Witness* (1985), starring Harrison Ford as a detective assigned to cover a case of a murdered policeman. A small Amish boy witnesses the brutal act, and through him Ford learns that the murder involves corrupt cops.

Poland's great filmmaker is **Andrzej Wajda.** He has been making films since World War II. Because he lives in a communist nation, however, Wajda must receive permission from the authorities before making any film. In the triology of films, *A Generation* (1955), *Kanal* (1956), and *Ashes and Diamonds* (1959), Wajda explored the themes of the regenerative power of love and the tragic nature of human destiny. He began looking at contemporary behavior in *The Innocent Sorcerers* (1960). It associates the growing materialism of Polish society with cynical and aliented young Poles.

In the mid-seventies, he received permission to film *Man of Marble,* modeled somewhat after Orson Welles' *Citizen Kane.* The film is about a graduate documentary filmmaker who is making, for her graduate requirements, a film with a politically naive bricklayer who becomes a hero because of his great productivity. The film was an immediate success throughout Poland, even after the scene of the death of the bricklayer was censored. Tickets sold on the black market for ten times their original price. In the United States, the film critics said it might be best film analyzing the effects of Stalinism. *Man of Iron* (1981) continues the story. It won the top prize at the Cannes Film Festival.

Of filmmaking, Wajda says, "My task as a director is not just to provide a nice evening's entertainment. The important thing is to tell the audience something, to make people think, to initiate a dialogue."* No one could describe better the most important objective in the study of film.

There are many other foreign directors who could or should be mentioned in this chapter. Most of them are not yet known to American audiences. Perhaps with the expansion of cable television, direct satelite-to-home communication and video cassette the works of these directors, and indeed, all filmmakers, will be seen by a larger audience.

Further Reading: *Check your library.*

Bach, Steven. *Final Cut: Dreams and Disaster in the Making of Heaven's Gate,* New York: William Morrow and Company Inc., 1985.

Blum, Daniel. *A Pictorial History of the Silent Screen,* New York: Putnam Publishing Group, 1982.

Castell, David. *Richard Attenborough: A Pictorial Film Biography,* Bridgeport, CT: Merrimack Publishing, 1984.

Champlin, Charles. *The Movies Grow Up: Nineteen Forty to Nineteen Eighty,* Athens, OH: Ohio University Press, 1981.

Crawley, Tony. *The Steven Spielberg Story,* New York: Morrow, 1983.

*Interview in *Cineaste* magazine, Winter 1980–81.

Desser, David and Diane Kirkpatrick. *The Samurai Films of Akira Kurosawa,* Ann Arbor, MI: University of Michigan Research Press, 1983.

Dworkin, Susan. *Brian DePalma & The Making of Body Double, A Film Study,* New York: Newmarket, 1984.

Kagan, Norman. *American Skeptic: Robert Altman's Genre-Commentary Films,* Ann Arbor, MI: Piernan Press, 1982.

Langman, Larry. *A Guide to American Film Directors: The Sound Era, 1929–1979,* Metuchen, NJ: Scarecrow Press Inc., 1981.

Liem, Mira. *Passion and Defiance: Italian Film from 1942 to the Present,* Berkeley, CA: University of California Press, 1984.

Pollock, Dale. *Skywalking: The Life and Films of George Lucas,* New York: Crown Publishers Inc., 1983.

Shipman, David. *The Story of Cinema: A Complete Narrative History from the Beginnings to the Present,* New York: St. Martin's, 1984.

Side, Anthony and Edward Wagenknecht. *Fifty Great American Silent Films,* New York: Dover, 1981.

Stratton, David. *The Last New Wave: The Australian Film Revival,* New York: Ungar, 1981.

Notes

1. J. A. Place, *The Western Films of John Ford* (Secaucus, NJ: Citadel Press, 1974).

2. Arthur Knight, *The Liveliest Art* (New York: New America Library, Mentor Book [paperback], 1979), p. 31.

3. Arthur Knight, *The Liveliest Art,* pp. 79–80.

4. American Film Institute, *Dialogue on Film.*

5. Paul McCuskey, *Movies: Conversations with Peter Bogdanovich.* (New York: Harcourt Brace Jovanovich, Inc.), p. 11.

6. Arthur Knight, *The Liveliest Art,* p. 43.

7. Arthur Knight, *The Liveliest Art,* p. 48.

8. Arthur Knight, *The Liveliest Art,* p. 51.

9. Roy Paul Madsen, *The Impact of Film.* (New York: The Macmillan Company, 1973), p. 292.

10. Arthur Knight, *The Liveliest Art,* pp. 114–115.

11. Essoe and Lee, *DeMille: The Man and His Pictures.* (New York: A. S. Barnes, 1970).

12. *Focus on Hitchcock,* ed. by Albert J. LaValley. (Englewood Cliffs, NJ: Prentice-Hall, 1972), p. 23.

13. *Focus on Hitchcock,* p. 45.

14. Arthur Knight, *The Liveliest Art,* p. 140.

15. Interview with Orson Welles by Juan Cobos, Miguel Rubio, and Jose Antonio Pruneda in *Cahiers du Cinema,* April 1965.

16. Robert E. Lauder, "Vittorio de Sica: Genius of Neorealism," *America,* March 8, 1975.

17. Paulene Kael, *Going Steady.* (Little, 1970).

18. André Bazin, *Jean Renoir.* (New York: Simon and Schuster, 1971).

Reflection

1. Howard Kazanjian, producer of *Return of the Jedi,* and himself a graduate of the Director's Guild of America Training Program, says a producer creates the film. Based on what you have learned from this course, do you feel that the producer or the director is more important in the creation of the film? Why?

Activities

1. Re-read the interview with director Ivan Reitman (*Ghostbusters, Meatballs,* and *Stripes*). Reitman says the director is the creative captain of the ship—responsible for all big and little decisions. Go through all the profiles in *Understanding the Film* and find examples where veteran professionals in other crafts defer to the director's wishes.

2. See at least two films by one director (preferably one of those listed in this chapter). Then see at least two films by another director. Write a short paper or give a presentation in class, comparing and contrasting the directors' style. You may find it easier to see films on video or even on television.

Appendix

Selected American Films

The authors of this book have selected 100 American films that we feel students should try to see. Naturally, everyone will not agree with this list, but most people would consider the films selected as worthwhile for a film-educated individual to see.

How many have you seen? Could you discuss them? Do you agree with the list of films or would you have different choices?

Adam's Rib (1949)
Courtroom battle between a woman lawyer (Katharine Hepburn) and her husband, the assistant district attorney (Spencer Tracy). Directed by George Cukor.

The African Queen (1952)
An adventurous, offbeat, love story of a prim missionary and a scruffy riverboat captain (Katharine Hepburn and Humphrey Bogart) who risk their lives traveling down a river in East Africa during World War I. Directed by John Huston.

All Quiet on the Western Front (1930)
A powerful antiwar film about a group of German recruits in World War I. Their idealism changes from horror to disillusionment. Directed by Lewis Milestone.

All the President's Men (1976)
Watergate was the big issue at the mid-seventies, and this film explores it with intelligence and dignity. Directed by Alan J. Pakula.

Amadeus (1984)
Amadeus tells the story of Mozart and Salieri, a rival composer. The music is superb and the setting in eighteenth-century Europe is breathtaking. The movie's themes deal with envy, deceit, and murder. Directed by Milos Forman.

American Graffiti (1973)
A film that follows the lives of four boys in their small town in 1962—their last night before each goes his own way. Directed by George Lucas.

Annie Hall (1977)
This Oscar-winning film starred Woody Allen, portraying a man who constantly experiences failed relationships; a man incapable of experiencing pleasure. It is a tender and introspective story. Directed by Woody Allen.

Ben-Hur (1959 version)
The second version stars Charlton Heston as Ben-Hur, who is betrayed by his boyhood friend, a Roman. Directed by William Wyler.

The Best Years of Our Lives (1946)
Set in post-World War II America, the film is about three soldiers and the frustrations and adjustments they experience returning from war to their families. Winner of four Oscars in 1946. Directed by William Wyler.

The Birth of a Nation (1915)
Considered to be the first major feature film, and still a powerful melodrama about the American Civil War. Directed by D. W. Griffith.

The Black Stallion (1979)
The first half of this film has little or no dialogue—the beautiful story of a boy who saves and loves a horse is told through images alone. This is a most remarkable film that uses the medium to communicate in its most basic and important element. Directed by Carroll Ballard.

Bonnie and Clyde (1967)
Banks are not safe in this film as Bonnie (Faye Dunaway) and Clyde (Warren Beatty) re-create the 1930s bank robbers. Directed by Arthur Penn.

Breaking Away (1979)
This film shows the trials and tribulations of growing up in America. A rare and very well done film. Directed by Peter Yates.

Citizen Kane (1941)
The story of a man who rises to the top, but dies unloved and lonely. Orson Welles, the director, introduced many new techniques to this masterpiece of cinema.

The Day the Earth Stood Still (1951)
A visitor from space tells Earth people that they must use their weapons for peaceful uses, but meets hostility and fear. A young woman, her son, and a scientist help him achieve his aim. Directed by Robert Wise.

Days of Wine and Roses (1962)
This film is a love story (Jack Lemmon and Lee Remick) as well as a powerful drama about the couple's fight against alcoholism. Directed by Blake Edwards.

Dr. Strangelove (1963)
This film is a chilling, funny satire about the possibilities of an accidental nuclear war. Directed by Stanley Kubrick.

Doctor Zhivago (1965)
A beautifully photographed love story set in turbulent revolutionary Russia. Directed by David Lean.

Duck Soup (1933)
One of the best and most famous Marx Brothers films. Directed by Leo McCarey.

Easy Rider (1969)
A turning-point film. "Captain America" and Billy (Peter Fonda and Dennis Hopper) set out on their motorcycles to find America, but their search ends in violent tragedy. Directed by Dennis Hopper.

The Endless Summer (1966)
A beautiful film of surfing all around the world. Directed by Bruce Brown.

E.T.: The Extra-Terrestrial (1981)
If perhaps you are one of the few people who has not seen this all-time best-selling film, *E.T.* is about a visitor from another planet who befriends a young boy on Earth. Directed by Steven Spielberg.

Fantasia (1941)
One of the best animations of Walt Disney, to a background of classical music.

Five Easy Pieces (1970)
This film is about a man's discovering himself, escaping from his childhood and his relationships with his family and friends. Directed by Robert Rafelson.

Fury (1936)
About a man (Spencer Tracy) suspected in a killing even though he is innocent. When the jail burns down after a mob tries to get him, he escapes to come back to take revenge. Directed by Fritz Lang.

Gandhi (1983)
Gandhi is the epic-scaled biography of the Indian non-violence leader of 1940s India. Ben Kingsley is superb in the title role. Though the film is quite long, the pacing is excellent, making it a very watchable, informative, and entertaining film. Directed by Richard Attenborough.

The General (1924)
Buster Keaton at his best, in one of his funniest yet most dramatic films. It is about a group of men who make their way to Atlanta during the Civil War to seize a train. Directed by Keaton and Clyde Brickman.

The Godfather (1972)
A dramatic story of organized crime, with Marlon Brando as the head of a Mafia family. Directed by Francis Ford Coppola.

Gold Diggers of 1933
The first of a long string of spectacular dance films. Directed at first by Mervyn LeRoy with Busby Berkeley, later by Berkeley alone.

The Gold Rush (1925)
Charlie Chaplin goes north to Alaska to find gold. One of the classic Chaplin films and the funniest. The famous boot-eating scene is in this film. Directed by Charlie Chaplin.

Gone with the Wind (1939)
Still the most-often-revived film. A spectacular story of the Civil War, as background to the romance of an adventurer (Clark Gable) and a strong-willed Southern belle (Vivien Leigh). Directed by Victor Fleming.

The Graduate (1967)
A turning-point film, about an inexperienced college graduate (Dustin Hoffman) who has an affair with an older woman (Anne Bancroft) and ends up falling in love with her daughter (Katharine Ross). Directed by Mike Nichols.

The Grapes of Wrath (1939)
Pushed off their farm by the Depression and the Dust Bowl, a young man (Henry Fonda) and his family travel west to look for work in California. Directed by John Ford.

The Great Train Robbery (1903)
The first western film. Directed by Edwin S. Porter.

Greed (1924)
One of the great silent films. It is about money and its power to corrupt. Directed by Erich von Stroheim.

The Gunfighter (1950)
A quiet man, trying to flee his reputation as the deadliest shot in the West, finds he must stay on top until someone shoots him off. Directed by Henry King.

High Noon (1952)
A marshal (Gary Cooper) is left alone to fight a notorious outlaw, when everyone else in town is afraid. Directed by Fred Zinnemann.

How Green Was My Valley (1941)
The lives of the Morgan family, caught up in a strike of Welsh coal miners in the nineteenth-century. Directed by John Ford.

The Human Comedy (1943)
Homer (Mickey Rooney) is a teenager who delivers telegrams at night during the war years. His older brother (Van Johnson) goes off to war and Homer becomes the male head of the family. Directed by Charles Brown.

The Hustler (1961)
Paul Newman plays the role of an itinerant pool shark who challenges the best in the country, Minnesota Fats (Jackie Gleason). He sacrifices everything and everyone until he realizes, almost too late, that the price is too high. Directed by Robert Rossen.

I Am a Fugitive from a Chain Gang (1932)
A man (Paul Muni) escapes from a chain gang in the South. Based on an actual event, this film was so shocking that an aroused public demanded reforms. Directed by Mervyn LeRoy.

The Jazz Singer (1927)
The first American talking picture. Al Jolson plays a man caught between devotion to his family and love for jazz music, which his father feels is sacrilegious. Directed by Alan Crosland.

Jezebel (1938)
Usually considered Bette Davis' best role. She plays the part of Julie Marstan in a bittersweet love affair in antebellum New Orleans. Directed by William Wyler.

Julia (1977)
In this film set in pre-World War II, Jane Fonda plays Lillian Hellman, a writer. Vanessa Redgrave plays her friend, Julia. The film is a psychological characterization of Julia's political commitment and, most of all, the study of friendship. Directed by Fred Zinnemann.

The Killing Fields (1984)

Perhaps one of the best films in the last decade, *The Killing Fields* tells of a *New York Times* correspondent's account of his experience in Pol Pot's Cambodia. The film is not easy to watch with its many gut-wrenching sequences of man's inhumanity to man as the reporter and his Cambodian friend try to survive a man-made hell. Directed by Roland Joffe.

King Kong (1932)

The first major monster movie. A gigantic gorilla captured on a remote island falls in love with a girl (Fay Wray). Directed by Merian C. Cooper and Ernest B. Schoedsack.

Kramer vs. Kramer (1979)

This film is about a failed marriage and the subsequent custody fight over a child. The director and actors go far, in what could have been a lesser film, by showing that nobody wins. Directed by Robert Benton.

The Last Picture Show (1971)

A story about a young man growing up, dreaming of greatness, and surrounded by mediocrity. The film is set in a small town, and directed by Peter Bogdanovich.

The Life of Emile Zola (1937)

The film is about the unjust persecution and trial of Alfred Dreyfus, a major scandal in France. Paul Muni plays Zola, the author who defends him against intolerance. Directed by William Dieterle.

Little Caesar (1930)

This film portrayed the first of the movie gangsters, epitomized for all time by Edward G. Robinson followed soon after, by James Cagney, George Raft, Humphrey Bogart, and others. Directed by Mervyn LeRoy.

Lonely Are the Brave (1962)

John W. Burns (Kirk Douglas) plays the role of the last cowboy caught in a world of jeeps, prisons, and fences. He pits individualism against helicopters and walkie-talkies in a final chase scene. Directed by David Miller.

The Long Voyage Home (1940)

A British merchant ship on its way home is ordered back to pick up ammunition in the U.S. Then it is discovered that there is a saboteur aboard. Directed by John Ford.

The Lost Weekend (1945)

One of the best-known social dramas, *The Lost Weekend* is about a man (Ray Milland) who is trying to kick the habit of alcohol. Directed by Billy Wilder.

The Maltese Falcon (1941)

One of the best and most famous of "private eye" films. Humphrey Bogart plays Sam Spade who, along with an assortment of colorful characters (Mary Astor, Peter Lorre, Sidney Greenstreet, and Walter Huston, father of John), goes after the jeweled falcon of Malta. Directed by John Huston.

The Man with the Golden Arm (1955)

This film about heroin addiction is still one of the most powerful films about social problems in America. Directed by Otto Preminger.

Marty (1955)

Marty is a Bronx butcher (Ernest Borgnine) who is unmarried and used to it. He is so used to his dull life that he doesn't want to meet girls anymore. One night he meets a girl who is very much like him. This film is simple in its plot and magnificent in its theme. Directed by Delbert Mann.

M*A*S*H (1970)

The famous war comedy-drama, in the tradition of the Marx Brothers but with serious undertones. It is about a team of surgeons in a Mobile Army Surgical Hospital during the Korean War. Directed by Robert Altman.

Midnight Cowboy (1969)
Jon Voight plays the role of a naive Texan who is convinced he can live in the city. Dustin Hoffman, in his best performance, is a downtrodden, crippled con artist and petty thief. The two unexpectedly become friends. Directed by John Schlesinger.

The Misfits (1961)
The last film of Clark Gable and Marilyn Monroe. Three jobless cowboys see, in the one woman who keeps house for them, a mother, wife, sweetheart, and mistress. Directed by John Huston.

Mr. Smith Goes to Washington (1939)
A young idealist from Montana (James Stewart) steps into history and the United States Senate to fill the unexpired term of a senator who had died. Directed by Frank Capra.

Moby Dick (1956)
Taken from Herman Melville's classic novel. In this powerful film, Captain Ahab (Gregory Peck) is the tyrannical man whose lust for vengeance against a mysterious white whale takes his ship and crew into tragedy. Directed by John Huston.

Modern Times (1936)
One of Chaplin's finest feature films. He plays his usual tramp role as he attempts to find work during the Depression. Directed by Charlie Chaplin.

Mutiny on the Bounty (1935 version)
Captain Bligh (Charles Laughton) is a symbol of vicious naval discipline that leads to rebellion by his crew. Christian (Clark Gable) is the officer who leads the revolt. Directed by Frank Lloyd.

Nanook of the North (1922)
The famous documentary film about an Eskimo and his family and their everyday battle to survive. Directed by Robert Flaherty.

Nashville (1976)
This film told the stories of various people in Nashville. It focuses on many issues about America in that year, such as politics, race problems, class problems, the media, music, and human vanity. Directed by Robert Altman.

A Night at the Opera (1935)
Another of the more famous Marx Brothers films. Directed by Sam Wood.

North by Northwest (1959)
Shooting in famous spots like Mt. Rushmore, Alfred Hitchcock created one of his best films. An advertising man (Cary Grant) is mistaken for a CIA agent by foreign agents. They try to kill him in the most ingenious ways.

An Officer and a Gentleman (1982)
Richard Gere stars as a traumatized son of a drunken sailor who signs up for the Naval Aviation Officers Candidate School in Washington. Here Gere is forced to confront himself and his weaknesses. Directed by Taylor Hackford.

On the Waterfront (1954)
A great film about crime and corruption on the waterfronts of New York. Marlon Brando plays the minor hoodlum, and Karl Malden is a fearless priest out to smash the rule of the crooked longshoreman's union. Directed by Elia Kazan.

Our Daily Bread (1954)
One of the social problem films of the Depression, Our Daily Bread is about a migrant family's attempt to make a go of farming after fleeing the Dust Bowl. Directed by King Vidor.

The Ox-Bow Incident (1943)
A serious, dramatic western about a group of men who are captured by a posse and lynched. Directed by William Wellman.

Paths of Glory (1957)
Kirk Douglas as a lawyer in the French army during World War I. When a hopeless attack fails, the commanding general fires on Douglas' men and, to cover up his misjudgment, selects three

soldiers for execution for cowardice. Douglas defends them. Directed by Stanley Kubrick.

Patton: A Salute to a Rebel (1970)
About the tough, famous general of World War II. Directed by Franklin Schaffner.

The Phantom of the Opera (1925 version)
Even though there are other versions, this may be the best film of the phantom. Lon Chaney plays the part of a man who inhabits an opera house and scares everyone with his chilling appearances. Directed by Rupert Julian.

The Plow That Broke the Plains (1936)
A famous documentary film (with a fine musical score) about the economic and social history of the Great Plains. Directed by Pare Lorentz.

Psycho (1960)
One of the most famous psychological thrillers, *Psycho* is about a girl who is murdered—but a murder that is certainly impossible to forget. Directed by Alfred Hitchcock.

Raiders of the Lost Ark (1981)
One of the most popular films of all time, *Raiders of the Lost Ark* follows the adventures of Indiana Jones and his daring pursuit of the Ark of the Covenant. The film is reminiscent of the old Saturday afternoon serials and cliff hangers. It is high adventure—exciting and fast moving. Directed by Steven Spielberg.

Rebel Without a Cause (1955)
The 1950s film that started a trend in youth movies. James Dean plays the part of a youthful rebel who is at odds with his affluent parents. Directed by Nicholas Ray.

The Right Stuff (1983)
This film records the Mercury space program and the early astronauts involved in America's entry into the space race. The film is a fairly good example of irony, showing how the nation sometimes puts publicity, public relations, politics, and

national interests ahead of human lives. Directed by Phillip Kaufman.

Rocky (1977)
Rocky is a triumph of the human spirit; a down-and-out fighter finds himself. *Rocky II* (1979) is one of the few sequels that has also proved popular at the box office. Directed by J. Avildsen.

Romeo and Juliet (1963)
From the classic play by Shakespeare. The actors are the youngest yet to play in a film of this tragic love relationship. Directed by Franco Zeffirelli.

Shane (1953)
The story of a bold and stubborn homesteader (Van Heflin), fighting for his land with the help of the mysterious drifter, Shane (Alan Ladd). The late Brandon de Wilde plays the part of the boy who idolizes Shane. Directed by George Stevens.

Singin' in the Rain (1952)
One of the greatest movie musicals. It features Gene Kelly, Donald O'Connor, and Debbie Reynolds. Directed by Gene Kelly.

Stagecoach (1939 version)
The classic western about a group of people and their overland venture via stagecoach. Directed by John Ford.

Star Wars (1977)
Fantasy, adventure, excitement, romance, evil and good forces, and heroes are all words that define this film set in a galaxy a long time ago. Directed by George Lucas.

The Sting (1974)
This may be one of the best films ever made about a confidence game. Paul Newman and Robert Redford are two con men who fool everybody, even the audience. Directed by George Roy Hill.

Sunset Boulevard (1950)
A forgotten silent film star (Gloria Swanson)

slowly goes mad as a young scriptwriter (William Holden) exploits her illusions. Directed by Billy Wilder.

The Ten Commandments (1956 version)
This is the famous film in which Moses (Charlton Heston) leads his people out of bondage, with some amazing special effects. Directed by Cecil B. DeMille.

Three Women (1977)
Three Women is about women of all ages. It concerns the relationships, fantasies, and dreams of three women who find themselves together. Directed by Robert Altman.

To Kill a Mockingbird (1963)
A beautiful, atmospheric film, based on the novel. Two children in a small Southern town in the 1920s must face the tensions caused when their father, a lawyer, defends a black man in a rape trial. Directed by Robert Mulligan.

Tootsie (1982)
Dustin Hoffman, in a remarkable role, is an out-of-work actor who finds work by playing the part of a woman, Tootsie, in a daytime soap opera. Directed by Sidney Pollack.

The Treasure of the Sierra Madre (1948)
Two cowhands (Humphrey Bogart and Tim Holt) and an old prospector (Walter Huston), who look for gold in the mountains of Mexico. The theme of the story is the effect of "gold fever" and greed on the three. Directed by John Huston.

A Tree Grows in Brooklyn (1945)
A story about the triumph of the human spirit over death, poverty, weakness, and misunderstanding. Directed by Elia Kazan.

Twelve O'Clock High (1950)
One of the classic war films. It is about a general who accepts the challenge of rebuilding the morale of a bomber group that has suffered great battle losses. Directed by Henry King.

2001: A Space Odyssey (1968)
Science fiction at its best, made in collaboration with Arthur C. Clarke, the science fiction writer. It boasts some outstanding photography and interesting concepts about a future contact with aliens. Directed by Stanley Kubrick.

An Unmarried Woman (1978)
The film is about an unmarried woman, living in contemporary New York. Jill Clayburgh is a woman who thought she was happily married until her husband told her otherwise. Directed by Paul Mazursky.

White Heat (1949)
James Cagney once again as a mad killer, with a spectacular ending atop an exploding oil tank. Directed by Raoul Walsh.

The Wizard of Oz (1939)
Haven't you seen it on television? This film started Judy Garland's career, as she played a Kansas farm girl carried to Oz by a violent tornado. There she meets all kinds of strange characters, notably the Tin Woodman, the Cowardly Lion, and the Scarecrow. Directed by Victor Fleming.

Woodstock (1970)
Some critics believe *Woodstock* to be the best documentary made in many years. It is about the music rock festival with a cast—literally—in the thousands. Directed by Michael Wadleigh.

Yellow Submarine (1968)
One of the best animated features. A world of pure visual fantasy surrounds the Beatles and their songs. Directed by Heinz Edelmann.

Selected Foreign Films

The following is a list of 55 foreign films that we feel students should try to see. In some cases we have listed several films by one director.

Aguirre, the Wrath of God (1977, Germany)

This film is about a power-mad officer in the sixteenth-century who practically destroys the Amazon jungle in his search for gold. Directed by Werner Herzog.

The Ballad of a Soldier (1950, U.S.S.R.)

A young soldier traveling home on a pass witnesses the disorder, grief, and frustrations of people caught in war. The deceptively simple story makes a profound statement about the horror of war. Directed by Grigori Chukrai.

The Battle of Algiers (1966, Italy)

This film is almost a newsreel in its visual style, but it is a powerful example of outstanding filmmaking. It is about the people of the Casbah (the Arab section) and their revolt against the French. Directed by Gillo Pontecorvo.

The Bicycle Thief (1948, Italy)

This film is discussed in Chapter 12. Directed by Vittorio de Sica.

The Blue Angel (1930, Germany)

A middle-aged professor falls in love with a dance-hall girl (Marlene Dietrich in her first film role). They marry, but the tragic relationship ends in his destruction. Directed by Josef von Sternberg.

The Boat (Das Boot) (1982, Germany)

The Boat is an exciting and suspenseful film about World War II German U-boat sailors on patrol. When one watches this film, unlike most WW II films, one roots for the Germans rather than for the allies. Directed by Wolfgang Peterson.

Breaker Morant (1981, Australia)

This film tells the story of one of the most controversial military court-martials in history. Three officers are put on trial after several captives are mysteriously killed during the Boer War. Directed by Bruce Beresford.

The Burmese Harp (1965, Japan)

This film deals with war guilt and people's capacity to live together. At the end of World War II, one man attempts unsuccessfully to notify some last-ditch fighters at the end of the war. Later he becomes obsessed with burying the bodies of many Japanese soldiers. Directed by Kon Ichikawa.

Chariots of Fire (1982, France)

This film, based on fact, is the story of British athletes competing in the 1924 Olympics. The movie is thrilling and inspiring and is bound to become a classic for all to see and admire. Directed by Hugh Hudson.

The Cranes are Flying (U.S.S.R.)

One of the best films from Russia. In this tragic love story, youthful ambitions and love are shattered by the forces of war. Directed by Mikhail Kalatosov.

Dead of Night (1946, Britain)

This is a most bizarre and complex film, with an intricate plot. It is a shocking calendar of happenings that leaves the mind whirling. Directed by Alberto Cavaleanti.

Diva (1982, France)

An 18-year-old Paris mailman loves opera and is fascinated by an American diva (a distinguished female singer). She will not allow her voice to be recorded, but the mailman does it without her knowledge. Then two Taiwanese record pirates find out and the chase is on. This may not sound like a great foreign film, but it is a *tour de force* that shows an uncommon touch by the director and his cameraman. The scenes are like paintings. The acting is excellent and the direction is superb. Directed by Jean-Jacques Beineix.

The Emigrants (1972, Sweden)

Perhaps the finest film portrayal of the European immigrants who settled and built America. Liv Ullman and Max von Sydow are the young farm couple who undergo incredible hardships as they make their way to the rich lands of Minnesota.

The New Land continues the story. Directed by Jan Troell.

Fanny and Alexander (1983, Sweden)
This film by the Swedish film director, Ingmar Bergman, tells the story of a young boy and a young girl and their childhood in a small town in the early 1900s. There are the usual symbols and dream fantasies, but without the usual Bergman heavyhandedness.

Fitzcarraldo (1982, W. Germany)
The film is about a man driven to build an opera house in the remote jungles of the Amazon. On the surface the film sounds absolutely ridiculous, but the film is really a wonder to see—a masterpiece. Directed by Werner Herzog.

Forbidden Games (Jeux Interdits) (1952, France)
Two young children during the German occupation imitate the cruel adult life that surrounds them, collecting dead animals for their private cemetery. An excellent antiwar film that doesn't deal with actual warfare. Directed by René Clement.

The 400 Blows (1959, France)
A film about a delinquent young boy. This film is discussed in Chapter 11. Directed by François Truffaut.

Gate of Hell (1953, Japan)
This film has a simple theme about pride and desire. It takes place in twelfth-century Japan, where noble clans are fighting for control of the country. A samurai, a professional warrior, falls in love with a happily married woman. Stunning use of color and photography. Directed by Teinosuke Kinugasa.

Great Expectations (1946, Britain)
A memorable adaptation from the Dickens novel about young Pip, whose "great expectations" of a fortune come from an unexpected source. This film is admired for director David Lean's effective editing.

The Green Wall (1970, Peru)
One of the best Latin American films. It is about a young couple who take their young son and leave the city behind them to build a home and farm in the jungle. They live an idyllic life until the Land Reform Commission challenges their claim. Directed by Armando Robles Godoy.

Henry V (1944, Britain)
A colorful film version of Shakespeare's play about a young soldier-king. Sir Laurence Olivier, both star and director, followed it with *Hamlet* and *Richard III*.

Hiroshima Mon Amour (1950, France)
This film is a complex love story about a Frenchwoman and a Japanese man. Directed by Alain Resnais.

Ikiru (1952, Japan)
This film is discussed in Chapter 12. Directed by Akira Kurosawa.

Il Posto (Sound of Trumpets) (1961, Italy)
A youth begins his first job in a large factory. The film traces the process by which he willingly becomes another cog in the machine. Directed by Ermanno Olmi.

Jules and Jim (1961, France)
Jules and Jim, friends, love the same girl, and this story is about their love through 20 years. The film is a mixture of fun, comedy, tragedy, and drama. Directed by François Truffaut.

Kagemusha (1981, Japan)
This is an epic drama of feudal conflict in sixteenth-century Japan. It is a film to behold with images of power and boldness. The story is based on a real incident about a warlord who dies and is replaced by a man who looks exactly like him. Directed by Akira Kurosawa.

La Dolce Vita (1961, Italy)
This film is described in Chapter 12. Directed by Federico Fellini.

La Grande Illusion (1937, France)
This is the antiwar film described in Chapter 12. Directed by Jean Renoir.

The Last Laugh (1924, Germany)
A silent film about an elderly doorman (Emil Jannings) who is replaced by a younger man, but cannot bear to tell his relatives about his loss of position. Directed by F. W. Murnau.

The Last Wave (1978, Australia)
This is a haunting masterpiece of suspense from Australia. A lawyer takes the defense of some aboriginal tribesmen who are accused of murder. Directed by Peter Weir.

La Strada (1954, Italy)
This film is about a young girl and her relationships with two men. The film is discussed in Chapter 12. Directed by Federico Fellini.

Los Olvidados: The Young and the Damned (1950, Mexico)
This film is a study of juvenile delinquents living near Mexico City. It is almost a documentary, but really is about the effects of poverty and violence on the young. Directed by Luis Buñuel.

M (1931, Germany)
M was the first talking German film and gave Peter Lorre his first role, as the child murderer. (It is discussed in Chapter 12.) Directed by Fritz Lang.

Metropolis (1926, Germany)
A futuristic film about a revolt against the rulers of a city. Directed by Fritz Lang.

Miracle in Milan (1951, Italy)
This fantasy is about a social protest in Italy shortly after World War II. It concerns a group of beggars and poor people who fight against a rich man, who wants their land after discovering oil on it. Directed by Vittorio de Sica.

Olympia (1937, Germany)
This great documentary film shows the Olympic Games held in Germany before the beginning of World War II. It contains some of the best sports footage and beautiful sequences of any film. Directed by Leni Riefenstahl.

The Overcoat (1962, Italy)
Comedy and pathos are mingled with the treatment of humanity. A man needs a new overcoat and saves to buy one, but soon after the purchase, it is stolen. Directed by Alberto Latluada.

Paisan (1946, Italy)
Roberto Rossellini's great film shows the suffering and heartbreak of the people of Italy as the war progressed up the Italian peninsula. The film is discussed in Chapter 12.

Pather Panchali (1954, India)
Part of the "Apu" trilogy, this film, like the Gorky trilogy, follows a youth from childhood to maturity. It is a most beautiful and human story of love and devotion. Directed by Satyajit Ray.

Potemkin (1925, U.S.S.R.)
The use of montage and editing in this classic film of the Russian Revolution makes it a must for students of film. Directed by Sergei Eisenstein. We also suggest that the student see his *Ten Days that Shook the World* (1928) and *Ivan the Terrible*, Parts I and II (1944–46).

Rashomon (1951, Japan)
The main character of this film is accused of raping a woman and killing her husband. The event is retold through the eyes of each of the people involved. Directed by Akira Kurosawa.

Rules of the Game (1939, France)
This film of the French leisure class is described in Chapter 12. Directed by Jean Renoir.

The Servant (1963, Britain)
This film is a sardonic drama about the impermanence of power and exposes the hypocrisies of British upper class morality. Directed by Joseph Losey.

The Seven Samurai (1954, Japan)
Seven samurai (professional soldiers) come to save a village from bandits. It is a compassionate story of men struggling to keep their way of life and to be free. Directed by Akira Kurosawa.

The Seventh Seal (1956, Sweden)
The Seventh Seal is considered to be Bergman's best film. A knight (Max von Sydow) plays a game of chess with Death, while returning home from the Crusades as the plague ravages medieval Europe. The film is a stunning allegory of the meaning of life. Directed by Ingmar Bergman.

Shoeshine (1946, Italy)
Delinquency is the main idea of the film, but it probes deep into the social problems prevalent in postwar Italy. Directed by Vittorio de Sica.

The Shop on Main Street (1965, Czechoslovakia)
When the Nazis begin deporting Jews, a man risks his life to hide an old woman. This is one of the most acclaimed films of recent years. Directed by Jan Kadar and Elmar Klos.

The Third Man (1940, Britain)
A classic spy film set in grim postwar Vienna, with a zither playing the memorable theme music. Orson Welles and Joseph Cotten meet at the end in a remarkable final chase sequence. Directed by Sir Carol Reed.

Through a Glass Darkly (1961, Sweden)
A girl reads her father's journal describing the fact that she is an incurable schizophrenic and plunges into a series of hallucinations. Directed by Ingmar Bergman. We would also suggest seeing the following Bergman films as a thorough study of a great film director: *Wild Strawberries* (1957), *Winter Light* (1962), *The Silence* (1963), *Persona* (1967), and *Cries and Whispers* (1972).

Triumph of the Will (1934–36, Germany)
This film, perhaps more than any other documentary exposes the psychology of Germany during the Nazi regime. Hitler commissioned the director to make a film of the Sixth Annual Party Congress in Nuremberg. She had 30 cameras and a staff of 120 at her disposal. One must see this film to realize the full impact of Hitler's way of gaining power over a crowd. Directed by Leni Riefenstahl.

Two Women (1961, Italy)
The film is a story of a mother and daughter struggling to survive during World War II in Italy. It is the only time that an Oscar as Best Actress has been given for a foreign language performance—to Sophia Loren for her role as the mother. Directed by Vittorio de Sica.

Umberto D (1952, Italy)
This was the last great film of the postwar neorealism tradition. It is a simple story of an old man who faces eviction from his apartment so the landlady can rerent the room for more money. But like most films with very simple stories, there is much more to the character and theme of this film. Directed by Vittorio de Sica.

Viridiana (1961, Spain)
This may be Buñuel's masterpiece, but as with many "personal" filmmakers, the viewer must see a number of the director's films before any one can be fully appreciated. *Viridiana,* like most of Buñuel's films, is concerned with attacks on religion and society in general. We would suggest also seeing *Nazarin* (1958), *Simon of the Desert* (1965), *Tristana* (1970), *The Exterminating Angel* (1962), and *The Discreet Charm of the Bourgeoisie* (1972).

The Wild Child (1970, France)
This film is discussed in Chapter 12. Directed by François Truffaut.

Wild Strawberries (1957, Sweden)
An elderly scientist, traveling to receive an honorary degree, is confronted by haunting flashbacks which reveal and ultimately change his character. Directed by Ingmar Bergman.

Selected Short Films

These 43 short films are recommended by the authors for serious study by film study students. (A short film is usually a film less than 50–60 minutes.)

A
In animation, a gigantic "A" invades a man's room.

An American Time Capsule
A history of the United States in four minutes.

Blaze Glory
Blaze saves the day, in pixilation technique.

The Bolero
Music at its greatest. Academy Award for best short film of 1972.

Braverman's Condensed Cream of the Beatles
A look at John, Paul, George, and Ringo.

The Bride Stripped Bare
Not what you think it is.

Dinosaur
Dinosaurs come alive through the process of claymation (similar to *Mountain Music*) in a classroom of unruly fifth graders. They learn that dinosaurs can be fun, and so does the audience.

Dream of Wild Horses
A beautiful film poem.

Doubletalk
This film is intriguing, telling the story of a young man who goes to pick up his date. In overlapping sound tracks, we hear the dialogue of the characters, plus their thoughts. This technique produces great dramatic irony.

The Fable of He and She
On a nameless island, Hardybars hunt for food and Mushamels cook and take care of children. One day a disaster causes the island to split apart, separating the two groups. What they learn about the roles people play, we learn along with them by watching this interesting and well-made animation.

Frank Film
A look at Frank's film after he spent two years cutting pictures out of magazines and photographing them. Academy Award for best short film, 1973.

Gallery
A history of art in six minutes, using beautiful visual techniques.

Glass
A most beautiful film about the art of glass blowing—technically outstanding.

Hangman
When the hangman comes to town . . . from the poem.

The House
People in a house, the house is being torn down, more people, more of tearing the house apart, man executed, girl looking out window—a nonlinear film.

Jabberwocky
Children's toys and garments move through the technique of pixilation. It is a very clever film that is bound to have everyone talking.

John Henry
John Henry is a well-done stylized animation of the familiar folktale. Roberta Flack sings the story of the steel-driving man.

Krasner, Norman . . . Beloved Husband of Irma
A horror story at a pay toilet!

Leo Beuerman
Leo takes just one day at a time. A heartwarming, tender film.

Lines—Vertical and Horizontal
An abstract film of beauty.

Mint Tea
A study in observation and perceptions for students of film.

Moonbird
Children hunt for the "moonbird" in their backyard (in animation).

More
Everyone—children, teenagers, adults, city and country dwellers, people around the world—all want more. More of everything: toys, cars, houses, TV sets, lumber, oil, and food. What happens if there is no more? This short animated film suggests one possibility.

Mountain Music
This beautiful short film is done in animation, using clay. Will Vinton, the creator, calls the technique "claymation." The film is about the destruction of the environment by technology.

Neighbors
Two neighbors go to battle over a flower. Don't laugh; others have fought for less than that.

Night and Fog
This is a story about the horror of German concentration camps. Directed by Alain Resnais.

Nine Variations on a Dance Theme
This film explores a simple dance movement in nine variations of camera angles and editing techniques. The film is an excellent example of using film to explore artistic possibilities.

An Occurrence at Owl Creek Bridge
Powerful! You won't forget this film. Don't reveal the ending.

Peege
Perhaps the most moving short film ever made. It is about an old woman in a nursing home who receives a visit from her family.

The River
A 1930 classic documenty about the Mississippi and adjoining rivers. The film contains excellent examples of editing techniques.

60 Cycles
A filmic poem about cycling.

Ski the Outer Limits
One of the best films about skiing, showing movement and beauty.

Solo
An exciting and remarkable film.

The Star-Spangled Banner
Powerful film about life and death, war and peace.

The String Bean
An old lady grows a bean plant, her only companion. (This film is discussed in Chapter 10.)

That's Me
Alan Arkin, the actor, in a role that is elegant.

Threshold
A film full of symbols, and concerned with life and death.

Time Piece
A visual satire in the day of the life of a man.

Toys
A film about war toys that shoot it out in a department store window.

Two Men and a Wardrobe
A short film by Roman Polanski. It is about two men who carry a wardrobe around with them.

Index